BUTTERFLIES
AND MOTHS

BUTTERFLIES AND MOTHS

Text by Ivo Novák

Illustrations by František Severa

BLITZ EDITIONS

Text by Ivo Novák
Translated by Marie Hejlová
Illustrations by František Severa
Graphic design by Miroslav Barankiewicz

Designed and produced by Aventinum Publishing House, Prague,
Czech Republic
This English edition published 1999 by Blitz Editions,
an imprint of Bookmart Ltd.
Registered Number 2372865
Trading as Bookmart Limited
Desford Road, Enderby, Leicester LE9 5AD

ISBN 1-85605-440-3
Printed in the Czech Republic by Polygrafia, a.s., Prague
3/07/10/51-06

Contents

Preface

There are more than 120,000 species of butterflies and moths, representing a very conspicuous group of insects — the Lepidoptera. This group includes some of the most beautiful animals inhabiting our planet. They live from the tropics to polar regions, in high mountains and deserts. Their excellent capacity for flight has enabled them to occupy all potential habitats. Because butterflies and moths depend almost exclusively on plants for food, their existence is limited by conditions governing the life of plants.

The brightest colours and the greatest diversity of species occur among tropical Lepidoptera. In some areas primitive species have survived and help us to understand the early history of these insects, while in other parts of the world the evolution of new species is still taking place, even now. The fauna of some regions is characterized by a superabundance of Lepidoptera species; in others, butterflies and moths attain high population densities, but with a more modest species diversity.

In regions with a prevailingly mild climate there are few large forms, most species not exceeding quite limited dimensions. But they are diverse in their ways of life, responding to the seasonal climatic conditions, particularly the warm summers and severe winters. Butterflies and moths are on the wing all the year round (with even a few special moths appearing in the depths of winter); they animate fields and meadows, forests and mountains, and adorn the blossoms of plants with their presence. Brightly coloured nymphalids are among the pioneers of spring. After awakening from hibernation, brimstones shine with their radiant yellow in the verdant spring, and newly emerged whites display their dazzling reflectance. On sunny days the Kentish Glory and the Tau Emperor Moth flash through the woods. In addition to these species there are legions of less conspicuous early moths, including a lot of geometrids and noctuids. In the course of the year, the life-cycle of all the species gradually progresses, all timed by the phases of the ever-changing seasons.

Under the impact of civilization butterflies and moths are threatened, their numbers being greatly reduced, some species becoming extinct. Today a solitary white may be seen fluttering over clover fields formerly vibrant with butterflies and moths; the much admired Swallowtail is now a rarity. As the different species are associated with particular environments, butterflies and moths disappear hand in hand with the felling of forests, the draining of marshes, the ploughing of meadows and steppes. And man's technology is all the time extending to situations where Nature hitherto found refuge.

However, let us leave these gloomy deliberations about the survival of butterflies and moths, and concentrate on what still exists. This guide will, of course, enable us to unveil these riches only in part, even though it covers a great number of species. Attention is inevitably focussed on large and showy insects, or species that, for one reason or another, arouse our curiosity. The arrangement of coloured plates has been made to comply with this practical conception, with butterflies at the beginning and the relatively primitive, small moths at the end. Less well-known groups — that is families of minute moths with a great number of species — have not been omitted, however, and the book is intended to give an entire cross-section of this vast order, including all the major families. Species distributed predominantly in Europe are represented here. Many of them, however, are widespread throughout the huge Palaearctic or even the Holarctic region — that is Europe, northern Africa, Asia and North America. The illustrations of small butterflies and moths are magnified to facilitate an accurate reproduction of their beautiful colour patterns. With caterpillars and pupae only the more conspicuous forms, typical of particular families, are presented.

Traditionally, an interest in butterflies and moths has principally involved knowledge of their anatomy, identification, life-cycles and distribution. The study of butterflies and moths (lepidopterology) is now passing from this stage of collection, taxonomy and natural history to experimental and applied disciplines. Further, it is necessary to understand some ecology to appreciate the true significance of butterflies and moths and how they fit within the complex web of nature. We have included some practical suggestions to help those naturalists who might wish to study the Lepidoptera in greater depth.

Evolution

Our knowledge of the remote history of the evolution of life on Earth is very fragmentary: it is extraordinarily difficult to fill in the gaps, and the actual course of events will probably never be disclosed in all detail. Today the Earth is inhabited by an enormous number of different organisms, animals and plants, but we are incapable of supplying any exact answers to questions such as when these organisms appeared for the first time. The task for archaeologists is somewhat less difficult: on the one hand, they do not have to penetrate so far back in time, and, on the other hand, they find quite a number of remains (skeletons and artefacts) indicative of past activities; these sometimes enable human history to be reconstructed with a relatively high degree of accuracy. Palaeontologists are in a more difficult position. They certainly come across skeletal remains of vertebrates, fossil shells, etc., but the further we reach into the past, the fewer traces do we find. Insects, and particularly butterflies and moths with their delicate little bodies and wings, have left behind very little evidence to serve our present purposes. In the majority of cases, their past history can be inferred only indirectly, from the evolution of other insects and other animals, as well as from the evolution of plants on which, due to their way of life, butterflies and moths depend.

The oldest fossil remains of insects (much more primitive and simple than Lepidoptera) originate from the Palaeozoic, from the middle Devonian period, about 350 million years ago. Vestiges of real Lepidoptera are known from a much later period, the Tertiary, approximately 50 million years ago. In the Tertiary butterflies and moths were already well developed, and many species, preserved for example in amber, do not differ substantially from present ones. They may even be classed in contemporary families and genera. Thus we understand that Lepidoptera must have developed in the intervening period between the Devonian and the Tertiary, which lasted about 300 million years. Some direct precursors of butterflies and moths, resembling the present caddis flies, quite possibly appeared as early as the end of the Palaeozoic, in the Permian period. At that time the conditions of life, as well as the food essential to Lepidoptera, the land plants, were already in existence. It may be assumed, however, that the main development of this group had not started before the Mesozoic, probably during the Jurassic, about 135—180 million years ago. These ages and times are very approximate, and it must be clear to the reader that a few million years do not count for much in such estimates. In fact, what exact data could these estimates be based on?

Nevertheless, the result of this long development of the order Lepidoptera is about 200,000 living species of butterflies and moths. This is the present estimate of the number of species formed by this group throughout the world. More than 120,000 species have been formally described, while tens of thousands are estimated still to await recognition or discovery.

How the enormous multitude of forms assumed not only by the Lepidoptera but also by other animals and plants have come into existence continues to be a matter of guesswork. The only thing we can do is to draw indirect inferences based on comparing the structures and properties of individual species, the functions of separate organs, ways of life, and so on. Human life is too short to let us prepare a real experiment in evolution to test our theories!

Usually we are inclined to imagine Nature as a creator endowed with boundless possibilities, revelling in ideas, exploring the capacity of each species to survive, both in competition with others and under the impact of unfavourable external conditions. The ability to change and develop is a basic quality of living matter. In nature, two completely identical organisms can never be found. Even members of the same species differ from each other in many details. Deficient individuals are rejected, replaced by those better adapted to the conditions. It is only individuals possessing particularly advantageous combinations of qualities — for example powers of resistance, adaptability, reproductive capacity, ability to defend themselves, etc. — that can survive for long. What has been said about the variability of individuals applies also to higher units: to populations, species, genera, etc. Of the endless forms that have inhabited the Earth in the course of ages only those have prevailed which were well fitted for life. The variability of organisms, their capacity for reproduction, and the unremitting action of natural selection — these are the motive forces of evolution. The situation is made all the more complex by the changes in the conditions of inanimate nature to which all organisms are continuously required to adapt themselves. This is why, in the course of geological development, a great many species, and even whole groups, have become extinct.

It is precisely these changes of inanimate nature, and the different conditions prevailing in the separate areas of the Earth, which have created preconditions for the development of new species, so-called speciation. The survival of different forms that have come into being through the course of evolution is thought to be dependent on the emergence of barriers separating the different forms, allowing for their development in isolation — at least for the time necessary to attain a level of differentiation precluding the possibility of re-mixing. Today it is generally admitted that many, if not all, species came into being and multiplied on the basis of geographical (often called *allopatric*) speciation. The populations of a species distributed throughout a large territory were separated by — for example — the rise of mountain ranges, the separation of continents, the rise of oceans, climatic changes in a particular zone, etc., and they continued developing independently of each other in different conditions. After a long period of time, the differences among the populations were so great that the populations were no longer able to interbreed successfully, and they became independent species. These changes cannot be observed during a man's lifetime (the time estimated for the differentiation of even a 'subspecies' being 10—20 thousand years) but it is possible to be aware of more modest changes, as represented, for example, by the development of breeds and strains of animals and plants used in agriculture.

Biologists are now examining the possibility that speciation could take place in ways other than by geographical isolation. Could speciation occur within the confines of a species inhabiting a single undivided territory (so-called *sympatric* speciation)? It does seem possible that barriers other than territorial ones, separating individual populations of species, may arise. For example the time of occurrence of individual populations in the year may be shifted to a sufficient extent to prevent the populations from meeting and interbreeding. Evidence in favour of this assumption is supplied by the occurrence of pairs of closely related lepidopterous species one of which appears in late autumn and the other in early spring. Barriers might also be of genetic, physiological, ethological, or of some other nature.

It is characteristic of evolution that the same 'goal', functional adaptation, can be attained in various ways. This is perhaps best demonstrated by *convergence,* many examples of which can be found among butterflies and moths. Some remotely related insect groups imitate the same object, for example much-feared wasps, since a wasp-like appearance affords some protection against enemies. Other species have developed, in different ways, camouflaging colouration (*crypsis*) enabling them to merge with the environment wherein they live. Another example is the frequent dark colouration of Lepidoptera in high mountains. Here the main reason appears to be thermoregulation, and the need for solar energy. And so we could go on, presenting further examples.

If all these creative potentialities are combined within the vast aeons of time, the only likely result is the great variety of nature, a complex, dynamic system subjected to continuous change. Each time something new arises, something else may be faced with extinction. Not even today has evolution come to an end: the present also belongs to geological history.

Classification

The study of living organisms requires a classification system, helping us both to understand nature and to utilize our knowledge for scientific and practical purposes. This is why, from time immemorial, naturalists have tried to make classification systems to categorise the products of nature. Standpoints have varied, both practical and scientific, but primary attention has gradually turned to the elaboration of the so-called *natural system,* aimed at the truest possible description of conditions prevailing in nature. This in turn implies that the natural system should present a scheme of evolutionary or *phylogenetic* development, from the oldest lineages to the most recent, so expressing the kinship relations of living organisms. This is no easy task in view of the fact that all relationships in nature are the result of long and complex evolution, and relatively little evidence is available for the detailed reconstruction of evolutionary history. Moreover, nature is so complex that it cannot be forced to fit any simple scheme, however convenient this might be to us. Consequently, the natural system is only an ideal goal which may be approached in some measure, but which necessarily entails some simplification of reality.

Many attempts at elaborating a system have been made, but the first to solve this problem with relative success was an 18th century Swedish scientist, Carl Linné. He classified all the plants and animals known to him, and his book *Systema Naturae* has become the basis on which the present classification of organisms has been developed. Linné, who revised and added to his work several times, would perhaps be surprised if he could see how whole generations of scientists have developed his original system — but many of the underlying principles have remained unchanged.

As with all groups of animals, butterflies and moths have been organized within the Linnean system. There is general agreement with respect to the classification of the evolutionarily most progressive groups of Lepidoptera — the noctuids, hawkmoths, prominents, butterflies, etc. However, major problems arise with the classification of the primitive families, which are similar in a number of features to related orders of insects, particularly the caddis flies (Trichoptera). Some of the most primitive lepidopterous species have functional mandibles and do not feed on nectar, but on pollen. Thus they may represent that remote stage in the evolution of the Lepidoptera when flowers did not yet yield nectar. It is not surprising, therefore, that some researchers refrained from classifying this group among the butterflies and moths, but created for it an independent order of insects (the Zeugloptera). Recently, however, the placing of these most primitive moths within the true Lepidoptera has gained general acceptance.

Different scholars approach the problems of classification from different points of view. Higher systematic categories (genera, families, orders, etc.) are often regarded as artificial units, primarily of value to 'pigeon-hole' information; their delimitation is usually dependent on the weight ascribed by the individual specialist to particular morphological or other characteristics. The classification of butterflies and moths serves to demonstrate this very clearly.

During normal flight, the fore and hindwings of Lepidoptera are functionally joined. According to the way in which this is achieved, the Lepidoptera can be divided into Jugatae (whose wings are joined by a projection from the forewing *(jugum)* − Fig. 1a), and the Frenatae, provided with a more specialised organ interlocking the fore and hindwings: on the costal margin of the hindwing there are one or more tough bristles *(frenulum)* inserted into a lobe or fan of stiff setae *(retinaculum)* on the underside of the forewing (Fig. 1b, c). The Jugatae include the primitive families Micropterigidae, Eriocraniidae and Hepialidae; the Frenatae cover all the other moths and the butterflies.

Another character used for the classification of Lepidoptera is the wings. The veins of the fore and hindwings may either be the same in number, and the fore and hindwings similar in shape (Homoneura) (Fig. 2a); or the veins of the fore and hindwings differ in number and arrangement, and the wings are dissimilar in shape (Heteroneura) (Fig. 2b). Further, with respect to the number and location of the female sexual ducts, some families may be classed among the Monotrysia (with one sexual outlet), and others among the Ditrysia (having two outlets, one of which is used for copulation, the other for oviposition). In practice, the traditional division into Macrolepidoptera (butterflies and large moths) and Microlepidoptera (small moths) still continues to be adopted widely. But even though this arrangement cannot be denied its certain practical advantages, it makes no sense in terms of anatomy, nor of what we understand of the evolution of the individual subgroups of Lepidoptera.

The classification of the Lepidoptera may take on different aspects, even with respect to subdivision into families. According to some authors, the Lepidoptera can be divided into approximately 50 families, while according to others the number of families exceeds 120. Recently the splitting of large families into smaller units has reached a climax. Pyralids, now divided by many authorities into six independent families, serve as an example. At present, however, a number of authors seem to be returning to larger systematic units, and many groups treated for a while as independent families have been relegated to their former status as subfamilies or even tribes.

And so we might go on. Every researcher is anxious to contribute something new, to find new

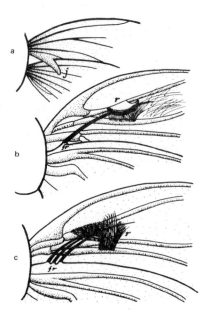

1 Wing-coupling apparatus in two suborders of Lepidoptera: a − Jugatae, b, c − Frenatae: b − in males, c − in females, j − jugum, fr − frenulum, r − retinaculum.

2 Venation of forewing and hindwing in two suborders of Lepidoptera: a — Homoneura, b — Heteroneura, j — jugum, fr — frenulum.

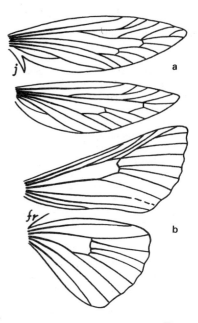

and more suitable criteria for classifying butterflies and moths in a natural system. These efforts are far from complete — yet in the course of time a particular sequence of families, from primitive to more advanced, has been established and is now generally accepted as a relatively satisfactory system.

The following scheme shows both the position of the Lepidoptera within the animal kingdom as a whole, and the breakdown of the order of Lepidoptera into superfamilies and families. This system includes all the major superfamilies, but only a selection of the larger or more important family units; many small or otherwise obscure families have been omitted.

In addition to the features described above, the classification of Lepidoptera into suborders and families is also based on the wing venation, that is, on the number of veins, their position and branching. Further important characteristics include the type of antennae, the shape and position of the labial palps and other mouthparts, leg and body structures, etc. More precise information about these aspects can be found in the key to the more important lepidopterous families

copulatory organs of males and females is of major significance. Some species can hardly be distinguished in any way other than by the form of these organs.

Kingdom: animals (Animalia)
  Phylum: arthropods (Arthropoda)
    Class: insects (Insecta)
      Order: butterflies and moths (Lepidoptera)
        Suborder: Homoneura (= Jugatae)
        Superfamilies (families in parentheses):
        Micropterigoidea (Micropterigidae — archaic moths)
        Eriocranioidea (Eriocraniidae; Agathiphagidae — primitive moths)

Hepialoidea (Hepialidae — hepialids, ghost and swift moths)
Mnesarchaeoidea (Mnesarchaeidae)
Suborder: Heteroneura (= Frenatae)
Superfamilies (families in parentheses):
Nepticuloidea (Nepticulidae — nepticulid moths, serpentine miners)
Incurvarioidea (Incurvariidae — includes the yucca moths;
    Adelidae — longhorns, fairy moths)
Cossoidea (Cossidae — goat moths)
Tineoidea (Tineidae — tineids, clothes and scavenger moths; Psychidae — bagworms;
    Gracillariidae — narrow-winged leaf miners, blotch miners; Lithocolletinae)
Yponomeutoidea (Sesiidae — clearwings;
    Yponomeutidae — ermine moths)
Gelechioidea (Elachistidae; Oecophoridae;
    Coleophoridae — case bearers; Gelechiidae — gelechiid moths)
Tortricoidea (Tortricidae — leaf rollers, tortrix moths)
Copromorphoidea (Copromorphidae; Alucitidae — many-plume moths)
Zygaenoidea (Zygaenidae — burnets and foresters;
    Limacodidae — slug-caterpillar moths)
Pyraloidea (Pyralidae — pyralid moths)
Pterophoroidea (Pterophoridae — plume moths)
Hesperioidea* (Hesperiidae — skippers)
Papilionoidea* (Papilionidae — swallowtails and apollos;
    Pieridae — whites and sulphurs;
    Nymphalidae — nymphalids, brush-footed butterflies;
    Satyridae — browns, satyrs and wood nymphs;
    Lycaenidae — blues, coppers and hairstreaks)
Castnioidea (Castniidae — castniid moths)
Geometroidea (Drepanidae — hook-tips; Thyatiridae;
    Geometridae — geometrids, inchworms, loopers)
Calliduloidea (Pterothysanidae; Callidulidae)
Bombycoidea (Endromidae; Lasiocampidae — eggars, lappet moths, lackey moths;
    Bombycidae — silkworms; Lemoniidae; Saturniidae — emperor moths)
Sphingoidea (Sphingidae — hawkmoths)
Notodontoidea (Notodontidae — prominents, puss moths)
Noctuoidea (Lymantriidae — tussock moths;
    Arctiidae — tiger and footman moths;
    Noctuidae — noctuids, owlet moths, millers)

---

* The closely related superfamilies Hesperioidea and Papilionoidea comprise the butterflies of well-known diurnal habits; all other Lepidoptera are classed as moths — even though many of them also fly in the daytime.

Nomenclature

Nomenclature is a subject which usually fills the beginner with fear or distrust. 'What's the good of constantly changing scientific names?' asks one. 'Not long after one gets used to a name it is declared invalid, and a new one proclaimed to be assuredly correct,' complains another. How are we to know that, for instance, *Scopelosoma satellitia* (L.) is the same as *Eupsilia transversa* (Hufnagel), or that *Thais polyxena* (Denis & Schiffermüller) is another name for *Parnalius hypsipyle* (Fabricius), or *Zerynthia hypermnestra* (Scopoli), and so on — to mention only two of the dozens of common and the hundreds of less familiar examples? A great many collectors of butterflies and moths entertain the deep-rooted feeling that continually recurring changes in the nomenclature make no sense whatsoever and result in nothing but chaos and misunderstanding. This impression may sometimes arise, but in reality the situation is not so bad. The names of butterflies and moths are formed in conformity with certain rules, the purpose of changes being the improvement of order within nomenclature, the correction of errors wherever the established rules have not been observed, and the adjustment of old names, formed at a time when our modern rules had not yet been formulated. The stumbling block lies in the fact that our own generation lives at a time when many of these problems are still actively being solved. It should be recognised that the present state of affairs is transitory, being a manifestation of an enormous upsurge in science all over the world. It is only today that scholars in many countries now have the opportunity for thoroughgoing studies in specialized disciplines, and are in a position to correct the errors handed down by tradition for several decades. In particular, old collections and treatises which have formerly escaped attention must be reassessed according to the standards of modern taxonomy (classification). But the supplies of old collections and treatises are not inexhaustible: the time is sure to come when practically all formal problems will have been solved and a relative stability in the scientific designations of Lepidoptera will be attained. Then the only changes will be those necessitated by new findings concerning kinship relations among butterflies and moths, so affecting their classification into the 'natural system of animals'.

Let us now consider some examples which may help us to reach a deeper understanding of the principles underlying the formation of the names of butterflies and moths. The same principles apply to all animals, including the other insects, as well.

The endeavour to assign names to living organisms is as old as human language. First Man gave names to the animals with which he most frequently came into contact — domestic animals and game. Then it was the turn of the more conspicuous wild species. The popular local and other vernacular names which arose have been in use until our time. But the development of science necessitated international understanding, and in Europe Latin was traditionally the language serving this purpose. The oldest scientific names had the character of Latin descriptions rather than 'labels': they were long and complex in translation, for example 'a big butterfly with yellow wings striped with black'. Many attempts at producing a universal nomenclature were never generally accepted, until Linné, through his book *Systema Naturae* (published during the 18th century and referred to above in connection with the general classification of animals and plants) established the Latin nomenclature which, in principle, is applied to plants and animals (and hence to butterflies and moths) even today.

Linné's system consists of two names for each species, and is therefore called *binominal nomenclature*. The first of these names is that of the *genus*, always written with a capital letter — for example *Papilio, Vanessa, Sphinx;* the second name designates the *species*, and is written with a small initial, even if it is derived from a proper name normally written with a capital letter. For example: *Luperina nickerlii* (a species named after the Czech entomologist Nickerle), *Celaena haworthii* (named after the English entomologist Haworth), *Scolitantides orion* (after the mythical hunter Orion). Similarly, the name of the species is written with a small letter if it is derived from the generic designation of a plant written with a capital letter — for example *Stauropus fagi* (based on *Fagus* — beech), *Cucullia verbasci* (based on *Verbascum* — mullein). In the literature of the last century these rules were not yet fully established or observed.

Linné's binominal nomenclature has been extended to a trinominal nomenclature, whereby the third name denotes the subspecies, written with a small initial in the same way as the species name. This third name is added where species give rise to different local forms or races, so-called subspecies. The names of the subspecies are often based on the name of countries or other geographical units, for example *Heliothis maritima bulgarica, Erebia epiphron carpathica, Parnassius apollo nevadensis,* etc. The race inhabiting the territory from where the species has been described is called the nominate race, and in its designation the name of the subspecies is identical with that of the species, examples being *Papilio machaon machaon, Parnassius apollo apollo,* etc. In what follows, if a subspecies is referred to within the framework of the species, it is denoted by the abbreviation ssp. — for example, ssp. *bulgarica.*

Generic names have the character of nouns. The species may be denoted by a noun either in the first or in the second case, or else by an adjective or another word, or even an arbitrary (but pronounceable!) group of letters not necessarily conveying any concrete meaning. In those cases where the name of a species has the character of an adjective, its grammatical suffix is of the same grammatical gender (masculine, feminine or neuter) as the respective name of the genus in Latin. If we place a species denoted in this way in another genus, the grammatical suffix of the name of the species must be made to correspond. For example, *Crambus permutatellus* is changed into *Catoptria permutatella* on transferring the species from *Crambus* to *Catoptria.* If the name of the species is not adjectival, then its form is not adjusted to the name of the genus. There are exact rules governing all these factors, and the authors who invent new names for hitherto undescribed genera or species are recommended to indicate the way in which the name has been derived, and its grammatical gender. Nevertheless, recently a tendency to preserve the species name in its original form irrespective of the grammatical gender seems to prevail.

Taxonomic units higher than the genus (families, orders, etc.) do not form a part of the name. On the other hand, the name of the butterfly or moth technically also involves the name of the *author* who was the first to describe the species or the subspecies, as well as the *year* in which the description was published — for example:

Heliothis maritima (Graslin, 1855)

Heliothis maritima bulgarica Draudt, 1938

The reader must often have noticed that the author's name and the year are sometimes put in *parentheses,* while at other times this is not the case. Even this detail has significance. If the species has until now remained within the same genus into which it was classed by the author who originally named and described it, the author's name is written down without parentheses, for example *Papilio machaon* Linné, 1758; or *Sphinx ligustri* Linné, 1758. If, however, on the basis of further studies the species has been re-classified in another genus, the author's name and the year are introduced in parentheses, for example *Acherontia atropos* (Linné, 1758), or *Parnassius apollo* (Linné, 1758). Linné's system was very simple in comparison with that of our time, and later scientists have divided Linné's original genera into a number of others. Hence it follows that Linné's name rarely appears without parentheses.

Often it is unnecessary to write down complete names, including the subspecies, author, year and parentheses. As a result and because of the insistence upon conciseness and space saving characteristic of our time, this practice has gradually been abandoned — with the exception of purely taxonomic publications. In faunistic studies, or in applied literature, abbreviations for the author's name are usually employed and the year and parentheses are dropped. Particular abbreviations have become established for classical authors: L. = Linné, Hw. = Haworth,

Tr. = Treitschke, Hb. = Hübner, D.&S. = Denis & Schiffermüller, etc. Thus we may write: *Papilio machaon* L. The names of less well-known or contemporary authors are usually still written in full.

Another rule indicates that, with the exception of the grammatical suffix in adjectives, the valid name must retain the form wherein it appeared in print when the species was named and described for the first time — even if the author used an incorrect form due to ignorance or other reasons, or if the name was composed contrary to the rules in force today. Even corrections of printing errors are permitted only in exceptional cases. Thus a new species of white was named after the Viennese collector J. Mann. The second case of the name Mann in Latin should be 'manni'. However, the description was published under the name *mannii*, and so it must remain, even though the grammatical form applied is incorrect. Thus the white's name is *Pieris mannii* Mayer, 1851. For similar reasons, the Dark Sword Grass moth is called *Agrotis ipsilon* (Hufnagel, 1766) even though in many languages 'ypsilon' would now seem to be a much better transliteration from the Greek: when Hufnagel introduced this name in 1766 he spelt it 'ipsilon', and so it must remain.

It may and frequently does happen that a particular species is named by two or more scholars independently of each other — either by coincidence, or simply because it escaped the attention of one of them that the species had already been described. In such a case it is expedient to apply the very important rule of priority which validates the older name, that is of the name published at the earlier date. The later published (younger) name is called a *junior synonym*. The older, valid name is called a *senior synonym*. It might seem possible that the discovery of older and older names could go on for ever, and that perhaps one day we might reach as far back as Aristotle who also had designations for animals! In order to avert such extremes, scholars have agreed upon a reasonable date from which the priority of scientific names commences. The date is the year 1758 when the tenth edition of Linné's book *Systema Naturae*, the first fully binominal classification, was published. The *rule of priority* is applied to the names of families, genera, species and subspecies. This and other rules are not necessarily applied to so-called infrasubspecific names or taxons, such as forms (f.) or aberrations (ab.), which lie outside the scope of internationally agreed rules governing the names of families, genera, species and subspecies.

Some people erroneously assume that all names used by Linné necessarily must remain valid. Could Linné himself have created synonyms? The answer is unambiguous: he not only could but did make quite a number of them, even within his famed *Systema Naturae*. And the tenth edition of this book was not Linné's last work. He continued to describe new species, and published further major works in 1761 and 1767. The rule of priority also applies to these later works, and thus it has come about that some other authors, who published descriptions in the intervening period betwen 1758 and 1761 or 1767, sometimes have priority over Linné — for example Clerck 1759, Schreber 1759, Scopoli 1763, Müller 1764, Hufnagel 1766, etc.

Invalid names may arise in other ways. According to another important rule of nomenclature, no two genera in the entire animal kingdom, and no two species within any genus, can bear the same name. If a new genus of butterflies or moths is given a name which has already been used in the past to designate, for instance, a fish or a fly, the name of the lepidopteron would be an invalid *homonym*. Generally it must either be replaced by the oldest synonym or, if a synonym is not available, a *new name* has to be proposed to replace the old. It sometimes takes several decades to discover such a discrepancy and the original author may have died in the meantime. Then, as a rule, the scientist who detects the error is expected to devise the necessary new name. A potential example included several species of common cutworm moths belonging to the family Noctuidae, which were classed under the generic name *Agrotis*. This designation was given to the genus by Ochsenheimer in 1816. It was realised, however, only a relatively short time ago that the name *Agrotis* had been used by Hübner in 1808 (several years earlier) to designate another, quite different genus of the family Noctuidae. Thus the name *Agrotis* appeared twice in the animal kingdom, which is inadmissible according to the rules. The priority is Hübner's, and as a result the generic name *Agrotis* would have become valid for the species group including *venustula* Hb., whereas the cutworm moths under Ochsenheimer's *Agrotis* would have had to be provided with another name. The oldest junior synonym of *Agrotis* O. is Hübner's *Scotia*, which he used to designate the cutworm moths in 1821, which would give these pests the names *Scotia segetum* (D.&S.), *Scotia exclamationis* (L.), etc. However, in this particular case the name *Agrotis* for the cutworms is so entrenched in the agricultural literature that the International Commission for Zoological Nomenclature has declared Hübner's *Agrotis* invalid, so as to conserve the application of *Agrotis* O. for *segetum, exclamationis,* etc; the generic name for *venustula* is now *Elaphria*, another of Hübner's names, proposed by him in 1818.

In fact, synonyms, homonyms and otherwise invalid names are probably more numerous than valid names, and in order to find our way in this labyrinth, at least an abbreviation of the author's name must be attached properly to each designation. As we have pointed out, *Agrotis* O. is not identical with *Agrotis* Hb. Equally, the specific names *aceris* Frey, *aceris* L., *aceris* Lep., or *catax* Esp. and *catax* L., denote totally different Lepidoptera.

More space has been devoted to the nomenclature of Lepidoptera than might at first sight, seem necessary. Yet all the problems have not been exhausted. We have mentioned only a few essential examples. In reality, problems often arise which rank with legal documents in their complexity and can be solved only by experts. The International Code of Zoological Nomenclature exists as a basis for this, while the already noted International Commission for Zoological Nomenclature (ICZN) is a permanent organisation set up to solve with authority all difficult questions of nomenclature. Its binding resolutions are published in its own international journal, where, for example, the vexing question of *Agrotis* Hb. versus *Agrotis* O. was dealt with.

Besides the scientific nomenclature of butterflies and moths, there also exists a set of common or vernacular names in every living language, usually based on popular names and traditions. It is far from being exhaustive. Names are given only to conspicuous, abundant or economically significant species, those frequently dealt with in textbooks or in popular scientific literature. Rare species usually have no vernacular names, or such names are not in common use. In some countries there exist more or less official lists of common names of butterflies and moths; in other countries the names are loosely applied and the same species can have several popular names. Most languages employ names which have nothing in common with the scientific, binominal nomenclature. For study purposes, publication and international communication, it is always best to designate animals by their scientific (Latin) names.

Life-cycles

Metamorphosis

Every butterfly or moth passes through a complex development, involving *metamorphosis,* in which several completely different growth stages follow in succession. A *caterpillar,* the principal feeding stage, emerges from an immobile *egg* laid by the female. When full-grown, the caterpillar turns into an almost inactive *pupa* — a transformation stage characterized by lack of feeding. The *adult* lepidopterous insect eventually emerges from the pupa as the final stage, the culmination of the developmental cycle and the founder of the next. Since the life-cycles of butterflies and moths include a pupal stage, we refer to them as insects with *complete metamorphosis* — in contrast to those insects (for example plant bugs, grasshoppers) which develop through a succession of more and more adult-like stages (so-called *partial metamorphosis*).

The development of a lepidopteron starts with the fertilization of the egg by a spermatozoon received during copulation. The main characteristics of the future individual are determined, including sex, at this time. It occasionally happens that some eggs escape fertilization; these simply dry up after being laid, without starting to develop: no caterpillars hatch from them. The development of caterpillars by *parthenogenesis* from unfertilized eggs is quite an exceptional phenomenon among butterflies and moths, but does occur, for example, in some bagworms.

What happens within the fertilized egg? This single cell, the *zygote,* which has received its hereditary instructions equally from unfertilized egg and the sperm, commences to divide. It has to undergo many divisions before the tiny developing embryo comes to resemble an animal, even remotely. The embryo is surrounded with a rich supply of yolk. There is just enough to provide the nourishment for the development of the whole animal — the small caterpillar. The embryo is protected by the eggshell, or *chorion*, not only against mechanical damage but also against external variations in temperature, humidity, light and oxygen levels.

The moment when the caterpillar gnaws its way out of the egg marks the beginning of its independent life. The yolk supply inside the egg is exhausted and the caterpillar now has to fend and feed for itself. The empty chorion serves many caterpillars as their first food, after which nothing remains of the shell but the base, still fixed to the support on which it was laid. Other caterpillars leave their abandoned shells untouched, going immediately in search of their main food.

In the course of its development the caterpillar passes through several *instars,* or growth stages. Usually there are five instars, but sometimes there may be more than ten. Slowly growing caterpillars tend to have more instars, and there may be differences even among caterpillars of the same species, often dependent on the seasonal generation to which they belong. The transition from one instar to another involves shedding the old skin *(moulting)* and developing a new, bigger and looser one. The skin is cast off inclusive of all appendages and setae — even the external linings of the air-tubes *(tracheae)* and mouthparts are removed from the body. The head capsule, including mandibles, antennae and maxillary palps, is shed as an independent unit. Each moulting is preceded by a short period of rest, taking one or two days. The caterpillar stops feeding, and in pale-coloured caterpillars the new skin can be seen under the old one. A caterpillar which has reached the last instar is transformed by one further moult into a pupa.

During development the caterpillar grows ten to twenty times in length, its head increases about six times in breadth, and its weight increases 2—3 thousand times from *eclosion* (hatching from the egg) until the moment immediately preceding pupation. The pupa, in contrast, is apparently inert, not taking food, nor moving from place to place. Inside, however, an almost incredible process is under way. Immediately after pupation *histolysis* occurs, by which all the organs of the caterpillar undergo dissolution, leaving the pupa filled with fluid. Out of this an apparently quite different organism, the future adult butterfly or moth, begins to take shape, developing from minute *germinal buds* — special little groups of cells from which all the adult structures and organs are formed.

When the development of the pupa nears completion, the pupal skin is filled by an animal possessing all the organs of the adult. In the last phase, the coloured wings, eyes and body of the butterfly or moth shine through the pupal cuticle. This foreshadows the imminent rupture of the pupal skin, from which the adult insect will emerge to complete its complex metamorphosis.

Anybody who might expect to see a butterfly or moth rising, in all its glory, and flying away immediately after its emergence from the pupa would be thoroughly disappointed. In fact, a peculiar long-legged creature with minute bag-like wings crawls out, quite unable to fly. At first the insect searches for a suitable support. This may be a twig, a tree trunk, a flower stem or a grass stalk, a wall or a stone — in short, some elevated place where it can hang by its forelegs and let its wings hang down freely. What follows are hardly perceptible motions of the body, a pumping by which the insect fills its wing veins with blood and its tracheae with air. This expands the wings to their functional size. If you are fortunate enough to see a butterfly or moth immediately after its emergence from the pupa you need no more than 10—15 minutes to follow this wonderful process. Not even then, however, can the insect take to the wing. It shifts the drooping wings to the position in which it will later rest (wings may be folded flat, in a roof-like manner, or they may remain slightly open) and waits another 1—2 hours until they become sufficiently stiff. At this moment the butterfly or moth has attained its final size and does not grow any more.

As we have seen, the development of butterflies and moths is far from simple. Moreover, in the various species of this vast order of insects the appearance, the way of life and the development of individual stages may be very diverse and remarkable.

The imago or adult

Butterflies and moths, like all insects, have a body consisting of three parts: *head, thorax* and *abdomen* (Figs. 3, 4). The whole body is clothed with minute hairs and scales. The head, joined to the thorax by the *cervix* (neck), carries a pair of large, hemispherical *compound eyes*, usually shiny and variously coloured: often they are light yellowish-green, sometimes black or even

3 The body of a lepidopterous insect consists of three basic parts: head, thorax (inclusive of legs and wings), and abdomen (see also Fig.4, for abbreviations).

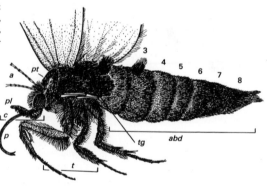

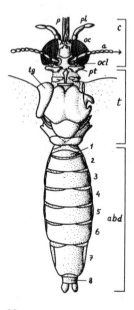

4 The body of a lepidopterous insect, seen from above, and denuded of scales: c — head (caput), t — thorax, abd — abdomen, p — proboscis, pl — labial palps (palpi labiales), oc — compound eye (oculus), ocl — simple eye (ocellus), a — antenna (only first few segments included), pt — patagium, tg — tegula (removed on right-hand side) 1 to 8 — abdominal segments.

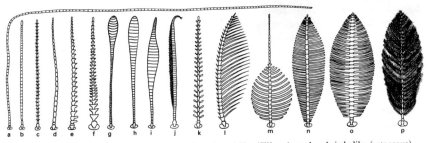

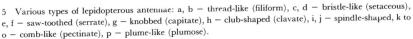

5 Various types of lepidopterous antennae: a, b — thread-like (filiform), c, d — bristle-like (setaceous), e, f — saw-toothed (serrate), g — knobbed (capitate), h — club-shaped (clavate), i, j — spindle-shaped, k to o — comb-like (pectinate), p — plume-like (plumose).

speckled. In some cases they are bare, in others they are clothed with fine hairs. A pair of simple eyes, or *ocelli*, is also present in some more or less primitive groups. Two conspicuous *antennae* are located on the head. They vary in the number of segments as well as in length and shape (Fig. 5). Most common are thread-like (filiform) antennae which can be found in noctuid moths, in many geometrids, and in numerous families of small Lepidoptera. Males of the small moths of the family Adelidae have very long antennae, exceeding the length of their wings about five times; thus they resemble certain caddis flies, to which the Lepidoptera are most closely related in terms of evolutionary descent. Comb-like (pectinate) antennae frequently occur in the males of numerous species of geometrids, eggars, tussock moths and some noctuids. The branches (rami) of the combs may be of various lengths, and are often longer on one side, so the antenna may be sword-like, lanceolate or oval in general outline. The antennae of some Lepidoptera, including bagworm moths, are of a peculiar shape. The lateral projections are long, thin and irregularly arranged, somewhat like a bird's down feathers. Burnets and foresters have club-shaped (clavate) antennae, gradually enlarging towards the tip, while antennae in hawkmoths are thick or angular, sometimes terminated with a little hook. Butterflies are characterized by fine yet stiff antennae which terminate in a little knob — hence their collective name of Rhopalocera (literally club-horns). Antennae of female Lepidoptera are, as a rule, simpler than those of the males; they are either shortly pectinate, serrate or aristate. This can be explained by the fact that in Lepidoptera the antennae serve as organs of smell helping their bearers to find mates. Males use smell for locating females and can do so from a great distance, perhaps as much as a kilometre.

Butterflies and moths usually have *suctorial mouthparts* (Fig. 6b), well illustrated by the conspicuous *proboscis* of a hawkmoth or a butterfly. Few people, even entomologists, are aware that biting *mandibles* are present in the primitive families, including the Micropterigidae and Eriocraniidae (Fig. 6a). Some of these species possess functional mandibles enabling them to feed on pollen instead of the nectar sought by most Lepidoptera. Usually, however, the mandibles are reduced to non-functional vestiges.

Almost all Lepidoptera, apart from the most primitive, have a proboscis, evolved from the jaws *(galeae)*. It is a double organ — two grooved halves joined by a seam to form a slender tube. Butterflies and moths use the proboscis to suck nectar from flowers, or other juices, on which they feed. The longest probosces are found in the hawkmoths, in which they may attain lengths of several centimetres. When not in use, the proboscis is coiled up in a spiral, and only fully extended during the act of sucking. Many butterflies (Rhopalocera) and noctuids are also provided with long probosces, but a number of Lepidoptera have much shorter probosces — sometimes even just a little spike, adapted to piercing soft fruits. In a great many families the

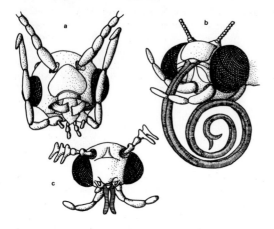

6 Various types of mouthparts in Lepidoptera: a — well-developed mandibles, characteristic of the most primitive Lepidoptera, b — typical well-developed suctorial proboscis, c — degenerate mouthparts, incapable of taking food.

mouthparts are reduced or entirely absent. The proboscis may, like the mandibles, also lose its function (Fig. 6c) and may be lost during the course of evolution. Eggars, emperors, goat moths, some tiger moths, prominents and others do not take any food at all as adults, acquiring all the energy they need from fat stored by the caterpillar. The adults of such species have only one function in life, to reproduce and so secure the continuation of the species.

In most Lepidoptera vestiges of other primitive mouthparts have been preserved. The *labial palps,* consisting of 2—4 segments, are all that usually remains of the lower *labium;* however, sometimes they form such conspicuous structures that they have become an important feature for identifying families according to their length, shape, position, size and pilosity. The palpi belonging to the second pair of mandibles *(maxillary palps)* are small and frequently degenerate.

The thorax comprises three parts: *prothorax, mesothorax* and *metathorax.* At first sight they form a compact whole. However, there are considerable differences in the shape of the separate parts or *sclerites* (hard parts of the exoskeleton locked together by strong seams, or sutures, so-called

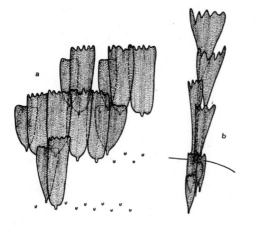

7 Scales covering the wings of Lepidoptera overlap each other like tiles on a roof: a — on wing area, b — at wing margin.

sulci) since the legs and wings are attached to some of them. The three pairs of legs are attached to each thoracic segment, and the two pairs of wings to the second and third segments. Rarely the wings (and even the legs) may be degenerate, a relatively rare but not unknown phenomenon in the Lepidoptera.

The wings, attached to the thorax by means of a complex system of tiny sclerites, are two-layered, membraneous structures thought to have evolved as sac-like expansions of the integument. They are densely clothed with tiny, usually coloured *scales,* orientated in one direction and overlapping each other like tiles on a roof (Fig. 7). The whole colourful splendour of the Lepidoptera lies in these small scales which either contain pigments, or produce colours physically by the diffraction or refraction of light. Such physical systems produce the metallic blues, greens, purples and other iridescent colours familiar in the blues, coppers and purple emperors. The individual coloured scales are arranged like a mosaic to form the elaborate wing patterns. The profusion of different patterns typical of butterflies and moths is dependent on this basic scheme. However, purpose usually prevails over chance, even here. In butterflies it is the forewings (sometimes the hindwings as well) that tend to be brightly coloured, while in moths the more conspicuous colours are restricted to the hindwings, concealed under the neutral shades of the forewings. Some of these colour patterns are of importance in thermoregulation, while others play a role in protective or warning colouration. In some cases certain

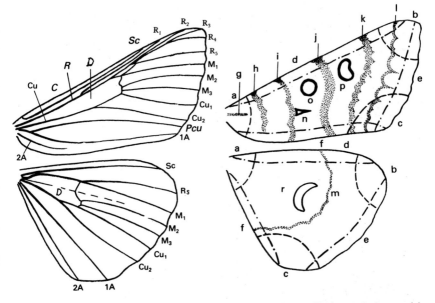

8   Left: Veins and cells of forewing and hindwing: C — costa (confluent with the costal wing margin), Sc — subcosta, R — radius and its branches (R_1–R_5), R_S — radial sector, M — media and its branches (M_1–M_3), Cu — cubitus and its branches (Cu_1, Cu_2), Pcu — postcubitus (in some families absent in hindwing), A — anals (1A, 2A). Corresponding cells are designated similarly (R_4, R_5, M_1, M_2, M_3, Cu_1, etc.), usually taking their name from the vein anterior to them; D — discal cell.   Right: Zones of lepidopterous wings and characteristic elements of the pattern: a — base of the wing, b — apex, c — tornus, d — costal (front) margin, e — apical (outer) margin, f — anal (inner) margin, g — basal line, h — basal cross-band, i — inner cross-band, j — median band, k — outer cross-band, l — wavy line, m — median band of the hindwing, n — wedge-shaped spot, o — circular spot, p — kidney-shaped spot, r — crescent-shaped spot.

special scales are connected with glands and emit an odour which may sometimes be perceived by humans. An intense lemon scent is produced, for example, by males of the Green-veined White. Such scents are thought to be involved in the normal courtship of males and females, as signals or aphrodisiacs.

The delicate wing membranes could not resist alone the pressure of the air during flight, which is why the wings are reinforced by longitudinal and transverse ribs, or *veins* (Fig. 8). These veins have little in common with the veins involved in the blood circulation of vertebrates. Throughout all Lepidoptera, and many other insects, certain homologous veins can be recognised: the *costa, subcosta, radius, media, cubitus, postcubitus,* and *anals.* The abbreviations of these names are written C, Sc, R, M. Cu, Pcu and A respectively. The little areas, or *cells,* enclosed by the veins, are designated by the name of the vein anterior to the cell. Some of the veins branch beyond the base, others remain single throughout their length. The wing veins of different groups of Lepidoptera vary in number, and their arrangement plays an important part in the classification of families, as noted above. Almost every family can be characterized by a particular type of *venation.*

The *legs* are attached laterally, one pair to each thoracic segment. They consist of the following basic segments: *coxa, trochanter, femur, tibia, tarsus,* and *praetarsus* (Fig. 9). The tarsus is five-segmented; the praetarsus bears a pad provided with two claws. The femur (or the tibia) is usually the longest of the segments. Differences may be observed between the three pairs of legs — for example, the forelegs of nymphalids are reduced, while pyralids and plume moths have very long hindlegs. The claws and other appendages also differ in form and number, and may be totally absent in some cases. These characters help to differentiate between the various lepidopterous genera and families. The greatest reduction of the legs is found in the females of certain bagworms, which cannot crawl, and so never leave their cases.

The *abdomen* is cylindrical and primitively consists of ten segments. The first 7—8 segments are very similar in shape and internal structure. The terminal segments (two in males and three in females) have been transformed into *copulatory organs,* entirely different from the other segments in shape. Within the abdomen there is a dorsal *alimentary canal,* a ventral *nerve cord,* branching respiratory tubes (tracheae), glands and *reproductive organs.*

The external sexual organs formed from the sclerites of the terminal abdominal segments function as mechanical organs for copulation. From group to group, species to species, they often differ greatly in form (Fig. 10). It seems likely that their evolutionary development has

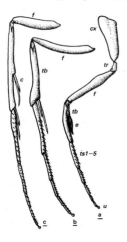

9   Legs of Lepidoptera: a — 1st pair (fore legs), b — 2nd pair (mid legs), c — 3rd pair (hind legs), cx — coxa, tr — trochanter, f — femur, tb — tibia, ts — 1st to 5th segment of the tarsus, u — praetarsus with a claw (unguis), c — spurs, e — appendage (epiphysis) for cleaning the antennae.

10 Male copulatory organs — examples of extraordinary variability:a, b — geometrids (Geometridae),c, d — noctuids (Noctuidae), v — valves, u — uncus, s — saccus, c — corona, h — harpe, p — penis (aedeagus).

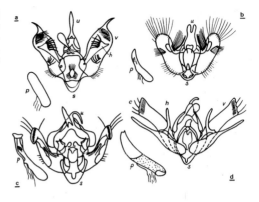

been relatively unaffected by the impact of the external environment. Thus similar forms of copulatory organs, bearing evidence of kinship relations, occur in cases where external appearances have been greatly changed under the pressure of natural selection to fit the rest of the organism to its environment. Similarly, the study of these reproductive organs helps to reveal how evolution, in similar conditions, may result in a convergence of otherwise remotely related groups, often producing butterflies or moths closely resembling each other both in shape and colouration of the wings. Male and female reproductive organs have thus become an indispensable aid in the systematics and taxonomy of Lepidoptera. They are so specific that, on their basis alone, we can classify most butterflies and moths into species without being aware of the colouration of their wings or the structure of other bodily parts. This enables us to identify damaged specimens in which the colour patterns are no longer distinguishable. Use can be made of this to discover what bats and insectivorous birds feed on — by analysing the content of their stomachs or crops and searching for the yet undigested, hard genital sclerites. Resort to the examination of these reproductive organs is also necessary where certain related species are so similar that they cannot be distinguished on the basis of colouration and pattern. In recent years several new species have been discovered in this way, even among the large Lepidoptera. These so-called *sibling species* have often previously escaped attention, notably in common species, as the idea of examining them in detail did not occur to anybody. The following examples are typical: *Hydraecia ultima,* very similar to the common moth *H. micacea;* and *Amphipyra berbera,* which differs only slightly from the abundant Copper Underwing, *A. pyramidea;* or the pair of similar species *Plusia festucae* and *P. putnami.*

The external male reproductive organs can be imagined as a pair of forceps or grasping *valves.* These valves, used by the male to hold the female, are most heterogeneous in shape, sometimes extremely complex, symmetrical or asymmetrical, and often armed with spiny protuberances or appendages, all of which have their names. Dorsal to these valves is the non-paired *uncus,* and on the ventral side lies the *saccus.* All these are modified sclerites of the terminal abdominal segments. The penis *(aedeagus),* connected with the testes by a duct, lies within the space bounded by these four sclerites. The penis is a tough cylindrical structure, often provided with tooth-like projections on the outside; within it contains an eversible *vesica,* frequently adorned with clusters of hooks and spines *(cornuti).*

The female reproductive organs (Fig. 11) are partly membraneous and mostly concealed inside the abdomen. The most conspicuous organ — the *bursa copulatrix* — is a membranous sac whose surface is often spinose. During copulation, *spermatophores* (sacs of sperm) supplied by the male are deposited within the bursa copulatrix, to give a reservoir of sperm which the female

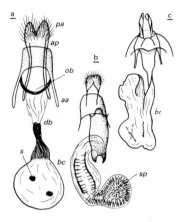

11 Female reproductive organs: a, b — geometrids (Geometridae), c — noctuids (Noctuidae), pa — papillae anales, aa — anterior apophyses, ap — posterior apophyses, bc — bursa copulatrix, db — ductus bursae, ob — ostium bursae (entrance to the bursa), s — sclerotized patch (signum), sp — spinules inside the bursa (spini).

gradually uses to fertilize the eggs as they mature in her ovaries. The bursa copulatrix is connected to the surface of the eighth abdominal segment by a passage, the *ductus bursae*, the orifice being called the *ostium bursae*. This opening, located beneath the *anal papillae*, is the only externally visible structure of the female genitalia.

The male and the female organs, with their species-specific structures, may form a system which prevents copulation with alien species in a similar fashion to the way in which a lock can only be opened by the right key. The importance of these genital organs for systematics and taxonomy is so great in the Lepidoptera that their morphology has been studied in great detail, and has been the subject of extensive articles published in scientific journals, and even of whole books. It is essential to study these structures when describing new species and subspecies, in trying to establish kinship relations amongst the Lepidoptera, and for the reliable determination of numerous species.

In contrast to the almost immobile pupa, the adult (imago) is an extremely active creature. The main 'mission' of the adult is reproduction, and almost all the activities of adult butterflies and moths are channelled to this goal. This requires that males and females of the same species can find each other to copulate and so effect fertilization. At the same time interbreeding among sibling and other species must be prevented, since offspring from such unions are reduced in fitness and fertility, totally sterile, or even inviable altogether. A great variety of different mechanisms have evolved to prevent *crossbreeding*, so ensuring that copulation occurs only between members of the same species.

The extreme scarcity of some species means that males may have the difficult task of finding a female at a distance of perhaps several kilometres. But this is not left to chance. Unfertilized females secrete a characteristic odour from special abdominal glands. The odour substance is called a *pheromone*. The odour is carried by the wind throughout the neighbourhood. The males fly to and fro in search of mates, and having extremely sensitive organs of smell on their antennae, they are able to perceive the female pheromone at great distances. Led by this scent, they try to locate her. In fact the males appear to be much more interested in the sexual scent than in the female herself! They can be allured to glands extirpated from a female, while the female herself sits nearby, unnoticed. Similarly, males will fly to the place where a female has been sitting and which still bears traces of her scent. If a virgin female is enclosed in a small cage so arranged as to prevent males from reaching and so fertilizing her, dozens of males may gather around the female overnight. When the female has been fertilized, the pheromone glands stop functioning and she loses her power to attract males.

Pheromones are often quite simple substances, chemically. Since the number of combinations is exhaustible, it happens that more than one species may use the same pheromone. Specific differentiation is achieved in various ways, sometimes through several other substances being mixed in various proportions to form a specific 'bouquet'. Other ways of preventing mistakes include different times of flight or seasons of occurrence, differences in the morphology and anatomy of copulatory organs (as already described), different stimulatory behaviour prior to copulation, etc. Many pheromones (or substances very similar to them) have been produced artificially and are used with considerable success to mislead the males of selected economically detrimental species. The males will gather at an artificial source of scent, instead of around their females, and here they can easily be caught. So many males can be destroyed in this way that many females are unfertilized, and the destructive caterpillars become far less numerous.

Males also emit sexual odours, from glandular scent scales or zones on the wings, abdomen or hind legs. Unlike the scents exuded by the female, which are used to attract males from a distance, those emitted by the male have a different function: to induce or excite the female to copulate.

Even the manner and timing of *copulation* varies in the different groups of Lepidoptera. Some species mate immediately after issuing from the pupa, others only after several days of adult life. Some species mate easily in captivity, whereas others, for example many butterflies, require a large volume of space and an appropriate environment before mating will take place. In some species the duration of mating is brief, yet others may remain coupled for up to two days. In some species the fertilization of a whole clutch of eggs can be secured by a single mating, while other species mate several times, and there may be an interval of a few days or even weeks between individual copulations, during which eggs are laid and feeding takes place.

Let us now return to events immediately following the eclosion of the adult. Females of some species already have their eggs prepared for fertilization and laying. They lure the males and are soon fertilized. Such species often do not take any food as adults, the supply of reserve substances in their bodies proving sufficient for all their needs. The batches of eggs are large in number, and all the eggs are laid within a short span of time. The desire to lay eggs may be so strong that females who have failed to find a mate will start laying unfertilized eggs. Other species, however, emerge from the pupa with their sexual organs immature. No eggs have developed in the ovaries of the females. If eggs are to mature, the insect must indulge in a period of intensive feeding. She sucks nectar from flowers or other nutritious substances. Even so, it takes several days for the first mature eggs to appear in her ovaries. In some cases ovarian development ceases for a long time, to start again only after winter hibernation, or aestivation (a state of dormancy during the hot summer). Those species in which eggs develop continuously in the ovaries tend to have a very lengthy egg-laying period, even if the greater part of the total supply of eggs is laid during the first few days. Eggs are laid one by one, as they successively develop. If each batch contains a considerable number of eggs, each laying is usually interrupted by a few days' rest.

If individuals of the same species are to meet, it is necessary that their eclosion takes place within a limited space of time. This is of great importance in species having a very short life span. The signal for the insects to emerge from the pupa is given by the length of the day, or by a combination of day-length with temperature. The total temperature regime experienced by the pupa may determine its period of development, and so the time of the insect's emergence. Knowledge of the effective temperature required for development can be turned to advantage, for example in forecasting the appearance of particular insect pests. In other cases the signal coordinating emergence of particular butterflies or moths may be a slight frost, this being typical of late-autumn species.

However, even within a single species it may commonly happen that not all individuals complete their pupal development at the same time. Here we refer not to those variations caused by microclimatic differences but to the fact that sometimes males appear earlier than females, while in other species the reverse is true. This has significance concerning the fertilization of females and reducing the possibility of crossbreeding among related species.

The early eclosion of males ensures that at the time when females start hatching, there is a sufficient number of males available for fertilization. A migration of males can take place preceding the emergence of females. As a result populations become thoroughly mixed (frequently over a vast territory) and *inbreeding* is greatly reduced. After the emergence of females there is often fierce competition among males. Individual males may occupy whole territories, chasing out all rivals. This has been observed in several butterflies. The appearance of males before females is typical of whites, sulphurs, blues, coppers, hairstreaks and many other Rhopalocera.

The emergence of females prior to males is a common phenomenon in species occurring at some unfavourable time of year, such as early spring or late autumn, or in species exposed to other difficult conditions. As a rule, the females of such species are relatively immobile, some even being wingless. They do not eat, but possess sufficient fat supplies on which they can live for a very long time, since energy requirements are reduced at low temperatures. The females of some spring geometrids (*Lycia, Nyssia,* etc.) may emerge in midwinter. They remain alive until spring, waiting for a suitable day when the males then emerge to fertilize them. Gradual emergence of males gives protection against adversity of the weather, for a whole population of these fragile male moths can be annihilated by a sudden rain or snow storm. The hardy females survive and wait for new males to appear as soon as the weather improves.

Apart from fulfilling the basic reproductive function, the excellent flight capacity of adult Lepidoptera enables them to travel great distances, and so spread to new, favourable habitats. In species where the females are wingless or incapable of flight, the males can carry the females some distance during copulation. This is small compared with the distances travelled by good fliers, and so species endowed with such a limited capacity for flight can only spread slowly.

The ovum or egg

The first stage in the life cycle of a butterfly or moth is the egg. The egg is encased in a solid shell (the *chorion*) containing the materials *(yolk)* necessary for the development of the embryo. The chorion has a minute opening or group of openings, called the *micropyle* (Fig. 13), through which sperm can penetrate to the female germ cell within. If the micropyle is located at the top of the egg, we speak of the egg as upright; if the micropyle is placed to one side, the egg is described as recumbent.

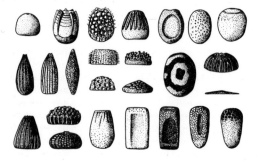

12 Various shapes of lepidopterous eggs.

13 Regular and irregular shapes of the micropylar rosette of eggs (the micropyle opening is situated near the middle).

Lepidopterous eggs (Fig. 12) are mostly spherical or hemispherical in shape, and are attached to a support by their base. However, there are also slender upright eggs of a conical, cylindrical or spindle-like form (many butterflies); others are low, drum-shaped, or scale-like suggestive of sea shells. These are typical, for instance, of some noctuids and leaf rollers. All these eggs are circular in horizontal section. A great many eggs are asymmetrical, angular, or bear elevations, depressions or small hollows on their surface — such variations are frequent in the geometrid family. Raised *ribs,* running from top to bottom of the egg, are a common ornament. Their number varies from about twenty to as much as fifty. They are either straight or sinuous, and may separate into branches. Ribbed eggs are characteristic of noctuids and some butterflies (e.g. nymphalids, browns, whites and sulphurs). The chorion may be finely granulated. Such eggs appear dull: the granulations can be seen only under a microscope. The granules may be relatively coarse, or the surface may bear starlike formations or reticular structures. Towards the micropyle the surface sculpture usually changes, a rosette of leaflike outgrowths frequently being formed — possibly for regulating the motion of sperms towards the micropyle opening (Fig. 13). In some species the surface structure of the eggs cannot be seen, as they are covered with a quick-hardening vitreous substance, with foam, or with hairs from the female's abdomen.

Newly laid eggs are usually yellowish-white and soft. A short time afterwards the chorion becomes hard and the eggs acquire their true colouring. They may be pale yellow, orange yellow, light green, reddish-brown or black. The eggs of moths of the genus *Catocala* and those of eggars are brightly coloured. The colouration may remain constant throughout the entire period of development, or it may change, reflecting the developmental stage of the embryo within. The yellowish-white eggs may acquire a reddish, wreath-like design; in other cases they may turn brown or grey, or develop a sheen. Towards the end of embryonic development the small caterpillar is usually visible through the chorion, particularly if the larva has a dark head and a body covered with tubercles, or if it is all dark.

The females may lay their eggs singly, in small groups, or in large *clutches* containing as many as several thousand eggs (Fig. 14). Large clutches are laid, for example, by the females of tiger moths, tussock moths, eggars, and a great number of noctuids. The clutches may be laid in a single layer, when the eggs are often neatly aligned in rows, or they may be arranged like tiles on a roof, or several layers may be heaped up without any apparent order. To protect their eggs against enemies, females sometimes insert them, using their narrow abdomens as 'ovipositors', into bark fissures, under leaf-sheaths, or into rosettes of leaves, buds or empty seed-pods. Sometimes, as already noted, they cover them with hairs from their abdomen, or by a solidifying secretion. In contrast, swift moths lay their eggs in a rather extraordinary manner. Their

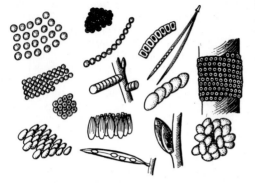

females do not produce any secretion for gluing eggs to a support, but, while flying about, simply let them drop freely into the grass. Species whose caterpillars feed on the parts of plants above ground would suffer great losses in this way, but the caterpillars of swift moths crawl into the soil to feed on roots.

Temperature is the most important external factor influencing the development of the egg. A change of several degrees may result in a substantial acceleration or retardation of development. At a temperature of 25°C it may take the egg 2—3 days to pass through the entire embryonic development, whereas at 10°C the development might last for several weeks or even months. The maximum temperature for most eggs is approximately 40°C, which they can stand for a short time, but several hours at this heat usually result in death. Sudden chilling to below freezing point may also kill eggs. Only eggs 'programmed' for low temperatures, for which they are physiologically prepared, are capable of surviving severe winters and bitter frosts without damage. Generally the development of the embryo within the egg comes to a standstill at the onset of low autumn temperatures, to continue in spring when the weather gets warmer. Sometimes the complete first instar caterpillar develops within the egg as early as autumn. However, it remains within the hard chorion (which has considerable protective value) until spring, when it emerges to continue development in favourable conditions.

Humidity may considerably affect the survival of eggs. Generally they are not capable of withstanding absolute drought, but excessive moisture can also be harmful. In fact, the temperature and humidity requirements of different eggs are very varied. Species living in the far north or south are necessarily adapted to low temperatures, whereas the development of tropical species requires resistance to entirely different conditions, including very high humidity.

The larva or caterpillar

This larval stage of feeding and growth usually has a cylindrical, vermiform body, in some cases flattened or spindle-shaped. All caterpillars have a head and thirteen posterior segments (Fig. 15). The first three of these constitute the thorax, the remaining ten form the abdomen.

The solid head (Fig. 15b) is shaped in two hemispheres. Between these, to the front, is a triangular forehead *(frons)* with the *vertex* at the top. Laterally there are six *ocelli*, usually arranged in a horseshoe pattern. These simple eyes are sometimes lacking, as in caterpillars of some storehouse pests which live in the dark for the greater part of their life. In front of the ocelli there is a pair of short, segmented *antennae*. The most outstanding structures of the head are the mouthparts. These consist of two powerful, wedge-shaped, toothed *mandibles*. Above, the mandibles are bounded by the upper lip *(labrum)*; below, by the lower lip *(labium)*. The labium carries a pair of inconspicuous *labial palps*. More prominent is the *spinneret*. This special organ, found only in the caterpillar and without analogy in any other developmental stage, is the outlet of the *silk gland*. Silk is produced by squirting out a fluid which rapidly coagulates on exposure to air. In this way caterpillars spin silken fibres, or use the fluid to glue together bits of leaves or wood, tiny lumps of clay and other materials. Although in the adults the second pair of jaws (the *maxillae*) are considerably reduced, in the caterpillars they are developed into powerful *maxillary palps*. These organs aid the mandibles by holding the food, and thus assist in mastication and shifting food into the pharynx. The voracious way caterpillars eat may readily be observed. For example, the caterpillar of the Spurge Hawkmoth employs its forelegs to hold a narrow leaf of the cypress spurge which, within a few seconds, then disappears down the insatiable gullet. Without delay, the caterpillar starts foraging for another leaf. Soon all that remains is a bald stem.

Each thoracic segment has a pair of jointed legs (Fig. 15c) consisting of similar parts to those observed in the adult. They differ only by being less complex: the tarsus consists of one segment only. In caterpillars the absence of thoracic legs is exceptional. The thorax also has paired ventilation openings *(spiracles)*, and in some species extrusible glands occur on the ventral or dorsal side. The double, horn-shaped protuberance *(osmeterium)* found in swallowtail caterpillars is a well known example of the latter.

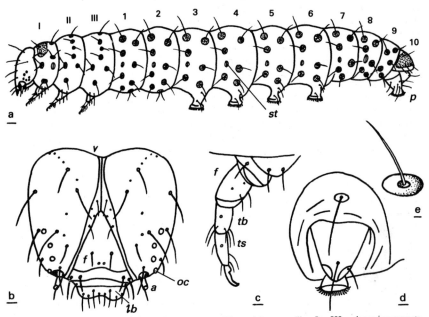

15   Caterpillar and principal parts of its body: a — usual form of the caterpillar: I to III — thoracic segments with thoracic legs and thoracic scutellum on the prothorax, 1 to 10 — abdominal segments with abdominal legs and suranal plate on the 10th segment, st — spiracles (stigma, stigmata), p — anal claspers. b — head of the caterpillar: a — antenna, f — frons, lb — labrum, oc — ocelli, v — vertex.   c — thoracic leg: f — femur, tb — tibia, ts — tarsus.   d — abdominal leg with a ring of hooks (crotchets).   e — seta arising from tubercle.

A further eight pairs of spiracles are situated on the abdomen; they are absent only from the ninth and tenth segments. Abdominal legs (so-called *prolegs* — Fig. 15d) are soft and muscular, and in contrast to the thoracic legs, they are not segmented. The tips are provided with a great number of hooks *(crotchets)* regularly arranged either in lines, arcs or circles. The number of prolegs varies according to family or species, and may also change in the course of the development of an individual species. Caterpillars usually have five pairs of prolegs — on the third, fourth, fifth, sixth and tenth abdominal segments. The first four pairs are similar, but the legs on the tenth segment are different. Being very important for crawling, they are particularly powerful, and are called *claspers*. Exceptions occur: the true claspers may be transformed, in some species, into protuberances or tiny whips, as is the case with prominents — here they do not serve for crawling at all, and the function of the claspers is taken over by the legs of the sixth segment. The prolegs are often reduced in number. Thus in moths belonging to the genus *Catocala,* for example, the legs of the third abdominal segment are absent, and those of the fourth segment are so reduced that they are of little help in crawling. Other noctuid moths (Plusiinae) usually have abdominal legs only on the fifth, sixth and tenth segments, representing a transition to the condition found in geometrids, the majority of which only have legs on the sixth and tenth segments. Their well-known 'looping' (inchworm) movement is a conse-

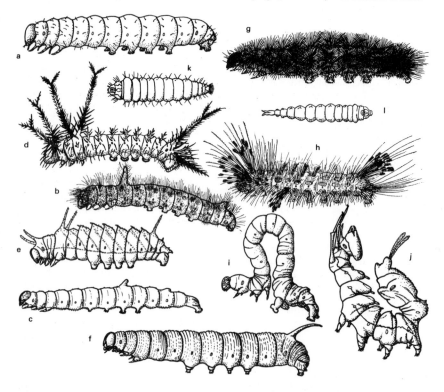

16   Various types of caterpillars: a, b, c — Noctuidae, d, e — Saturniidae, f — Sphingidae, g — Arctiidae, h — Lymantriidae, i — Geometridae, j — Notodontidae, k — Tischeriidae, l — Gracillariidae.

quence of this reduction. In some species (for example in the family Eriocraniidae) prolegs are entirely wanting. On the other hand, caterpillars of the family Micropterigidae have legs on all of the first eight segments, and caterpillars of the family Nepticulidae have legs from the second to the seventh abdominal segments.

The *integument* of caterpillars may either be almost bare, or more or less densely clothed with hairs; it also may be furnished with *setae, spinules* and *tubercles* (Fig. 16). Even the bodies of apparently naked caterpillars are set with fine cilia. The location of the cilia or setae *(chaetotaxy)* is sufficiently varied yet regular that it has become an important character for the identification of caterpillars to species (Fig. 15). In hairy or spinose caterpillars this fine, so-called primary setation is concealed under the numerous secondary hairs, which either grow out of big tubercles, or are enlarged spinules of the exoskeleton.

Peculiar outgrowths make some caterpillars assume a bizarre shape. Such outgrowths are used by geometrid caterpillars to simulate twigs with buds or thorns, withering and deformed leaves, husks of various herbs, etc. The caterpillars of prominents bear conspicuous excrescences suggestive of leaf cankers. Hawkmoth caterpillars are characterized by a peculiar horn at the end of the abdomen. The larvae of many nymphalids, including the fritillaries, are markedly spiny; in some species the spines are branched or covered with coarse tubercles. Caterpillars of some emperor moths, equipped with hard, star-shaped spines and coloured tubercles, have an extremely weird appearance and are capable of injecting urticating chemicals into human skin! — an unpleasant property shared by many larvae.

The pattern and colouration of caterpillars present inexhaustible variations. However, these patterns, even the most extreme examples, show certain regular features. Pigments are either arranged into longitudinal, transverse or oblique lines and bands, or dispersed all over the body as spots. In many caterpillars there is no pattern at all — they are green, yellowish or brownish, or the pattern is quite simple. Pigments are often virtually absent in caterpillars living inside plants, or underground, but some species abound in bright-coloured markings, such as the Spurge Hawkmoth, the Bedstraw Hawkmoth, and the Swallowtail.

The size of larvae is, naturally, very variable. Full-grown caterpillars of some miners do not exceed 4mm in length. At the other extreme caterpillars of noctuid moths (particularly of those belonging to tropical species) can grow to as much as 150mm in length and 20—30mm in breadth. Mature caterpillars of most of the European tiger moths, noctuids and prominents are 30—50mm long, while the larger butterflies produce caterpillars as much as 20—40mm in length. Geometrids have slender, long caterpillars, burnets and foresters have short and thick ones, and those of hairstreaks and blues are short and flat, rather slug-like in appearance.

Caterpillars are for the most part herbivorous, specializing on green plants, but many feed in other ways. Some species bore in dry wood or feed on decaying leaves and seeds. In nature, larvae of the Clothes Moth live on the hair and horn of mammals, or on birds' feathers: so in human homes they are content to eat woollen clothes and furs. The caterpillars of a few species feed on bees' wax and can be destructive parasites in beehives. Caterpillars sometimes occur on decaying animal remains, excrement and rubbish-heaps. Fungi are also consumed by Lepidoptera — an example being the macropore fungi tunnelled into by larvae of the specialized genus *Morophaga*.

Most caterpillars specialize in consuming particular plant parts. Some gnaw roots, others bore inside bulbs and tubers. Larvae of goat moths and clearwings bore galleries in tree trunks, branches of shrubs, or plant stems. The caterpillars of the pyralid genus *Nymphula* and its relatives live under water, eating waterlilies, duckweed and other aquatic plants. Most of these aquatic species absorb oxygen from the water through a layer of air with which they are surrounded. An exception is the pyralid *Parapoynx stratiotata,* in which the breathing organs (tracheae) protrude from the body to form gills.

Even the manner in which caterpillars eat green leaves, apparently so familiar to us, shows great variation between species. Some always start eating the leaf from the side, others begin in the middle and gnaw holes between the leaf veins. Such leaves may look as if they have been shot at. As a rule, young larvae do not make complete holes in the leaf, but leave one layer of translucent skin undamaged — usually on the upper surface of the leaf. Leaf roller caterpillars curl a leaf up and fasten it with silk to prevent it from unfolding. In the tube thus formed they spend the greater part of their life, leaving their abode only when they go foraging nearby for food. Flowers, seed-pods and fruits also provide a home for caterpillars of various noctuids, leaf rollers and geometrids. The colouration of some of them is exceptionally well adapted to their environment: only those very familiar with their habits are likely to perceive them. For example, caterpillars of small geometrids of the genus *Eupithecia* are very frequent inhabitants of flowers: unless they move it is extremely difficult to distinguish them from the pistil, on which they feed. After destroying the pistil in one flower, they move to another. Often they are brought into the home in a vase of flowers: they may then betray their presence by tiny droppings falling onto a clean table-cloth.

Caterpillars of the families Psychidae, Coleophoridae and Adelidae live in cases (Fig. 17) which they carry wherever they go. Sometimes the whole case is spun from silk, or made up of a pale, parchment-like substance, or it may be fabricated by the larva from leaf fragments or bits of straw. Some case bearers turn a partly bitten out piece of leaf into a case, which they then separate from the leaf with a final cut. The caterpillar never leaves this case but gradually enlarges it by adding further materials and spinning additional parts. It only moves the anterior part of its body out of the case opening, in order to reach for food. When full-grown it spins the opening of the case against a leaf or other support, and then turns round to face the end of the case which has little valves the larva uses to eject its droppings; then it pupates. The adult eventually emerges from the case, making its way out between these valves at the free end. The females of some bagworms remain in their case, where they are fertilized and may even lay their eggs. The caterpillars crawl away to a fresh part of the host plant. The shape of the cases, and the materials of which they are made, are characteristic for each species. If we also know the foodplant, we can confidently identify the bagworm caterpillars to species.

The life of caterpillars of the smallest moths, with wingspans lying within the range of 4–8mm, is of great interest. Most belong to the families Gracillariidae and Nepticulidae, involving a great number of species. Caterpillars of these little moths are so tiny that they can live inside buds or, more frequently, in leaves, where they drive tunnels or galleries, so-called *mines*. If the cross-section of a thin leaf is examined under a microscope, several cell layers become visible. The upperside and the underside of the leaf are covered with a soft 'skin', the epidermis, consisting of a single layer of cells. The intervening space is filled with a green tissue

17 Larval cases of the families Coleophoridae and Psychidae (the psychids, or bagworms, are the last two on the right-hand side).

on which the tiny caterpillars feed, leaving the epidermal layers intact. Like a miner excavating a gallery in a coal seam, so the tiny larvae leave a tunnelled gallery behind them — the mine (hence their name: miners). At the head of the gallery the caterpillar works away, depositing its droppings in the cavity behind. The mines create various patterns on the leaves — sometimes spiral or zigzag lines, sometimes circular, like little blisters. If the miner feeds closer to one of the two epidermal layers (often closer to the underside of the leaf), the thinner skin contracts and the opposite side of the leaf bulges out. This may result in a local deformation or in the distortion of the whole leaf. The workings of the miners show great variety. The forms of the majority of mines are so typical of individual species of these small moths that, on this basis alone, it is possible to determine the species without ever having seen the moth or the caterpillar. As a rule, a species starts mining the leaf at a particular place (for example, at the base of leaf veins, at the tip of the leaf, etc.); it forms similar curves or undulations in the course of its mine, and also the droppings are deposited in the mines in the same way — in continuous chains, in broken chains, in groups, in one place only, irregularly, etc. The full-fed caterpillar of a species also behaves in a constant fashion. In some species they leave the mine and pupate in the ground, or on the leaf surface. Others pupate directly within the mine, in a spun cell which remains behind after the adults emerge.

In some lepidopterous families the larvae typically form large colonies. If the female lays a large number of eggs in one cluster, this does not necessarily imply that the caterpillars are going to live gregariously. For example, caterpillars of most tiger moths, noctuids and geometrids — the females of which often lay their eggs in clusters — wander away on hatching to lead solitary lives. In contrast, the larvae of many eggars, tussock moths, and the tiny ermine moths live together for a long time, in some cases for their whole life. Caterpillars of gregarious species often spin a web-like nest of silk to protect themselves against bad weather and enemies; the nest also helps to keep the colony together. The grey, pear-shaped nest formed by the larvae of the Small Eggar moth is spun of dense fibres, and is visible on an infested tree from a great distance. Burdened by dozens of large dark caterpillars and their droppings, a slender branch on which the nest is formed may hang down conspicuously. A multitude of silk threads leading from the nest to the tree top guide the larvae on their way back to the nest after a day's feeding. The nest is so solid that it is far from easy to get inside. When the caterpillars rest on its surface they are protected by the almost invisible threads extending to the surrounding twigs, which discourage birds from attacking. A cross-section through the nest reveals a number of layers. If cold weather sets in, the caterpillars creep deep into the interior layers, where they are well protected and insulated.

Brown-tail and Lackey moth larvae build similar nests to that of the Small Eggar, but as they mature they no longer return to the nest: this remains abandoned among the defoliated twigs. The mature Brown-tail caterpillars live freely in the crown of the tree. Caterpillars of the Lackey weave an extensive pad of grey silk in a fork of two strong branches, where they congregate to moult and rest. In sunny weather several hundreds of them may be seen. When disturbed all of them start shaking the anterior part of their body, only settling down when the disturbance ceases. Sometimes the movement of several caterpillars becomes a signal for a general exodus: hundreds of caterpillars rain down in search of safer shelter in the undergrowth. Only when all is clear do they climb back again.

Experiments have shown that the gregarious life in caterpillars of some species is so important that the well-being of individual caterpillars is dependent upon the group. When isolated they develop much more slowly and often fail to complete their development altogether.

The gregarious larval habit also occurs in numerous butterflies. Generally, however, they do not weave nests. Even when they do, they soon abandon them — as in the Black-veined White in which the nest serves for the purpose of hibernation only. Caterpillars of the Large White live gregariously for a long time: only in the last instar do they wander apart — because the food in a confined area could never satisfy all their needs. Caterpillars of the Small Tortoiseshell behave in a similar way, but larvae of the Camberwell Beauty and the Large Tortoiseshell stay together throughout their life, separating only to pupate. All such gregarious species tend, of course, to defoliate plants: such damage can often be seen on fruit trees, willows, birches, aspens and sallows.

The pupa or chrysalis

Full-grown caterpillars wander about in search of a suitable site for pupation. Butterflies usually pupate freely, that is, without the protection of a cocoon. The larva usually spins a small pad of silk on a support, to which it then fastens itself by means of its anal claspers. After pupation has taken place, adhesion to the silk pad is maintained very firmly by the *cremaster*. Butterfly chrysalides either hang upside down, suspended from the cremaster (as is the case in nymphalids), or they are fastened in a more or less upright position, the weight bearing on the cremaster, the position being maintained by a girdle of silk fastened round the thorax. This mode of pupation is typical of pierids and papilionids. The chrysalides of some butterflies lie loosely on the ground, wrapped only in a flimsy web which serves as a rough or simple cocoon.

The caterpillars of moths almost always seek or make a shelter of some kind for pupation. This may simply be a fissure in the bark of a tree, a knot-hole, or a gap between stones. A hollow foodplant stem is a favourite place for the pupation of many species. The caterpillar forms a little chamber within the cavity and partitions it off. Before pupation the larva gnaws away at the wall of the chamber, to leave a weak zone formed only by the epidermal layer. The pupa is still well hidden from its enemies. The emergence of the moth from the cell is made possible by the pupa's abdominal segments being set with spines. Using these to get purchase, the pupa can force a way through the pre-prepared weak zone, and so protrude from the chamber, to allow the easy emergence of the adult moth. The empty pupal cuticle usually remains jutting out of the stem. This mode of pupation occurs in such genera as *Archanara* and *Nonagria*, some oecophorids of the genus *Depressaria*, some goat moths, clearwings, etc.

Caterpillars of a great many species seek shelter for pupation on the ground, or underground. Plant fragments and decaying leaves are suitable material to make a tough cocoon. Sometimes the caterpillar merely joins such fragments with a few strands of silk, before pupating inside. Such simple cocoons are made by the Tau Emperor Moth, many geometrids and tiger moths, and some hawkmoths. The majority of moth larvae enter the ground to pupate, forming little solid walled *cells*, sometimes lined with a soft fabric of spun silk. On digging up such cells, they look just like little lumps of earth — only their regular oval shape indicates their animal origin. Hawkmoths, such as the Death's Head, Privet and Convolvulus hawks, make their large cells deep in the soil. Moths of the genus *Cucullia* produce solid, firmly spun cells. It is amazing how such fragile moths can force their way from deep in the earth to the surface.

Of great interest and importance are the more or less densely woven *cocoons* spun by certain caterpillars prior to pupation. The regularly spun cocoon of the Silkworm is perhaps the finest example. Commercial silk thread is obtained by unwinding the cocoon in the direction opposite to that in which it was spun. Similar cocoons are also produced by many species of eggars and emperor moths, but their fibres are usually grey or dirty brown, not the pure white, yellow or pink so characteristic of the Silkworm. In constructing such cocoons, most larvae bind in various extraneous materials with the silken threads — particles of leaves, or, as is the case with tiger and tussock moths, hairs from the caterpillar's body. Sometimes the silk takes a long time to harden; the threads then coalesce to form a solid, lustrous parchment-like cocoon. Such compact, hard cocoons are found, for example, in eggars of the genus *Eriogaster*. Burnet and

18 Three types of lepidopterous pupae: a — decticous exarate pupa (typical of Eriocraniidae): antennae, tarsi and wing sheaths are free, not fused together, and the mandibles are also visible, b — adecticous incomplete pupa (Cossidae): body appendages are not free but their shape is distinctly outlined on the pupa, and the abdomen is very mobile, the rows of spines giving purchase when the pupa works its way out of the cocoon, c — adecticous obtect pupa (typical, for example, of Noctuidae): sclerites only slightly protrude, and the abdomen is restricted in movement, or completely immobile.

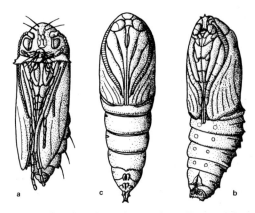

forester larvae produce yellow or white cocoons glistening with a vitreous sheen. Eggars of the genus *Malacosoma* have softer cocoons incorporating yellow dust capable of causing dermatitis ('caterpillar rash'). All these are methods of protecting the otherwise helpless pupae.

The hardest cocoons are spun by some species of the prominent family, notably puss moths of the genera *Cerura* and *Furcula*. The silk is mixed with masticated chips of leaves, wood or bark, giving a tough-walled cell placed in a fissure of bark or the fork of a branch. Even though it is quite large it so perfectly resembles a canker or scar that it is most difficult to find.

A number of caterpillars neither form cocoons nor cells, but pupate instead in a rolled-up leaf, drawn together with silk to form a little tube. Some take advantage of the natural position of adjacent leaves, joining them together with threads. These pupae are not very well protected and may easily fall prey to birds, predatory beetles, or other enemies, but situated among the foliage they are supplied with the required humidity, since water is being constantly evaporated by the transpiring leaves. The majority of leaf rollers and pyralids pupate among leaves in this manner. Among the larger Lepidoptera, this habit is adopted by moths of the genus *Catocala* and the Red Admiral butterfly.

The pupa has a hard, compact case, on which the outlines of the future adult can be discerned. Mobility is usually limited to just some of the abdominal segments.

In the Lepidoptera, three basic types of pupae can be distinguished (Fig. 18). The most primitive of these is the *decticous exarate pupa* in which some appendages are partly separate and even slightly mobile. In these species the mandibles are still visible on the head, as in the adult, and are used to help escape from the cocoon. This primitive type of pupa bears some resemblance to the pupae of caddis flies, and is characteristic of the two ancient families of Lepidoptera — the Micropterigidae and Eriocraniidae.

The second type, the *adecticous incomplete pupa*, occurs in other primitive families, including goat moths, hepialids, burnets and foresters. Wings and limbs are partly free, but immobile. The number of mobile abdominal segments is reduced, the pupae are more solid than those of the preceding type, and they are usually furnished with some device for tearing open the cocoon.

The most widespread and evolutionarily advanced type is the mummylike chrysalis, or *adecticous obtect pupa*. It forms a compact structure with clearly outlined sclerites. The abdomen, consisting of ringlike segments, is visible from the first segment dorsally, but on the ventral side only from the fifth. The first four segments are covered by thoracic sclerites. Mobility is restricted to the fifth and sixth abdominal segment at most, or is entirely lacking. Spiracles are visible laterally on the abdominal segments. The proboscis sheath in some hawkmoths (for

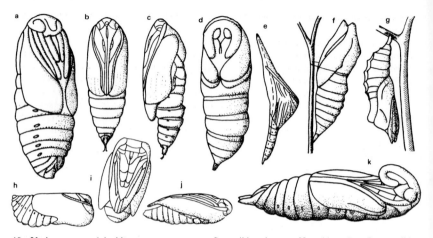

19 Various types of lepidopterous pupae: a — Saturniidae, b, c — Noctuidae, d — Lymantriidae, e — Pieridae, f — Papilionidae, g — Nymphalidae, h — Lycaenidae, i — Nepticulidae, j — Yponomeutidae, k — Sphingidae.

example the Convolvulus and Privet hawks) forms a very conspicuous structure in these and some other moths. The tenth abdominal segment of the pupa forms the cremaster, a somewhat elongate, hard and compact structure bearing a conspicuous sculpture characteristic of each species. The tip is usually provided with several anchor hooks.

To determine the sex of a caterpillar is usually very difficult without studying and dissecting the rudiments of the sex organs within the body, but in pupae males may be distinguished from females on the basis of external features, according to the openings on the ventral side of the eighth and ninth abdominal segments. In species characterized by distinct sexual dimorphism, such as differences in the size or shape of the antennae, the sex of a pupa may also be distinguished by the size and form of the sclerites covering the particular structure.

The size of pupae (Fig. 19) ranges from 2—3mm in the smallest Lepidoptera to large hawkmoth pupae, attaining 60—70mm in length. The pupae of giant emperor moths are not particularly long, but are extremely bulky. In general it holds that the size and shape of the pupa corresponds closely with the body dimensions of the future adult.

The colouring of pupae is often variegated in butterflies but relatively uniform in moths. The pupae of butterflies are often yellowish or green, frequently marked with black spots or shiny patches. The pupae of moths are green, light or dark brown, brownish-red or black. The pupae of moths of the genus *Catocala* are dusted with grey or blue.

Variation

Individual variation

To give a detailed description of a particular lepidopterous species usually entails difficulties: individuals belonging to the same species, or even to the same population, are by no means all the same, often differing in many details. The same situation occurs in our own species: we are all members of *Homo sapiens*, yet there are great differences in stature, head shape, skin, hair and eye colour, resistance to diseases, mental faculties, etc. Such *variability* is a general phenomenon in nature.

In sexually reproducing species this variability can be traced to both the unique *genetic inheritance* of individuals, and the inevitable inequalities of the *environment*, ensuring that no two individuals develop with either the same potentialities or in exactly the same conditions. In the course of evolution variability has probably been selected for, insofar as variable species have a good chance that at least some of their number will have the ability to cope with the ever-changing vicissitudes of life, and so survive to found succeeding generations. The wholesale application of insecticides, for example, frequently results in the rapid development of resistant strains or populations of insects: these are founded by just those individuals who possessed, by chance, some inherent and heritable resistance to the chemicals toxic to their former brethren.

In the sections that follow, some of the principal types of variation, both continuous and discontinuous, are briefly reviewed.

Geographical variation

A great many species inhabit extensive territories, ranging, for example, from western Europe as far as eastern Asia and Japan. The climatic differences which occur over so vast an area have marked effects on the variability of organisms. Over long periods of time different populations of a species tend to adapt to the local conditions. This can result in such great variations in appearance or biology that we may find it hard to decide whether or not one or more independent species is involved. Where these different forms replace or represent each other in different parts of the total range, they are usually classified as *geographical races* or subspecies, using the trinominal nomenclature referred to above (p. 13). An important criterion for recognising a *subspecies* is the condition that more than one geographical race cannot simultaneously inhabit the same region — in other words, they must be isolated territorially. The most likely situation in which to find subspecies is where the range of the species is divided by physical barriers — seas, lakes, wide rivers, mountains, deserts, etc. Ideal conditions for the evolution of subspecies occur on islands, in high mountains, or in 'ecological islands' — for example, the peat-bogs of central Europe, which have much in common with the northern tundra, but from which they are territorially separated. The same applies to isolated steppe habitats which once formed a part of the steppes of central Asia, but are now separated from them. The higher mountain ranges of Europe afford isolated retreats for a fauna which probably enjoyed a continuous distribution in glacial times. All such places are likely to promote the origin of geographic races. The multitude of races of the Apollo butterfly, as described from individual mountain systems of Europe, serves as a good example. Several subspecies are known in the copper *Lycaena dispar*, the brown *Erebia epiphron*, the white *Pieris bryoniae*, and in hundreds of other species.

Such geographic variation can formally be recognised by the trinominal system — but it must be remembered that individuals of every subspecies, and every population of a subspecies, also show individual and further local variability.

Seasonal polyphenism

Some insect species have only one generation in the year, while others, developing at a more rapid rate, manage to produce two or even more generations. It sometimes happens that individual generations differ considerably from each other in appearance. This is called *seasonal polyphenism* (formerly polymorphism), many examples of which can be found in butterflies. A well-known case is the Map butterfly, *Araschnia levana*, whose spring generation (f. *levana*) has brown wings with a black pattern, whereas the summer generation (f. *prorsa*) has black wings marked with yellowish-white spots and reddish lines. Experiments reveal that this effect is evoked by day-length during larval development. Caterpillars developing in spring, when the day is long, produce black butterflies characteristic of the summer generation. Caterpillars developing in the short days of autumn give rise to the brown butterflies of the spring generation. Although not so striking, seasonal differences also occur between the generations of certain other nymphalids, the Bath and Green-veined whites, many blues and coppers, and some moths. Seasonal polyphenism may also be manifest in developmental stages other than the adult.

Sexual dimorphism

Males and females always differ in the structure of the internal and external primary sex organs; sometimes, however, the differences may extend to their general appearance, including size and colouration. Such a marked difference between males and females is called *sexual dimorphism*.

Examples of sexual dimorphism abound among butterflies. Many blues only show characteristic metallic blue colouring in the males, the females being dark brown. In the common Large White, the male has black markings on the apical parts of his forewings only, while the female's wings are marked with additional black spots. The male Orange-tip is decorated with bright orange on the forewings, whereas the female lacks this colour. The male of the Brimstone is a beautiful lemon yellow, but the female is much paler, greenish-white in colour.

Many moths show marked structural differences between the sexes. The Gypsy moth has a big, yellowish-white, clumsy female with a thick abdomen, and a smaller, brown, rapidly fluttering male. A more complex example is supplied by the Wood Tiger: the hindwings of the male are yellow in the lowlands, while in the mountains they are almost white. The female is reddish in all situations.

Sexual dimorphism frequently involves size. Females are usually bulkier than males, even in butterflies, but they are particularly so in eggars, tigers and prominents among the moths. Female geometrids often have reduced wings, as found in the well-known Winter Moth, and species of the genera *Erannis* and *Lycia*. Vestigial wings are also found in females of some leaf rollers *(Exapate)*, occophorid moths *(Diurnea)*, and vapourer moths *(Orgyia)*. (Fig. 24).

In many moths sexual dimorphism is manifest in the shape of the antennae. Males often have comb-like (pectinate) antennae, whereas their females have smaller or simpler ones — either with short pectinations or small serrations, or they are thread-like (filiform). This is often the case in geometrids, eggars, emperor moths, prominents, and some noctuids. Frequently the antennae are much longer in males than in females. Small moths of the family Adelidae are extreme in this respect, the male antennae exceeding those of the females by as much as three or four times. (Fig. 5a).

Geographical distribution

Lepidopterous insects are creatures of dry land. Species whose caterpillars live in water are a rare exception. Over the land surface of the globe, butterflies and moths are absent only from the most inhospitable regions of extreme cold and drought: from the Arctic and the Antarctic, from the highest mountains and the most extreme deserts. Directly or indirectly, their life depends on vegetation, and thus they occur wherever plants grow. In addition, they now inhabit places where Man has created artificial conditions suitable for them, in his habitations and storehouses. Transiently, when actively migrating or being carried by air currents, butterflies and moths may also appear in localities otherwise unsuitable for them.

The science concerned with the distribution of animals and plants on the Earth's surface is called *biogeography*. It is based primarily on geological research, the findings of palaeontologists, and evolutionary systematics — notably *comparative morphology*. Comparative morphology supplied the impulse for much of the work, once it became apparent that organisms living on distant continents may have much in common, and not all aspects of biogeography can be explained by dispersal or migration. In many cases it is most reasonable to assume that present-day species have developed from common ancestors which inhabited a common and unbroken territory. The continuous areas became disjoined by major geological events, and so separate biogeographic regions came into existence. A number of theories have been developed along these lines, the most famous being Wegener's well-known theory of *continental drift*, now well corroborated by modern geological evidence.

Nineteenth century scholars, notably Alfred Russel Wallace and Percy Sclater, attempted to divide our planet into regions characterized by the kinship relationships among animals. More recently it has been accepted that biogeographic divisions can also be made on the basis of ecology. Ecological biogeography *(chorology)* takes as its basis the existing distribution of life forms, and divides the Earth into oceans, freshwater habitats and dry land. On dry land, forest, steppe, desert and tundra zones, etc., can be distinguished. Regional biogeography is fundamentally historical in approach. An attempt to classify the biogeographic regions of the earth, based mainly on historical considerations, is given below (see also Fig. 20):

Biotic kingdom: Megagaea (= Arctogaea)
  Biotic region: Holarctic region
    Palaearctic subregion
    Nearctic subregion
  Biotic region: Oriental region
  Biotic region: Afrotropical region
    African subregion
    Madagascan subregion

Biotic kingdom: Neogaea
  Biotic region: Neotropical region
Biotic kingdom: Notogaea
  Biotic region: Australian region
    Continental Australian subregion
    New Zealand subregion
    Polynesian subregion

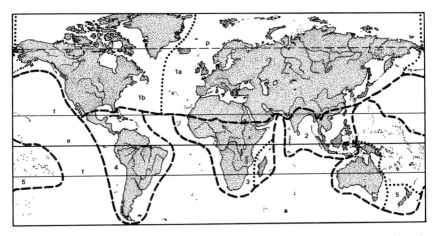

20 Biogeographic division of the world: 1 — Holarctic region, 1a — Palaearctic subregion, 1b — Nearctic subregion, 2 — Oriental region, 3 — Afrotropical region, 4 — Neotropical region, 5 — Australian region; e — Equator, t — tropics, p — Arctic Circle.

Most distinct among the biogeographic kingdoms is Notogaea, including Australia and the adjacent islands, New Zealand and Polynesia. In terms of land area it is the smallest of all the kingdoms, and is characterized by many ancient and primitive *endemics* (animals occurring nowhere else in the world). This is the home of such peculiar vertebrates as the kangaroos, the Duck-billed Platypus, and the Kiwi. Among the Lepidoptera, the primitive families Micropterigidae, Mnesarchaeidae and Hepialidae are represented in this region by a relative multitude of species. Some of the hepialids attain a remarkable wingspread of about 200mm, a size unparalleled by these moths elsewhere in the world.

Neogaea mainly represents present-day South America. Its northern boundary passes through Central America and the Antilles.

Megagaea (also called Arctogaea) is the largest of all biotic kingdoms, covering the remainder of the Earth. Situated mainly in the northern hemisphere, it extends to the southern hemisphere only in Africa. Three subregions are delimited here: the Oriental region covers the peninsulas of southern Asia (to the south of Tibet) and Indonesia. The Afrotropical region is restricted to Africa south of the Sahara desert; it is divided into continental Africa and the island of Madagascar, inhabited by a very distinctive fauna including many endemic forms. It seems that the Madagascan fauna has been developing in isolation for a very long time.

In this book we are primarily concerned with the Holarctic region, consisting of two subregions: the Nearctic subregion, which comprises North America and Greenland, and the Palaearctic subregion, covering northern Africa, the whole of Europe and the major part of Asia (with the exception of some southern territories belonging to the Oriental region). Sometimes an Arctic region is distinguished as an independent zone, and similarly the Antarctic region in the southern hemisphere.

Europe is situated in the vast Palaearctic subregion, extending from the Canary Islands and northern Africa as far as eastern Asia. The eastern outposts of the Palaearctic subregion are Japan, the Kurile Islands and Kamchatka. Surprisingly, the fauna inhabiting this vast Palaearctic zone, measuring over 15,000km from one end to the other, is relatively uniform. A great number of European lepidopterous species occur, in an only slightly modified form, as far as eastern Siberia. Further, the Palaearctic fauna has much in common with that of North America. In the two regions, numerous noctuids, geometrids, butterflies and other species belong to the same genera. Some species are distributed throughout the entire Holarctic region, that is, they occur in Europe, Asia and North America. This is consistent with the assumption that these subregions formed a continuous whole at a relatively recent period — but it must be remembered that the faunal similarity of two areas may also result from climatologically determined ecological similarities. During the Quaternary period (about the last one million years) the Palaearctic region has been affected strongly by glaciation, the last 'ice-age' ending only about 10,000 years ago. Europe was then held for long periods in the grip of an icy subarctic climate, the effects of which can still be traced, even to the south of the region. Many warmth-loving species that inhabited Europe in the Tertiary (the long geological period before the Quaternary) became extinct, or were driven south to warmer refuges — often only to be cut off by the mountain ranges of northern Africa or the Himalayas. Some of these species returned north from their refuges during the warmer interglacial periods, and in the recent, postglacial epoch. While the glacial epoch drove out a considerable number of such thermophilic species, it also pushed many subarctic species southwards and enabled alpine species to spread widely, being adapted to the cold climate then prevailing even in the lowlands. After the glaciers had retreated and the weather ameliorated the cold-adapted species found refuge in high mountains or by retreating northwards. Such species that occur both in the north and in the European mountains are designated Boreo-Alpine; species inhabiting the mountains only are known as Alpine, and species living exclusively in the north as Boreal. Similar faunal shifts took place in Asia and North America, but these areas appear to have been less affected by glaciation.

The Lepidoptera provide much data for biogeographers. The great number of butterfly and moth species and the popularity they enjoy among naturalists has facilitated much research and helped formulate important theories concerning the origin and dynamics of the world's fauna.

Increasing altitude results in rapid climatic change. In Europe a 100m change in altitude is roughly equivalent to moving 1,000km to the east or 100km to the south. In central Europe, which has a moderate climate, elevations up to 300m have a warm lowland climate, while elevations up to 700−800m have a submontane climate accompanied by a decrease of the average annual temperature of 2−3°C. The temperature drops still further with increasing elevation, so that at an altitude of about 1,500m the average annual temperature is about 0°C. Together with such changes in temperature there are substantial changes in the vegetation − from lowland steppes and oak forests through to beech and fir forests. Above a certain altitude (the so-called treeline) no trees will grow. Changes in vegetation have a marked effect on the composition of the lepidopterous fauna. Butterflies and moths can live at high mountain altitudes if the conditions allow suitable food-plants to exist. In the northern Palaearctic, Lepidoptera do not occur above an elevation of about 1,000m, but in the south they may live at up to 3,000m.

Species permanently residing *(autochthonous)* in mountains should be distinguished from individuals of other species arriving there by chance during migration, or passively carried up by air currents. Most of the world's true mountain species occur at altitudes of 2,000−4,000m, but some rare species, which never descend to lower elevations, live as high as 5,000m. These are mostly inconspicuous insects whose caterpillars feed on tough grasses or lichens.

Migrating Lepidoptera may appear in passes between glaciers at an altitude of about 5,000m, and stray individuals may be found still higher, often blown helplessly onto the snow. Most frequent amongst these visitors are butterflies and big, conspicuous species of moths, such as hawkmoths. These are often noticed by mountaineers. In Tibet, satyrid butterflies have been recorded at an altitude of about 6,000m, and in mountaineering literature some unspecified Lepidoptera are claimed to have been found at 6,300m. Death's Head and Convolvulus hawkmoths, known to undertake long migrations, have often been found in the snowfields. In the Hindukush Mountains, butterflies and moths have been collected at 4,000−4,500m, and in the South American Andes a number of species are recorded from 4,700m or more. Further south Lepidoptera can be found up to 4,000m. In Europe the boundary line of semi-permanent snow and ice is at 2,500−3,000m, marking the upper limit at which Lepidoptera can live.

Ecology and behaviour

The study of the dynamic relationships between organisms and the environment in which they live is termed *ecology* − a relatively young, but already very complex science. Animals form an integral part of nature, responding to and dependent on the world which surrounds them, at the same time contributing to and forming an important part of the environment for other organisms.

The ecology of all living things is partly controlled by *inanimate nature,* including the geological substrate and physical factors such as temperature, humidity and light, inorganic chemicals, and so on. These operate together with the complex *biotic factors* of the living world. One of the most dominant biotic factors is food, and this leads to various relationships among organisms − such as *competition, symbiosis, parasitism,* etc. Competition arises not only for food but also for living space. Each such factor can affect the organisms at the level of individuals, populations, species, or whole communities. And the influence of the organisms on the environment may have repercussions for individuals, populations, or higher ecological units. Ecology involves unceasing processes of interaction. Individuals, species or communities that fail to fit into the whole complex process become extinct. Survival often depends on the plasticity of an organism, its so-called *ecological valency*. Species possessing broad valency are adaptable and can live in a wide variety of available habitats. The Lepidoptera include species which can range from lowlands to high mountain elevations, from the Mediterranean region to northern Europe. The catholic taste in food of some species testifies to their wide ecological valency. Their adaptability has enabled a great number of species to survive or even invade man-made environments, in conditions radically different from those otherwise prevailing in nature. On the other hand, species with a narrow ecological valency are less adaptable and can only tolerate specific conditions. In habitats which satisfy these, they survive well, but any change, however small, may jeopardize their very existence. They may overcome change by migrating to other places offering suitable conditions, insofar as these remain unexploited. A narrow ecological valency is characteristic of high-mountain Lepidoptera that are specialized for the harsh conditions of mountain climates. These insects are rarely capable of holding out in competition in a less harsh environment. Similarly, *monophagous* species (those specializing exclusively on one kind of foodplant) have a narrow ecological valency. If, for some reason or other, their foodplant dies out, they are usually doomed to extinction.

An important but rather difficult concept in ecology is the *ecological niche*. Imagine a landscape where life has been exterminated — for example after a forest or steppe fire, or a ploughed field. Animals invade such a place if there is a 'niche' for them in which to live. A shrub or tree with no inhabitants may represent a spatial niche. A niche may be represented by some food for which no consumer has yet arrived (for example, a fresh corn supply in the grainstore; a temporal niche is a season of the year in which no potentially competing species occur. In general niches are more complex than this, being delimited by a combination of several factors operating simultaneously, some of which may be of major importance for the particular species. One niche might be the crown of a tree, having specific humidity, air flow and exposure to the sun. Another part of the same crown, perhaps that part not exposed to sunshine, may represent another niche. Different species may subdivide the resources (notably food and shelter) available within a niche. In the example just given, one of them may live on young shoots, another on old leaves, one in spring, another in summer, and so on. Some species require a niche taking up only a small space — for example, merely a leaf of a particular plant, or even just some part of it. Niches of this kind are occupied by leaf-miners, and here an explanation may be found why some species make their mines close to the base of the leaf, others in the centre of the blade, one on the underside, and another on the upperside of the leaf, etc. A temporal niche may be a certain part of the year characterized by rainy weather, by a certain length of the day, by a particular spectrum of flowering plants, etc. Where more than one species occupies the same niche, or are endeavouring to do so, the result is a competitive struggle for life. This often results in driving one of the competitors into another niche — insofar as it is capable of finding and existing in one. To continue its existence, such a species must adapt in some way, by occurring earlier or later in the year, exploiting a different part of the foodplant, choosing another foodplant, or making some response involving a shift to a different niche.

The physical environment

Temperature is a basic factor controlling the life of butterflies and moths. Activity can only take place within a certain temperature range. The Lepidoptera are cold-blooded, and so their temperature is largely determined by the external environment. They are warmed either directly by sunshine or by the atmosphere. Once they have reached some minimum temperature in this way they can raise their bodily temperature somewhat further by flapping their wings. Most butterflies do not take to the wing in dull weather, usually because they are too cold to fly. This is obvious in mountain regions, where we ourselves may also feel chill whenever the sun is covered by clouds. When this happens all the butterflies settle, only to reappear with the sun. The colouration of Lepidoptera is partly determined by the need for heat. Many mountain butterflies and moths are darkly coloured, apparently to increase their absorption of solar energy.

Each species has a certain minimal temperature for survival, the so-called *lower temperature threshold*. This temperature generally ranges from 2—10°C, but varies for different types of activity. The minimum temperature for life lies within the approximate range of minus 40 to plus 5°C. Below the minimum temperature for a species death ensues within a few days. Another threshold is the *developmental minimum,* usually between 5 and 10°C. Below this temperature caterpillars stop developing, both caterpillars and adults cease to take food, and the development of the adults' reproductive organs stops. All activity is reduced to the basic physiological processes required for survival. Temperature thresholds vary greatly from species to species, and during the year, as well as in different climatic zones. Hibernating caterpillars searching for food in the first few days of spring may be ice cold to touch. Tropical species require relatively high temperature for activity, the low temperatures easily survived by temperate species being lethal to them. The cold-hardy species inhabiting high mountains, the far north, or active in late autumn and early spring, fly, take food, mate and reproduce at temperatures approaching freezing point.

Temperate-zone Lepidoptera are most active at temperatures between 20—25°C. Moths show far greater activity on warm nights. Moth collectors using light traps have learned that if the evening temperature falls below 10°C in summer, few insects will be caught. Good catches are only obtained when the temperature does not fall below 18—20°C.

The development of eggs, caterpillars and pupae takes the least possible time at optimal temperatures. This is well known to those who breed caterpillars for experimental purposes. The common Silver-Y moth may serve as an example. At a temperature of 25°C the eggs need about three days to develop, at 20°C approximately one week, and at 15°C about 15—20 days. The development of the caterpillars which takes 10—12 days at 25°C may take twice as long at a lower temperature, or may even come to a standstill. However, some Lepidoptera, particularly the larvae of subterranean and aquatic species, are very sensitive to high temperatures.

The bodies of animals consist largely of water, required both as an essential part of their living protoplasm, and as a means for transporting dissolved substances to and from the tissues through the blood system. This is why the provision of water is of vital importance for all animals. This is one reason why humidity, already discussed, can be so important, as it controls, in conjunction with temperature, the rate of water loss from the body — a high temperature coupled with low humidity (as in deserts) being fatal for many animals.

The water requirements of butterflies and moths can be satisfied in two ways: by means of good water 'economy' (devices to restrict loss by evaporation, and make good use of metabolic water derived from food), or simply by drinking (which implies the need for an adequate supply). Some species are well adapted to life in the driest conditions: thick hair or a waxy cuticle prevents water loss, their eggs have a strong drought resistant chorion, and their cocoons maintain a suitable humidity for the survival of the pupae.

Other species frequent environments with suitable humidity levels. Females lay eggs in places where the required humidity obtains — in leaf-rosettes, tufts of grass, in the soil, on the underside of leaves, etc. Larvae of some noctuid moths (*Nonagria, Gortyna,* etc.) live inside stalks where the humidity is always high. Similarly, the tiny caterpillars of moths belonging to the families Gracillariidae and Nepticulidae live in mines: if taken out of them, they soon dessicate. Caterpillars of leaf rollers and other small moths weave themselves into sprouting leaves and buds, on which they feed, or roll up leaves to form little chambers in which the humidity always exceeds that of the surroundings — because of the transpiration of the leaves. Some caterpillars take advantage of the moist environment in the ground and live there, also feeding on plant roots, or just seeking shelter there during the daytime, when the atmospheric humidity outside is at its lowest. The nocturnal activity of many caterpillars partly reflects their need for high humidity levels.

Pupae, even though they are enclosed in relatively hard cases, are also sensitive to humidity. When rearing butterflies and moths it is necessary to sprinkle the pupae regularly with water, to prevent them from drying out. In nature pupae are often formed among leaves fastened together by silk, in cocoons, or in the ground, all places where the humidity is relatively high.

Neither eggs, pupae, nor those adults with degenerate mouthparts are equipped for drinking. Their water must be obtained biochemically, mostly by burning fat reserves. Butterflies and moths with a well developed proboscis can obtain water easily. They may take in a lot of water when feeding on nectar or rotting fruit. Swarms of whites, blues and swallowtails may be seen sucking salty water from moist sand or mud. Purple emperors and white admirals may be found sucking at mud like this, along wet woodland rides. In dry summers noctuids gather during the evening on tree trunks moistened with wet sugary bait, or even plain water. Most caterpillars obtain sufficient water from the cell sap of the green leaves on which they feed.

Sunlight is the basic energy source for life on Earth. For Lepidoptera, sunlight is also important with respect to signalling and orientation. Lepidoptera can detect wavelengths beyond those included in the spectrum of light visible to Man: in particular, they can perceive light in the near ultraviolet. Most noctuids are allured by ultraviolet light. However, some Lepidoptera (for example, certain tiger moths) assemble in great numbers at red light. It has been discovered that the spectrum of vision in some butterflies and moths is 'broken': they react to short- and long-wave radiations, but are blind to radiations of intermediate wavelengths, such as green light. Whatever the spectral sensitivity of a particular species, we can be fairly sure that to Lepidoptera the world is seen in quite different colours to those perceived by us. Butterflies and moths may even react to thermal radiation, and to electric and magnetic fields. They are able to distinguish the colour of the sky at night and react to the light of stars. They are sensitive to changes in light during the day, and the level and quality of illumination may operate as a signal triggering certain activities, or inhibiting others. The rhythms of many species can be explained in terms of these remarkable abilities. The activity of most butterflies is concentrated in the morning; at a certain time in the afternoon they start looking for a shelter for the night. Particular moth species show their greatest activity in the late afternoon (for example males of some eggars), in the early evening hours (hawkmoths and many noctuids), or in the morning, when the weather is sunny (emperor moths, the Kentish Glory) — all these moths, however, are also on the wing at night. Not even truly nocturnal moths are on the wing for the whole night: each species has particular, characteristic hours for flight. Those who have used light traps for collecting moths at night are well acquainted with this fact. Some tiger moths *(Eucharia casta, Diacrisia caesarea)* gather to light at nightfall, and then again at day-break. The large-bodied, brightly-coloured Garden Tiger does not come to light before midnight, but then it arrives in great numbers.

The onset of dawn and dusk are signals for day and night-time activity. Temperature and humidity tend to fluctuate widely at all times, but the alternation of day and night, or changes in the length of the day during the year, show regular and exact rhythms. The intensity of light is, of course, affected by cloud cover, but the basic rhythms have continued for millions of years without change: long enough for butterflies and moths to adapt themselves to these rhythms and make good use of them.

Dormancy

The change of seasons in the year leads to an alternation of periods favourable and unfavourable for the life of butterflies and moths. These changes are particularly marked in the temperate zone of the northern hemisphere: summer with its warm temperatures and abundance of food passes into winter, which, if such conditions were to occur in summer, would exterminate many insects. Even in the tropics dry periods are succeeded by rains, and not all weathers are suitable for the development of particular species. Somehow the insects have to survive seasons unfavourable to them, both severe winters and hot, dry periods.

The winter sleep, or hibernation, of many vertebrates is a familiar phenomenon. Similar periods of *dormancy* occur in the lives of butterflies and moths. During dormant periods food consumption is limited, the animal surviving on accumulated fat supplies. To do this for months on end, say to survive a northern winter, metabolic and energy requirements must be reduced to a minimum. Movement is limited, and physiological and biochemical processes within the body are slowed right down. Dormancy, really a state of arrested development or suspended animation, may either affect all bodily functions, when the animal lapses into a state of torpidity, or it may affect only some functions — most often the reproductive system. In such cases the insect may run, fly and take food, but cannot reproduce because of arrested development of the sexual organs. Dormancy may occur at any stage of the life-cycle: egg, caterpillar, pupa or adult — whichever is most suitable for the survival of the particular species. During development a butterfly or moth may fall into dormancy several times — but this need not always be of the same type. In species producing several generations in a year, dormancy may occur in one of them while another generation may develop without interruption; or only part of a population may become dormant, giving rise to *partial generations*.

Dormancy involves many complex phenomena. Several attempts at classifying the various types of resting stages have failed to accommodate the new discoveries of ecologists and physiologists which are still being made.

Like all characteristics, the ability to become dormant has evolved in the course of phylogenesis in response to the impact of the external environment. Closely related species may utilise entirely different types of dormancy, so adapting in different ways to different, or even the same conditions. Two main types of dormancy can be recognised. The first involves an immediate and direct response to a change in conditions, and is designated *quiescence*. Dormancies of the second type *(diapause)* prepare the organism for the onset of an unfavourable period and are usually closely synchronized with the annual climatic cycle, not directly with the unfavourable conditions.

Quiescence lasts only as long as the unfavourable conditions obtain. It is usually controlled by temperature, or, less frequently, by humidity. Quiescence, which is reversible, can be recognised by the absence of a preparatory phase, and is important for overcoming a sudden change of conditions, particularly frost. In the Lepidoptera, quiescence is typical of mountain or arctic species which must take advantage of every suitable occasion to feed, yet be able to survive abrupt falls of temperature and unexpected snow-storms — nothing unusual even in summer. The development of such species can be interrupted by several periods of quiescence, and may thereby be prolonged by as much as several years.

The various types of true diapause, as opposed to simple quiescence, are governed primarily by day length. Other factors — temperature, humidity and food quality — may also play a certain role. As discussed above, day length and changes in it signal the onset of different periods (for example, shortening of the day foreshadows the arrival of winter). On this basis organisms can 'estimate' the most likely time at which the weather will change. Thus an insect can start making preparations for winter as early as summer or autumn, accumulating fat and looking for suitable shelter while conditions still hold good.

The Pine-tree Lappet moth shows an intermediate type of dormancy in which, as in quiescence, the resting stage is brought to an end by the same factor which evoked the dormancy in the first place. In autumn the caterpillars of this moth *(Dendrolimus pini)* stop their development under the influence of the shortening day length, lapsing into a gradually deepening sleep. With the increase of day length in spring the caterpillars slowly re-awaken to attain full activity at the appropriate time — when new pine needles appear.

Many Lepidoptera exhibit true diapause, a very sophisticated way to survive unfavourable periods. True *diapause* has several peculiarities distinguishing it from other types of dormancy. First, it is irreversible. Once set in motion it must continue without stopping until the end, even if the factor which induced it has long ceased to operate. In many Lepidoptera only one developmental stage is sensitive to the diapause triggering impulse, and then only for a short time — for example, during the third or fourth larval instar. If this sensitive period is somehow missed, diapause will not occur and the insect endeavours to go on developing, without interruption. A further characteristic feature of true diapause is that it is *induced* by one factor (most often day length) but *terminated* by another (often temperature or humidity). Moreover, specific conditions are necessary for breaking diapause, otherwise the insects may die without re-awakening to active life. Those who rear butterflies and moths are familiar with the fact that hibernating pupae must be 'frost-bitten', that is they must pass through a period of quite severe cold if any insects are to emerge in spring. Pupae of many species kept continuously in a warm room do not give rise to any adults, even though the pupae may live for a long time.

Not only the termination of diapause but its induction may also depend on temperature. Caterpillars of a particular species may go into diapause only if the temperature falls below 20°C, while in another species temperatures below 15 or 16°C may be necessary. At 25°C all attempts to induce diapause in such species will result in failure.

The fact that the signal for inducing diapause occurs before the actual period of dormancy can produce some interesting effects. Very often the induction occurs during the larval stage, but the diapause only takes place subsequently, in the pupal stage. Larval diapause may be controlled by an induction affecting the egg. Eggs prepared for diapause may rapidly develop to a certain point, the caterpillar appearing within the chorion, sometimes still provided with a rich supply of yolk. At this stage the eggs may then become dormant.

In some species induction may be effected by passing the so-called critical day length, after which further shortening or lengthening of the day has no effect. Other species require a very slow change in day length. Still other species respond to relative differences in illumination. Spectral composition of the light can also be significant, experiments demonstrating that in some species diapause can only be induced by particular colours.

Diapause usually consists of several phases. The first is often the deepest. After some time this stage passes into quiescence, and the re-awakening of the insect may only be dependent on temperature. In temperate species winter diapause is intense from November to January — the most unfavourable time for the insects to wake up. They must not succumb to any 'temptation' to awake provided by a temporary spell of warmer weather. In two or three days new frosts could set in and prove fatal for them. Various other safety mechanisms exist: the caterpillars of some eggars (the Fox Moth, for example) do not wake up until they are abundantly sprinkled with water at a sufficiently high temperature. Thus they are awakened by only that combination of factors which herald the onset of the spring growing season.

In spite of considerable efforts, all experimental attempts to affect the diapause of some Lepidoptera — for example of the common Winter Moth — have proved unsuccessful. According to current explanations the physiological cycle of these species has been stabilized to such an extent that it has become genetically determined and hence relatively independent of external conditions.

Diapause may occur for periods longer than one year. Those who have reared butterflies and moths are familiar with cases where the pupae of hawkmoths, prominents and numerous noctuids may lie dormant for several years before the adult moth makes its appearance. This could be of advantage where adverse conditions obtain in the first year — if, for example, the entire adult population were extinguished by extremely bad weather. Diapause can also secure the *synchronization* of populations. In species producing more than one generation during the year, individuals develop in different microconditions so that, towards the end of the season, the adult insects may be emerging almost at random in relation to each other. If this were to go on indefinitely, particularly in short-lived species, the probability of meeting partners and effecting fertilization might be severely reduced. All this can be corrected by the winter diapause, so that in spring all the individuals emerge in synchrony again.

Collectors are often puzzled by effects caused by diapause. Some succeed in breeding adult insects by autumn. Others do not see any adults before spring, or these may fail to emerge altogether — although the caterpillars apparently pupated successfully. The explanation may be quite simple: in one case the caterpillars were kept in a room without any artificial illumination, where only the daylight rhythm made itself felt. In another case we might have read a thrilling novel and kept the light on late into the night, just at the critical time for the induction of diapause. The complexities of diapause mean that the proper hibernation of caterpillars in artificial conditions is extremely difficult.

Food

Butterflies and moths, being heterotrophic organisms, cannot feed on inorganic substances. Like all animals, they are dependent on organic materials produced by autotrophs, notably green plants, or must feed on other animals. Plants supply the adult insects and caterpillars of most species with their nourishment. Animals serve as foods for Lepidoptera only exceptionally — more often they represent competition for food or enemies. Thus complicated relationships may arise between Lepidoptera and other living things.

The main nourishment of butterflies and moths is obtained from living plants. Caterpillars live on leaves, flowers, fruits or wood, adults suck nectar from flowers, sweet juice from fruits, or sap from injured trunks. The ability of caterpillars to live on different foods is not equal in all species. *Polyphagous* caterpillars may live on a variety of plants belonging to various families, and survive very well on all of them. For example, caterpillars of the Silver Y Moth have been observed on more than 220 plant species belonging to 51 families, and caterpillars of the Fall Webworm (introduced to Europe from America) on more than 130 plant species. Species feeding on plant roots or boring in wood will often accept a very wide range of host species.

Many caterpillars are more specialized. They live on nourishment obtained from only a few plant species, belonging to the same family. Examples of such *oligophagous* species include the Spurge Hawkmoth (which lives on various kinds of spurges); the Death's Head Hawkmoth (on several species of Solanaceae — potato, woody nightshade, thorn apple); and the Peacock butterfly (on nettles and hops). Oligophagy is sometimes determined by factors other than the systematic affinity of plants — for example, by the environment. Thus caterpillars of the moth *Archanara sparganii,* a species which breeds by ponds, were found on cattails (reed mace), branched bur-seed and swordflags. It is difficult to draw a hard line between polyphagy and oligophagy — both types gradually merge into each other, and represent a spectrum of abilities. Oligophagous species may, in case of need, survive on plants they would not otherwise eat.

Monophagous Lepidoptera represent the most specialized group. They feed on only one kind of plant, sometimes just on a particular part, such as the flower or the fruit. They sporadically occur in all families, yet purely monophagous Lepidoptera are relatively scarce. Oligophagy is the most common situation. Just like every narrow specialization, monophagy entails risks. The extinction of the foodplant irrevocably seals the fate of any Lepidoptera dependent on it. The activities of Man are tending to eliminate certain natural biotopes. Consequently, formerly abundant plants are disappearing, and with them a number of butterflies and moths. Most afflicted are the species inhabiting bogs and marshes, now mostly drained, or living in steppes, which, with the exception of small areas, have been turned into arable land.

Many caterpillars live on dead plant material. This is typical, for example, of the geometrid genus *Idaea*, which includes a great number of species: the caterpillars eat dry, decayed leaves, hay, etc. Caterpillars of the species *Epizeuxis calvaria* feed in very much the same way. Caterpillars of the moth *Laspeyria flexula* and of some geometrids belonging to the genus *Boarmia* eat mosses and lichens, while caterpillars of the moth *Parascotia fuliginaria* and certain species of the family Tineidae live in withered fungi.

Consumers of fruit and food products form a special group. They have become storehouse pests. Most of them belong to the families Tineidae, Pyralidae, Gelechiidae and Tortricidae. The family Tineidae includes species which exclusively eat substances of animal origin: fur, wool, feathers, etc. In nature they live in birds' nests, in lairs of mammals and on dead animals.

Although very rare, even in the Lepidoptera we may come across predatory caterpillars, which attack other caterpillars or other animals. Very abundant are the species *Cosmia trapezina* and *Eupsilia transversa*, which eat tiny caterpillars. These predatory larvae may frequently be found in the cocoons of pyralids or leaf rollers, having settled there following the liquidation of the former inhabitant. Besides such meat, however, they also eat leaves. The caterpillar of the scarce *Porphyrinia communimacula* eats scale insects on fruit trees.

The quality of food affects both the development of caterpillars and the fertility of adults. The nutritive value of every food varies, including various substances such as glycosides, vitamins, alkaloids, pigments, etc. A high or low content of any of these may make the food unsuitable for a particular caterpillar species. The quality of food is significantly influenced by the development of plants during the vegetative season. Caterpillars may react to changes by looking for more suitable plant species, younger shoots, by passing from withered flowers to leaves, from trees to herbs, etc. For the most part, the selection of an adequate food supply is effected by the female, who finds an appropriate plant to lay her eggs on. But caterpillars taste the food before they begin to consume it.

Enemies and disease

Butterflies and moths are consumers of plants, but in turn they themselves serve as food for other animals: vertebrates, other insects, spiders, and even lower animals. They are often affected by parasitic organisms, including fungi, protozoa, bacteria and viruses. Parasites and enemies limit the reproductive capacity of these insects, so regulating their numbers and maintaining the existing balance of nature.

The most notorious disease affecting caterpillars is *polyhedrosis*, caused by a polyhedral virus. Infested caterpillars hang helplessly upside down on plants. Their guts dissolve into an unpleasant-smelling brown liquid containing vast quantities of the virus, which, in favourable humidity and temperature, represents a source of further infection. Caterpillars mostly pick up the disease by eating stained food. An abundance of caterpillars helps to spread the disease. *Granulosis* is another virus disease, manifested by a whitening of the caterpillars, and ultimately by dissolution of the body tissues.

The most well-known bacterial disease is caused by *Bacillus thuringiensis*. This bacterium can be produced artificially on a vast scale and used to make a suspension applied to crops for caterpillar-pest control. Unlike chemical agents it is harmless to Man.

Some protozoa cause disease symptoms similar to those caused by bacteria. Either a particular organ or the whole body of the caterpillar is attacked. The infection usually results in intestinal disturbances. Even if the caterpillar survives the infection, the protozoa may still cause the death of the pupa or infertility in the adult.

Caterpillars attacked by bacteria or viruses usually undergo dissolution. Diseases caused by fungal parasites are different. The fungus grows through the whole body of the caterpillar, which then turns rigid. In due time it either falls into pieces containing spores, or, if conditions are favourable, thalli carrying spores grow out of the dead body. An abundant fungus which causes the blackening of moth caterpillars is *Tarichium megaspermum*. Caterpillars, and especially pupae, covered with a white mildew may have fallen victim to the fungus *Beauveria bassiana*. Rather like *Bacillus thuringiensis,* it has proved possible to culture this fungal parasite on a huge scale, and it has also become a useful organism for the biological control of economic pests.

Butterflies and moths, in all developmental stages, have many enemies among parasitic and predacious insects. Eggs are pierced by the ovipositors of tiny wasps, whose larvae then develop inside the eggs. Larvae of braconid, ichneumonid and chalcid wasps, and certain flies (tachinids) parasitize caterpillars. Parasitic larvae do not kill the caterpillar immediately but live on its fat deposits, leaving the vital organs intact. Shortly before the parasite is full-grown and ready to pupate, it switches to feeding on the vital organs, and the caterpillar soon dies. Sometimes the parasite pupates inside the body of the dead caterpillar, or it may perforate the body wall and pupate outside, next to the caterpillar or in the ground. Sometimes there is only one large parasite larva (ichneumon wasps, tachinid flies) per caterpillar, in other cases there are dozens of minute larvae with which the caterpillar body is literally packed in the last hours of its life. Cases are known when the caterpillar still manages to pupate and the parasite completes its development within the pupal case. A number of ichneumon wasps inject their eggs into pupae; in this case, of course, it is not a butterfly or moth but an ichneumon that emerges from the pupa. Parasitism is a common phenomenon in nature: consequently it may be difficult to rear even a few butterflies or moths from a large number of wild-caught larvae.

Predators such as ladybirds and lacewings feed primarily on aphids — but they are quite partial to lepidopterous eggs as a variation in diet. Ravenous bugs of the genus *Nabis* and other genera pierce and suck the juices of young caterpillars. Fierce enemies of caterpillars are predatory beetles. The most outstanding among these are the insatiable ground and carrion beetles. They may even climb trees in search of caterpillars. Pupae hidden in the soil often fall prey to rove beetles (Staphylinidae). Further enemies include digger wasps and other hymenopterans which, having stunned the caterpillar with their sting, carry this living food supply to their larvae waiting in nests. Many caterpillars are eaten by spiders, particularly by ground hunting species which do not use webs. Ants are very dangerous enemies of caterpillars. Wood ants have been observed to clear all caterpillars within a range of several dozens of metres from their anthill, and forage up to a distance of 100m.

It would seem that adult butterflies and moths are least threatened by predators. Yet even they are exposed to danger. Predacious robber flies (Asilidae) swoop at lightning speed on victims that have settled too close — robust species of this family venture to attack even a large butterfly or moth. Tiny, gaily coloured crab spiders are concealed in flowers. When a butterfly alights to drink nectar, the spider assaults the most sensitive part of its body — the head — with its venomous fangs. Generally, only small Lepidoptera die in spider webs: the spider itself helps to disengage a big butterfly or moth, to prevent it from tearing its web to pieces.

Insectivorous vertebrates have to consume a considerable amount of food. Birds are almost untiring at the time of feeding their young, catching thousands of caterpillars, pupae and adult Lepidoptera. We can witness how a small songbird, perhaps a sparrow, follows in loops a disturbed noctuid or geometrid moth — which has little chance to escape. Titmice, redstarts, wagtails and other birds systematically search through hiding-places, fissures in bark, ledges and other places where moths seek shelter during the day, or where their eggs and pupae might be concealed. The Cuckoo is well known for eating, without any difficulty whatsoever, the hairy tussock moth, eggar and tiger moth caterpillars avoided by other birds. Starlings flock to forests where a population explosion of caterpillars of the Green Oak Tortrix Moth or the Winter Moth has taken place. Crows and gulls walk about freshly ploughed fields picking out insect larvae and pupae.

Many pupae are destroyed by moles, shrews and hedgehogs, while plump caterpillars are not considered unworthy even by cats and foxes. The greatest enemies of nocturnal moths are the bats. With the aid of their exceptionally developed sonar sense organs they can find and catch their prey even in the dark. Bats can often be seen flying around street-lamps, catching the moths attracted in abundance.

Even this brief and incomplete survey shows that the enemies of adult butterflies and moths, as well as their developmental stages, are very abundant indeed, and Lepidoptera are practically incapable of active self-defence. As a result they must depend on passive means for defence: repel, hide or flee from the enemy. Through natural selection, evolution has produced in each species one or more characteristic ways by which they defend themselves.

Butterflies and moths frequently imitate the background of plants and lifeless objects: foliage, little twigs, withered leaves, droppings of birds. An adult or a caterpillar may, by so merging with the environment, escape the eyes of predators. This phenomenon is called camouflage or *crypsis*. Genuine masters of this art are geometrid caterpillars. Their tuberculate brown skin resembles the bark of twigs covered with small buds. The caterpillar holds on firmly to a twig by its claspers, the angle it forms with the twig being suitable to simulate a side branch, a thorn or a broken leaf-stalk. Many caterpillars of very small geometrids of the genus *Eupithecia* living in flowers are characterized by bright colours matching the interior of the flower. The yellowish-brown caterpillar *Eupithecia silenata* is almost invisible in bladder campion flowers. Other such cryptic species inhabit the flowers of foxgloves, pear and blackthorn blossoms, petals of goldenrod, etc. It is amazing how easily the large caterpillar of the Privet Hawkmoth, several inches long, can escape attention when sitting motionlessly on a shoot of privet, how caterpillars of noctuid moths of the genus *Cucullia* merge with the wormwood on which they live, and how indistinguishable caterpillars of prominents can be from leaves distorted by the galls of aphids or mites.

Butterflies and moths at rest can resemble various objects. An example is the Lappet moth — at rest it looks like a withered leaf. The same applies to the Poplar Hawkmoth. Minute Lepidoptera frequently resemble birds' droppings: then they quietly sit on a leaf or twig, since the probability of their discovery is small. Such a colouration is typical of the geometrids *Epirrhoe alternata* and *Xanthorhoe fluctuata*. Still more perfect is the simulation of birds' droppings by small leaf rollers of the genus *Hedya,* which may easily deceive even an experienced lepidopterist. It is only when the moth flies away that we recognise our error. Gaily coloured nymphalids and large satyrids are perfectly camouflaged when sitting with their wings closed on tree trunks; other species are indistinguishable on the ground or among grass.

Protection of another type is provided by *mimicry* — usually involving the simulation of much-feared insect species, chiefly hymenopterons, or of special butterfly or moth species that are distasteful to many predators. A well-known example of mimicry is provided by the clearwing moths, which resemble wasps, bees, and hornets. Their specific names have been made to correspond: *vespiformis* (*Vespa* = wasp), *apiformis* (*Apis* = bee), *crabroniformis* (*Vespa crabro* = hornet), etc. The appearance of caterpillars of the lobster moths is rather bizarre: the very elongate forelegs and the forward bend of the abdomen give their larvae the appearance of a large spider. The yellowish tiger moth *Spilosoma luteum* has evidently based its defence on its close similarity to the species *Spilosoma lubricipeda,* which appears in nature a few weeks earlier, and is considered unpalatable by most birds. These learn to avoid this species on sight, and they mistakenly continue to respond in the same way when a species more palatable but similar in colouration takes to the wing. The poisonous and conspicuous tropical butterflies of the family Danaidae afford protection to a whole host of similarly coloured, but unrelated, non-poisonous mimics.

Flash colouration is an alternative to crypsis or mimicry, or may provide a second line of defence for a cryptic species which has been detected. For example, in moths of the genus *Catocala,* brightly-coloured hindwings are concealed beneath grey forewings, to be suddenly exposed in case of disturbance. Fiery red or yellow wings marked with a contrasting dark design usually succeed in giving birds a real scare, and the moths use the moment of surprise to make good their escape. An eye-like design is very common in both butterflies and moths. We find it on the wings of emperor moths, some hawkmoths and many nymphalids, especially in the tropics. It can even be found in some caterpillars, for example, the Elephant Hawkmoth. Large eye-spots, suddenly exposed, can induce a moment of panic in predators, who may 'think' they are being confronted by a large rival — again, the insect can use this moment for escape.

An effective means of defence in some caterpillars is their abundance of long hairs, which may make them difficult to swallow, or defeat parasitic wasps. The hairs of some species break off and may cause persistent itching or skin eruptions. They may produce eye inflammations, or even bleeding. A common reaction of caterpillars to disturbance is a sudden regurgitation of food through the mouth. Some species can emit drops of foul-smelling secretion from glands, or thrust out coloured appendages — as in Swallowtail butterfly and Puss moth larvae. Protection by leaves tied together by silk, cases, and spun nests for caterpillars, and by cocoons or cells for pupae, have been described above (p. 34–35).

Attack and defence involve an evolutionary 'arms-race'. If butterflies and moths succeed at one time in developing an effective protective system, some predator will later develop an 'answer' to take advantage of this otherwise untapped food source. The Cuckoo whose digestive system has become adapted to consuming hairy caterpillars without any ill-effects has already been mentioned. It may be assumed that at night Lepidoptera are protected by darkness against those insectivores which hunt by sight. However, as we have already noted, the bat has based its search for prey on a new principle. Now it might seem that there would be no defence for moths against echolocation. But this is not so. Moths are capable of intercepting the ultrasound sonar signal emitted by bats and respond by zigzag flight or rapidly dropping to the ground. Further, some moths can even respond with their own 'signals', so interfering with or jamming the echolocation of the bats. Every advance in attack or defence is counterbalanced by a new adaptation — if not, predators or prey are likely to become extinct.

Behaviour

Most butterflies and moths live solitarily. Occasionally individuals assemble, but the reasons for this are not as in social insects (such as ants and bees) which form organized communities. The mass occurrence of adult or larval Lepidoptera is rare but very conspicuous. The most common causes are migration, hibernation or aestivation, or concentration at a source of food or water.

A well-known example of migratory insect is the American butterfly *Danaus plexippus.* The butterflies, which cannot survive the cold northern winters, migrate south for hibernation purposes. They assemble, year after year, on particular trees (at sites in California and Mexico) which they literally cover with their bodies. It is not known why it is just these and no other trees that exercise so much attraction for the butterflies. To prevent interference with this remarkable phenomenon, these 'butterfly trees' are protected by law in California. In southern Europe, the Jersey Tiger Moth assembles in large colonies. In summertime, when this species is on the wing, the assembly places of these brightly-coloured insects provide an attraction for tourists. An Australian noctuid moth, *Agrotis infusa,* gathers in large numbers on hilltops to survive the unfavourable tropical summer. Masses of individuals often throng in a small space between stones and rocks. Some species of the family Pieridae (whites and sulphurs) make mass-migrations. Clouds of sulphurs have been observed in Africa, and massed flights of the Black-veined White and *Colias* butterflies may be witnessed in Europe. Reports of 'snow-covered' fields, strewn thick with whites, will be found in old literature. Some nymphalids (for example the Painted Lady and the Red Admiral) or clouded yellows *(Colias)* appear all of a sudden without anybody having noticed their arrival. If we are lucky enough to observe a migration, individual butterflies may be seen flying past at intervals of a few seconds, sometimes shorter, sometimes longer. These flights have most often been observed in mountain passes, through which the butterflies fly in order to get most easily over the obstacle in their way. In mountains where the butterflies do not normally occur, they are very conspicuous, particularly if they appear at a time when the terrain is still covered with snow.

Migration occurs not only in butterflies but also in certain moths. Year after year, migration brings to central Europe populations of the Silver Y. Another migrant is the Dark Sword Grass. Since flights take place by night, they have escaped the attention of observers for a long time. Sometimes the moths arrive in such multitudes that their offspring, voracious caterpillars, cause serious damage to agricultural produce. Well-known solitary migrants include the large hawks: the Death's Head, Convolvulus and Oleander hawkmoths. Although it is impossible for them to hibernate in the temperate zone, in summer they find central Europe has an adequate climate for reproduction. Year by year they come to southern and central Europe from Africa, sometimes they are also caught in the far north. The distances the butterflies and moths must fly are to be reckoned in hundreds and thousands of kilometres. During their flight they often take advantage of air currents, and thus their arrival is usually connected with a certain type of weather. Not surprisingly, many migrant butterflies and moths perish on the way.

A concentration of butterflies and moths around food can most easily be obtained by smearing some sweet, fermenting juice on a tree trunk in dry, warm weather. If we are lucky, several hundred moths may assemble on one trunk. This tends to happen naturally wherever sap oozes from an injured trunk. Whites settle in numbers on damp sand or muddy ground, at places where a little stream crosses a path, where moisture has been left after rain, or on patches of dung or urine. Flowering clover fields may be inundated by butterflies from the entire neighbourhood, while plants of the pink family are enticing to night-flying moths.

Caterpillars mostly lead solitary lives, trying to keep as far from each other as possible. They react in an ill-tempered way to the presence of a neighbour, and if many of them are confined to a limited space they may even resort to cannibalism. Some species possess means of dispersal. Small caterpillars of the Gypsy Moth are tufted with very long hair, which enables them to be borne away by the wind. Predacious caterpillars usually represent the extreme of solitary life.

However, the caterpillars of some species spend a part of their life, or even the whole of it, in a more or less numerous colony. The caterpillar colonies of eggars and tussock moths have already been mentioned (p. 33). Caterpillars of the Buff-tip Moth stay close together, eating off one leaf, then a whole branch of a lime, a hazel, or a birch. Caterpillars of the Camberwell Beauty, Large Tortoiseshell, Small Tortoiseshell and some other nymphalid butterflies behave in very much the same way. It is not until they reach the last instar, or even immediately prior to pupation, that they wander apart. Caterpillars of the Brown-tail, Lackey and Small Eggar live gregariously in nests. The yellow and black caterpillars of ermine moths live together in thousands, covering whole blackthorn shrubs, apple trees, spindle trees and bird-cherry trees with their greyish cobwebs. Different species of shrubs are host to ermine moths of different species.

The caterpillars of processionary moths (Thaumetopoeidae) wander from place to place in search of food in Indian file, all the individuals maintaining head-to-tail contact. Sometimes this procession assumes a wedge-like shape: further back more and more caterpillars move along side by side. This behaviour is reflected in the name of the most common European species, *Thaumetopoea processionea*. An experiment with an American species is worth mentioning: a long file of caterpillars was made to form a closed circle. The caterpillars then continued to move around the circle for days on end, until they were exhausted. The circle could be interrupted at any place and the caterpillars would follow the individual that happened to be in front. Hence it follows that the processionary behaviour is instinctive and that no individual caterpillar is predetermined or selected to occupy the leading role.

Community ecology

Butterflies and moths live in organized contact with the rest of nature, and form part of it. The more complex nature becomes, the more complex are the interrelationships and ties. These relationships have evolved by natural selection, the sacrifice of inadequate individuals and species. A balance is always attained — a *community of species* dependent on prevailing conditions and on each other.

If we study a particular locality, we see that it is characterized by a particular type of vegetation. For example, a forest will have a certain tree structure, with a number of shrubs in the understorey, and a forest-floor herb layer comprising particular species. This vegetation, dependent on the geological substrate, forms the living environment of numerous animals. The plants are supplied by the soil with the nutrients required for growth, herbivores feed on the plants, and the predators on them in turn. Normally the loss of material and energy from the system does not exceed the rate at which it can be replaced. The complex of plant and animal organisms is a system which inherently maintains the established balance through the interlinking relationships of the organisms themselves. Such a community or association of biologically interdependent organisms is called a *biocoenosis*. If the link with the geological substrate is also taken into account, we may speak of a geobiocoenosis, or an *ecosystem*. A biocoenosis is a system which is relatively independent of adjacent such systems. Whatever the caterpillars and other herbivores within a system eat is replaced by the system itself. The overproduction of herbivores is prevented by predatory animals. These in turn have their own enemies — either more efficient or larger beasts of prey, or parasites, or various diseases.

The balance of a biocoenosis is usually only disturbed by interference from outside. After some time the balance is re-established, or, if the interference has been too great and persistent, the old biocoenosis is eliminated and replaced by a new one corresponding to the changed conditions. Natural disasters can interfere strongly with biocoenoses: forest or steppe fires, extensive floods, relatively permanent changes of climate, etc. To this must be added interferences by Man: felling forests, building dams, highways, settlements, application of chemical pesticides, etc.

Examples of biocoenoses are the communities of organisms inhabiting deciduous forests, peat-bogs, mountain forests, alpine meadows, steppes, etc. These are balanced communities evolved in specific conditions. A biocoenosis is never fully homogeneous, nor is it static. In a forest trees grow and change in form, affecting penetration of sunlight to the undergrowth. On the forest-floor plants germinate, flower and mature, while established deciduous shrubs alternatively acquire and lose their foliage. Different microclimates characterise the separate parts of a biocoenosis, determined by the plant layer, by exposure to sunlight and to shade, by wind and humidity. In this way the theoretical niches discussed above take on a concrete reality, as functional units. Plants and animals are incessantly filling free niches, releasing others, destroying some, creating new ones, so giving rise to multifaceted relationships. Niches on the ground and in space are filled by plants, while plant and space niches are filled by animals. A particular animal in a particular niche forms a part of a complex niche for another animal, such as a parasite or a symbiont. Numerous plant or animal species have only a short period of activity, during a particular part of the year. The eggs and pupae of insects, though forming part of a biocoenosis, have no immediate food requirements, and so the species leave their food niches open to others during these stages of their development.

It is on this ecological basis that the abundance of Lepidoptera species found in many biocoenoses is currently explained and understood. Species living in tree tops and on the forest floor, consumers of wood, withered leaves, flowers and fruits — all these exist side by side. Some species occur early in spring, others in summer or in autumn. Together with all the other organisms they make up a temporal and spatial mosaic. Of course, the number of species living in an ecosystem must necessarily be limited, so as to let all of them have enough room and food. If too many species occur competition arises, and the most capable or adaptable species usually come to occupy the available niches, while the other species are eliminated.

The abundance of species and the nature of their interrelationships vary in different biocoenoses. The interrelationships and even the number of species may also change in the course of the year, depending on climatic and other abiotic influences. The underlying principle is the supply of *energy* and its *transfer*.

The sun is the ultimate source of nearly all the energy necessary for life on our planet, and the only organisms capable of intercepting this energy and using it to make organic substances are green plants. Green plants are *autotrophic,* that is, they are capable of producing their own food from energy and substances provided by inorganic nature. They are the fundamental producers of living matter. All other organisms, primarily animals, are *heterotrophic,* living on the energy accumulated by plants. Animals live at the expense of other organisms, from which they acquire energy in the form of food; this energy is partly utilized by them, partly wasted, and partly passed on — insofar as they themselves represent food for other organisms in the so-called *food chain.* If every organism in a food chain utilizes some energy for its life processes, it follows that each subsequent link of the chain is somewhat poorer in energy. At the end of each chain there are the top predators, animals, including Man, which rarely fall prey to other species. These obtain only a small part of the energy originally gathered by the plants.

Microorganisms can cut short the food chain at any point and complete the cycle: they bring about the destruction of living matter and return the remaining energy to inorganic nature. If plants are the only organisms capable of utilising solar energy, it is logical that the abundance of species in the further links of the chain is dependent on their productive capacity. In unfavourable conditions for plant life (insufficient light, warmth, or water and essential inorganic materials), the primary production of living matter is insufficient to maintain a great abundance of individuals or species. The result may be an ecosystem poor in species, where relatively simple interrelations prevail among the organisms involved, and which can easily become subject to disturbance by many outside influences. Such a biocoenosis may lack the inherent forces necessary for its regeneration. This is actually the case in high mountains, polar regions, deserts, poor and arid zones, etc. But wherever conditions are favourable for vegetation, there is a great abundance of species and the natural ecosystem has corresponding regenerative capacity.

Population cycles

The reproductive capacity of insects is immense. It is not uncommon for butterfly or moth females to lay 100—300 eggs. Females of some species of tussock moths, eggars and noctuids lay batches consisting of several thousand eggs. If a population density similar to that of the parent generation is maintained, this means that, on average, only two reproductively successful adults develop from each whole batch. Thus the total mortality for all developmental stages comes close to 100%. For batches of 1,000 eggs it represents 99.8%. In the course of normal development the population is actually decimated in this drastic way. If, for one reason or other, more individuals manage to survive, the density of the population increases. If favourable conditions and reduced mortality persist in the following generations, the number of individuals will rise rapidly. Unless adverse conditions set in at the last moment, the result is a population explosion of the species. But such a situation rarely persists for long. The first consequence is a quick consumption of suitable food. And hungry caterpillars behave in a different way than usual. Often they resort to cannibalism, fail to complete their development, grow weak, or succumb to various diseases. In response to their abundance, parasites and predators grow in number, and birds come from afar to feed on the bloom of insects. More or less rapidly, everything returns to normal. The growth of the population from normal to the peak and back again is called a population cycle, and usually takes several years.

Characteristic of the population cycles of individual species is a certain periodicity which is determined by the reproductive ability of the species in given conditions (recently this has been discussed as the *strategy* of species) on the one hand, and by the state of natural conditions on the other. There are species in which rapid population growth does not take place in any circumstances — it is not in their nature. In contrast, other species have a great tendency for rapid increase ('boom and bust' species). In a balanced ecosystem there are few major fluctuations in population densities. The less well balanced an ecosystem, the more frequently do population explosions occur.

Man severely interferes with nature almost wherever he lives, and produces many artificial, poorly balanced communities. Fields, gardens, monocultures, open ground or plantations, all would immediately start returning to something close to their original state if Man stopped tending them. Even semi-natural ecosystems are frequently disturbed: swamps are drained, cattle graze in the mountains, and wherever Man cannot penetrate directly, the waste-products of his activity (air and water pollution caused by industry) may make themselves felt. Below we will look at several examples of the results of disturbed ecological relationships.

The havoc wreaked by larvae of the Black Arches Moth among spruce plantation monocultures represented a real menace to forests at the beginning of our century, and compelled the foresters to reconsider forest economy. The Green Oak Tortrix Moth can bring disaster to oak forests. Its population cycles used to take approximately six to seven years; however, after the introduction of insecticides for controlling this pest, in many places outbreaks of this species now occur every other year due to the reduced number of the natural enemies. The natural regulative forces of nature have been impaired. The foliage of orchard and woodland trees is consumed by Winter, Brown-tail and Lackey moths. On a world-wide scale enormous damage is done to apples by *Cydia pomonella,* the Codling Moth, and to plums, apricots and peaches by the Plum Fruit Moth, *Cydia funebrana.* Massive losses of field crops are caused by the Turnip, Dark Sword Grass and Silver Y moths, while in mountain meadows the Antler Moth occasionally causes damage by population outbursts. The now widely distributed European Corn Borer endangers corn production throughout the world. Many other species of otherwise inconspicuous Lepidoptera may undergo population explosions on sugar-cane, rice and cotton plantations, as well as in tobacco and vegetable fields.

Particularly favourable conditions for the build up of huge populations occur in storehouses containing grain, seeds and other food products. Thousands of tons of grain may easily be spoilt by caterpillars of the Angoumois and European grain moths. Mills and bakeries may be infested by the Mediterranean Flour Moth or the Meal Moth.

From a human standpoint, this presents the worst aspect of the life of butterflies and moths. But we can hardly blame them for something Man has brought on himself by disturbing the natural balance.

Lepidoptera and Man

Man, although he himself forms a part of nature and cannot survive without it, has assumed a contradictory attitude toward the natural world: on the one hand he would like to preserve all its variegation and luxurious abundance, be it for aesthetic and cultural reasons, or for the sake of instructing future generations; on the other hand he endeavours to master the forces of nature and to make them subservient to his own interests. He uses former woodlands and steppes to make fields and settlements; he inundates large areas with water for reservoirs; his industrial wastes interfere with life in seas and lakes; he penetrates into wildernesses and mountains to control and harvest the forests for timber production. In spite of some partial successes, this activity has usually resulted in the impoverishment of nature rather than its transformation and control.

Butterflies and moths are a sensitive and valuable indicator of the state of nature. In the forties of the present century, for example, 46 abundant butterfly species could be found in the fields and meadows of central Europe, and 28 species in the forests. Now, about 40 years later, only 11 species occur in the fields and 9 in the forests that could be described as abundant. The populations of the others have decreased to such an extent that they are considered uncommon, or even rare. All available evidence seems to suggest that this unfavourable trend is going to continue. Already many species can be found only in collections and museums. The reason is simple: the living environment of butterflies has literally been consumed by agricultural and industrial development. Meadows swarming with brightly coloured butterflies and woodland glades dancing with insects belong to the memories of an older generation rather than to present-day reality. In fact, much of this change has occurred within the life-span of one human generation! The question arises as to how long this can go on, and are there limits to the destruction of the natural environment? If we base our judgement on butterflies and moths, and on many other living forms, we may have already gone beyond the critical point.

It would be difficult to estimate the real significance of butterflies and moths in nature. Through their variety and abundance of form and biology, the Lepidoptera contribute to the complexity of nature as a whole. If ecological aspects are taken into account, butterflies and moths represent, inclusive of their developmental stages, a considerable mass of living matter. This *biomass* may be conceived as a colossal store of utilizable energy. They form an important link in many food chains, and so supply energy to higher-level consumers, among which are many of great interest or importance to Man.

Lepidoptera play a significant role in relation to plants. As *herbivores,* they represent one of the regulators of plant production. At the same time they are important *pollinators.* Some tropical plants have adapted the shape and colouration of their flowers to suit particular butterflies and moths, offering them nectar in return for their pollinating services. In some cases these plants are entirely dependent on Lepidoptera for successful pollination.

In relation to Man, butterflies and moths can contribute to the enrichment of human life from cultural and aesthetic aspects. It is a matter of individual choice, interest or aptitude as to what extent we make use of this potential. In the past Man has often only honoured irrational gods or personal greed: many now feel that nature, on which we truly depend, is the more worthy of serious study.

If we leave apart the pollinating activity of butterflies and moths mentioned above, the number of directly useful species of Lepidoptera is not very high. Probably the best-known is the Silkworm. In Oriental countries it was bred for silk production as early as 4,000 BC, and only introduced to Europe at a much later date. The secret of silk production was strictly guarded and attempts at exporting the moth illegally were punishable by death. As the story goes, in the sixth century AD two monks smuggled some Silkworm eggs, concealed within the cavities of their bamboo walking sticks, to Constantinople. Hence the breeding of Silkworms spread to Europe.

Silk is unwound from the pupal cocoons. One cocoon yields 800—1,000m of silken thread. It requires about 50,000 cocoons to produce 1kg of raw silk. We may calculate the huge number of cocoons needed to satisfy the demands of industrial production, currently about 30,000 tons of pure silk per year. It is extremely difficult to breed such vast multitudes of caterpillars. The Silkworm is a domesticated species, not to be found free in nature. Numerous strains have been bred, differing in biology and in the colouration of eggs, caterpillars and cocoons. In the age of artificial or man-made fibres, the significance of the Silkworm has somewhat decreased — nevertheless, because it has inimitable qualities, natural silk continues to be important in a number of applications. Silk is also obtained from several species of the eggar and emperor moth families, but this production is not so extensive and, as can be imagined, the silk obtained is of a different quality to the traditional product.

Several monophagous species have been investigated as potential agents for the *biological control* of weeds. Successful attempts have been made at introducing the pyralid *Cactoblastis cactorum* into Australia, where introduced cacti of the genus *Opuntia* had become a danger to sheep. Of recent years, geometrids of the genus *Aplocera* have been imported to America, in an attempt to control *Hypericum* (St John's wort), an unobtrusive European plant which has become a troublesome weed in the USA. Attempts at introducing insects for weed control are risky and must be made with great care. It may happen that the imported species transfers its attentions to some indigenous plant and thus, instead of being a help, it becomes a troublesome pest itself.

In considering the usefulness of butterflies to Man we may note that many species are important subjects for various biological experiments. Due to the ease with which they can be bred, the pyralids *Galleria mellonella* and *Ephestia kuehniella* and other lepidopterous species have become as common as laboratory animals for the biologist as the white mice, rats, guinea-pigs and rabbits used in medical research. They can be used in ecological investigations, they are subjected to genetic and physiological experiments, they can operate as models in the search for new methods of protecting plants and products, and in the elucidation of the general laws of nature.

Another practical use of a lepidopteron involves the little wasps of the genus *Trichogramma*, egg parasites of various noctuid moths, which can be multiplied artificially in the eggs of the stored product moth *Sitotroga cerealella*. Subsequently the wasps are released in millions into the fields to help prevent the multiplication of cutworm and other destructive noctuid species.

Because of interferences with natural ecosystems many formerly harmless species have turned into pests. The low number of plant and animal species in agricultural systems gives rise to many unoccupied niches which may be populated by adaptable lepidopterous species endowed with a high reproductive capacity. As a result the population density rapidly increases and may lead to an outbreak of economic importance. Sometimes a number of species, each of little importance when taken in isolation, may all feed together, and their total destructiveness may become economically significant.

Migratory polyphagous species appearing unexpectedly in a region represent a source of danger. Females lay their eggs in millions and the caterpillars can cause devastation. Thousands of square kilometres all over Europe have sometimes been devastated in this way. In 1921—1924 masses of hungry caterpillars of the Silver Y Moth, moving to new fields in pursuit of food, repeatedly stopped trains, the wheels of which would spin on their crushed bodies as they swarmed across the tracks. At other times a hundred or more caterpillars could be found on a single sugar-beet plant. If we calculate that about 100cm^2 of leaf area are needed to satisfy the needs of a single caterpillar during its life, it can be seen that such a plant with a leaf area of about 0,3m^2 can be defoliated in two or three days.

Imported species can be very dangerous because, if they come to a region devoid of natural enemies, and they find the climate suitable, little can prevent them from multiplying. This can be exemplified by the Fall Webworm (*Hyphantria cunea*) which was brought from America to Europe during or after World War II, and caused havoc in orchards. The Gypsy Moth, the European Corn Borer and a number of tortricids living on deciduous or coniferous trees have moved in the opposite direction, from Europe to America, where they too have proved very troublesome.

The number of destructive and economically significant lepidopterous species is too high to allow individual attention. Species inhabiting fields, orchards, plantations and gardens are dealt with in the ample literature on agricultural entomology, while species inhabiting forests are widely discussed in the equally voluminous studies on forest entomology. Almost every species has been described in detail, their ways of life examined, and methods for controlling them have been devised.

Collecting

Adults

With the exception of the frosty winter months, many butterflies and moths can be collected the year round. Early species appear on the wing at a time when the snow is thawing, the last ones can be found in late autumn. In those parts of Europe which do not have extreme winters, specialized species also occur even in mid-winter. The hibernating species emerge early in spring — numerous nymphalids and the brimstone butterflies, and moths including many noctuids, geometrids and various small species.

Butterflies can be found in woodland margins, flowery meadows, clearings, along streams in lush valleys, and in drier localities such as steppes and stony hillsides. Some species have to be sought in their exclusive haunts. On sunny days, butterflies settle on flowers or on the leaves of plants and shrubs, sometimes on moist ground. Many species can be attracted by evil-smelling substances — for instance, purple emperors and white admirals like to settle on cattle dung, rotting meat, etc. In daytime even small Lepidoptera may be put up from undergrowth by tapping the plants with a stick. Moths, unless carefully concealed, rest by day on tree trunks and stones, mostly on the side away from the sun. Some moths that are usually considered night-fliers may sometimes be seen on the wing in daytime. Certain noctuids, eggars, tussock moths and geometrids are active chiefly in the afternoon.

Butterflies and moths are collected in various ways. The simplest of these is by catching them in an entomological or 'butterfly' net (Fig. 21). Resting butterflies, particularly in late afternoon, can be shaken off trees or shrubs, or, like caterpillars, swept from vegetation with a sweep-net. The majority of moths of nocturnal habit can be collected by attracting them to light or to bait, while males of a great many species can be allured by a freshly hatched female. Certain species, such as leaf-miners, including the smallest Lepidoptera, are most easily obtained by rearing them from eggs, caterpillars or pupae. This has the added benefit that we learn more about the species, and obtain perfect specimens at the same time.

Entomological nets are made of fine fabric — bobbinet, mosquito netting, organdie or nylon. They are shaped like a bag, gently rounded at the bottom, and fastened to a metal ring of about 300mm in diameter. The bag must be deep enough to fold over the edge of the ring, and so trap the captured butterfly or moth inside. The ring is either made of one piece, or, for convenience in travelling, may be collapsible into 3—4 parts; it is circular or pear-shaped and attached to a wooden, bamboo, or metal stick. It is either fixed or provided with a screw fastener enabling us to separate the ring from the stick and so stow them separately. The length of the stick is optional. A relatively long stick is required for hunting butterflies as these are very wary, and it is almost impossible, however stealthily, to approach members of some species. Others like to sit on the branches of high trees, or above water, and cannot be reached with a short-sticked net. A short handle is often convenient for collecting moths and certain smaller butterflies. A stick consisting of extendable sections can be very useful. Some practice and dexterity are needed to use a net properly, as the wings of Lepidoptera are easily damaged by clumsy or too vigorous action.

Butterflies may be caught by net throughout the day, until dusk. At night we cannot do without illumination. A strong torch will render some service, but a petrol or kerosene pressure lamp brightly illuminating the whole neighbourhood is much better, and it can be placed on the ground to leave both hands free. Alternatively, we can illuminate the ground in front of us as we walk, and hunt for moths feeding on flowers or fluttering in the lamplight. Hunting at night involves handling the lamp, wielding a net, and carrying killing bottles and further apparatus. So an assistant is always welcome.

The use of light at night also takes advantage of the well-known weakness of moths: the strong attraction light has for them. Kerosene, petrol or gas pressure lamps have proved very practical for field work, but access to electricity enables us to use a mercury discharge lamp.

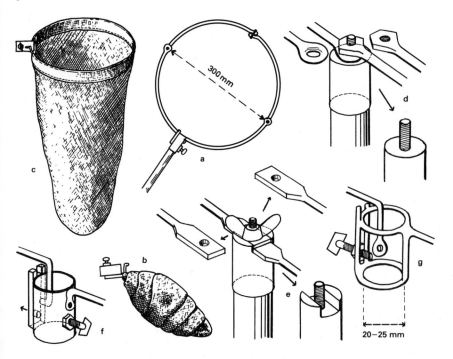

21 Entomological net: a — collapsible ring, b — folded net, c — unfolded net, d to g — various mechanisms for fastening the net to a stick or handle: d, e — stick with a metal ending, f, g — devices for fastening the net to any kind of stick.

The ultraviolet radiation emitted by such lights has an extraordinarily strong effect on moths. When using an ultraviolet lamp it is essential to shield our eyes with protective goggles, and, for sensitive people, to smear our faces with anti-sunburn oil. Electricity may be supplied by a car battery or portable generator, many types of which are now available. In addition to the source of light we need a white sheet with an area of $1-2m^2$, (some collectors prefer a much larger sheet), vertically attached so that its lower edge touches the ground. The light source is placed on a stand, or hung from a branch, at a distance of about $50-70$cm from the sheet, so that the sheet is strongly illuminated. In a good locality (the most productive being an elevated place partly overgrown with vegetation where the light can still penetrate into a wide neighbourhood) many moths arrive and settle on the sheet or in the grass nearby, or keep moving and flying all over the sheet. From these we select the specimens required, usually capturing them directly by clapping a killing bottle over them. Collectors should always endeavour to kill only those moths wanted for the collection, without exterminating others not required.

A more refined method employing light involves capturing moths in an automatic light-trap. Moths attracted to the light fall into a collecting container where they are killed by chloroform or some other substance. The trap is switched on in the evening and off in the morning by an automatic timer. The bottle containing the captured moths must be removed once a day, to be replaced by an empty one. At this time the killing fluid is topped up, and any repairs necessary are carried out. Dozens of light-trap types are now available. Most of them, however, fail to satisfy the requirements of collectors as the material captured is usually too damaged for the collection. They are used primarily in scientific research aimed at surveying the abundance and phenology of species rather than accumulating collection specimens. Light-traps help us to record sudden and unexpected occurrences in relation to time of year or the weather, to study migratory species, or the population changes in agricultural or forest pests. As the trap can function day after day, rare species are often caught. The data from traps are collected and passed to scientific data banks. Reliable conclusions can often be based on several years' observations. In many countries whole networks of observation centres equipped with light-traps have been established to help protect agricultural crops. Light-traps are also very valuable for faunistic research.

The use of baits provides an excellent method of capturing those Lepidoptera which feed at night. Although baiting can be practised all the year round, the best results are obtained at a time when there is a lack of plants in flower — in spring until May, and from midsummer to the end of the season.

The best substance for baiting is fermenting, sweet-smelling liquid. A convenient and much-recommended bait is beer boiled with a few spoonfuls of honey, syrup, or fruit juice, to which some apples cut in small pieces may be added. Dried fruit slices or bits of porous material attached to strings are then dipped into this liquid. Before nightfall, these are hung on branches of trees and shrubs in the locality to be investigated. Another kind of bait is fruit pulp prepared from mixed or stewed fruit. Several hours preceding its application, it is warmed and yeast is added to evoke fermentation. The pulp is spread with a spatula or brush on tree trunks, branches and leaves.

The preparation of baits is something like culinary art: many collectors have secret recipes for baits effective beyond comparison with those prepared by anyone else!

If we intend to use bait we must reach the locality before sunset. Baits are hung or spread about $1-2$m above the ground, most usually in woodland margins, along forest paths and rides, around groups of bushes, and on solitary trees. This preparation must be finished before nightfall. The first moths appear at dusk, sometimes even in daylight, but it is after nightfall that they arrive in greatest numbers. The baits are examined by means of a lamp; red lamps are often recommended as least disturbing to the moths. Most can be placed straight into the killing bottle, but some species are very shy and drop down into the grass from the bait at the slightest disturbance. They can also alarm the other moths, and the bait may be abandoned within seconds. A special net placed ready beneath each bait can help overcome this problem.

Virgin lepidopterous females may emit a particular odour appealing to their males, which may be effective even at a great distance. These chemical sexual lures (pheromones) are released from abdominal glands. Females reared in natural conditions so that they emerge at the natural time of flight of the given species can be used for attracting males. A virgin female is placed in a small cage and taken to a suitable place where the species is likely to occur. One female can sometimes entice several dozen males. This technique is most useful for eggars, tussock and tiger moths. The time must be adjusted to the activity of the species in nature − usually the early evening.

Some pheromones have been synthetically produced to bait traps used in agriculture for catching the males of destructive lepidopterous species. This is a good method of control, as it is normally specific to the particular pest involved − unlike pesticides and other poisons.

An effective, though rather tiring method of collecting Lepidoptera in spring is by beating. This can be used to investigate trees on a frosty morning following a series of nice days when a number of butterflies and moths have already emerged. We must get up early to reach the wood shortly after daybreak. Besides the usual entomological equipment we need a rubber truncheon, mallet, or heavy stick wrapped in soft material to beat the tree trunks and branches. After such blows, many butterflies and moths that have been sitting in the trees fall to the ground, stiff with cold. Even a net is not needed, since the half-frozen insects are unable to fly and can be collected directly into the killing bottle from the ground. By spreading a fairly large sheet under each tree we can obtain wingless females which otherwise would be overlooked in the grass. Moreover, it is surprising how many other insects (beetles, plant bugs, etc.) are living on the trees at such an early time of the year. As soon as the sun rises and it starts to get warm, it is time to stop work. By this method we may get all species of geometrids of the genus *Archiearis,* various other geometrids, the Kentish Glory, moths of the genera *Orthosia* and *Tethea,* and hibernating as well as spring leaf rollers.

In the evenings it is also worth while dislodging moths from flowering sallows, aspens, poplars, maples, etc., where many species come to feed. After unfolding a sheet under the tree or shrub, we beat or shake the trunk. The moths fall to the ground and, for a short while, remain motionless. It is not exceptional for several dozen moths to come falling down from a single flowering shrub. There is usually time enough to examine them by lamplight and pick out those of interest. This method produces many moths of the genera *Conistra, Orthosia, Xylena, Lithophane,* and others.

A rather different technique must be applied for collecting the smallest mining Lepidoptera. These are, for the most part, reared in their mines. It is possible to collect the adults directly, but they are not easy to transport in a killing bottle without damage, and to pin them it is often necessary to use a magnifying glass. Once these minute moths have dried and stiffened, they are practically impossible to prepare properly, and can only be included in the collection in an unset state. We therefore catch them, one by one, into small glass tubes (about 10 × 50mm), and use these to transport the living specimens. At home or back in the laboratory we can then kill them and prepare each one immediately. Naturally, it is necessary to take a considerable supply of small tubes into the field for this purpose.

Eggs, caterpillars and pupae

Butterflies and moths captured in nature are often damaged. Many collectors who are keen to have undamaged specimens in their collection rear their butterflies and moths, from eggs, caterpillars or pupae.

Eggs may often be obtained very easily if we succeed in catching a female. In most cases she has already been fertilized. We place the living female into a little box and take her home. Sometimes females will lay eggs on the inner surface of the box almost immediately, but others must be kept in captivity for a longer time, and fed with a solution of honey or fruit juice. A piece of cotton-wool or filter-paper is dipped into the solution for the insect to suck from. Females of some species are more difficult: they refuse to deposit their eggs anywhere but on their food-plant, or in small fissures (for example in crumpled or corrugated paper), or else in some moist environment. Other females, especially those of butterflies, require sufficient room to fly — otherwise no eggs can be obtained from them. These may be released in a room with windows or in a suitable greenhouse, with a supply of fresh caterpillar food-plant. Slight narcosis may induce the females of many moths to lay their eggs. There are cases, however, where all efforts end in failure. Perhaps the females need some special condition we cannot supply in captivity. The advantage of obtaining eggs directly from a female is that we know from the start what species is involved. This makes it possible to seek information in the literature about the larval food-plants, and thus make adequate preparations for rearing the livestock.

The collection of eggs in nature is laborious: one needs to be very lucky to find a whole batch. By examining a shrub, leaf after leaf and branch after branch, we may sometimes be surprised by the multitude of eggs discovered — for the most part, however, we are unlikely to be able to ascertain the species to which they belong. Without a great deal of experience, the identification of eggs is extremely difficult. Note should always be taken of the kind of plant on which the eggs have been found: this may help us to select the food-plant for the caterpillars, as they are often laid on the correct plant. Each type of egg should be kept separately.

It is sometimes possible to observe a female in the act of oviposition (most likely a butterfly) and to collect the eggs laid immediately after she has finished.

Caterpillars are obtained by searching for them individually, or by beating or sweeping. In the first case we patiently examine one plant after another, leaf by leaf, flower by flower; attention should also be paid to branches and trunks, as caterpillars can be found almost anywhere. Their occurrence is often indicated by traces of their feeding. Numerous species live underground and may be unearthed by digging. Hunting caterpillars at night with a hand-lamp is usually very profitable, for a great many caterpillars are nocturnal in their habits. In the lamplight they may be seen from some distance, but sometimes any shaking of the ground makes them fall into the grass — hence it is necessary to walk with care. In spring the caterpillars climb bare branches in search of the first greenery. In the course of a single evening many hundred specimens can be caught. Common species of cutworm moths prevail, but rare species may be found among them which are difficult to obtain in any other way.

Beating is a very effective method. A beating-tray, a sort of white umbrella with its handle at the side (in case of need, a real umbrella can be pressed into service!), is held below a suitable branch. A sharp blow to the branch with a stout stick will dislodge caterpillars, which either fall directly or descend on silk threads into the beating-tray.

Sweeping is done with a sweep-net, rather similar to but heavier than a butterfly net. The bag is made of coarse white cloth attached to a firm frame (the shape need not necessarily be circular). The handle must also be stronger, as the sweep-net must be able to stand strong blows against plants, and the cloth must not get torn by the first branch. Such a heavy tool cannot be managed with one hand only: we have to use both. We walk about the undergrowth, sweeping the net from side to side, as if we wanted to scythe off the tops of plants. Caterpillars fall into the sweep-net, together with a multitude of various other insects and debris. The fragile larvae must be picked out after a few sweeps, otherwise many will be injured against sharp sticks or spiny leaves.

In collecting caterpillars, knowledge is a great asset. Special manuals can furnish us with information about the time of occurrence and the food-plant of caterpillars of those butterflies and moths we seek, or about the traces of their feeding and where these should be looked for. All this raises the probability of success.

Some groups of caterpillars require special collecting methods. Caterpillars of clearwings and goat moths tunnel in branches and roots, while caterpillars of many other species do so in rotten tree trunks, stumps or under bark. Their collecting is laborious and usually requires spades, saws, chisels and similar tools.

Mining caterpillars have to be searched for on selected plant species, as they are often monophagous. A mined leaf is plucked off and enclosed in a container in which high humidity and turgor of plant tissues can be maintained, where the caterpillars complete their development — a well-sealed polythene bag is often ideal. Owing to high mortality, good results can only be expected if we succeed in catching almost full-grown caterpillars. The detachment of the leaf is soon followed by a change in the osmotic pressure and chemical composition of the cell sap, to which the caterpillars are very sensitive. One of the best times for collecting mines is in autumn, prior to leaf-fall. At this time full-fed caterpillars may be found in the mines. These larvae pupate and complete their development immediately after emerging from hibernation. The results are less favourable in the summer generation.

Parasitism often frustrates our efforts to get adult Lepidoptera from caterpillars captured in nature. In spite of considerable care devoted to them, the results are often nil. But it is not right to wreak vengeance upon ichneumon, braconid and chalcid wasps, egg-parasite wasps (Proctotrupidae), tachinid flies and other such 'vermin' by just annihilating them. After killing them, put them into a clean tube provided with a label giving data on the locality where the larva was found and its species, close the tube with a tight cork and put it aside for a parasite specialist. Such specimens, with good data, are of immense scientific value and would be gratefully received by any serious hymenopterist (collector of hymenopterous insects) or dipterist (collector of two-winged flies), or by any properly equipped natural history museum.

Lepidopterous chrysalides occur in a variety of places, dependent on the caterpillars' way of life. Quite a lot of relevant information is included in the chapter on the life-cycles of butterflies and moths. Great attention should be paid to fissures and cracks in bark, to the forks of branches, and to rolled-up leaves. Here pupae can be found wrapped up in flimsy or more solid cocoons. Pupae can also be raked out of the soil or forest litter. The results, however, are often poor, and digging for pupae may cause damage to trees.

Rearing

So we have obtained the various individual stages — what is to be done with them? Most difficult of all is to rear Lepidoptera right through from the egg stage. Eggs are best placed in small tubes or other receptacles made of glass or transparent plastic, and kept from excessive drought or direct sunshine. However, as the requirements of individual species differ, experience is important. Prior to hatching (usually signalled by a change in the egg colour), a little piece of a leaf of the food-plant — insofar as this is known to us — should be placed in the tube to enable the caterpillars to move on to it immediately after emergence. If the food-plant is unknown, we must try out several plant species, including the so-called universal or emergency food-plants. These consist of plant species eaten by numerous kinds of caterpillars — among herbaceous plants these include dandelion, plantain and nettle, and among trees, oak, willow and birch. If the caterpillars take to any of them, the battle is usually won. The rearing receptacles for small caterpillars must not be too spacious, the optimal size being $50-100cm^3$, and the caterpillars should find food anywhere they crawl. The receptacle should be covered with a light yet sufficiently fine fabric to prevent them from crawling out. Care must be taken not to let the walls get wet (caterpillars easily drown in drops of water), yet the food must not be desiccated either. If need be, the receptacle may be covered with a lid. As they grow the caterpillars are gradually separated into smaller groups and kept in bigger jars or boxes. Later on they may be placed in a breeding-cage, but only species living gregariously in nature survive collective rearing well (and may even depend on it).

A breeding-cage consists of a wooden box approximately 25 × 25 × 10cm. A wooden frame about 40cm high fitted with fine mesh wire netting is built on top of it. A little door or a removable glass panel at one side of the cage is useful for removing *frass* (caterpillar droppings) and supplying fresh food. Breeding cages are unsuitable for species which prefer creeping about all the time instead of keeping to their food-plant. It is also difficult to preserve in a fresh state those food-plants that wither rapidly, even in a vase. Glass jars offer some advantages. Being usually more easily available than breeding-cages, it requires less effort to change them, and keep them clean. They do not occupy much space and the food keeps fresh for a longer time. Sometimes, however, they promote excessive humidity which, particularly in combination with a high temperature, considerably increases the danger of infection. Glass jars containing larvae should never be exposed to direct sunshine.

In rearing caterpillars it is necessary to supply fresh food almost daily, and to remove the frass which very soon becomes covered with mildew and may provide a source of infection. If an infection does break out in some stock, it is best to kill the whole lot without delay and disinfect the breeding-cage or glass jar. As a rule, in an infected stock most of the caterpillars are afflicted and hesitation can bring about the destruction of all your other stocks.

Caterpillars are reared either solitarily or en masse, according to their nature. Some species develop cannibalistic tendencies. The larvae of wood-boring species must be kept in glass jars, as they would soon gnaw their way out of wooden or paper boxes.

When pupation time draws near, caterpillars become restless, lose all interest in food, and crawl about the breeding-cage until they succeed in voiding all food remains from their guts. At the same time they search for an adequate pupation site. Some species require a layer of earth in which each caterpillar makes a little cell in which to pupate. Some caterpillars need sawdust, paper or other materials to build up a suitable cocoon. If we fail to provide the right conditions during the prepupal period, the caterpillars lose their ability to burrow in the ground or to build a cocoon, and just pupate freely on the bottom of the jar or cage. Such pupae are frequently damaged or incompletely formed; insofar as anything emerges from them, it will be a deformed butterfly or moth.

Eggars, tussock, emperor and tiger moths, some noctuids and various butterflies and other moths spin a variety of cocoons — some tough, others weak. For these they choose rolled-up leaves, twig forks, or a corner of the breeding-box. They often like to use some material for reinforcing their cocoons.

Pupae do not require very much care. Do not take them out of the webs of cocoons spun by the larvae. Free pupae are best put on a layer of moist sand and, until the time for eclosion is near, covered with a piece of linen cloth or filter-paper to help maintain a moderate humidity. From time to time they should be sprinkled with water. To avoid trouble due to diapause, if possible leave pupae in natural conditions — in an unheated room with natural light, at a cellar window, in a garden arbour, etc. Of course, some safety measures must be taken to prevent, for example, mice from eating them. Attention must be paid to supplying the butterfly or moth with something on which to crawl after emergence — bare twigs are usually ideal.

The development of pupae can be speeded up only after the end of diapause, in January or February, by taking them to a room with a higher temperature. Then the adult insects appear much earlier than in nature, although deviations from the typical colouration may be produced as a result.

Killing and initial care of specimens

Butterflies can be killed in two ways. We may take advantage of the moment when a butterfly calms down in the net and clasps its wings together. In this position we hold it in the netting and carefully pinch the thorax from below. In its death spasm a butterfly will often re-open its wings. In order to prevent this, wait for a few seconds before releasing the pressure of our fingers and the net. If, nevertheless, the butterfly does open its wings, immediately use a pair of entomological forceps to return it to the wings-closed-over-the-back position. To make sure it is dead, the butterfly should be put into a killing bottle for a while. Smaller butterflies, noctuids and minute moths are transferred directly from the net, or from plants and trunks, into killing bottles.

Killing bottles are usually made from relatively small, wide-necked glass jars or tubes. The atmosphere inside is saturated with deadly fumes produced by some chemical agent. This is soaked into a layer of cotton-wool crammed at the bottom. Chloroform is quite suitable for killing Lepidoptera, since it kills quickly and reliably without affecting the colouration. Diethyl ether or ethyl acetate, used with success in killing beetles, Diptera and other insects, often affects butterflies too slowly and these may then be damaged by fluttering in the killing bottle. Frequent use is made of killing bottles containing potassium cyanide placed below a layer of cotton-wool or sawdust. Liquid Plaster-of-Paris is then poured over this, and allowed to harden. Fumes of hydrogen cyanide, released from the cyanide under the influence of carbon dioxide and humidity, penetrate through the porous plaster into the killing bottle and quickly kill the majority of butterflies and moths. Only burnets and foresters and some geometrids are able to resist the fumes for a long time. Consequently, in their case, a killing bottle of this type is of little use. Cyanide killing bottles are very practical because one may last for a whole season, often longer. Their disadvantages include the decolourization of some red or green-coloured Lepidoptera exposed to the fumes, and the fact that both cyanide and hydrogen cyanide are very dangerous to human life. In the majority of countries potassium cyanide can only be obtained on special licence, and cyanide killing bottles should never be handled by young or inexperienced people. Handled properly, no accidents need happen, but the loss of such a killing bottle is very serious, since it may be found by an uninformed person or a child. The splinters of a broken killing bottle may also be dangerous, so that cyanide bottles are now usually made of plastic instead of glass, and firmly bound with tape as an extra precaution. It should be pointed out, however, that most clear plastics are not suitable for chloroform or ethyl acetate killing bottles since these solvents dissolve such plastics.

In practice, one killing bottle is insufficient. Only one live butterfly or moth should be placed in each killing bottle at a time. Dead specimens can, for a time, be placed together in greater numbers, so long as we leave the killing bottle motionless. Different-sized killing bottles for lepidopterous insects of various sizes are useful — their number and assortment are determined by the collector's interest in a particular group of butterflies or moths. A collector of butterflies will need to be equipped with larger killing bottles having a neck of 6—10cm in diameter, while a collector of moths and small butterflies will prefer a supply of smaller killing bottles with a 2—3cm opening.

Large Lepidoptera, such as hawkmoths and eggars, are best killed by injecting ammonia into the thorax from below, by means of a fine-needled syringe. Alternatively, a sewing-machine needle will suffice, if the eye can be filled with a sufficient amount of deadly liquid. Carbon dioxide (often now available in little pressure containers for producing soda water or inflating car tyres) may be used for stunning Lepidoptera for the purposes of short-term manipulation or injection. A butterfly or moth, if transferred from carbon dioxide to fresh air, recovers very soon.

Caterpillars and pupae can also be killed by chloroform, ether, or hydrogen cyanide fumes.

Pupae, which have a very low respiratory rate, must remain in a killing bottle for a long time, sometimes even for several days. For all the early stages it is best, however, to kill them by dropping them into hot (60°C) water, followed by fixing in a preservative liquid — alcohol, 'Pampel's fluid', formalin, etc.

As soon as they are dead, or as soon after as possible, adult specimens should be removed from the killing bottle and pinned into a suitable box. A box of tin-plate or plastic, with a moistened layer of peat forming the bottom will render good service. Sufficient humidity is maintained in such a box to keep the butterflies and moths relaxed until they can be set at home or at base camp. But if this cannot be done within a few hours, as may occur on a long expedition or because of having other work to do, the insects must be dried to prevent the formation of mildew. They may either be pinned in a dry box or placed between layers of absorbent paper or wadding (not cotton-wool), so as to prevent their movement or mutual contact. In this way they can be transported home or even mailed in a box with safety. If material is to be left for any appreciable time, we must not forget to attach a label giving the date, locality and any other relevant data concerning their capture.

Preparing specimens for the collection

First the dead butterfly or moth must be pinned. For this purpose, stainless steel *entomological pins*, produced in black or white, 36—38mm long, and of various thicknesses, are supplied. The thinnest ones are designated 000, slightly thicker ones 00; these are followed by 0, 1, 2, 3, 4, 5, etc. A no. 5 pin is quite stout, suitable for the robust bodies of hawkmoths. For the smallest Lepidoptera, however, even no. 000 is too thick. Minute *micropins* are available for these: they are about 15mm long and not thicker than 0.2mm. Numbers 1 and 2 pins are used for the majority of European butterflies, nos. 2 and 3 for most medium sized moths, etc. Since it is often difficult to insert exceedingly thin pins into the bottom of collection boxes, the small Lepidoptera should be pinned with the stoutest size of pin their bodies can withstand. The pin is inserted through the centre of the thorax of the butterfly or moth so that it is at right angles with both the longitudinal and the transverse axes of the body. Specimens should be positioned about $^2/_3$ of the way up the pin.

Butterflies and moths to be included in a collection are usually 'set' or 'spread', and each must be labelled individually with the basic data concerning capture. *Setting* essentially involves spreading the wings out flat, with the hind margin of the forewings, and the fore margin of the hindwings at right angles to the body — in fact, in the attitude in which lepidopterous insects are usually illustrated in identification manuals. This manipulation not only increases the aesthetic appearance of the specimens, but facilitates their full and accurate comparison, and improves the neatness of the collection.

The preparation of butterflies and moths is relatively simple, but does need patience and sensitive, dextrous hands. The equipment required can be obtained from a commercial entomological dealer, but it is not too difficult to make it for oneself. The necessary items include setting boards, entomological pins, pins with glass heads, strips of shiny paper, setting needles and various forceps. The preparation of the smallest Lepidoptera requires a magnifying glass.

Easiest to prepare is a freshly killed butterfly or moth which has been kept for a few hours in a damp box: it is supple and pliable. Dry insects, from old supplies of unprocessed material, must be *relaxed* before preparation. For this we need a dish containing previously washed and sterilized moist sand to which a few drops of creosote or other chemical agent are added to prevent moulding (cellulose wadding is often used as a substitute for sand). The butterflies and moths to be relaxed are put in envelopes on the top of the sand, or, if already pinned, they are pinned into the sand. The dish is then covered with a lid, the best thing being a glass bell enabling us to look inside. Relaxing takes about one day for average-sized Lepidoptera, but two days or more for the larger insects. Minute specimens are ready for preparation in 8−10 hours, sometimes even sooner. There are no exact instructions. Relaxing is very difficult, if not impossible, for three lepidopterous groups which should be prepared immediately after capture. These involve, on the one hand, the smallest Lepidoptera pinned on micropins, which are in danger of being badly damaged by humidity − especially their delicate wing fringes. The second group are the most robust species, hawkmoths, eggars, and so on. If the necessity does arise to prepare old or dried material of these big moths, they should be placed on moist sand for 1−2 days, and then hot water injected into the thorax at the wing bases. Despite all this, these big moths remain rather stiff and show a tendency, even after preparation, to *spring* − that is, they often return to the position in which they originally dried. Skipper butterflies (Hesperiidae) are also much more difficult to set from old rather than fresh material. The last group includes some green coloured moths, which change their natural colouration to yellow after having passed several hours in a humid environment.

The actual preparation is effected on the setting board. This consists, in essence, of two wooden boards slightly tilted towards a groove situated between them. Setting boards are of various types and sizes, to accommodate the various sizes of insects. The groove is usually about 25mm deep and lined at the bottom with some soft material suitable for receiving pins. To commence preparation we place the pinned insect's body into the groove so that the pin is perpendicular both to the vertical and the horizontal axes of the setting board, and so that the outspread wings are poised just above the surface of the board. In working with them, care must be taken not to touch the butterflies and moths other than with the setting needles and forceps. Fingers easily rub off the scales covering the wings and body. The wings are spread out on the board and covered with a glazine setting strip. First one strip is fastened in front of the left-hand wings by two pins, or we lightly hold it with the fingers of one hand. The setting needle is inserted into the base of the left forewing, and, with its help, the wing is advanced into the desired position, that is the hind margin of the wing and the longitudinal axis of the setting board are made to form a right angle. It may be necessary to insert a pin next to the body, to stop it twisting. Then the hindwing is moved up, to pass beneath the forewing by a small amount. Once both left wings are in the correct position, we press the setting strip down with our fingers and secure it in place by pins inserted around the wings. The same procedure is then repeated on the right-hand wings. In order to make the work more accessible, we may turn the setting board the other way round. Finally, the abdomen is supported with a wisp of cotton-wool or two crossed pins to assume a natural position, and the antennae are arranged under the setting strip approximately in parallel to the costal margin of the wing.

The prepared butterfly or moth must then be allowed to dry out on the setting board. In a dry room this takes 3−4 days for small insects, and 7−10 days for butterflies and common moths. Insects with thick abdomens must dry for 2−3 weeks. If sufficient setting boards are available, it is worthwhile to leave the insects in place for a longer time, to ensure that their wings will not spring later.

More exacting is the preparation of the smallest Lepidoptera pinned on micropins. The working principle is the same, though all the instruments applied are more delicate. What we need is special small setting boards provided with a groove 1−2mm in breadth. We can easily produce them ourselves by using a razor to make a small groove in a piece of soft cork, polystyrene or 'plastozote' foam. Forceps and setting needles must be particularly fine. Good work may be done with a setting needle which has its end turned through a right angle. Sometimes it suffices to blow the finely fringed wings apart from behind to get them into the right position. Some moths may be so small that we require a lens to magnify them about 5−10 times. Once dried, a micropinned specimen is then mounted on a little stick, first by passing the micropin tip through one end, and then a large, thick entomological or other suitable pin through the other: this process is called double-mounting. The large pin, which now bears the tiny moth or butterfly affixed to the little stick, is used to handle the specimen in the collection, and to carry the labels. The little sticks for double mounting (in size of approximately 10 × 3 × 3mm) can be made from elder or maize pith. The best double mounts of all are made from the dry bracket fungus *Piptoporus betulinus,* gathered in autumn from withered birch trunks. Many collectors now use 'plastozote' plastic foam, cut into suitable pieces, for this purpose.

Caterpillars can be preserved either by drying or in a liquid preservative. Drying involves the following procedure: after killing the caterpillar, its anus is cut open and the entrails are pressed out, from head to tail, with the aid of a small roller. By way of the anus, the empty skin is next pulled over the narrowed end of a tube and fastened to this by a small clamp. The caterpillar is then dried in a little oven, or over an asbestos or similar fireproof plate heated from below by a gas burner, while air is forced through the tube into the caterpillar, so keeping it inflated until it is completely dry. The dry caterpillar is finally impaled on and glued to a suitable length of straw, the end of which receives a suitable pin for the labels and handling in the collection. Drying perfectly preserves some colours (many of them change), the patterns and the hairs, but the specimens are very fragile. Large caterpillars, however, are quite often preserved in this way.

Another method involves freeze-drying of the dead caterpillar. This is first rapidly frozen and, in this state, dried at a low temperature in a vacuum. This usually preserves the colours very well indeed. The caterpillars are put into glass tubes each plugged by a piece of cotton wool.

Nowadays preference is given to keeping caterpillars in liquid preservatives. Before being put into the liquid, the dead caterpillar is briefly boiled in water. Alternatively, the larva can be killed by immersion in hot water, as already noted. The colours fade hereby, but all morphological structures are clearly visible on the now taut skin. The caterpillar is then placed in a small tube filled with 70% alcohol. For special purposes other liquids are used. Tubes provided with data labels are closed with a cotton-wool plug and placed in series into large preserving jars containing alcohol, in which the tubes are submerged. A caterpillar collection should include a register with a description of the colouration and patterns of the living caterpillars. An album of colour photographs or slides is an excellent complement to any caterpillar collection.

Hard, strongly sclerotized pupae are killed, dried and deposited, in a dry state, in tubes or collection boxes. Softer pupae are easily deformed by drying and are therefore preserved in liquid, in the same way as caterpillars. The empty pupal cuticles *(exuviae)* are not without value either − those who rear Lepidoptera often make the mistake of disposing of them. In pupae, most features characteristic of the species are found on the abdomen, especially the cremaster. This part remains undamaged after emergence of the adult. We know from the adult to what species the exuviae belong − and this is a great advantage. Also the cocoon, the web in which it is wrapped, the cell made up of earth or other material belonging to the pupa can all usefully be preserved. As a matter of common practice, cases formerly containing the caterpillars and chrysalides of bagworms and case bearers are added to the collection by being pinned directly with the insect that has emerged from them. The cases are often of help in the identification of the species of these families, whose adults are very similar in appearance.

Lepidopterous eggs are collected by rather few people. Eggs with a hard chorion (for example, those of eggars and tussock moths) can be killed and preserved dry. Softer eggs should be fixed and preserved in liquid: methods and formulations for this may be found in special manuals. And the empty shells may be preserved − unless, of course, they are eaten by the caterpillars on hatching (an important first 'meal' in some species). To study eggs seriously it is necessary to have a strong magnifying glass or, better still, a microscope. Valuable data may be gathered by measuring the eggs in a fresh state, noting their shape, and by describing the colouration and structure of the chorion.

It is also possible to collect caterpillar mines. Mined leaves and other plant parts damaged by feeding are dried between layers of blotting-paper or newspaper, and glued to sheets of paper on which data concerning the occurrence and locality are entered.

The great advances in the technology of photography make it quite easy to produce colour macrophotographs either in slide or print form. In fact, with due regard to the needs for conservation, many collectors now prefer to 'hunt' with the camera rather than the net. Colour photography can just be a complement to other collecting methods, or it can be an independent activity aimed at illustrating Lepidoptera in all their developmental stages in the natural environment.

As we have already noted, to identify many species of Lepidoptera it is essential to make preparations (dissections) of the male and female reproductive organs. The basic method will now be described. The objects of our interest are the solid, sclerotized parts that must be excised from the abdomen and cleaned to remove hairs, various membranes and other tissues. First detach the whole abdomen from a specimen and place it in a 75 × 15mm test-tube. To this add sufficient 10% potash solution to just cover the abdomen and carefully boil the tube in a water-bath (a large beaker is suitable) for 5−15 minutes. The potash solution is prepared by dissolving (care!) one unit by weight of potassium hydroxide (KOH) in nine units by weight of distilled water. Remember that potash is caustic, so handle it with care, and do not spill it on your skin or clothes. The boiling potash dissolves the soft tissues, and makes the hard parts flexible. The amount of time required depends on the specimen (especially its size). In the course of time we gain experience as to how long the abdomens of variously sized butterflies and moths should be boiled. The abdomen is next transferred to a dish of water or dilute alcohol. All further work is done in this dish with the use of a large magnifying glass or low power binocular microscope enlarging 10−20 times. The genital organs are removed from the tip of the abdomen with forceps and cleaned of membranes, hairs and various debris with the aid of dissecting needles, fine forceps and brushes. It is often necessary to separate the aedeagus (penis) and other organs by dissection, for critical examination, but great care is needed to avoid damaging any of the parts because they often bear important identifying characters. After examination the genital organs are preserved either by placing them in a small tube containing glycerol and ethyl alcohol, or by making them into a permanent microscope slide preparation. Many textbooks describe procedures for doing this. The tubes or slides are provided with data labels and deposited in a store. Each preparation has its own serial number: this number is also attached to the pin of the butterfly or moth from which the given preparation was made and a serial entry made in a preparation register. Recently it has become common practice to insert the preserved genitalia into a small ampoule filled with glycerol, which is then closed and located on the pin of the insect concerned. Although this is time and space saving, it can cause chaos in the collection if any of the ampoules break loose.

A collection of butterflies and moths with detached abdomens, 'sacrificed' for the sake of making microscope preparations, is by no means lacking in value. On the contrary, it testifies to the serious approach of the collector, and his or her desire to add to our scientific knowledge of these insects.

Making data labels

The collection is of full value only insofar as each butterfly, moth or caterpillar, each tube, sheet or box, each microscope slide or other preparation, is provided with a label giving exact data about capture. The data labels should include the date of capture, the locality (with the local region and country to which it belongs), the elevation above sea-level, the collector's name, and any other relevant details.

In the field there is rarely time or opportunity for writing labels. At this stage we usually supply the collected specimens with a provisional collective label, or with references to some notes in a diary. However, in any kind of manipulation with a specimen we must never forget to include the data labels relating to it, to prevent confusion that might otherwise (so easily!) arise. A few false or inaccurate data labels can cause a disproportionate amount of trouble, and may render the entire collection of questionable value. It is safest to write labels simultaneously with the preparation of the insects and pin them at the edge of the setting board in a sequence corresponding to that of the butterflies and moths. After these have dried and as they are removed from the boards, the appropriate label is assigned to each of them and mounted on the same pin. Thus all danger of confusion is ruled out. Some collectors prefer to write their labels in one lot, during the winter, making use of the time when there is little opportunity for field work. If this is done great care must be taken to avoid confusion. Further, the writing of several hundreds or even thousands of labels at once represents a daunting prospect, and, moreover, use of the collected material is impossible until all the labels have been attached.

In order to make the data labels serve their purpose, some principles must be observed. First, the data must be put down in a way understandable to anybody who may need to examine the butterfly or moth − that is, legibly, concisely and clearly. On principle, proper names and local geographical designations are never abbreviated, with the exception of those few abbreviations which are in general international use. The name of the collector should be followed by the universally applied Latin abbreviation *leg.* or *lgt.* (= *legit,* collected by). Wherever possible, fix the locality precisely by inclusion of a grid reference, or, in poorly known regions, by longitude and latitude. Material that has been obtained by rearing can be designated by common abbreviations: e.o. − *ex ovo* (from the egg,) e.l. − *ex larva* (from the caterpillar), e.p. − *ex pupa* (from the pupa). The date of capture of the developmental stage should also be entered. This is of greater significance than the date of the insect's emergence, since the adult butterfly or moth may appear in captivity at an atypical time − for example during winter. The data are written in Indian or some other permanent ink. If access to the necessary equipment is possible, typewritten labels, reduced in size by photographic methods, or labels printed directly in a small type-face are very convenient. The following are examples of data labels:

| England
Hampshire
New Forest
mv light 24. vii. 1980
J. O. Brown | WALES:
Snowdon, 1,100 m
1. vi. 1980
leg. A. L. Jones | SCOTLAND
Aviemore, Inverness.
1. on bilberry vii. 1979
em. 5. v. 1980
M. McKenzie leg. |

We must always bear in mind that, through museums or by way of exchange and lending services, our material might be sent to the other end of the world for scientific study, or perhaps our data might be deciphered by scholars after several decades. This has happened to the collections of Linné and other 18th century entomologists. A properly labelled collection is always of value, and should we want to dispose of it, a museum or private collector might well be willing to buy it. Unlabelled material or material provided with questionable data has at most some aesthetic value, or might be used for instructional purposes. Its value, both scienfitic and monetary, is always less than if it had been properly labelled.

Storing the collection

A collection of Lepidoptera is ideally housed in glass-topped, airtight boxes or drawers within a good cabinet, where they can easily be viewed. If the lid is not transparent the box must be opened at every inspection, and the butterflies and moths easily suffer damage by the continual inrush of air. The bottom of the box is lined with a layer of cork, plastic foam or some other soft material suitable for receiving pins. Butterflies and moths are arranged in the boxes in accordance with a classification system, specimens of the same species always being kept together — either side by side in lines, or one after the other in columns. At the beginning or end of each line or row, every species is provided with a label giving its name. On the outside of the box is a label bearing the names of the Lepidoptera inside, together with the name of the family. The size of boxes is, unfortunately, very variable, no standard ever having been fixed. Convenient for big butterflies and moths are boxes about 50 × 50cm and 6—7cm in height; for small Lepidoptera boxes of 40 × 30cm are often preferred. Collectors usually employ boxes of a size corresponding in some unit fashion to the dimensions of the cabinet or cabinet space available to them. Boxes are placed in the cabinet side by side — either vertically like books in a bookcase, or in a horizontal position. Glass topped boxes or drawers can be made to move on individual runners, which is particularly convenient. Within the cabinet the butterflies and moths are protected against light (which causes them to fade) and, to some extent, against pests.

Besides collection boxes, a great number of smaller working boxes are needed. Use can be made of a variety of discarded empty boxes, provided that they are deep enough for a pin. We only need line the bottom of each with a thin layer of soft material suitable for pinning. Well made boxes are needed for expeditions, whereas small, light yet strong boxes are used for sending material by mail.

Every collection must be frequently checked and protected against potential pests, of which there are several. The most damaging is the small Museum Beetle *(Anthrenus museorum)*, about 2mm in length, whose thickly-haired larvae eat, among other things, the dead insects included in collections. An infested specimen may be recognised by a fine, greyish-brown powder which appears below it on the bottom of the box. The beetle larva feeds on the surface of small butterflies or moths, while the bodies of more robust Lepidoptera may sometimes be eaten away completely. Other destructive pests, particularly in damp conditions, are the light brown booklice, about 1mm long. Again, fine dust on the bottom of the box or drawer betrays their presence, but they usually only damage the wing areas between the major veins. From time to time it is necessary to disinfect the collection against pests. Paradichlorbenzene in various commercial formulations and Lindane are commonly used, but some organophosphates (for example Shelltox strips) are also currently applied. All these are poisonous, so precautions must be taken in using them. The selection of a pesticide must be carefully considered for boxes which are lined with synthetic material. Paradichlorbenzol, for example, dissolves polystyrene. Naphthalene is often employed in an attempt to discourage pests from entering the insect boxes.

The extent and layout of a collection of Lepidoptera depends on the purposes the collection is to serve. The collection of an amateur working with butterflies and moths for pleasure and instruction will probably not contain extensive series of individual species, but will include representatives of most local forms. The collection of a specialist who has concerned himself with a particular group of Lepidoptera will be completely different: it will be poorer in species but will contain extensive series of specimens necessary for studying variation, or materials from various parts of the entire range of distribution, etc. Again, a collection used for the purposes of school instruction will differ markedly from a collection of destructive species intended to assist workers in agriculture or forestry. The largest collections are kept in major natural history museums. These collections are used almost exclusively for scientific research, and only a small part of them is usually accessible to the public seeking information or instruction.

A collection of caterpillars, pupae or eggs is not so aesthetically pleasing as a collection of adult butterflies and moths. However, as surprisingly little is known about these so-called pre-imaginal stages, such collections are of considerable scientific value. The larvae and pupae of many butterflies and moths have yet to be found and described, to say nothing of the eggs. Even few major museums can boast of having a large collection of lepidopterous developmental stages.

Keeping records

An entomologist who is not content with merely accumulating butterflies and moths, but intends to devote detailed attention to entomological problems and the life of Lepidoptera in general, should keep a working diary. A diary need not necessarily be conceived as a notebook wherein activities are to be recorded day by day. We add to the diary only when there is something worth recording. The diary may have the form of separate sheets which, later on, may be bound, or stored in folders. Also file cards of notebook format have proved useful, because they permit ready arrangement according to a given system. If, in the course of time, we decide to change our precise interest, we can reclassify the cards according to the needs of the moment.

The diary consists of detailed records and notes. These refer to various things which, in our opinion, might be of interest to us in future or prove helpful in our work or for publication. For instance, notes may be written down about some completed expedition. This is the most frequent case with collectors, whereby the basic data contained in the data label of a butterfly or moth can be expanded in detail: the locality is described, its geographical position is given, the elevation above sea-level is recorded, mention is made of the weather at the time of capture, of plants in flower, of collecting methods, etc. A list of species observed in the locality is compiled. Abundant or common species are not collected on every excursion, as this would lead to an uncontrollable and undesirable expansion of the collection. It is, however, convenient to record their presence by a note in the diary. An observation of some species, details about an unexpected abundant occurrence of a rare species, a description of some experiments carried out, or of rearing techniques, etc. — all these may be included in the notes. The diary may also contain our own opinions and doubts, those of our colleagues, and a number of other matters of interest. Some notes may cover 2—3 lines, others may consist of several pages. The heading of each entry should include the date, and a concise indication of what the entry refers to. This will facilitate any future search. Each entry should be written down so as to be understandable to everybody — only this discipline can give us confidence that, after a lapse of time, we shall be able to comprehend it ourselves! We must not rely on our treacherous memories. We may come to value our diary records greatly in the course of time, after having gained a more profound knowledge of Lepidoptera, or when we start to publish our findings.

Key for the identification of major families

The key given here for identifying the families of Lepidoptera is of the dichotomous type. At each numbered point in the key the user is faced with a pair of alternatives; either the specimen should fit the first half of the 'couplet', or the second half. Once we have decided which half of the couplet is right for the particular specimen in hand, we proceed to a later couplet as directed, and so on. For example, if our specimen fits the second half of couplet 1, we proceed to couplet 10. If it fits the second half of this couplet, we move to couplet 50, etc. We arrive ultimately at a point not referring to a further number but giving us the name of a family; this brings us to our goal. In specialized literature keys may be found to genera within families, and even to the species within the genera (although, for many groups, no up-to-date keys to species yet exist).

Although many of the features used in the key can be seen with the naked eye, a magnifying glass or hand lens giving a 5−10fold magnification will be of great assistance. Reference is often made to the position of veins, which are usually covered with scales and so not easily seen. There are two possibilities: either we sacrifice a poor specimen (if a series of the species is available) and carefully brush or bleach the scales off the wing, or we can dip the whole wing into xylene, benzene, ether, or some similar wetting agent. So treated, the venation becomes clearly visible until the solvent evaporates, when the wing regains its former appearance. Applying this latter technique to small Lepidoptera is likely to result in damage to their fringes.

Let us make a small test and use the key to identify the family of, first, a member of the butterfly family known commonly as whites, and then an eggar moth.

Starting with the white at couplet 1, we find that its features correspond to the first alternative: the antennae are terminally dilated to form a club, the body is slender and the wings are broad. We therefore proceed to couplet 2. Here, on comparison with the venation diagrams, the specimen will be found to fit the second half of couplet 2, from where we proceed to number 4. At number 4 we examine the labial palps and, finding them to be short, we consequently proceed to number 5. The eyes of the white are round, not oval; this fits the second half of couplet 5, which thus directs us on to number 7. At couplet 7 we find that our butterfly corresponds to the second point: its anterior legs are normally developed and the wings are essentially white. This refers us to number 9. At number 9 we consider the anal margin and the vein 2A of the hindwings. Since this vein is developed, we have reached the final point: family Pieridae − whites and sulphurs.

In a similar way we can check how to use the key by identifying an eggar. Here we gradually proceed in accordance with the following points (where (a) = first half, and (b) = second half, of any given couplet): 1(b), 10(a), 11(b), 13(b), 15(b), 33(b), 34(b), 41(b), 42(b), 45(b), 46(b), 49(b): Lasiocampidae − eggars.

Sometimes we may make one or two mistakes in examining the butterfly or moth, or else certain features are obscure or difficult to interpret, or we might have chosen accidentally a specimen in which some of the characters are developed atypically. As a result, our attempts at identification will probably lead us into a blind-alley; we can do nothing but retrace our steps number by number. To facilitate this retrograde search, in some places of the key the number of the previous couplet in that route is given in parentheses. Such a feature is of great help in keys involving a multitude of taxa, with many hundreds of couplets. In such cases, retrograde search is extremely difficult without the help of back-references.

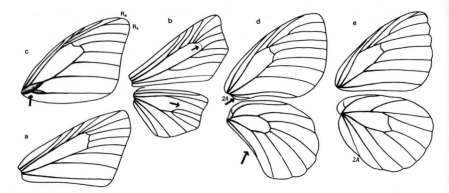

22 Various types of wing venation in Lepidoptera: a — Hesperiidae, b — Thyrididae, c — Satyridae, d — Papilionidae, e — Pieridae.

Key

1 Antennae slender, apically dilated, forming a gradual or abrupt club (Fig. 5g, h); body slim, wings broad 2
— Antennae generally of a different shape (filiform, pectinate, etc.), but if they are club-like they are thick, or the body is more robust in relation to its length 10
2 Veins in the apical part of the forewing unbranched (Fig. 22a, b) 3
— Some radial veins (for example R_3 or R_4) bifurcated; R_5 present 4
3 Discal cell of both wings not closed distally (Fig. 22b), wings angular in outline, no tuft of hairs at the base of antennae (medium-sized moths with translucent areas on the wings; diurnal in habit; approximately 700 species, mainly tropicopolitan, only two species in Europe)

Thyrididae — leaf moths

— Forewing with discal cell completely closed (Fig. 22a), a tuft of hairs at the base of antennae, wings rounded (small to medium-sized, heavy bodied butterflies with robust broad heads and terminally dilated antennae, frequently terminating with a hook; caterpillars with large head, naked or finely haired; more than 4,000 species, most occur in South America, only several dozen species known in Europe) . . . . **Hesperiidae** — skippers
4 Labial palps (Fig. 3) as long as thorax (small family of medium-sized butterflies with clavate antennae and very long labial palps; only one thermophilic species — *Libythea celtis* (Fuessly)
— found in Europe . . . . **Libytheidae** — snout butterflies
— Labial palps much shorter than thorax 5
5 Eyes oval (Fig. 30b), edged with white scales 6
— Eyes round, lacking white marginal scales 7
6 Precostal vein present in hindwings (Fig. 23a); two rows of white spots and a series of black dots on the underside; upperside of brownish-red wings bears a black pattern, but no metallic sheen present (small variegated butterflies with short palps; approximately 1,500 species distributed mainly in tropical America; in Europe one species only, *Hamearis lucina* (L.))

Riodinidae — metalmarks

— Precostal vein absent in hindwings (Fig. 23b), wings on both upperside and underside marked with a pattern different from the above, colouration reddish-brown or blue with bright metallic lustre, or brown to black with orange or blue spots along wing margins, or in the centre of forewing (small, at most moderately sized butterflies often showing marked sexual dimorphism: males often glisten with bluish or reddish metallic sheen, while the females are dark brown or spotted; capitate antennae attached close to eyes; caterpillars clothed with fine hairs, short and flat, slug-like, sometimes living in anthills; approximately 6,000 species, about 100 in Europe) . . . . **Lycaenidae** — blues, coppers and hairstreaks

7 Forelegs reduced, clawless (Fig. 29a); usually brown, reddish-brown or black, variegated butterflies 8

— Forelegs normal and terminating in a claw; butterflies essentially white, or yellow with black or coloured design 9

8 Base of forewings with one or more veins enlarged to form inflated vesicles (Fig. 22c) (small to large-sized butterflies, yellowish to brown, wings usually with small marginal eye-spots, variegated cryptic patterns often present on the underside; antennae slender, with only weakly developed club; caterpillars spindle-shaped, bare, often longitudinally striped, with two processes at the end of the body; family rich in species occurring in high mountains, polar regions, steppes, etc; about 100 species in Europe)

Satyridae — browns, satyrs and wood nymphs

— Forewings with veins not inflated at base (medium to large-sized, multicoloured butterflies with clubbed, porrect antennae; hindwing with large anal cell; caterpillars with excrescences on the head, or spiny all over and clothed with fine hairs; very abundant family comprising about 4,000 species, predominantly tropicopolitan; about 70 species in Europe

Nymphalidae — nymphalids (brush-footed butterflies)

9 Hindwing with more or less concave anal margin; vein 2A developed as a very small vein on the forewing, absent on hindwing (Fig. 22d) (large, varicoloured butterflies; hindwings often with tails; antennae with marked club; caterpillars hairless, often variegated, often with

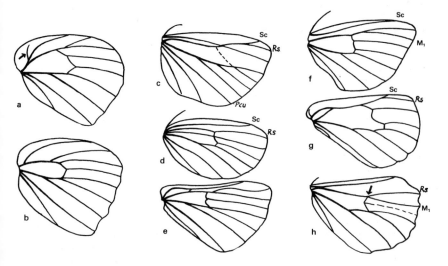

23 Various types of hindwing venation in Lepidoptera: a — Riodinidae, b — Lycaenidae, c — Pyralidae, d — Psychidae, e — Lemoniidae, f — Notodontidae, g — Drepanidae, h — Geometridae.

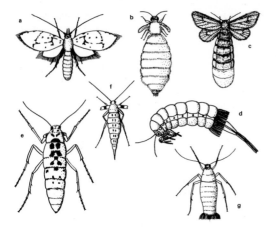

24 Lepidopterous females with reduced wings, or no wings at all: a — Oecophoridae, b, c — Lymantriidae, d — Psychidae, e, f, g — Geometridae.

protrusible osmeterial gland behind head; about 700 species, mostly in the tropics, 10 species in Europe) . . . .**Papilionidae** — swallowtails and apollos — Hindwings with anal margin not concave; vein 2A indiscernible on the forewing, but normally developed on hindwing (Fig. 22e) (butterflies of moderate size; wings usually white or yellow, with black or coloured maculae; marked sexual dimorphism quite common; antennae clavate, gradually dilating towards the tip; caterpillars yellowish or green, covered with short hairs, head small; approximately 1,500 species, 45 in Europe)

Pieridae — whites and sulphurs

10(1) Wings well-developed, insect capable of flight 11
— Wings reduced, or absent altogether (Fig. 24) 50
11 Wings deeply cleft into separate, plume-like divisions (Fig. 25a, b); if not so, at least hind tibiae exceed femora by more than twice their length (Fig. 29d) 12
— Wing margins either entire or only slightly notched; hind tibiae less than twice length of femora 13
12 Both wings divided into six plumes (Fig. 25a) (very small, fragile moths with wings divided into twelve cross-striped plumes; caterpillars live inside plant stalks; of 100 known species, less than 10 live in Europe) . . . . **Alucitidae** — many-plume moths

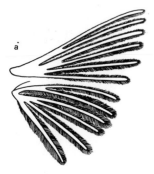

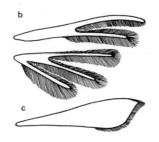

25 Wings of many-plume moths and plume moths: a — Alucitidae, b, c, — Pterophoridae.

— Forewings divided into two plumes or flaps, hindwings into three plumes, or wings not cleft at all (Fig. 25b, c) (very small to small, inconspicuous moths with narrow wings; antennae filiform, posterior legs very long; both caterpillars and pupae sparsely hairy; caterpillars often live in leaves spun together or inside stalks; 600 species, with more than 100 in Europe)

Pterophoridae — plume moths

13 Fore and hindwings·similar in shape and approximately equal in size; jugum present on forewing; hindwing with more than one radial vein (Fig. 2a) 14
— Fore and hindwings differ in shape; hindwings smaller, with only one radial vein, and usually one or more stiff bristles (frenulum: Fig. 2b) or with a lap-like amplexiform area (Fig. 33e, f) on costal margin, close to the base 15

14 Larger species, wing expanse at least 20mm, antennae short, not more than one quarter of the length of forewings (primitive, small to huge-bodied moths with wings coupled by jugum, venation of forewings and hindwings very similar; mostly inconspicuous moths, crepuscular in habit; caterpillars live in the ground, eat plant roots, and their development often takes several years) . . . . **Hepialidae** — ghost and swift moths (hepialids)
— Very small species, wingspan (European species) less than 20mm; antennae attain at least one half the length of forewing (primitive Lepidoptera possessing mandibles; caterpillars with as many as eight pairs of prolegs or only rudimentary legs, often living in mines; several dozens of species described, about 30 species in Europe) . . . . . **Micropterigidae** — archaic moths

Eriocraniidae — primitive moths

15 Hindwing with vein Pcu well developed (Fig. 23c), or else the moths are very small, wingspan less than 10mm 16
— Hindwing with vein Pcu absent (Fig. 23d, e), wingspan never less than 10mm 33

16 Lepidoptera resembling bees or wasps in appearance, hindwings (and often forewings also) with translucent, scale-less areas clearly showing dark venation (Fig. 26d); forewings narrow; abdomen black, frequently marked with yellow or red transverse stripes (Fig. 26d) (moths small to moderate in size; threadlike or slightly thickened antennae; abdomen terminated by a tuft or hairs; diurnal in habit; caterpillars bore in wood or plant roots and sometimes take many years to develop; about 1,000 species, primarily in South America; approximately 220 species in the Palaearctic, over 30 in central Europe . . . . **Sesiidae** — clearwings
— Lepidoptera different in appearance and colouration 17

17 Hindwings of various shape (Fig. 27g—m), mostly only slightly longer than broad, but not narrow or wedge-shaped (Fig. 27a—d); hindwings with fringes usually shorter than their breadth, often only forming a narrow zone along wing margin, somewhat broader along its inner part (Fig. 27k—m) 18

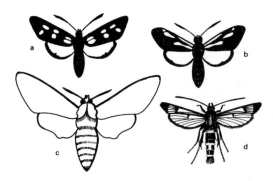

26 Characteristic forms of lepidopterous insects: a, b — burnets and foresters (Zygaenidae), c — hawkmoths (Sphingidae), d — clearwings (Sesiidae).

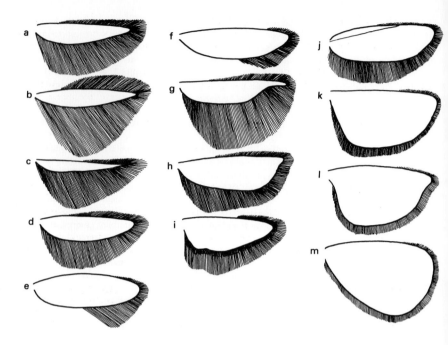

27 The length of the fringes and shape of the hindwings are characteristic of a number of families.

— Hindwings narrow and wedge-shaped (Fig. 27a—d), with defined costal and anal margins only, extended by long fringes equalling or exceeding the broadest part of hindwing in length (several families whose differentiation is extremely difficult, and practically impossible without a microscope)   . . . . **Nepticulidae** — nepticulid moths (serpentine miners)
Coleophoridae — case bearers
Gracillariidae — narrow-winged leaf miners (blotch miners) and other families of small Lepidoptera.

Nepticulidae—belong among the smallest Lepidoptera, their wingspan not exceeding 3—8mm; active at night; wings black or with metallic sheen, bearing pale spots; caterpillars mine in leaves; about 300 species, some 150 in Europe.

Coleophoridae — very small to small moths with wingspan less than 25mm, generally dull-coloured, with narrow wings bearing long fringes; nocturnal in habit; antennae densely covered with long scales arranged in lines; caterpillars live in cases (Fig. 17) and gnaw circular mines in leaves, with a small opening in the middle; about 1,000 species, widespread particularly in the northern hemisphere; more than 300 species in Europe.

Gracillariidae — very small moths with wingspread 6—10mm; active day and night; wings long-fringed, often variegated; caterpillars mine in leaves; about 2,000 species, more than 200 in Europe.

18 Hindwings with fringes longer than one third of the maximal width of hindwing (Fig. 27g—j); forewing often with long marginal fringes (27e, f)   19

— Hindwings with fringes shorter than one third of the maximal width of hindwing, often forming only a narrow margin (Fig. 27k—m); forewings with fringes always narrow 28

19 Vertex more or less smooth (Fig. 30a, b); labial palps longer than thorax and bent upwards in a falcate curve, or their middle segment considerably dilated with scales; or hindwings concave sub-apically (Fig. 27g, h); or else both features simultaneously present; proboscis always covered in scales; forewing with vein R₄ stalked with R₅ (Fig. 28a) (two related families of very small to small moths, with wingspans from 6 to 30mm, differing in the venation of hindwings; many species inconspicuous, many brightly coloured — especially in the family Oecophoridae; proboscis developed, antennae filiform; mostly nocturnal in habit; caterpillars live in decaying matter, under outer bark, within stalks, among spun-up leaves — many species mine leaves; about 5,000 species of the family Gelechiidae, about 4,000 species of the family Oecophoridae) . . . . **Gelechiidae** – gelechiid moths

Oecophoridae — oecophorid moths

— Vertex tufted with bristly hairs (Fig. 30c, d); labial palps shorter than thorax; hindwings with outer margin not concave 20

20 Legs covered with smooth scales, posterior tarsi provided with claws (Fig. 29c); labial palps with long tuft of scales and hairs on the second segment, so that the third segment seems to develop from the top of the second (Fig. 30e, f) (small family of minute moths active at night, wingspan less than 20mm; colouration mostly inconspicuous; antennae filiform, proboscis developed; caterpillars mine, or live in webs; about 300 species known to exist) . **Plutellidae**

— Tarsi without claws, palps of a different shape 21

21 Labial and maxillary palps absent (Fig. 31a); vertex with deep, rough vestiture (wings greyish with a silky lustre and indistinct reticular pattern, females wingless, caterpillars case dwellers) . . . . 32(a)

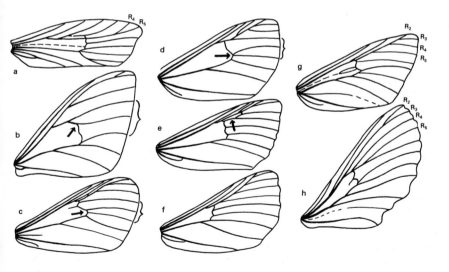

28 Various types of forewing venation in Lepidoptera: a — Oecophoridae, b — Saturniidae, c, d — Arctiidae, e — Thyatiridae, f — Lemoniidae, g — Endromidae, h — Lasiocampidae.

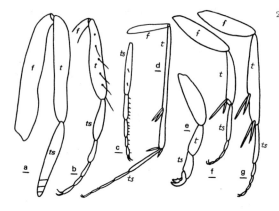

29 Various types of lepidopterous legs: f — femur, t — tibia, ts — tarsus.

— Palps (at least labial) developed, even though small; if absent, vertex with short flattened scales 22

22 Labial palps more or less smoothly scaled; hindwings with costal margin dilated in the basal third (Fig. 27j); hind tibiae smoothly scaled; head with vertex (only) tufted with bristly hairs 23

— Labial palps tufted with rough scales or hairs, or with tough bristles, or absent altogether; hind tibiae tufted with fine hairs 24

23 Antennae shorter than forewings; ocelli absent or indistinct (small moths with wingspan not exceeding 25mm, narrow forewings often thickly dotted with black on a lighter background; antennae filiform; nocturnal fliers; caterpillars often live gregariously on shrubs, enveloped with dense silken fibres; depending on conception of the family, about 1,000 species, with more than 100 in Europe) . . . . **Yponomeutidae** — ermine moths

— Antennae approximately same length as forewings; ocelli distinctly present (Fig. 30f) (small family consisting of only several dozens of species; minute nocturnal moths; caterpillars generally mine leaves) . . . . **Acrolepiidae**

24 Ocelli absent or indistinct 25

— Ocelli clearly visible (Fig. 30f) 27

25 Proboscis well developed, scaled at least at base; maxillary palps absent; antennae as long as forewings , occasionally several times longer (Fig. 5a) (small moths with long antennae, particularly so in males; wings often variegated, sometimes glistening with metallic sheen; flight activity mostly diurnal, in some species also nocturnal; caterpillars mine leaves or live in cases; 250 species, 120 in the Palaearctic, about 30 in Europe)

Adelidae — longhorns (fairy moths)

— Proboscis always devoid of scales, usually more or less degenerate; in species with long antennae, maxillary palps always distinct 26

26 Maxillary palps long, curved to form an angle (Fig. 31b); wings clothed with scales and microscopic spinules; antennae often exceeding forewings in length (small family of minute, inconspicuously coloured moths; wings sometimes patterned with pale spots; antennae filiform, sometimes pectinate; caterpillars often mine, at least when young; about 75 species known to occur in the world) . . . .**Incurvariidae** — incurvarids, including yucca moths (Prodoxinae)

— Maxillary palps absent or short; spinules absent from the wing area; antennae not exceeding forewings in length (minute to small moths, mostly with inconspicuous colouration; antennae filiform or plumose; active usually at night, some species also in daytime; caterpillars often live on food of animal origin, but also on seeds and remains of decayed plants; about 2,000 species, approximately 350 in the Palaearctic, 60 in Europe)

Tineidae — tineid moths (clothes and scavenger moths)

27 Forewing with vein R_4 stalked with R_5 (Fig. 28a) . . . . 32(a)

— Forewing with vein R_4 not stalked with R_5 . . . . 26(b)

28(10) Hindwing with vein Sc closely approximated to vein Rs and often fused with it for a certain distance (Fig. 23c) (small to moderate-sized moths often with long, forward-directed palps and wide fan-shaped hindwings; antennae filiform; moths nocturnal in habits; plainly coloured caterpillars invested with long bristles, with various modes of life, in spun-up leaves, inside plant stems, in seeds and plant products; a vast family comprising about 20,000 species, but often divided into several smaller families; approximately 300 species in central Europe)

Pyralidae — pyralids

— Hindwing with vein Sc free, not approximated to vein Rs (Fig. 23d) 29

29 Tibiae of hind legs provided with medial and terminal spurs (Fig. 29g); body narrower than 3mm; antennae never spindle-shaped, if pectinate, labial palps also developed 30

— Tibiae of hind legs with terminal spurs only (Fig. 29f), if medial spurs also developed, antennae spindle-shaped, or body thick, hirsute, and broader than 3mm, or antennae pectinate and wings almost or totally devoid of pattern 31

30 Labial palps oval or triangular, directed forwards, strongly dilated by scales, third segment largely concealed in scales of second segment (Fig. 31c, d); hindwings generally trapezoidal in shape (Fig. 27k, l) (minute, at most small moths with short, filiform antennae and usually well-developed mouthparts; moths active at night, often hibernate; caterpillars greyish-green, with relatively long, simple setae, often living in rolled-up leaves, fruits, but also under tree bark; about 5,000 species distributed predominantly in the temperate zone — more then 2,000

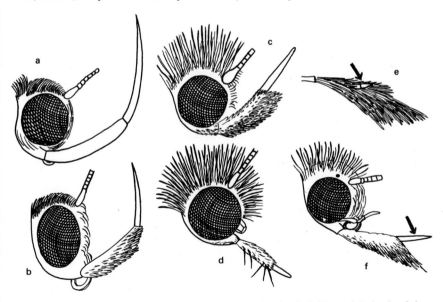

30 Features important for the differentiation of some families involve the hairiness of the head and the length, shape and position of the labial palps (the antennae are shown cut short): a — Oecophoridae, b — Gelechiidae, c, d — Tineidae, e, f — Plutellidae.

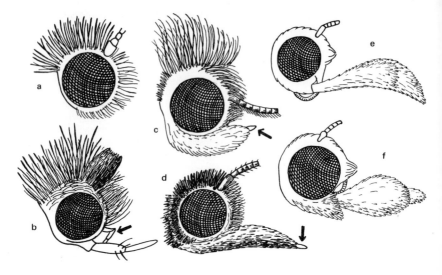

31 Heads of various lepidopterous insects, in lateral view (antennae cut short): a — Psychidae, b — Incurvariidae, c, d — Tortricidae, e — Noctuidae, f — Arctiidae.

species in the Palaearctic, almost 500 in central Europe; closely related to the family Tortricidae is the family Cochylidae, embracing about 400 species known in the world)

Tortricidae — leaf rollers (tortrix moths)

— Palps of a different shape, not dilated, or their terminal segment directed upwards (Fig. 30b)

Gelechiidae and several other small families of minute moths

Bradyptesidae, Orthotaelidae, Glyphipterigidae, etc.

31 Moths with red, yellow or white spots and metallic blue or green scales on otherwise black wings (Fig. 26a, b); wings sometimes devoid of pattern and metallic green to black all over, with a metallic, greenish lustre; antennae often spindle-like (see Fig. 5i) (small to medium-sized moths with well developed mouthparts; diurnal in habit; antennae either gradually clubbed or pectinate; caterpillars short and thick, with retractile head, sparsely covered with bristles; pupae enveloped in smooth, shiny, spindle-shaped cocoons; about 1,000 species, with rather more than 50 in Europe) . . . . **Zygaenidae** — burnets and foresters

— Moths with a different colouration, antennae not spindle-shaped 32

32 Labial palps not visible without microscopic examination; wing colouration inconspicuous — grey, brown, black, pattern either absent or reticular; small moths, wingspan less than 25mm (very small to small moths with degenerate mouthparts and marked sexual dimorphism; males: inconspicuously coloured wings and plumose antennae, crepuscular and nocturnal in habit, less often diurnal; females: apterous, legs often totally reduced, never leaving their cases; caterpillars live in cases of plant fragments held together by silken threads (Fig. 17); about 900 species, predominantly tropicopolitan, about 100 species in central Europe)

Psychidae — bagworms

— Labial palps distinct, wings usually marked with conspicuous patterns; moths with wingspan exceeding 20mm (primitive, dull-coloured moths with degenerate mouthparts and short, in males sometimes pectinate, antennae; species of small or exceedingly large size — some tropical species amongst the largest Lepidoptera known; nocturnal fliers; caterpillars equipped with strong mandibles to bore in wood or within stalks, bulbs, tubers, etc.; in some species development takes several years; about 600 species, most prevalent in the tropics, in Europe less than 10 species) . . . . **Cossidae** — goat moths (wood borers, carpenters)

33(15) Antennae thick, spindle-shaped or angular, nearly always hooked (Fig. 5j); body robust, spindle or torpedo-shaped (Fig. 26c) (large to gigantic moths; forewings narrow, hindwings small and oblique; mouthparts well-developed, often a very long spiral proboscis; mostly crepuscular and nocturnal, a few species diurnal; caterpillars bare, posterior end often equipped with a projecting horn; approximately 1,000 species living predominantly in the tropics, about 20 species in Europe) . . . . **Sphingidae** — hawkmoths
— Antennae and body of a different shape 34

34 Forewing with vein M_2 situated halfway between M_1 and M_3, or closer to M_1 (Fig. 28b)   35
— Forewing with vein M_2 closer to M_3 than to M_1 (Fig. 28c, d). 41

35 Large moths (wingspan exceeding 50mm, often as much as 150—200mm), wings broad, usually with an eye-spot on the centre (large to huge moths, some tropical species amongst the largest Lepidoptera of the world; antennae pectinate with rami longer in males; mouthparts degenerate; moths active in night hours, some species also in daytime; caterpillars stout, varicoloured, body invested with tubercles and coarse bristles, head relatively small; pupae enclosed in coarse, tough cocoons; about 1,200 species, particularly in the tropics and in the Orient; less than 10 species in Europe) . . . . **Saturniidae** — emperor moths
— Wings with proper eye-spots not developed; or if eye-spots are present, small species with wing expanse 30—40mm 36

36 Hindwings with veins Sc and Rs approximated or stalked (Fig. 23g) 37
— Hindwing with vein Sc not approximated to Rs (Fig. 23f) 39

37 Forewing with apex prolonged into a falcate projection; or, if not so, then hindwing with vein Sc stalked with Rs (Fig. 23g) (small to medium-sized moths with broad, usually falcate wings; proboscis short or absent; antennae short, pectinate with shorter rami, or serrate; moths of nocturnal habits; caterpillars nearly bare, but usually having some projections, green or brightly coloured, last segment acuminate; about 400 species, only 7 species in central Europe; family absent from South America) . . . . **Drepanidae** — hook-tips
— Forewing with non-falcate apex; hindwing with veins Sc and Rs widely separate (Fig. 23e) 38

38 Areole present in forewing (Fig. 28e); frenulum well-developed (Fig. 1b, c); pattern lacking in conspicuous yellow colour; forelegs without large claws (medium-sized moths with hirsute body suggestive of a noctuid; proboscis well developed, palps relatively long, roughly scaled; moths active at night; large-headed caterpillars live among spun-up leaves; a small family of approximately 150 species, about 10% of these living in Europe) . . . . **Thyatiridae**
— Areole absent from forewing (Fig. 28f); frenulum wanting; colouration of wings predominantly yellow or bearing a yellow pattern; forelegs each terminated with two large claws (Fig. 29e), which help the moth to force a way through the grass (small family consisting of a single genus and several species inhabiting the Palaearctic; of two species living in central Europe, one is nocturnal, the other diurnal in habit; medium-sized, hirsute moths with degenerate proboscis and pectinate antennae; caterpillars densely covered with hairs thickened to form transverse bands) . . . . **Lemoniidae**

39 Body slim, proboscis usually well developed; if body stout and hairy and proboscis degenerate, then hindwings with vein Rs not stalked with M_1, or stalked only shortly (Fig. 23h), or forewings with serrate apical margins; head with chaetosemal organ (Fig. 32) (small to medium-sized moths with broad wings, in females wings sometimes degenerate; antennae filiform, in males often pectinate; moths predominantly nocturnal in habit; caterpillars slim, often variegated, body often covered with tuberculous skin bearing various projections; family sometimes divided into several smaller ones, about 4,000 species, of which some 800 live in

32 A ciliated organ on the head (the chaetosema) is conspicuous in geometrids (Geometridae).

Europe, particularly in the forested areas)... **Geometridae** — geometrids (inchworms, loopers) — Body relatively stout and hairy; proboscis degenerate (Fig. 6c) or absent; hindwing with vein Rs stalked with M_1 for a relatively long distance; chaetosema absent 40

40 Hindlegs with tibiae provided with two pairs of spurs (Fig. 29g); if only one pair, then wingspan exceeds 40mm; female has no curly deciduous hairs on terminal abdominal segment (medium-sized, generally inconspicuously coloured moths, nocturnal in habit; antennae short, pectinate or setose; mouthparts degenerate; caterpillars smooth, or with bizarre projections, or hairy, longitudinally striped with various colours, hindlegs sometimes transformed into horns equipped with protrusible whips; about 2,000 species, mainly in South America, about 40 species in central Europe) . . . . **Notodontidae** — prominents (puss moths) — Hind tibiae with one pair of spurs (Fig. 29f); species smaller, wingspan less than 40mm; the female has a dense tuft of curly, deciduous hairs on the posterior part of the abdomen (family consisting of a small number of species of medium-sized, dull grey moths; body tufted with hairs, mouthparts degenerate, antennae pectinate; the hairy caterpillars live gregariously; about 80 species, only a few of them in Europe) · · **Thaumetopoeidae** — processionary moths

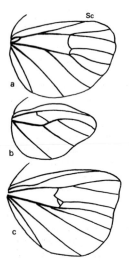

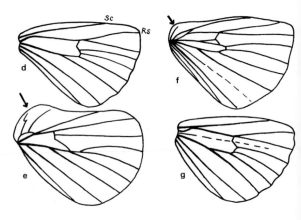

33 The venation and shape of the hindwings are characteristic of many families: a — Arctiidae, b — Ctenuchidae, c, d — Lymantriidae, e — Lasiocampidae, f — Endromidae, g — Noctuidae.

41 Hindwing with vein Sc absent (Fig. 33b) and considerably smaller than forewing (small to medium-sized, small-headed, stout moths; antennae long, filiform; mouthparts in the form of spiral proboscis; moths of diurnal habit; caterpillars densely clothed with hairs; 2,300 species, mainly in South America, South Africa and the Orient; less than 10 species in Europe)

Ctenuchidae — ctenuchids

— Hindwing with vein Sc well-developed, and not markedly smaller than forewings, normal in size (Fig. 33a) 42

42 Hindwing with vein Sc fused with radius from base, or shortly free near base only (Fig. 33a) 43

— Hindwing with vein Sc free at first but runs close to or becomes fused with the radius some distance from base, or remains free throughout its length (Fig. 33c, d) 45

43 Forewings with groups of rough scales; labial palps long, if viewed from above they project beyond the head by a distance approximately equal to the length of the head; wingspan generally less than 30mm 44

— Forewings with all scales smooth; labial palps shorter; wingspan generally more than 30mm (stout-bodied, medium to large-sized moths with broad, often very brightly coloured wings; antennae filiform, or pectinate in males; mouthparts usually reduced but proboscis present in some groups; moths of predominantly nocturnal habits, some species also diurnal; caterpillars hairy, brown or variegated, usually extremely active; 8,000 species, family most abundant in South America, about 60 species live in central Europe)

Arctiidae — tiger and footman moths

44 Labial palps with wedge-shaped second segment, terminally dilated (Fig. 31e) . . . 48(b)

— Labial palps with oval second segment, not terminally dilated (Fig. 31f) . . . . 43(b)

45 Hindwing with vein Sc free at base but otherwise fused with radius for a long distance; late autumn moth . . . . 39(a)

— Vein Sc different or fused with radius for a short distance only 46

46 Hindwing with frenulum consisting of one or more bristles (Figs. 1b, c;) 47

— Hindwing with frenular bristles absent, furnished instead with a lap-like amplexiform area (Fig. 33e, f) 49

47 Proboscis atrophied; vein Sc free for most of its length, then approximated to radius or connected with it by a short cross-vein (Figs. 33c, 23e) (moderate-sized moths with marked sexual dimorphism; males smaller, slender, with pectinate antennae, flight often zigzag and darting, females more robust, often with stout abdomen, flight cumbersome, or wings degenerate; moths of nocturnal habits, males of some species active also in daytime; caterpillars hairy, brightly coloured, with dorsal glands or thick tufts of hair, often living gregariously; 1,800 species, most of them in South Africa and the Orient, 17 species in Europe)

Lymantriidae — tussock moths

— Proboscis usually well-developed; vein Sc approximated to radius near base, then diverging again (Fig. 33g) 48

48 Abdomen red, marked with a black pattern, hindwings similar . . . . 43(b)

— Moths different in colouration (small to large moths; colouration nearly always cryptic, but more conspicuous in some groups; antennae filiform, less often pectinate in males; mouthparts usually well-developed; palps very long in some groups; moths mostly nocturnal in habit, diurnal activity very rare or only in case of emergency; caterpillars mostly bare, with scattered setae, less often hairy, 3—5 pairs of prolegs; largest family of Lepidoptera comprising 20,000 described species, a number of which survive in extreme conditions; at least 1,100 species live in Europe; family sometimes divided into several smaller ones)

Noctuidae — noctuids (owlet moths, millers)

49 Apex of forewing marked with three light triangular spots aligned in a slightly curved row; veins R_2—R_5 all stalked (Fig. 28g) (a monotypic family comprising one genus and one species

only — *Endromis versicolora* (L.)); antennae pectinate, mouthparts degenerate; moth active at night, males also fly on sunny mornings; caterpillar green with white diagonal stripes and black dots   . . . . . .`. . . . .**Endromidae**
— Pattern different; veins R_2—R_5 not all stalked together (Fig. 28h) (medium to large-sized, thickset, densely hirsute moths with broad brownish or greyish wings bearing a simple pattern; antennae short, pectinate, with longer rami in males; mouthparts atrophied; moths of nocturnal habits, in some species males flying about rapidly before dusk; caterpillars tufted with hairs, and having a long development time; approximately 1,300 species, absent from New Zealand and Oceania, most abundant in South America and in tropical regions of other continents, rather more than 20 species in Europe)

Lasiocampidae — eggars (lappet moths, lackey moths)

50(10) Moth living in water (some females wingless, genus *Acentria*)   . . . . **Pyralidae**
— Moth not living in water   . . . .`. 51
51 Moth (female), if living inside the case left by the caterpillar (Fig. 17), then scales and legs almost absent; or, if living in close vicinity to the case, then only sparsely covered with scales (Fig. 24d); abdomen often spherical, filled with eggs   . . . . **Psychidae** — bagworms
— Female not a case-dweller, and body normaly covered with scales and hairs   52
52 Legs short and weak (Fig. 24b, c); body and legs clothed with curly hairs

females of families **Arctiidae** and **Lymantriidae**

— Legs long and well-developed (Fig. 24a, e); hairs and scales often short and smooth   . . 53
53 Labial palps longer than head and clearly visible from above (Fig. 24a)

females of the families **Gelechiidae** and **Oecophoridae**

— Labial palps shorter, scarcely visible from above   54
54 Antennae shorter than forewings, ocelli present

females of the genus *Exapate,* family **Tortricidae**

— Antennae longer than forewings (Fig. 24e—g) (if wings not absent altogether), ocelli absent
. . . . females of the family **Geometridae**

(Note: the following families, mostly small, are not included in the above key though they are represented in the colour plates: **Danaidae; Dilobidae; Ethmiidae; Scythrididae; Elachistidae; Argyresthiidae; Lyonetiidae; Tischeriidae.**)

Plates

Family: **Papilionidae** — **swallowtails and apollos**

1 *Papilio machaon* L. — Swallowtail. 50—75mm. One of the most handsome European butterflies, it has a wide distribution not only in Europe but also in northern Africa, in the temperate zone of Asia as far as Japan, and in North America. Very local in England and absent from Ireland. The nominate race or subspecies (ssp. *Papilio machaon machaon*) occurs in Sweden. Throughout its vast range the species has produced a great number of geographical forms which include ssp. *gorganus* Frhst. in central Europe, ssp. *britannicus* Seitz in England, and ssp. *aliaska* Scudd. in North America. In the north it has one generation, in southern Europe and in Africa 2—3 generations. In central Europe there are two broods: the first is on the wing from April to June, the second from July to August. The butterfly flies in grassy and steppe localities, and in the mountains up to an altitude of 2,000m. The English race, ssp. *britannicus*, has a different ecology, being restricted to wet fenland. Caterpillars live on umbelliferous plants, primarily carrot, caraway and fennel. When irritated the caterpillar protrudes two red glandular structures (osmeteria) in the shape of little horns (1b) behind the head. Chrysalides are of two colours: green (more frequent in the summer brood) and grey-green (more frequent in the hibernating brood).

2 *Iphiclides podalirius* (L.) — Scarce Swallowtail. 50—70mm. More thermophilous (warmth-loving or requiring), with a smaller distributional range: its northern boundary passes across Poland and Germany; in Sweden and England only stray specimens have been captured. Eastwards it ranges across Asia Minor and Transcaucasia to western China. In central and southern Europe it inhabits forest-steppe localities. Its occurrence approximately coincides with that of the blackthorn, the most usual food-plant of the caterpillars. Two generations are produced in central Europe, three in the south. In spring it flies from April to June, in summer from August to September. Caterpillars (2b) live solitarily on blackthorn, hawthorn, rowan trees and on various fruit trees, for example apple. The chrysalis is supported by the cremaster and girdled with silken threads. As in the Swallowtail, the summer chrysalides tend to be green and the hibernating ones are brown (2c). In some countries both species are protected by law; they are apparently very sensitive to changes produced by Man's activities, and in recent decades they have become exceedingly rare, particularly in areas subject to increasingly intensive agriculture. Bans on collecting seem to contribute little to their survival, since their gradual disappearance is evidently connected with the destruction of suitable biotopes.

3 *Parnalius polyxena* (D. & S.) — Southern Festoon. 45—55mm. A thermophilous species, the southern part of central Europe being the northern limit of its distribution. Its main habitat is in the eastern Mediterranean region, from where it ranges into Asia Minor. It is absent from Spain. Lowland, coastal and low-lying meadow biotopes are its favourite haunts. One generation, on the wing in April and May. Caterpillars (3b) live in May and June on *Aristolochia*, often in great numbers. Long and slender chrysalides may be found on plant stems, in an upright position, supported by the cremaster (3c). In some countries it is protected by law. Formerly abundant here and there, it suffers from coastal developments, especially the treatment of suitable biotopes against gnats and the drift of insecticides from neighbouring crops, and is gradually becoming a rarity.

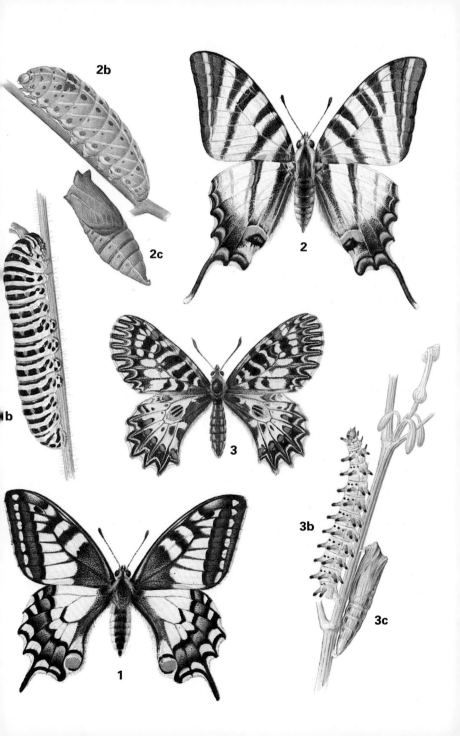

Family: **Papilionidae — swallowtails and apollos**

1 *Parnassius apollo* (L.) — Apollo. 65—75mm. The Apollo ranges from western Europe, including all the European mountains, the Carpathians, and the Caucasus, east as far as Transbaikalia and Mongolia in Asia. In eastern Asia it is represented by other species of the same genus. This butterfly inhabits mountain valleys and meadows, preferring rocky biotopes with a limestone substrate. In suitable localities it may be found at an elevation of only 200m above sea-level, but it often lives high up in the mountains — in the Alps, for example, up to 2,200m. The discontinuous nature of its occurrence seems to have given rise to a great number of local races, particularly in Europe, where several dozen have been described. The Apollo is considered to be a relic of the Tertiary period that survived the glacial epoch in Europe. It has only one generation a year, which flies from June to September, according to altitude and exposure of the given locality to sunshine. The eggs often hibernate; the caterpillars (1b) sometimes hatch in autumn, but do not then attain full size until spring. It feeds on various kinds of stonecrops and houseleeks (1c — pupa). Since this species is considered to be one of the veritable jewels of the butterfly world, collectors have taken a great fancy to it. And its behaviour contributes to its own downfall: it flies about slowly in sunny weather and settles on flowering thistles so peacefully and calmly that it can be caught by hand. At the same time, it is a species extremely sensitive to environmental changes. It has become extinct in many localities, and is becoming increasingly rare in places where it does still occur. It has become an item on the list of the World Red Book of endangered animals and in many European countries it is strictly protected by law.

2 *Parnassius phoebus* (F.) — Small Apollo. 50—60mm. Closely resembles the preceding species in colouration and way of life. Its occurrence in Europe is confined to the higher altitudes of the Alps (1,500—2,500m), eastwards it can be found in the Urals, China and Siberia, and in North America in the Rocky Mountains. Within its range of distribution it has formed a number of geographical races. The caterpillar lives from autumn or spring until summer on saxifrages and houseleeks.

3 *Parnassius mnemosyne* (L.) — Clouded Apollo. 45—60mm. Distributed in various parts of Europe, with the exception of the British Isles, Iberian peninsula, and northernmost regions of Norway. The eastern limits of its range lie in central Asia. It inhabits damp, grassy localities in hilly landscapes, and outskirts of deciduous forests supplied with a rich undergrowth. The Clouded Apollo displays a marked preference for lowlands, but can also be found in mountains up to an elevation of about 1,500m. There is only one annual brood. In the lowlands it starts flying early in spring, sometimes as early as April, while in the mountains it may still be on the wing in July. The female lays her eggs either freely, or on various objects in places where the food-plant of caterpillars, *Corydalis,* can be found; this, however, is already withered at the time of the butterfly's flight. Caterpillars hatch early in the following spring, grow rapidly to full size, and, after a short pupal stage, the adult butterfly appears. Despite the fact that the foodplant of the Clouded Apollo is widely distributed throughout Europe, the butterfly is getting exceedingly rare and has disappeared in a great many localities. As a result it is protected by law in some countries. Yet it might be more effective to protect its haunts from the undesirable effects of pollution.

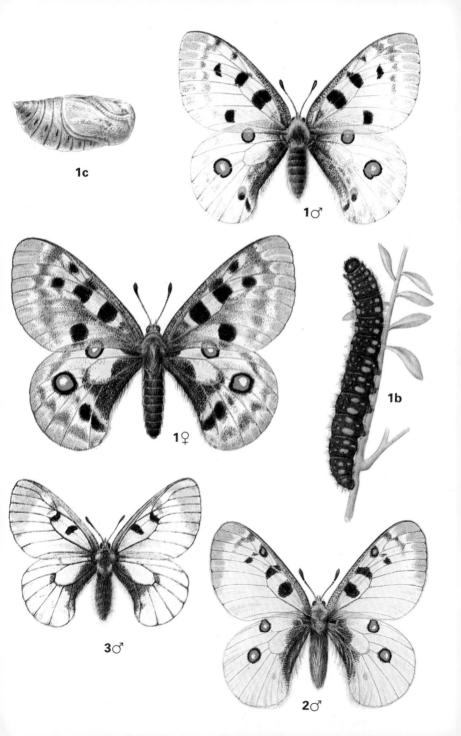

1c

1♂

1♀

1b

3♂

2♂

Family: **Pieridae — whites and sulphurs**

1 *Aporia crataegi* (L.) — Black-veined White. 50—65mm. Widely distributed in the Palaearctic, with the exception of northern Scandinavia and the British Isles (extinct). It is noted for its mass occurrence and migrations, as a result of which it may appear unexpectedly in quite atypical localities. In this century the butterfly has markedly decreased in number, and the notorious devastation of fruit trees by its caterpillars now occurs predominantly in warmer regions. Only one generation occurs, from May to July. Caterpillars (1b) develop in summer, hibernate collectively in a silken nest, and wake up in spring to complete their development. This is also the time when they cause the greatest damage. They feed on hawthorn, blackthorn and many cultivated fruit trees (1c — pupa).

2 *Pieris brassicae* (L.) — Large (Cabbage) White. 50—65mm. Widespread throughout Europe, with the exception of the northernmost regions, and in northern Africa. Its range extends as far east as the Himalayas, and just into China. This is one of the most abundant butterflies and a notorious pest of cruciferous vegetables. In most areas it has two generations, which fly from April to August. In hot regions it may have several generations. The yellow eggs are glued in batches on the underside of leaves, and the caterpillars live gregariously for a long time (2b), on various kinds of crucifers, mainly on cabbage, kohlrabi, etc., in the fields and gardens. Chrysalides of the second generation hibernate. The butterfly is sexually dimorphic, the female having more black spots on her wings.

3 *Pieris rapae* (L.) — Small White. 40—50mm. Perhaps the most abundant European butterfly. Originally only distributed in the Palaearctic, it has also now been introduced with vegetables to many parts of the world. The Small White often causes serious damage to agricultural and horticultural produce. It is well adapted to life in agricultural habitats and can be found in warm lowlands as well as high in the mountains. One to three generations occur, depending on climatic conditions. In central Europe there are usually two generations which, being somewhat different in size and pattern, are an example of seasonal polyphenism. The caterpillars (3b) feed on crucifers but also on mignonette, *Tropaeolum*, etc. The chrysalis hibernates.

4 *Pieris napi* (L.) — Green-veined White. 35—45mm. An extremely variable species generally distributed in the Palaearctic and ranging to North America. A great number of geographical races inhabiting this region have been described, and the species also shows marked seasonal polyphenism: in particular, the spring generation is most strongly patterned (4a adult of first generation — underside of wings, 4♀ belongs to second generation). The Green-veined White has one to three generations a year merging into each other: thus the butterfly appears on the wing practically from spring till autumn. The caterpillar lives on wild crucifers (only rarely attacking crops); the chrysalis hibernates.

5 *Pieris bryoniae* (Hb.) — Dark-veined White. 35—48mm. A very local species in the mountains of Europe, Asia and Alaska (up to an elevation of 2,000m), with a more continuous distribution in the north. Characteristic of this glacial relict species is the formation of geographical races in isolated localities, many of which have been described. Its sexual dimorphism is rather interesting: the male is white and resembles *Pieris napi,* while the female is very dark, or at least has strongly dark-dusted veins and, sometimes, a yellowish hue. The butterfly is on the wing, in two or three generations, from May to August. The caterpillar feeds on wall-cress, *Biscutella* and penny-cress. The chrysalis hibernates.

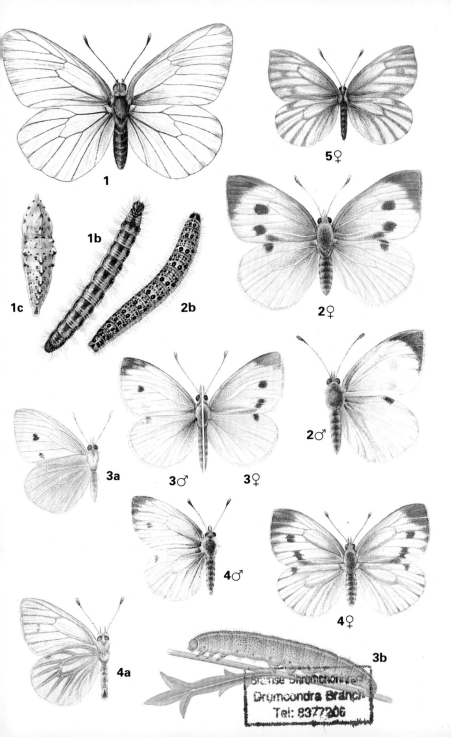

1

1b

1c

2b

5♀

2♀

2♂

3a

3♂

3♀

4♂

4♀

4a

3b

Family: **Pieridae — whites and sulphurs**

1 *Pontia daplidice* (L.) — Bath White. 35—45mm. This species is distributed throughout the temperate Palaearctic from northern Africa to Japan. It reaches about 60°N but occasionally appears even further north. In central and western Europe it is a regular migrant. Though not indigenous in northern Europe or in the British Isles, it has frequently been caught here. Stray specimens have also been reported from Iceland. In central Europe there are two generations: one in April and May, the other in July and August. In the south the butterfly is on the wing continuously from February until October, several generations merging into each other. The seasonal polyphenism of this species is noteworthy, the spring generation having been described as f. *bellidice*. There are also differences in the colouration of males and females, the latter having a stronger black pattern. The caterpillar lives from May to June, and again in autumn, on crucifers and mignonettes. The chrysalis hibernates.

2 *Anthocharis cardamines* (L.) — Orange-tip. 35—45mm. Described by Linné from Sweden, but its range extends over the whole vast Palaearctic region from western Europe as far as China and Japan. Its main haunts are in the lowlands, yet it also occurs in mountain valleys as high as 2,000m above sea-level. It is one of the first spring butterflies, and may be seen flying about in meadows till June, in flowery margins of open deciduous woods, and among trees bordering streams. In the mountains it may appear as late as July. The sexual dimorphism of this butterfly is very marked, the outer half of the forewings being orange in males, black and white in females. Gynandromorphous individuals, in which one wing is coloured orange as in the male and the other black and white as in the female, have sometimes been caught. The Orange-tip produces only one generation in the year. The caterpillar (2b) lives from May to August on crucifers, mainly on *Cardamine, Turritis* and *Sisymbrium*. The chrysalis (2c) hibernates. The Orange-tip has lately declined in numbers, the obvious main reasons being drainage of damp localities, ploughing of meadows and their fertilization, and the effects of insecticides.

3 *Leptidea sinapis* (L.) — Wood White. 30—40mm. One of the smallest European whites. With the exception of Scotland and the northernmost regions of Europe, it is distributed throughout Europe as far as the Caucasus, and in Asia Minor as far as Syria. The two generations produced in Europe from May to June (3c) and from July to August (3d) differ from each other in colouration. There are also differences between males and females. The female is almost pure white all over, while the male has a more or less well pronounced grey or even black patch in the apical part of his forewings. The caterpillar (3b) can be found from May to September in dry meadows — particularly on meadow-pea. The chrysalis, which hibernates, tapers to a point and is girdled by a silk thread and attached to a pad by the cremaster. A very similar white, Fenton's Wood White (*Leptidea morsei* Fenton), occurs in some localities in the eastern parts of central Europe, and further eastwards as far as Japan. It was not discovered until the end of last century, when it was described as a variety of *L. sinapis*. But more detailed research revealed it to be an independent species, differing in the shape and greater size of the wings, its later occurrence, and somewhat different ecological requirements (including the food-plant of the caterpillars).

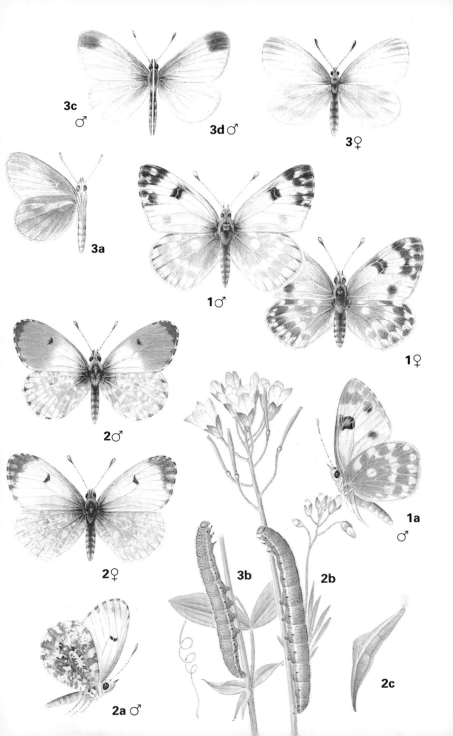

3c ♂

3d ♂

3 ♀

3a

1 ♂

1 ♀

2 ♂

2 ♀

1a ♂

3b

2b

2c

2a ♂

Family: **Pieridae — whites and sulphurs**

1 *Colias palaeno* (L.) — Moorland Clouded Yellow. 40—50mm. Widespread throughout the northern parts of the Palaearctic; related species live in North America. It is a typical relict of the glacial epoch. The only generation is on the wing in June and July, mountains and peat-bogs being its main haunts. The caterpillar feeds on leaves of the bog bilberry, and hibernates while half-grown. It reawakens in spring to complete its development, and the eclosion of the adult takes place after a short pupal stage. Like many species with a discontinuous distribution, this clouded yellow shows a tendency to form geographical races. The nominate ssp. *palaeno* L. lives in Sweden, the well-known ssp. *europome* Esp. occurs in central Europe, while in the Alps the smaller and darker ssp. *europomene* O. has become established. Sexual dimorphism manifests itself by the males' yellow and the females' whitish colouring. Occasionally yellow females can also be found, designated as f. *illgneri*.

2 *Colias chrysotheme* (Esp.) — Lesser Clouded Yellow. 32—40mm. This is a species peculiar to Asiatic steppes, ranging as far as the Altai; its western borderline in Europe runs through Vienna. The occurrence of this species in Europe is marginal, and it is rare here. From time to time it appears more abundantly as a migrant, as was the case in 1954. Its two generations emerge in May, and in August to September. The caterpillar lives on hirsute vetch.

3 *Colias croceus* (Geoffroy) — Clouded Yellow. 35—50mm. A typical migrant appearing in central Europe very abundantly in certain years, but often scarce for a long time to follow. The northern boundary of its range has probably shifted southwards in recent years. It inhabits northern Africa, the whole of warmer Europe, and western Asia as far as Afghanistan. The two or three generations fly from April to May, and then from July until autumn. The caterpillar lives on papilionaceous plants, including lucerne, and subsequently hibernates. The female differs from the male by having orange spots within the black wing margins. In addition, a certain number of whitish females of the f. *helice,* and sometimes transitional forms, may be found.

4 *Colias hyale* (L.) — Pale Clouded Yellow. 40—45mm. Widespread throughout the warmer regions of Europe, it is often to be found in steppes, meadows, and fields. It ranges eastwards to the Altai. A tireless flier, it occasionally appears even in areas which it does not normally inhabit, such as high up in the mountains. Thus it has been reported from the vicinity of St Petersburg, from Finland and Sweden, and from the Alps up to an altitude of 2,000m. The female is paler than the male. There are two generations of this butterfly, occurring from April to June and from July to September. The caterpillars (4b), which live on lucerne, hibernate as half-grown larvae; in the following spring it takes them only a short time to complete their development (4c — pupa).

5 *Colias australis* Vrty. — Berger's Clouded Yellow. 35—45mm. This species was confused with the preceding for a long time and was described only in 1911. However, the taxon apparently includes specimens described by C. Ribbe as early as 1905 as *Colias alfacariensis,* and consequently this should probably be the butterfly's correct name. This clouded yellow differs from those described above by, among other things, the more rounded forewings and less pronounced yellow dusting at their bases. It flies in two generations, particularly in arid steppe localities. The caterpillar lives on sicklewort and horseshoe-vetch.

Family: **Pieridae — whites and sulphurs**

1 *Gonepteryx rhamni* (L.) — Brimstone. 50—55mm. The range of this sulphur butterfly extends throughout the mild regions of the Palaearctic, from northern and western Africa to Siberia. Although not a very variable species, its sexual dimorphism is conspicuous. The lemon-yellow male is well-known, but the greenish-white female, when on the wing, is often mistaken for a white. There is little similarity between the life cycle of this species and that of other butterflies (although it may be compared with *Libythea celtis*). A single generation is produced during the year. Caterpillars (1b) live towards the end of spring on buckthorn, and perhaps also on spindle-tree and common privet. They develop relatively quickly, and butterflies emerge from the pupae (1c) in early summer. These soon go into aestivation, and can be seen on the wing only for a short time in autumn. They then hibernate (that is the second, this time winter, dormancy), and in spring they are one of the earliest butterflies to appear. They fly most abundantly in lowlands and on submontane slopes; their occurrence in mountains (up to 2,000m) is exceptional.

Family: **Danaidae — milkweed butterflies (monarchs, wanderers and crows)**

2 *Danaus plexippus* (L.) — The Monarch, Milkweed, Wanderer or Black-veined Brown. 85—95mm. Although not a true inhabitant of Europe, it has been captured repeatedly in Portugal, Spain, France and the British Isles. It is a North American butterfly, noted there for its long migrations from north to south and back again. As a result of its migratory tendencies, it has become established in several continents, and now occurs, for example, in Australia and New Zealand. In America the caterpillar lives on *Asclepias curassavica* and other milkweeds, but in its new habitats it has become accustomed to other food-plants — including *Gossypium arboreum* and *Euphorbia mauretanica*. It occurs in a number of widely overlapping generations, throughout the year. The adult hibernates.

Family: **Libytheidae — snout butterflies**

3 *Libythea celtis* (Fuessly) — Nettle-tree Butterfly. 30—40mm. This thermophilous species is widespread in northern Africa and throughout southern Europe and Asia, the eastern limit of its range being Japan. This small butterfly is conspicuous with its peculiar wing shape, striking colouration and long palps. The antennae also differ from those of most butterflies, gradually dilating into a club-like enlargement. The butterflies are on the wing during June, sometimes a little later, and reappear after hibernation, in March to April. They spend both summer and winter in a state of dormancy; in summer they sometimes migrate to cooler elevations in the mountains or in the north. The caterpillars live on *Celtis australis*.

Family: **Riodinidae — metalmarks**

4 *Hamearis lucina* (L.) — Duke of Burgundy Fritillary. 25—28mm. A pretty little species distributed from Spain, across central and southern Europe, to central Russia. It prefers open woods and meadows at low or moderate elevations; in mountains it never ascends above 1,300m. Individuals of this species are somewhat larger in warm southern regions than in the north. In the course of recent decades this butterfly has rapidly decreased in numbers almost all over Europe. The reasons are unclear — perhaps it is sensitive to the general changes of the countryside. Usually there is only one generation a year, on the wing from April to June, but in the warmest regions a second brood is produced. The caterpillars live on primroses, sorrel, etc., from August throughout the winter until the following spring. In some circumstances the chrysalis may hibernate.

4a

2

4

3

1 ♀

1 ♂

1c

1b

Family: **Nymphalidae — nymphalids (brush-footed butterflies)**

1 *Apatura iris* (L.) — Purple Emperor. 55—65mm. Together with the Lesser Purple Emperor this species is noteworthy for the iridescent, metallic violet-blue sheen of the wings of its males. It is fond of damp, deciduous forests in the vicinity of streams, rivers and ponds, where it settles on the foliage of trees overhanging the water. Sometimes it comes to muddy woodland rides where it sucks water or settles on cattle dung. The Purple Emperor is distributed in the deciduous-forest belt throughout the mild regions of Europe and Asia, ranging eastward as far as Japan. In mountains it ascends to about 1,300m. The adult flies from June to August. The caterpillar's (1b) life starts in August, to be interrupted by hibernation, and continues again in spring, feeding on sallows, other willows, and on aspens.

2 *Apatura ilia* (D. & S.) — Lesser Purple Emperor. 50—60mm. This butterfly occurs in similar biotopes to the preceding species, but being more thermophilous, its distribution area, from Spain to Japan, is shifted to the south. It produces one brood, on the wing from May to July; in the south a second brood often occurs, flying from July to September. The caterpillar is half-grown when it hibernates. It lives on aspens and other poplars, and on sallows and other species of willow. Besides normal individuals (2) it is possible to come across f. *clytie* (2c) with an ochre ground-colour, and various intermediate forms.

3 *Limenitis populi* (L.) — Poplar Admiral. 65—80mm. Inhabits damp deciduous forests in lowlands and mountain valleys and is reckoned among the most beautiful European butterflies. Its distribution area includes the temperate zone from France to Japan and extends far to the north. There is only one generation in the year, on the wing in June and July. The caterpillars, which feed on aspen, hibernate.

4 *Limenitis reducta* Stgr. — Southern White Admiral. 45—50mm. This thermophilous butterfly occurs from Spain across southern Europe to Iran. It is rarely found in central Europe. Evidently it produces two generations a year; these may be seen on the wing from May to September. The caterpillar lives and hibernates on various species of honeysuckle.

5 *Limenitis camilla* (L.) — White Admiral. 45—52mm. Together with the purple emperors, this species likes to fly in the vicinity of brooks and streams. Its distribution area coincides with that of *L. populi,* except that it does not extend as far north, nor as high in mountains. It has been decreasing in number recently. The time of flight of the only generation is from May to July; the caterpillars hibernate in leaves of honeysuckle joined together by silk.

6 *Neptis sappho* (Pall.) — Common Glider. 40—45mm. The western boundary of its distribution passes through central Europe. Originally described from the Volga Basin, it ranges eastward to Japan. A denizen of lowland deciduous forests and slopes covered with forest-steppes, where it can be seen flying about on sunny days from May to July. The caterpillar, which feeds on spring vetchling, is almost full-grown when it hibernates.

7 *Neptis rivularis* (Scop.) — Hungarian Glider. 42—50mm. Its range of distribution is similar to that of the previous species, except that it extends west as far as France. A generally more abundant species, it is chiefly an inhabitant of woodland margins and various damp localities where its food-plant, *Spiraea,* can be found. The single generation flies from May till August. The caterpillars hibernate.

Family: **Nymphalidae — nymphalids (brush-footed butterflies)**

1 *Nymphalis antiopa* (L.) — Camberwell Beauty. 55—75mm. A common butterfly to be found in lowlands, mountains, forests, watersides and parks. It inhabits the whole of Europe (except several Mediterranean islands, southern Spain and the British Isles — where it is a rare migrant), all Asia and North America. Although it does not breed in the far north, it is a regular frequenter of these regions. Its one generation is on the wing from June or July, then it hibernates, to reproduce in the following spring. After emerging from hibernation the butterflies like to suck the sap of injured birches and oaks. At the end of summer they gather around fallen and over-ripe fruit. Toward the end of the spring and the beginning of summer, the caterpillars (1b) can be found living gregariously on birches, willows and aspens, of which they may completely defoliate the branches and twigs. The numbers of this species have fluctuated widely in recent years.

2 *Nymphalis polychloros* (L.) — Large Tortoiseshell. 50—55mm. In comparison with the Camberwell Beauty, the range of this species is shifted westwards and southwards. It also occurs in northern Africa, extending eastwards to the Himalayas, but is absent from the northernmost parts of Europe. Its way of life is very similar to that of the Camberwell Beauty. Caterpillars develop in spring and feed on the leaves of willows, elm, poplars and fruit trees. The butterflies hatch in June and July, following a short chrysalis stage. After hibernation, they like to visit flowering sallows.

3 *Inachis io* (L.) — Peacock. 50—60mm. One of the most common butterflies, distributed throughout the whole Palaearctic, with the exception of northern Africa. It has one or two generations, depending on climate. The adults hibernate. The caterpillars (3b) live gregariously on nettles or hops. The Peacock seems to be one of the few species relatively unaffected by civilization — probably due to the increasing amount of waste ground rich in nitrogen providing favourable conditions for nettles. The adults find plenty of nectar in clover fields and city flower-beds. In spring the Peacock and other vanessid butterflies are amongst the most beautiful signs of the reawakening of nature.

4 *Vanessa atalanta* (L.) — Red Admiral. 50—60mm. A thermophilous species which manages to hibernate only exceptionally north of the Alps. Its home is northern Africa and southern Europe eastwards it expands to central Asia. Year by year it migrates throughout Europe. It also occurs in North America. The dark greyish-yellow, spiny caterpillars lead a solitary life in spun-up nettle leaves. Towards the end of summer the newly emerged butterflies concentrate on over-ripe fruit, especially on pears and plums in orchards, and stay here until late autumn. The upperside of their wings bears a showy pattern, but their intricately coloured underside merges perfectly with the tree trunks on which they like to sit with closed wings.

5 *Vanessa cardui* (L.) — Painted Lady. 45—60mm. With the exception of parts of South America this familiar subtropic butterfly is distributed all over the world. In central Europe it is to be found abundantly, but it does not hibernate there. It arrives between April and June and, before leaving again, produces one or two generations over the summer. The caterpillars live on thistles, stinging nettles and hops. There are occasional records of damage caused by this species to agricultural crops, mostly in the warm regions.

Family: **Nymphalidae — nymphalids (brush-footed butterflies)**

1 *Aglais urticae* (L.) — Small Tortoiseshell. 40—50mm. The most abundant nymphalid species of Europe. If in winter a hibernating butterfly is discovered in the cellar, in a cold out-house or in the loft, it is most frequently just this one. The butterfly often appears flying at a time when the ground is still covered with snow. The Small Tortoiseshell is widely distributed in the whole of Europe and Asia. In the cold regions of the north and in mountains it can be so plentiful that it sometimes literally covers the blooms of hawkweed and other flowers. In the Alps it commonly appears at altitudes of about 3,000m, in the Himalayas it has been observed above 5,000m. Local migrations from lowlands to the mountains take place from time to time. This pretty butterfly has adapted well to the civilized world. Being quite harmless to crops and other cultivated plants, they are sometimes reared in large numbers and let out in towns and cities to enliven flower-beds and parks. There are two or three generations a year, and the caterpillars (1b) may be found during the summer in various stages of development, massed together on nettles which they frequently strip of all their leaves.

2 *Polygonia c-album* (L.) — Comma. 42—50mm. Widespread in the whole Palaearctic, with the exception of the far north. Although subject to wide fluctuations in population size, it is still regarded as one of the common species. In spring, after emerging from hibernation, the butterflies lay eggs from which two types of adults emerge. One type resembles the typical butterflies (2) and makes ready for hibernation by the end of summer. The second sort takes a shorter time to develop from caterpillars and hatches earlier — in May and June. These butterflies are rather different in both wing shape and pattern and are known as f. *hutchinsoni*. They reproduce in summer, and it is only the next generation that joins the hibernating adults of the first group. This difference in ecological answer of individuals to summer weather conditions thus gives rise to a partial second generation. The caterpillars (2b) live solitarily on stinging nettles, hops, gooseberries and other plants. The Comma is an extremely variable species: in particular, a whole series of variations has been described, involving various shapes of the 'C' spot on the underside of the hindwings.

3 *Polygonia egea* (Cr.) — Southern Comma. 40—45mm. A Mediterranean species extending to Asia Minor and Iran. The upperside of the wings bears some resemblance to that of *P. c-album*, but the underside is finely striped and much paler (3a). There are two generations in the year — the first flies in May and June, the second in August. The latter hibernates. Caterpillars live on pellitory, and less often on nettles and other plants.

4 *Araschnia levana* (L.) — Map. 28—40mm. Besides being the smallest European vanessid, it is noteworthy for its seasonal polyphenism. While the spring f. *levana* is reddish-brown (4♂), the summer f. *prorsa* is almost black (4♀). Occasionally a third brood develops in autumn whose colouration is intermediate to these two forms. This species is widely distributed in the temperate zone of the Palaearctic and is one of the few butterflies that have become more abundant in the course of recent decades. The caterpillars (4b) develop on nettles. They are sluggish and fall to the ground when disturbed. They live in groups and do not separate until the last instar. The butterfly occurs in lowlands, on river banks and along brooks, and along the margins of damp woods.

Family: **Nymphalidae — nymphalids (brush-footed butterflies)**

1 *Boloria pales* (D. & S.) — Shepherd's Fritillary. 30—37mm. A butterfly locally distributed at higher elevations in European mountains. It is found in the Pyrenees, Alps, Carpathians and on the Caucasus; in Asia it ranges to western China. It tends to produce local forms in the circumscribed areas to which it is confined. The single generation is on the wing above the timberline, up to 3,000m, from June to August. The caterpillar lives on violets and spends the winter in hibernation.

2 *Boloria aquilonaris* Stich. — Cranberry Fritillary. 30—35mm. Closely resembles the preceding species both in colouration and pattern, yet its range and ecological requirements are rather different. The distribution of this typical Boreo-Alpine butterfly is continuous in northern Europe, but local in the mountains situated to the south. It is fond of peat-bogs, and wherever these occur it descends as low as 200m. It may be seen flying about in June and July. The caterpillar lives on cranberries and hibernates while very young, usually inside plant stems. Its total distribution is not well known, especially in Asia, since the species has often been confused with the similar *B. pales* (D. & S.) and *B. napaea* (Hffm.).

3 *Proclossiana eunomia* (Esp.) — Bog Fritillary. 28—40mm. Another species with a Boreo-Alpine distribution. In the north its range is continuous, almost circumpolar, extending from Scandinavia across Russia and Siberia as far as the Amur, and also in North America — both in the north and in the mountains. Its distribution in central Europe is discontinuous; the butterfly can be found in the neighbourhood of peat-bogs and fens, from lowlands up to 1,500m. It is on the wing from the end of May to July. The caterpillar (3b) hibernates. It lives on knotgrass, also on violets and bilberries.

4 **Clossiana selene* (D. & S.) — Small Pearl-bordered Fritillary. 28—38mm. Widely distributed throughout the temperate zone of Europe and Asia, extending also to North America. It ranges from lowlands to highlands up to an altitude of 2,400m and can be found in woodland margins, in meadows and in bushy biotopes. There is a tendency for the species to produce darker forms in the north. In cooler conditions there is only one generation, in central Europe there are usually two, which fly from May to July and from August to September. The caterpillar lives on violets and bilberries, and hibernates.

5 **Clossiana euphrosyne* (L.) — Pearl-bordered Fritillary. 32—40mm. Differs from the above species in the pattern on the underside of the hindwings. Its distribution is similar (with the exception of America); in Europe it extends further to the south. It is at home in open woods interspersed with grassy clearings or in dry meadows up to the timberline. In central Europe there are two generations, flying from April to June and from August to September. The caterpillar lives on various species of violets, and is the stage which hibernates.

6 *Clossiana dia* (L.) — Violet Fritillary. 27—35mm. Widely distributed in the temperate zone of Europe and Asia, as far as western China. It is one of the smallest fritillaries and occurs in two or three generations from April, flying almost all the year round. It prefers grassy woodland clearings, slopes and meadows, and is conspicuous for the dark violet-brown underside of its wings. The caterpillar (which hibernates) feeds on violets and blackberries.

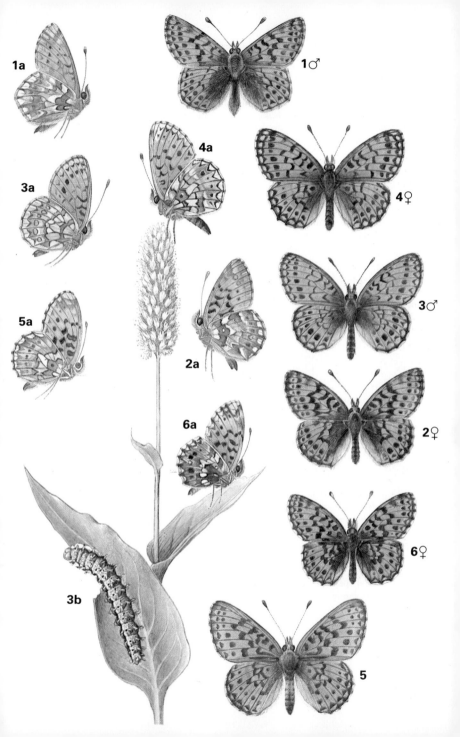

Family: **Nymphalidae — nymphalids (brush-footed butterflies)**

1 *Pandoriana pandora* (D. & S.) — Cardinal. 60—70mm. This, the largest European fritillary, is widespread in northern Africa, all southern Europe, and further east in western Asia and northwestern India. The northern limit of its distribution in central Europe roughly coincides with the upper Danube. Recently it has vanished from many of its old localities. The adults are sexually dimorphic, the females being larger and darker than the males. The butterflies occur from May to October, in one generation, and like to assemble in the open country on slopes and banks rich in flowering thistles. The caterpillar lives on violets, particularly on pansies, and hibernates.

2 *Argynnis paphia (L.) — Silver-washed Fritillary. 55—65mm. Although one of the most common large fritillaries of Europe, it has recently been declining in numbers and remains abundant only in areas undisturbed by civilization. Its flight is associated with the coming of midsummer, when it frequents forest clearings, grassy rides and damp meadow with blooming thistles and other plants on which it likes to settle. This beautiful species is generally distributed in the temperate regions of the Palaearctic, and flies from July till September. The caterpillar feeds on various species of violets, and hibernates. The females are polymorphic, the dark, blackish-green *valesina* form appearing at low frequencies in most localities in addition to the normally coloured females.

3 **Mesoacidalia aglaja* (L.) — Dark Green Fritillary. 50—55mm. An inhabitant of grassy woodland clearings, rides and slopes with an extensive vertical range — from coastal dunes to mountain meadows. In the mountains it has been observed at altitudes of more than 3,000m. At present it is becoming scarce in all biotopes. Its distribution area extends throughout Europe and Asia to Japan; in Africa it has been reported only from Morocco. Several geographical races have been described. This fritillary can be distinguished from the similar species *F. adippe* (D. & S.) and *F. niobe* (L.) by the pattern adorning the underside of the hindwings. The butterfly is on the wing from June to August. The caterpillar lives on violets, and hibernates.

4 **Fabriciana adippe* (D. & S.) — High Brown Fritillary. 42—55mm. Being highly variable, this species has many described geographical and individual forms. Very common is f. *cleodoxa*, in which the silvery spots on the underside of the hindwings are missing. The distribution of this species is similar to that of the Dark Green Fritillary — except that it extends more to the south, the High Brown being more thermophilic. On the wing throughout the summer, from June to August, it favours grassy woodland clearings and margins — particularly in uneven, hilly country. The caterpillar, which hibernates, feeds on various species of violets.

5 *Fabriciana niobe* (L.) — Niobe Fritillary. 42—55mm. The range of this species extends from western Europe across central Russia and Asia Minor to Iran, occurring in habitats similar to those of the preceding species. It may be found even high in the mountains above the timberline, up to an altitude of 2,500m. This extremely variable butterfly can produce dark forms (f. *obscura*), while the greenish to nacreous violet spots are frequently absent from the underside of the wings (f. *eris*). A characteristic feature of the species is the longitudinally divided black stripe on the underside of the hindwings. The butterfly is on the wing from June to August; the caterpillars feed on various species of violets, and hibernate.

Family: **Nymphalidae** — nymphalids (brush-footed butterflies)

1 *Issoria lathonia* (L.) — Queen of Spain Fritillary. 35—45mm. Distributed from northern Africa across Europe and Asia to the Himalayas and western China. However, it does not appear to be indigenous to the northern parts of this range, where it is nevertheless fairly abundant: year by year it arrives here from the south and produces one or two generations during the summer. This migrant butterfly is extremely shy and flies very swiftly. Most frequently associated with fields and steppes, where it likes to settle on the ground. Though its pattern presents many variations, it cannot be mistaken for any other species, because, on the underside, its hindwings are sprinkled with bright, silvery, almost mirror-like markings (which occasionally, most often in reared butterflies, fuse to form continuous bands — f. *paradoxa*). The Queen of Spain Fritillary flies from April — in the south from February — till October, in a series of overlapping generations. The caterpillars (1b) can also be found all the year round in favourable conditions. They feed on dog violets but also on other field and steppe plants.

2 *Brenthis hecate* (D. & S.) — Twin-spot Fritillary. 30—40mm. Locally distributed in southwestern and southern Europe, its range extends continously eastwards from the Balkans across southern Russia and Asia Minor, to central Asia. It inhabits forest steppes and grassy hillsides in warmer regions where the caterpillars' food-plant — *Dorycnium* — is sure to occur. It is one of the earliest fritillaries on the wing, the flight of its one and only generation being during May and June. The butterflies flutter always close to the undergrowth. The caterpillar hibernates.

3 *Brenthis daphne* (D. & S.) — Marbled Fritillary. 40—50mm. The distribution of this thermophilic species bears some resemblance to that preceding, but is more continous and extends eastwards as far as Japan. A rare fritillary, it displays a marked preference for warm, dry, grassy biotopes where it likes to settle on various flowers. It is conspicuous for its rounded wings bearing a bold black pattern, but it can safely be distinguished by the markings on the underside. There is only one generation of this butterfly, on the wing at the beginning of summer. The caterpillars live on various kinds of violets and brambles, and they hibernate.

4 *Brenthis ino* (Rott.) — Lesser Marbled Fritillary. 32—40mm. With the exception of the British Isles, this species is widespread throughout the temperate zone of Europe, ranging far to the north and across the whole of Asia to Japan. In southern Europe it may be found only locally, since it prefers damper and cooler localities. It occurs in the mountains to an elevation of 1,500m, in damp meadows and peaty areas. Its flight is slow and fluttering, and it often settles on the blooms of thistle, bramble, field-scabious, etc. In its haunts it is usually fairly abundant, but hand in hand with the disappearance of water meadows due to drainage schemes this butterfly has vanished from many of its old habitats. The time of flight starts in June and ends in July. The female lays yellow, broadly ribbed, tall eggs from which light brown, spiny caterpillars with a yellow dorsal stripe emerge. The caterpillars feed on bramble, *Filipendula ulmaria* and wood goatsbeard. They complete their development after emerging from hibernation.

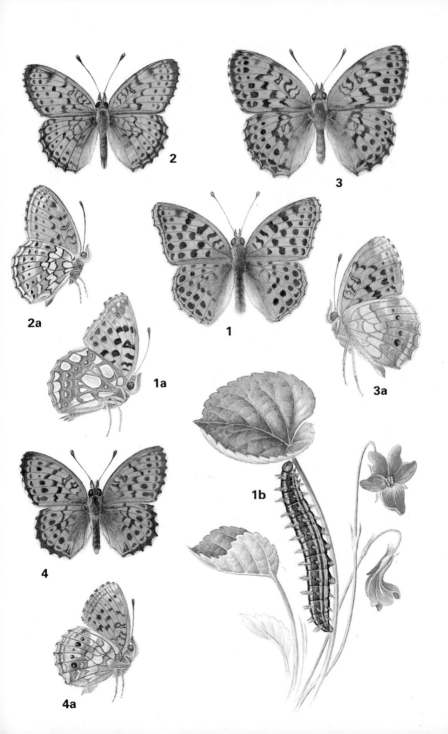

Family: **Nymphalidae — nymphalids (brush-footed butterflies)**

1 *Melitaea cinxia* (L.) — Glanville Fritillary. 33—40mm. Distributed in Morocco and the whole of Europe, with the exception of most Mediterranean Islands and the northern parts of Scandinavia; in Great Britain it is restricted to the Isle of Wight. In Asia it extends to the Amur. It has a particular liking for flowery meadows, from low elevations to 2,000m. The caterpillar lives on plantain and other low plants. Two broods are produced, whose flight period is from May to July and from August to September.

2 *Melitaea phoebe* (D. & S.) — Knapweed Fritillary. 32—42mm. A thermophilous species occurring in northern Africa, central and southern Europe and central Asia from where it extends to northern China. Within the range of its distribution it has produced a great number of geographical forms. The two generations of the butterfly are on the wing from April to June and from the end of July to August. The caterpillar lives on cornflower and plantain.

3 *Melitaea didyma* (Esp.) — Spotted Fritillary. 30—40mm. A thermophilous species absent from northern Europe which never ascends higher than 1,000m in mountains. Its distribution extends from northern Africa across Europe to central Asia. It is one of the most variable fritillary butterflies. Females are darker than males, sometimes almost black; there are differences between generations, and also geographical races are sharply delimited. The nominate race (illustrated) comes from Bavaria; the mountains of central and southern Europe are inhabited by ssp. *meridionalis* Stgr., and southern and southwestern Europe is the home of ssp. *occidentalis* Stgr. In central Europe the Spotted Fritillary has one generation which emerges over a long period, while in warmer localities two broods are produced. The butterflies may be seen flying from May to August on dry hillsides and steppes. The caterpillars feed on plantain, speedwell, woundwort, etc.

4 *Mellicta athalia* (Rott.) — Heath Fritillary. 25—38mm. Widespread all over Europe and in the mild regions of Asia, its eastern limit being Japan. It is an abundant butterfly, usually producing only one generation, which may be seen flying from May to August. It is frequently associated with open woodland, also with meadows and steppes, but decidedly prefers damp localities. Adults like to settle on moist ground, and as many as several dozen may assemble in a small area. This species presents great variations which make it difficult to distinguish it from several related species. The caterpillar (4b) lives mainly on plantain, and hibernates.

5 *Euphydryas maturna* (L.) — Scarce Fritillary. 35—42mm. Distributed in scattered localities throughout central and northeastern Europe, in Asia it extends to the Altai. A local species which is tending to become very rare, it is protected by law in some countries. Damp forests in the lowlands are its main habitat. The caterpillars remain for a long time in their nests on ash trees and poplars; only after hibernation do they separate, moving then to herbaceous plants, such as plaintain, speedwell, etc. The flight period of the single generation is in May and June.

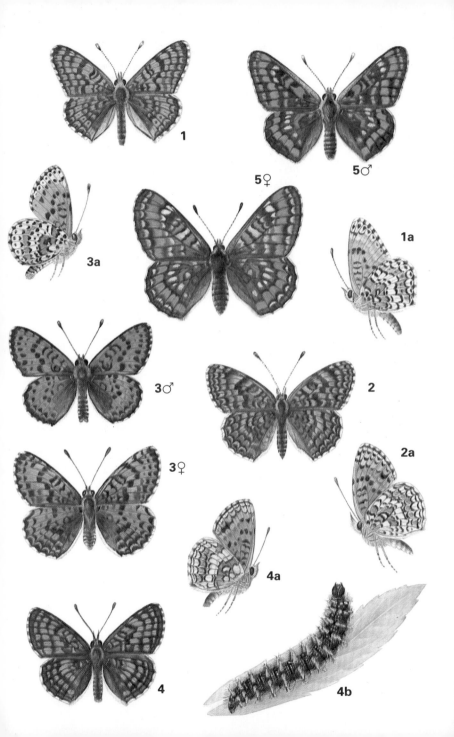

Family: **Satyridae — browns (satyrs and wood nymphs)**

1 *Melanargia galathea* (L.) — Marbled White. 37—52mm. Widespread in northern Africa and in the temperate parts of Europe, as far as the Caucasus. It has one generation which remains on the wing for a long time, from June to August. It is an inhabitant of meadows and steppes, but also of open woods rich in grassy clearings. The butterfly greatly varies in colouration: there are differences in the size of the black markings, as well as in the ground colour, which ranges from white to yellow. The form *procida,* with a greatly reduced pale pattern, is particularly notable. Some geographical races have been described, including ssp. *lachesis* Hb. from southern France and ssp. *lucasi* Rmbr. from northern Africa. The caterpillars feed on various grasses (*Phleum, Holcus,* etc.) and hibernate.

2 *Hipparchia fagi* (Scop.) — Woodland Grayling. 60—70mm. Distributed in southern, central and southeastern Europe as far as southern Russia. It is one of the largest and most conspicuous browns — a local species which of late has been vanishing from many of its old haunts. It shows a marked preference for warm, open woods and their outskirts, or for forest-steppes where it flies on sunny days or enjoys sitting on tree trunks with wings clasped. The colouration of the underside of its wings enables it to merge perfectly with the background. The only generation flies from June to August. The caterpillar lives predominantly on grass *(Holcus)* and hibernates.

3 *Hipparchia semele* (L.) — Grayling. 48—55mm. The total range of this species covers all Europe (with the exception of the northernmost regions) and ends, as far as is known, in Armenia. It inhabits forest-steppes and rough fields, preferring those with a sandy substrate, or clayey and stony hillsides. On sunny days it likes to rest on the warm ground and bask in the sun. Like the majority of large browns, it is very shy. Of late this species has been rapidly decreasing in number and has become a rarity in many of its old haunts. The Grayling flies from June to September; its caterpillar feeds on various grasses, and hibernates.

4 *Chazara briseis* (L.) — Hermit. 45—60mm. Occurs in northern Africa, in southern and central Europe, in Asia as far as the Altai Mountains and the Pamir. Being thermophilous, it favours steppes and rocky hillsides where the butterflies settle on the ground or on stones in full sunshine. They also like to suck nectar from flowering scabious plants. Within the range of its distribution, the Hermit has a number of geographical races, differing in size and intensity of the pale markings on their wings. One of the interesting individual forms is f. *pirata,* in which an orange-brown colouration replaces the pale spots on the wings. The Hermit produces one generation, on the wing from June to September. The caterpillar lives on grasses of the genus *Sesleria,* and hibernates.

5 *Arethusana arethusa* (D. & S.) — False Grayling. 40—45mm. A thermophilic species associated with steppes, distributed throughout southern and central Europe and eastwards to central Asia. A species which usually occurs in colonies in which it is often found in great abundance. Given to great variation, the butterfly is on the wing towards the end of summer, in August and September. The caterpillar lives on fescue grasses, and hibernates.

Family: **Satyridae — browns (satyrs and wood nymphs)**

1 *Minois dryas* (Scop.) — Dryad. 45—60mm. When on the wing this butterfly appears completely black. It has a characteristic flight suggestive of hops and skips in the air. Locally distributed in the temperate zone of Europe, it ranges eastwards as far as Japan. Recently it has become extinct in many of its former European habitats. The Dryad occurs in meadows and open woods with grassy clearings, and ascends to an elevation of 1,500m. It produces one generation, flying from July to September. The caterpillars feed on a variety of grasses, especially *Avena elatior,* and are the stage which hibernates. The male is smaller than the female and has fewer eye-spots on its wings.

2 *Brintesia circe* (F.) — Great Banded Grayling. 55—65mm. One of the most conspicuously patterned browns. The colouration of the underside is perfectly adapted to tree trunks, on which the butterfly likes to sit with its wings folded together. It is distributed in the warm regions of Europe and Asia, extending eastwards to the Himalayas. Fond of warm, mostly oak forests and forest-steppes, where it swiftly flies about on sunny days in June and July. The caterpillar lives on grasses of various kinds, including brome; it hibernates.

3 *Erebia ligea* (L.) — Arran Brown. 37—45mm. A butterfly of northern Europe, in central Europe living only within the range of 500—1,000m above sea level, its eastern outposts are in Japan. It can be found in mountain valleys of the forest zone and in meadows at submontane elevations. Depending on elevation, it flies from June to August. The caterpillars live on crab and millet grasses; they hibernate.

4 *Erebia euryale* (Esp.) — Large Ringlet. 33—40mm. A butterfly occurring at higher elevations of European and Asiatic mountains, including the Urals and the Altai. Its typical environment is the natural fir zone above 1,000m. Here it is often found in large numbers, settling on hawkweed and other mountain plants. Flowering groundsels are frequently meeting places for these butterflies. Usually a single generation occurs, on the wing on sunny days in July and August. The caterpillars live on a variety of grasses, and hibernate.

5 *Erebia epiphron* (Knoch) — Mountain Ringlet. 30—35mm. A typical species of European mountains, with the exception of Fennoscandinavia. Its domain is alpine meadows at an elevation of 1,000—2,000m, or meadows in the zone of dwarf mountain firs. In some of these localities it flies very abundantly, and forms a great number of subspecies. The butterfly is on the wing in July and August. In autumn and in spring, after awakening from their winter sleep, the caterpillars live on various mountain grasses — chiefly on tufted hair grass.

6 *Erebia medusa* (D. & S.) — Woodland Ringlet. 32—40mm. Only a few species of the abundant genus *Erebia* appear at lower elevations: they are, for the most part, montane species. The Woodland Ringlet is one of the exceptions, and can be found from lowlands up to an altitude of 1,500m. In lowlands it lives in damp meadows and damp, grassy forests; in the mountains it favours meadows and pastures. There is only one generation, on the wing from May to July, depending on elevation. The caterpillar lives on various grass species, particularly on crab and millet grasses, from summer until the following spring.

1♂ **1♀** **3** **2** **4a** **3a** **5** **4** **6**

Family: **Satyridae — browns (satyrs and wood nymphs)**

1 *Erebia gorge* (Hb.) — Silky Ringlet. 32—36mm. A typical mountain species, occurring on stony and rocky slopes of hills and mountains from 1,500—3,000m. It flies only on sunny days, in places with scarcely any vegetation and likes to settle on the flowers of hawkweed growing from cracks in the rock, often flying over the scree and settling on rocks warmed by the sun. It has a limited distribution in the mountains of Europe, from the Pyrenees across the Alps and the Tatras to the Balkan Mountains; it is absent from the north. The butterfly can be seen on the wing from June to August; the caterpillar lives on a variety of grasses, and hibernates.

2 *Erebia pronoe* (Esp.) — Water Ringlet. 38—45mm. Another mountain butterfly confined to European mountains. It occurs at somewhat lower altitudes than the preceding species, from approximately 1,000—2,000m above sea-level. At these elevations there are sparse coniferous forests, dwarf mountain firs and damp grassy meadows: these are its favourite habitats. The butterfly is remarkable for its flight period — from the end of July until the end of September. The caterpillar hibernates. It feeds on various kinds of grasses, especially on meadow-grass.

3 *Erebia pandrose* (Bkh.) — Dewy Ringlet. 35—40mm. In contrast to the mountain ringlets (Erebias) referred to above, this species has a Boreo-Alpine distribution. In addition to the mountains of Europe and, in the east, those of central Asia, it has a continuous range in the northern polar regions, where it naturally occurs at lower elevations. In central Europe this butterfly never descends below 1,600m. On sunny days it flies over Alpine grasslands, among dwarf mountain firs, and even above the timberline — up to 3,000m. Immediately the sun disappears behind a cloud, the butterflies settle. They can be seen from June to August. The caterpillar, which hibernates, feeds on a variety of grasses, mainly fescue and meadow-grass. This species shows great variability.

4 *Maniola jurtina* (L.) — Meadow Brown. 40—48mm. This is a species distributed in northern Africa and practically all over Europe, across Asia Minor as far as Iran. Even though it has been on the decline in recent years, it still can be reckoned an abundant species, largely resisting the effects of intensive agriculture. Formerly it used to be a typical species of meadows and unploughed margins, at present it survives in open, grassy woodlands. It flies in one, exceptionally two generations, from June to September. The caterpillar, which feeds on various grasses, hibernates.

5 *Hyponephele lycaon* (Kühn) — Dusky Meadow Brown. 37—43mm. The range of this species extends throughout the temperate regions of Europe, eastwards to central Asia. It occurs in dry, grassy localities, favouring those with a sandy substrate. Of recent years it has been rapidly disappearing. The butterfly is notable for its sexual dimorphism. On the wing from June to August, the caterpillar feeds on meadow-grass.

6 *Pyronia tithonus* (L.) — Gatekeeper. 30—38mm. Although it can be regarded as a thermophilic butterfly, it is abundant in England and Ireland, but otherwise absent from the whole of northeastern and northern Europe. The butterfly may be seen flying in thin deciduous forests, or more open countryside, but has of late vanished from many of its European localities. The caterpillar lives on various grasses.

Family: Satyridae — browns (satyrs and wood nymphs)

1 *Aphantopus hyperantus (L.) — Ringlet. 35—42mm. One of the most abundant butterflies, found in meadows and open forests, which it enlivens from June to August, sometimes even later. In the mountains it ascends to 1,500m. Its range extends across all the mild regions of Europe and northern Asia to the Ussuri Basin. In Europe it is absent from the Mediterranean and Arctic regions. Individual variations are innumerable — notably in the number of ocelli on the wings; there are also differences between the male and the female. However, no geographical forms are currently recognised. The caterpillar lives on a variety of grasses, and hibernates.

*Coenonympha tullia (Müll.) — Large Heath. 30—35mm. The Large Heath has a preference for cool and moist biotopes. It is absent from southern Europe, but widely distributed from northwestern Europe across all Asia to the Pacific, and in North America along the western mountain ranges to California. This highly variable species forms a great number of geographical races. Its favourite haunts in central Europe are damp meadows, marshes, mosses and bogs up to an altitude of 2,000m. The drying up or drainage of suitable habitats leads to its gradual disappearance. The butterfly is on the wing in June and July. The caterpillar feeds on various marsh grasses, and hibernates.

3 *Coenonympha pamphilus (L.) — Small Heath. 23—33mm. Widespread in northern Africa, throughout Europe, and in Asia as far as Siberia. It is one of the most abundant butterflies, withstanding the effects of agricultural change with relative success. This unobtrusive species lives in several overlapping generations, practically from spring until autumn. In the mountains it ascends to 2,000m and there produces one generation only. The female is somewhat larger but does not differ much from the male in colouration. The caterpillar lives on a variety of grasses, and hibernates.

4 Coenonympha arcania (L.) — Pearly Heath. 28—35mm. A species peculiar to open grass woodland, ranging from lowlands to about 1,000m above sea-level. The butterfly has one generation, which is on the wing in June and July, and shows a predilection for settling on leaves in the crowns of shrubs and lower trees. It is distributed from western Europe to the Urals and, for the most part, is still an abundant species. The caterpillar lives on grasses, especially on melick.

5 Coenonympha glycerion (Bkh.) — Chestnut Heath. 27—32mm. Widespread from western Europe to Siberia, but absent from Spain, British Isles, the greater part of Scandinavia and the Mediterranean regions. It has one generation which flies in June and July, haunting submontane meadows. The caterpillar lives on a variety of grasses, and hibernates.

6 Coenonympha hero (L.) — Scarce Heath. 28—33mm. Though very local and relatively rare, it is widely distributed in the central and northern parts of Europe, and in Asia as far as Japan. It can be found in highlands up to an elevation of about 1,300m. The butterflies of the single generation may be seen fluttering about by the end of May and in June, damp woodland clearings and grasslands being their favourite habitats. The caterpillar lives on grasses, chiefly the species Elymus arenarius, and hibernates.

Family: **Satyridae — browns (satyrs and wood nymphs)**

1 *Pararge aegeria* (L.) — Speckled Wood. 32—42mm. The range of this species extends from northern Africa throughout Europe to central Asia. It inhabits open deciduous woods, and oak and beech forests. In the mountains it never occurs above the upper limit of deciduous forest, i.e. approximately 1,000m. Annually there are usually two generations of this butterfly: the first flies very early in spring, from March to May, the second from July to September. The species is given to great variation, and forms several distinct geographical races. The nominate ssp. *aegeria* L., with an orange ground colour to its wings, lives in southern Europe and northern Africa. Central Europe is inhabited by ssp. *tircis* Btl. (illustrated), known also under the synonym *egerides* Stgr., whose wings have a light ground colour. The caterpillar lives in summer and in autumn on couch and other grasses. In Europe it is evidently the chrysalis that hibernates.

2 *Lasiommata megera* (L.) — Wall Brown. 35—45mm. The distribution of this butterfly is similar to that of the Speckled Wood, the only difference being a slight shift of its range to the south. However, its ecological requirements are very different: it prefers warm, open localities with a clayey or stony substrate. There are two generations in the year, on the wing in May and June and in August and September, while three generations may appear in the southernmost parts of its range. The butterfly may be seen fluttering about in grassy areas and in fields; it is fond of resting on low walls and stones. The caterpillar lives on grasses.

3 *Lasiommata maera* (L.) — Large Wall Brown. 37—50mm. Shares the range of the foregoing two species; in Asia it extends to the Himalayas. It occurs in thin, grassy woods and their margins, on hillsides and clearings, where the butterflies like to settle on stones or trunks of felled trees. Two broods develop during the year: the first flies in May and June, the second in July and August. In the mountains there is only one generation, flying up to the altitude of 2,000m. The caterpillar (3b) lives on various grass species, and hibernates. Of recent years this species has become rather rare in Europe.

4 *Lasiommata petropolitana* (F.) — Northern Wall Brown. 34—40mm. In central Europe this butterfly can be found only in mountains, but its range becomes more continuous in Scandinavia, Russia and Siberia, where it extends to the Amur. It is very similar to the Large Wall Brown but for the smaller and yet more conspicuous ocelli on the wings and the different position of the dark stripes on the underside of the forewings. It is also somewhat smaller. Its main generation is on the wing from April to July, and only occasionally a second one appears in September. The caterpillar feeds on fescue grass, and hibernates.

5 *Lopinga achine* (Scop.) — Woodland Brown. 45—55mm. Distributed in the temperate Palaearctic as far as Japan, absent from both southern and northern Europe and the British Isles. This species is characteristic of open deciduous woodlands; though confined to scattered localities, it is to be found in them very abundantly. It does not occur in mountains. There is one generation which flies from June to August; the caterpillar lives on grasses, and hibernates.

6 *Kirinia roxelana* (Cr.) — Lattice Brown. 50—60mm. Widespread in southeastern Europe, Asia Minor, Syria and Iraq. This thermophilic species shows conspicuous sexual dimorphism. Its only generation is on the wing from May to July. Males appear far earlier than females. The biology of the early stages is apparently unknown.

1

2♂

2♀

4

3

6

3a

4a

3b

3c

5

Family: **Lycaenidae — blues, coppers and hairstreaks**

1 *Thecla betulae* (L.) — Brown Hairstreak. 32—37mm. With the exception of southernmost and northernmost regions, this species ranges throughout Europe and Asia, Korea being its eastern limit. It is characteristic of deciduous forests and shrubby hillsides up to 1,000m. The caterpillar lives on blackthorn, plum trees, birches and hazels in May and June. The pupal stage lasts for a relatively long time, with the result that the adult does not appear on the wing until August to October. The female differs from the male in having orange markings on her forewings. The egg hibernates. The Brown Hairstreak has been diminishing in numbers and is now a rare species in some of its old habitats.

2 *Quercusia quercus* (L.) — Purple Hairstreak. 28—33mm. This species occurs in oak forests of Europe and the Near East, extending as far as Armenia. The butterflies flutter in tree tops and settle on the leaves — often attracted by honeydew, on which they feed. The single generation is on the wing from June to August. The male differs from the female in colour. The caterpillar (2b) develops inside the egg during summer but does not hatch until the following spring, when it completes its development, feeding on oak leaves. Due to its tree top life, this abundant species often escapes attention.

3 *Nordmannia ilicis* (Esp.) — Ilex Hairstreak. 26—30mm. Distributed in the warmer regions of Europe, Asia Minor and Lebanon. A single generation of butterflies may be seen on the wing in June and July in the vicinity of oaks — from lowlands to 1,500m in the south. The caterpillar lives on various species of oak; the egg hibernates.

4 *Strymonidia spini* (D. & S.) — Blue-spot Hairstreak. 27—32mm. The distribution of this hairstreak is similar to that of the preceding species; eastwards it ranges to Iraq and Iran. There is only one generation in the year, which is on the wing in June and July. Its favourite haunts are dry, shrubby localities where it flies about blackthorns and buckthorns, the foodplants for the caterpillars. The egg hibernates. Of late this butterfly has disappeared from many of its old localities.

5 *Strymonidia w-album* (Knoch) — White-letter Hairstreak. 27—30mm. Widespread in mild regions from central Europe to Japan. Its one generation flies from June to August, in margins of deciduous woods, or about groups of trees in open country. The butterflies like to visit flowering danewort, hemp-agrimony, etc. The caterpillar lives on elm and other deciduous trees; the egg hibernates.

6 *Strymonidia pruni* (L.) — Black Hairstreak. 25—28mm. Found in the temperate zone of Europe, and eastwards to Korea. It is locally distributed in lowlands, in warm, shrubby biotopes overgrown with blackthorn, sporadically also in plum orchards. The time of flight is from June till the beginning of August. The caterpillar lives in spring on blackthorn and plum trees, and the egg hibernates.

7 *Callophrys rubi* (L.) — Green Hairstreak. 24—28mm. This butterfly is distributed in the Palaearctic; closely related species live in North America. It produces one or two generations, depending on climatic conditions. The butterflies can be found on dry hillsides rich in blackthorn, in high mountains, or on peat-bogs. The green underside immediately distinguishes it from any other European species. The polyphagous caterpillar, which hibernates, feeds on a variety of plants, including broom, bramble, and bilberry.

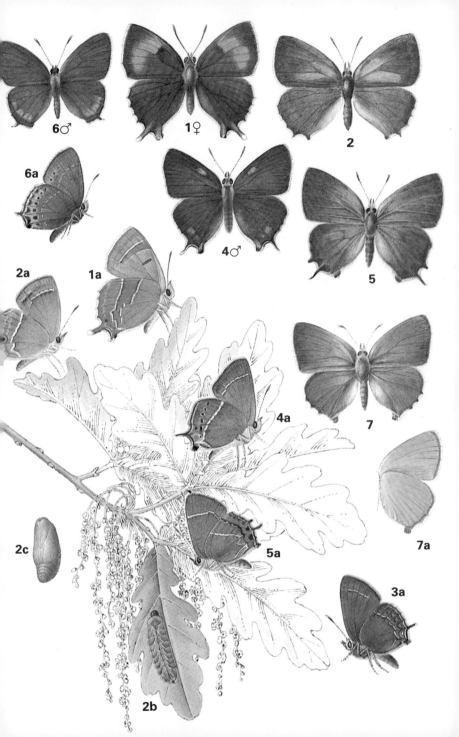

Family: **Lycaenidae — blues, coppers and hairstreaks**

1 *Lycaena phlaeas* (L.) — Small Copper. 22—27mm. In addition to its Palaearctic distribution, this species also inhabits North America. Its favourite haunts are dry, flowery places, open country or forest-steppes. In the mountains it ascends to an elevation of 2,000m. There are a number of subspecies, one of which (ssp. *polaris* Courv.) was described from northern Europe: its wings have the undersides grey. This species produces two or three broods, depending on locality. On sunny late autumn days it can be seen flying about in the fields. It is a shy butterfly and a swift flier. The caterpillar, the hibernating stage, feeds on sorrel and knotgrass.

2 *Lycaena dispar* (Hw.) — Large Copper. 27—32mm. Distributed in scattered localities throughout Europe and Asia, extending east to the Amur Basin, this pretty species has vanished recently from many places, since its environment — damp and swampy lowland meadows — is disappearing due to land drainage. Originally described from England, where it occurred in fenland, it became extinct there about 1850. Since then ssp. *batava* from continental Europe has been introduced to Britain, but seems incapable of surviving unaided. Central Europe is the home of the ssp. *rutilus* Wernb. (2, 2a). Its one generation is on the wing in June and July; sporadically two generations appear from May to August. The caterpillars feed on sorrel.

3 *Heodes virgaureae* (L.) — Scarce Copper. 27—32mm. This copper is distributed throughout the Palaearctic, except the northern regions. It is an inhabitant of meadows and forest clearings, with a particular liking for the profuse flowering vegetation along streams. In the mountains it ascends to 1,500m. As with most of the coppers, *H. virgaureae* is sexually dimorphic; it also shows remarkable geographical variability. The single generation flies from June to August. The caterpillar hibernates, and feeds on sorrel or goldenrod.

4 *Heodes tityrus* (Poda) — Sooty Copper. 23—30mm. The distribution of this butterfly is similar to that of the preceding species — only shifted more to the south, and with its eastern outposts in the Altai region. Favourite haunts are steppe country and dry mountain meadows up to 1,500m. It has two or three generations, emerging from April to August. The caterpillar lives on sorrel and hibernates.

5 *Heodes alciphron* (Rott.) — Purple-shot Copper. 30—38mm. Widespread from western Europe across Asia Minor to Iran, absent from northern Europe. It may be found in June and July in lowlands and at submontane elevations to 1,000m, where it favours dry, flowery meadows. Due to its great variability in colouring and size, several subspecies have been described, including ssp. *melibaeus* Stgr. from Greece and ssp. *heracleanus* Blach. from Morocco. In recent times the butterfly has been in decline. The caterpillar lives on sorrel, and hibernates.

6 *Palaeochrysophanus hippothoe* (L.) Purple-edged Copper. 28—32mm. Distributed throughout almost the whole of Europe, this species reaches east as far as the Amur. It is absent from the British Isles and the warmest parts of Europe. In the mountains it has been reported to occur above 1,000m, yet it prefers submontane elevations, where it flies in damp and peaty meadows or by springs and streams. The caterpillar feeds on sorrel and bistort. The only generation is on the wing from May to July. This Copper also includes a number of geographical races: the nominate race was described from Sweden, ssp. *stiberi* Gerh. lives in Lapland, ssp. *eurydame* Hoffmsg. in the High Alps and ssp. *leonhardi* Frhst. in the Bulgarian Rila.

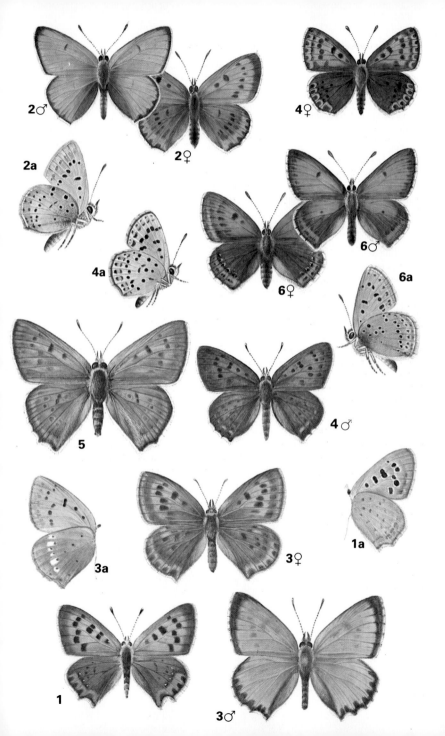

Family: **Lycaenidae — blues, coppers and hairstreaks**

1 *Everes argiades* (Pall.) — Short-tailed Blue. 20—27mm. This blue ranges from Spain to Japan and also occurs in North America; it is, however, absent from the cold regions of Europe and Asia. Found locally in various damp lowland meadows, or deep mountain valleys, it produces two or more broods annually. The caterpillar lives on clover, medick and other legumes; those of the last generation hibernate.

2 *Cupido minimus* (Fssl.) — Small Blue. 18—22mm. With the exception of the southernmost and the northernmost regions, this species inhabits the whole of Europe and temperate Asia, the eastern limit of its distribution being the Amur. It occurs in both dry steppe and damp mountain localities, up to 3,000m. According to climatic conditions it produces two or three generations during the year. The caterpillar lives on blooms and fruits of papilionaceous plants. The Small Blue has of late vanished from many localities, particularly from low-lying ones.

3 *Celastrina argiolus* (L.) — Holly Blue. 23—30mm. A species which inhabits northern Africa, the whole of Europe and Palaearctic Asia, and in North America reaching south to New Mexico. Characteristic of shrubby lowlands localities and damp forests, often occurring plentifully in clearings rich in flowers, it likes to sit on the leaves of shrubs and trees. There are two or three generations in the year. The caterpillar lives on various shrubs, notably holly, ivy and buckthorn. The pupa hibernates.

4 *Glaucopsyche alexis* (Poda) — Green-underside Blue. 23—30mm. This butterfly has a similar range to the Holly Blue, but is much rarer. It frequents dry meadows, the outskirts of woods and clearings, from low elevations up to 2,000m. It flies from April to June in one generation; in warmer regions it produces two broods. The caterpillars live on various papilionaceous plants, for example on milk-vetch and *Cytisus,* especially in the vicinity of ant colonies. The larvae overwinter fully developed and pupate in spring. The pupal stage is of very short duration.

5 *Maculinea arion* (L.) — Large Blue. 28—38mm. A notable species, inhabiting the temperate regions of Europe and Asia, being absent only from the northern and southernmost zones. The caterpillars feed on thyme, but the older larvae live in anthills and eat the larvae and pupae of their hosts, supplying them in return with a special secretion from glands located in the posterior parts of their body. The species is thus dependent on a combination of a suitable turf including thyme, and the nests of particular ants. Gradually deprived of its living conditions, the Large Blue has become nearly or quite extinct in many localities. One of the largest and most conspicuous of Blues, its single generation flies from May to August.

6 *Maculinea teleius* (Brgstr.) — Scarce Large Blue. 27—35mm. With a range which stretches in a narrow belt from central Europe to Japan, this butterfly keeps to damp meadows from lowland to submontane elevations. The only generation it produces is on the wing from the end of June to August. The caterpillar first lives on wild burnet and later in anthills.

7 *Maculinea nausithous* (Brgstr.) — Dusky Large Blue. 28—33mm. Its range more or less coincides with that of the preceding species but does not reach further east than the Urals and the Caucasus. This species also favours wetter biotopes, such as swampy meadows, ranging from lowlands to 2,000m above sea level. The butterfly is on the wing in July and August. The caterpillar lives from autumn till spring first on wild burnet, but later on it is to be found in anthills.

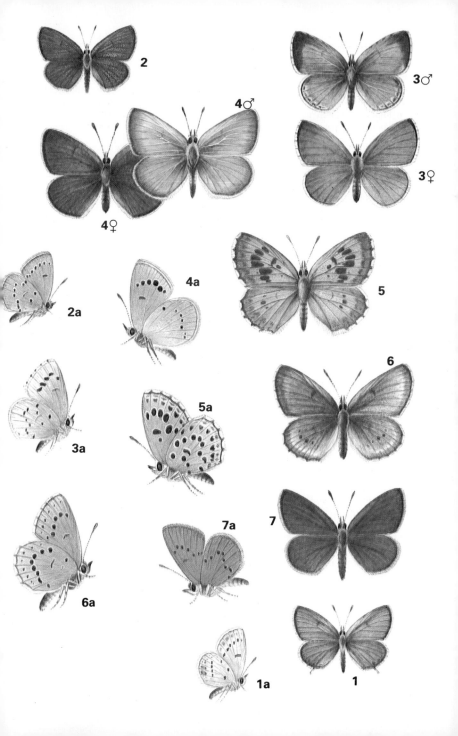

Family: **Lycaenidae — blues, coppers and hairstreaks**

1 *Philotes baton* (Brgstr.) — Baton Blue. 20—25mm. Distributed in western, southern and central Europe, this is one of the earliest blues, flying from April to June; a second brood is on the wing from July to September. It is found in dry localities overgrown with thyme, being fond of settling on the blooms of this plant which is also the food-plant of the caterpillars. Found even high in the mountains, to an altitude of 2,000m, it is, however, nowhere abundant. Recently it has generally become very rare.

2 *Scolitantides orion* (Pall.) — Chequered Blue. 22—28mm. This species, described from the Volga Basin, has an interesting disjunct distribution: one part stretches from Spain across central and southern Europe eastwards to Japan; the other zone lies to the north, in southern Scandinavia. The first generation appears early in spring, the second in July and August. Where the climate is cooler, only one generation develops. It flies on dry slopes exposed to the sun. The caterpillar feeds on orpine and white stonecrop. The pupae of the second generation hibernate.

3 **Plebejus argus* (L.) — Silver-studded Blue. 20—23mm. A species inhabiting the whole of Europe and Asia (with the exception of the northernmost regions) as far as Japan. Within this vast territory a number of geographical forms occur. Sometimes hundreds of individuals assemble on moist ground in the vicinity of brooks, drying pools, etc. It can be seen fluttering in damp meadows, heaths, and elsewhere in open country. The caterpillars live on papilionaceous plants, usually surrounded by ants. There are two broods of this species in the year, flying from May to June and July to August.

4 *Vacciniina optilete* (Knoch) — Cranberry Blue. 22—25mm. Distributed throughout central and northern Europe, and the cooler zone of Asia as far as Japan. A typical inhabitant of peat-bogs, it haunts the tundra in the north; in central Europe it may be found only locally. The single generation is on the wing from June to August. The caterpillar (4b) feeds on species of the genus *Vaccinium*, chiefly on *Vaccinium uliginosum;* it hibernates (4c — pupa).

5 **Aricia agestis* (D. & S.) — Brown Argus. 22—27mm. There is no trace of blue colour in this species which, moreover, bears great resemblance to its very close relative, *A. artaxerxes* (F.): since the two were confused for a very long time, the distribution of the Brown Argus is not known exactly. It probably ranges from southern Britain and France across Europe through the temperate zone of Asia to the Amur Basin. There are two generations per year, the first from April to June and the second from July to September. Caterpillars live on *Erodium*, geraniums and rock-roses.

6 *Cyaniris semiargus* (Rott.) — Mazarine Blue. 25—30mm. A species characteristic of submontane hillsides, it ascends in the mountains to 2,500m. Commonly found in hilly country scattered with woods, where it can be seen fluttering about in damp meadows, it ranges from Morocco across all Europe (extinct in Britain) and Asia to Mongolia. There is, as a rule, only one generation which flies from May to July; in warmer regions a second generation may appear in August and September. The caterpillar, which hibernates, feeds on clover, kidney-vetch, melilot, crown-vetch, etc.

Family: **Lycaenidae — blues, coppers and hairstreaks**

1 *Agrodiaetus damon* (D. & S.) — Damon Blue. 34—38mm. Occurs in widely scattered localities in Europe and Asia, from where it probably extends to Mongolia. Rare in all its habitats, it is found in mountainous regions at various elevations, the uppermost limit being about 2,500m, and shows a preference for biotopes with a limestone substrate. Its only generation emerges in July and August. The caterpillar lives in spring on sainfoin. The presence of this plant, which grows on dry slopes and in stony fields, is a good indicator of biotopes likely to be inhabited by this butterfly. The caterpillar is myrmecophilous (attended by ants).

2 *Plebicula amanda* (Schn.) — Amanda's Blue. 30—35mm. Widespread throughout the temperate zone of Europe and Asia as far as Mongolia, and perhaps extending even further eastwards. It is a rare species, occurring only locally in dry, flowery meadows, and on slopes in lowlands and submontane regions. The caterpillar lives on *Vicia cracca* and hibernates; it is myrmecophilous (attended by ants). The single generation of this species is on the wing from the end of June to August.

3 *Meleageria daphnis* (D. & S.) — Meleager's Blue. 30—35mm. This species is distributed in the warmer regions of Europe and eastwards to Iran. One of the beautifully coloured, thermophilic blues characterized by conspicuous sexual dimorphism. The male is of a brilliant light blue, while the female is more brown with dark blue scales, or with blue zones on her lobed wings. The butterfly is upon the wing in one generation, from June to August, and has a particular liking for flowery wastelands with a limestone substrate, situated in low hills or downs. The caterpillar, which hibernates, feeds on milk-vetch, sainfoin, and other legumes.

4 *Lysandra coridon* (Poda) — Chalk-hill Blue. 30—35mm. A species apparently confined to Europe, within which it does not spread to the southernmost or coldest regions. It prefers dry, sunny places in steppes and forest-steppes, particularly those having a limestone substrate. It is single-brooded and flies from July to September. The blue males appear on the wing somewhat earlier than the brown females. The caterpillar lives on papilionaceous legumes, for example on sicklewort and horseshoe-vetch; it hibernates. The Chalk-hill Blue has of late become rather rare in many localities.

5 *Lysandra bellargus* (Rott.) — Adonis Blue. 27—32mm. A species whose range includes the warmer parts of Europe and Asia Minor, as far as Iraq and Iran. It lives in dry, sunny biotopes with a calcareous substrate, and produces two generations per year: the first flies in May and June, the second from July to September. There is marked sexual dimorphism: males possess sky-blue wings edged with black and white chequered fringes, while the females are brown. Although they occur predominantly in lowlands, the butterflies may also be found in mountains up to 2,000m. The caterpillars feed on papilionaceous plants, particularly horseshoe-vetch, and hibernate.

6 *Polyommatus icarus* (Rott.) — Common Blue. 25—30mm. One of the most abundant blues, and capable of surviving on agricultural land. This might partly be due to the fact that the caterpillars (6b) can feed on lucerne, cultivated for cattle fodder. The Common Blue has a Palaearctic distribution and ranges to the Pacific, occurring both in lowlands, and in highlands up to 2,000m. Annually there are one to three overlapping generations, depending on the climatic conditions of the locality. The caterpillar hibernates.

Family: **Hesperiidae — skippers**

1 *Pyrgus malvae* (L.) — Grizzled Skipper. 18−22mm. With the exception of the northernmost parts of Europe, this species occurs throughout the temperate zone of the Palaearctic, reaching eastwards to the Amur. It is fond of flowering meadows, bogs, and other grassy places. The two generations it produces fly from April to August. The caterpillar lives during the autumn; the pupa hibernates.

2 *Pyrgus serratulae* (Rbr.) — Olive Skipper. 22−25mm. Widely distributed in the warmer regions of Europe and Asia, including the Transbaikalian region. A local species favouring dry, rocky places on hills and downs. The single generation is on the wing from May to July. The caterpillar, which lives in autumn and hibernates over the winter, feeds on cinquefoil and wormwood.

3 *Pyrgus fritillarius* (Poda) — Safflower Skipper. 27−33mm. This skipper occurs throughout the whole of warmer and central Europe and reaches to central Asia. Its two generations fly from May to August, in open steppe or other treeless habitats exposed to sunshine. Local but very abundant in places where it does occur, it ascends the mountains to 2,200m. The caterpillar lives towards the end of summer on cinquefoil, marsh mallow and mallow.

4 *Spialia sertorius* (Hffmsg.) — Red Underwing Skipper. 22−24mm. Widespread in northern Africa, southern and central Europe, it spreads across central Asia to the Amur. It is fond of dry, warm situations, from lowlands up to 2,000m. Two generations make their appearance in the year — the first in May and June, the second in July and August. The caterpillar lives on wild burnet, bramble and cinquefoil, and hibernates.

5 *Carcharodus alceae* (Esp.) — Mallow Skipper. 23−30mm. This species lives in northern Africa, southern and central Europe, extending eastwards to central Asia. Sunny, dry biotopes and grassy banks between fields are its favourite haunts. Since the two or three generations produced in the year merge into each other, it may be seen on the wing practically continuously **from April to September. The caterpillar (5b), which hibernates, lives on mallow, marsh mallow and** *Hibiscus*.

6 *Carcharodus lavatherae* (Esp.) — Marbled Skipper. 25−32mm. The distribution of this butterfly in Europe and Africa is similar to that of the preceding species, but in the east it reaches only to Asia Minor. This local and rare species can be found on sunny hillsides with a calcareous substrate. Its single generation is on the wing from June to August. The caterpillar feeds on woundwort, and hibernates.

7 *Erynnis tages* (L.) — Dingy Skipper. 23−26mm. Though absent from northern Europe, its range extends from western Europe across the whole of central Europe and Asia to China. One of the most abundant skippers, it frequents dry, grassy sites and steppe localities. Two generations are produced in the year; one flies early in spring, the other in July and August. The caterpillar lives on bird's-foot trefoil and eryngo, and also on scorpion vetch and crown vetch.

8 *Heteropterus morpheus* (Pall.) — Large Chequered Skipper. 30−35mm. Absent from southern and northern Europe, otherwise sporadically distributed from Spain across Europe and Asia to Korea. Tolerating many types of habitat, it can be found in damp meadows, dry grassy places and woodland clearings. The single generation flies from May to the beginning of July. The caterpillar lives on various grasses, and hibernates.

Family: **Hesperiidae — skippers**

1 *Carterocephalus palaemon* (Pall.) — Chequered Skipper. 22—28mm. Being a species characteristic of forests in the temperate zone, it is absent from southern Europe. Its range embraces all Asia and also North America. It is found in meadows and grassy woodland clearings, frequently it also occurs in mountain valleys up to an altitude of about 1,500m. Butterflies of the single annual generation fly from the beginning of May till July. The caterpillar lives from autumn till the following spring on a variety of grasses, especially brome grass. Of recent years, this butterfly has vanished from many of its old haunts and has become a rare species in all areas affected by Man.

2 *Thymelicus acteon* (Rott.) — Lulworth Skipper. 22—25mm. Distributed in northern Africa, southern and central Europe, and further eastwards to the Near East, this thermophilic species favours arid localities and steppes. Though it sometimes appears as early as May, in general it is a late species that can be seen on the wing in July and August. It produces a single generation. The caterpillar feeds on a variety of grasses.

3 *Thymelicus lineola* (O.) — Essex, or European Skipper. 22—26mm. With the exception of northernmost regions, it occurs from northern Africa over the whole of Europe and Asia and extends to the Far East. It also occurs in North America, most probably introduced through human agency. Its one generation flies from June to July in dry meadows, forest glades and clearings, sucking nectar from flowers of the Compositae, including thistles and cornflowers; it also likes to sit on damp ground and drink water. Caterpillars live from April to May on various grasses. The egg hibernates.

4 *Thymelicus sylvestris* (Poda) — Small Skipper. 24—27mm. In the western parts of its range, its distribution roughly coincides with that of the preceding species; in the east, however, it reaches only to Iran. It is one of the most abundant skippers, flying in a single generation from June till August. It can be found in all grassy, relatively dry biotopes abounding in flowers, and also in forest clearings and rides, etc. In the mountains it may ascend to 2,000m. The caterpillar lives on a variety of grasses, and hibernates.

5 *Hesperia comma* (L.) — Silver-spotted Skipper. 25—30mm. This skipper extends further to the north than the preceding species, its total range being altogether greater, extending to the whole of Asia and to North America. In mountains it can be found as high as 2,500m. Its only generation appears from June to September and can be seen flying in similar habitats to the Small Skipper. The caterpillar lives on various grasses, and hibernates.

6 *Ochlodes venata* (Bremer & Grey) — Large Skipper. 25—32mm. At first sight this skipper seems very similar to the preceding species. Its range is shifted to the north: it is absent from northern Africa but occurs in Scandinavia. The eastern limit of its distribution is Japan. The populations inhabiting central Europe are included in ssp. *septentrionalis* Vrty. The butterfly is on the wing from June to August, in grassy biotopes and mountains, up to 2,000m. The caterpillar feeds on a variety of grasses, and hibernates.

Family: **Arctiidae — tiger and footman moths**

1 *Nola cucullatella* (L.) — Short-cloaked Moth. 16—18mm. An exclusively European species, which does not occur in any other region. Together with the following species it is classed among the smaller tiger moths, frequently included in a small, independent family, the Nolidae. It produces one generation, flying in June and July. In spring, its small hairy caterpillars (1b) may often be found on apple trees.

2 *Nola confusalis* (H. S.) — Least Black Arches. 16—18mm. The range of this species extends from Europe to Japan. In the mountains it ascends to the beech tree line. Its only generation is on the wing in early spring — in April and May. Occasionally a partial second brood may emerge in August. The caterpillar spends the summertime on oak and hornbeam; the pupa hibernates.

3 *Cybosia mesomella* (L.) — Four-dotted Footman. 25—33mm. Distributed in the mild regions of Europe, particularly the southeast, and towards the southern Urals. It favours biotopes having a sandy substrate, or damp, peaty meadows and sparse forests. There is only one generation a year. The caterpillar feeds on liverwort, and hibernates.

4 *Miltochrista miniata* (Forst.) — Rosy Footman. 23—27mm. Ranges from France to Japan. It is peculiar to deciduous or mixed forests and flies from June to August. The caterpillar eats lichen growing on tree trunks, and hibernates.

5 *Eilema lurideola* (Zinck.) — Common Footman. 28—35mm. Widely distributed in the forest belt of the whole Palaearctic, but occurs more abundantly in the mountains. Its one generation flies from June till September, depending on climatic conditions. The caterpillar feeds on lichens growing on tree trunks, and hibernates.

6 *Eilema complana* (L.) — Scarce Footman. 28—35mm. Distributed in the temperate regions of Europe and further eastward across the northern parts of Asia Minor to Transcaucasia. It is an abundant species associated with warm, dry localities and open woodlands. The hibernating caterpillar lives on lichens; the moth's one generation is on the wing from June to August.

7 *Atolmis rubricollis* (L.) — Red-necked Footman. 25—35mm. Widespread in central and northern Europe, in Asia it reaches the Amur. A locally abundant species showing scarcely any variation, its single generation may be seen flying about in both coniferous and deciduous forests, from May to July. The caterpillar lives in autumn, eating lichens growing on tree trunks. The pupa hibernates.

8 *Spiris striata* (L.) — Feathered Footman. 30—35mm. Inhabits the whole of Europe, Asia Minor and the warmer regions of Asia. Dark specimens (f. *melanoptera*) are commonly found in the southern and eastern parts of Europe. The moth flies in one generation, from May to August; the caterpillar is polyphagous and hibernates.

9 *Coscinia cribraria* (L.) — Speckled Footman. 30—35mm. Distributed throughout the temperate regions of Europe, spreading eastwards to the Urals. Its main haunts are heather-covered moors, or upland forests well supplied with an undergrowth of heather, preferably on a sandy substrate. Being a relatively local and rare species, it tends to produce local forms. The moth is on the wing from June to the beginning of August; the caterpillar lives on heather or fescue, and hibernates.

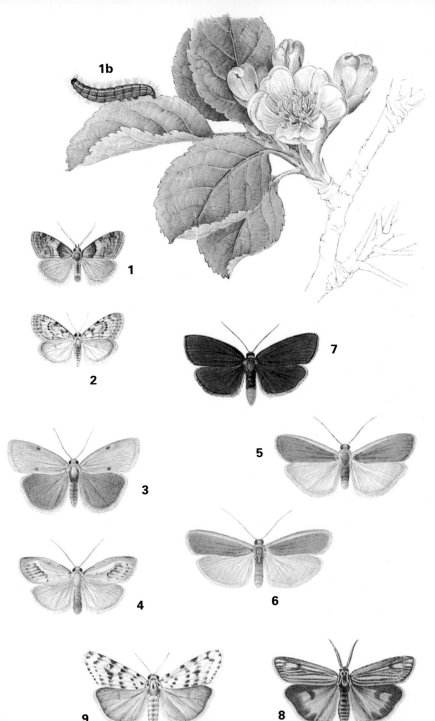

Family: **Arctiidae — tiger and footman moths**

1 *Phragmatobia fuliginosa* (L.) Ruby Tiger. 30—35mm. One of the most abundant tiger moths, often attracted to light. Its caterpillars can be found in many situations. The distribution of this species is Palaearctic, extending in the Far East as far as Japan. It can be seen flying even at high mountain altitudes. There are two generations from April to June and from July to September. The caterpillar is polyphagous; it hibernates when full-grown and pupates immediately after emerging from its winter sleep, forming a flimsy brown cocoon on the ground, or in various crevices, under stones, etc.

2 *Eucharia casta* (Esp.). 27—32mm. A thermophilic species distributed in southern and central Europe, ranging eastwards towards the Urals — but not beyond them. Sunny hillsides and open deciduous woods are among its favourite habitats. The only generation of these moths is on the wing in May; the caterpillars live in summer on bedstraw or woodruff. The pupa is the stage that hibernates. This moth presents a great number of variations.

3 *Parasemia plantaginis* (L.) — Wood Tiger. 32—38mm. Widely distributed throughout Europe and Asia as far as Japan. Its sexual dimorphism is remarkable: males are yellowish, while the females are reddish, and, moreover, males living at high altitudes are creamy white (f. *hospita* — 3c). The caterpillar hibernates when half-grown, and feeds on various herbs. In its single generation the moth flies from May to July, in grassy, moist biotopes and sometimes occurs above the timberline.

4 *Spilosoma lubricipeda* (L.) (= *menthastri* D. & S.) — White Ermine. 30—42mm. A common species seen on the wing in both lowlands and highlands, from May to July. It is widespread in the whole of non-polar Europe and Asia, showing a distinct preference for open country and biotopes with profuse vegetation. It is absent from the extreme south. The caterpillar (4b) is polyphagous; the pupa hibernates.

5 *Spilosoma luteum* (Hfn.) — Buff Ermine. 28—40mm. Occurs in Europe and Asia, the eastern limit being Korea. This single-brooded species is on the wing in June and July, somewhat later than the White Ermine, and is to be found in steppes, fields and waste ground. The caterpillar (5b) is polyphagous; the pupa hibernates (5c).

6 *Hyphantria cunea* (Drury) — Fall Webworm. 25—40mm. This moth of American origin was introduced to Europe during World War II. Since then it has managed to establish itself in all the warmer regions of central and southeastern Europe. There are two generations: one flies in May and June, the other in August. The caterpillars (6b) are polyphagous, and often cause serious damage to fruit trees. They live gregariously in nests among leaves spun together, and separate only prior to pupation. The pupa (6c) of the second generation hibernates in webs spun in the branches, in crevices, beneath bark, etc.

7 *Diaphora mendica* (Cl.) — Muslin. 28—38mm. Distributed in the temperate zone of Europe and Asia, where it extends to the Altai. There is one generation of this moth which flies in spring from April to June, usually in low-lying grassy biotopes. The caterpillar is polyphagous. The pupa hibernates.

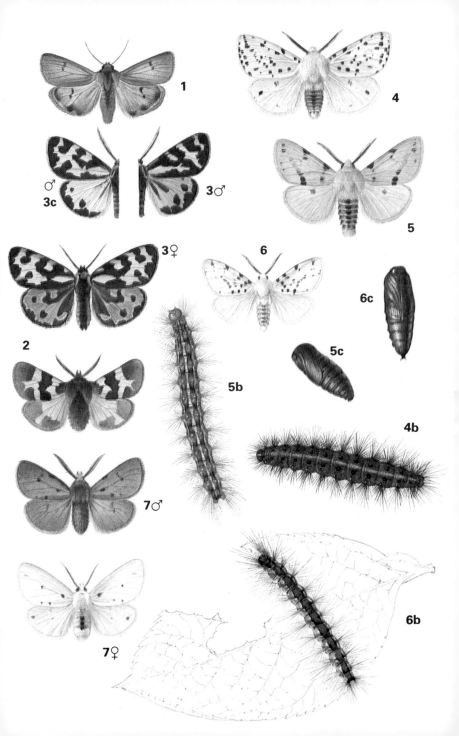

Family: **Arctiidae — tiger and footman moths**

1 *Diacrisia purpurata* (L.). 38—48mm. Widespread in all mild and warm regions of Europe and Asia, ranging eastwards to Japan. This extremely variable species occurs in dry localities and on warm hillsides in June and July; in the south a second brood may appear on the wing in September. The caterpillar (1b) is polyphagous but is partial to bedstraw, bramble and plantain. It hibernates when almost full-grown.

2 **Diacrisia sannio* (L.) — Clouded Buff. 33—45mm. Abundantly distributed throughout Europe, and widespread in Asia as far as the Altai. Though mostly associated with lowland habitats, it is also found in mountains up to 2,400m. The males can be lured to light at night, but on sunny days they are also active and can be found on dry slopes, in forest clearings, meadows and glades. The females are often practically immobile, many of them have somewhat reduced wings and are incapable of flight. In Europe this species appears in one or two generations, almost continuously from April to August. The caterpillar is polyphagous and hibernates.

3 *Diacrisia caesarea* (Goeze). 35—40mm. This thermophilic species occurs in widely separated localities in central and southern Europe and further eastwards, its eastern limit being Japan. It may be seen on the wing in dry, grassy and steppe localities, where it occurs in two generations, flying from May to June and again in August. The caterpillar is polyphagous, the pupa hibernates. This moth's habits are very interesting: it responds to light early in the evening, and then again at day-break. Recently this species has become rare, disappearing from many of its old haunts.

4 *Hyphoraia aulica* (L.). 30—38mm. Though widely distributed in all Europe and in central and eastern Asia, it is relatively rare in all its haunts. Moreover, it has of late become extinct in many localities. It shows a preference for warm, flowery biotopes, favouring those situated on a sandy substrate. The developmental rate of the caterpillars tends to be variable, even among those coming from the same batch of eggs. Thus the possibility arises for the more rapidly developing individuals to form a partial second generation. As a rule, however, there is only one brood, which is on the wing from May to July. Caterpillars (4b) are polyphagous and hibernate while half-grown. The patterning of these moths presents innumerable variations and many aberrations have been described.

5 **Tyria jacobaeae* (L.) — Cinnabar. 32—42mm. Distributed throughout Europe and Asia Minor, this species also penetrates to central Asia. It is found in both warm and cool meadow and steppe biotopes, occurring in the mountains to an elevation of about 1,600m. A more or less local species, not very abundant in any situation, the single generation is on the wing from May to July. The caterpillars (5b), marked with yellow and black transverse bands, represent an exception among tiger moths in that they live gregariously: this is a characteristic of the species. They feed on common kinds of field and meadow groundsels. By the end of summer they grow to full size and subsequently pupate, in which stage they pass the winter.

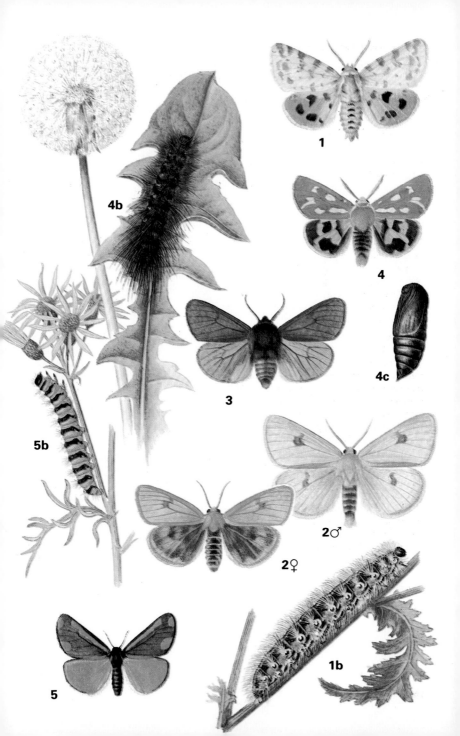

Family: **Arctiidae — tiger and footman moths**

1 *Pericallia matronula* (L.). 65—80mm. Although widely distributed in the temperate zone of Europe and Asia, from where it ranges to the Amur (its eastern limit), this is a very local and rare species. Moreover, no recent records have been reported from many of its old haunts where it was captured during the last century: this probably means that the moth is gradually approaching extinction. It is relatively more abundant in eastern Europe, including the valleys of the Carpathians where it may be found in deciduous forests having a dense, shrubby undergrowth. Though it shows considerable variation, no exhaustive investigation of its individual variability has been possible, because of its rarity. The only brood produced in the year is on the wing in June and July. Males are nocturnal in habit, but on sunny days they also take to the wing in the morning. The females are clumsy, and largely immobile. The caterpillar is polyphagous and can be found on shrubs and herbs. It apparently takes a very long time to develop, and it is said to hibernate twice and not to pupate until the second spring.

2 *Arctia caja* (L.) — Garden Tiger. 45—65mm. Distributed throughout Europe, Asia and North America. A moth at home both in low-lying agricultural ground and mountains, where it ascends to 2,000m, but its greatest abundance occurs at submontane elevations of about 600m. The species is given to such great variation that it would be extremely difficult to find two specimens with patterns identical in all details. This variability mainly involves either suppression of the chocolate colour, making the moths very pale (2c) or, alternatively, suppression of the pale-coloured parts of the wings, resulting — with the exception of a few pale splashes — in a fusion of the dark markings (2d). The hindwing pattern also exhibits considerable variation. A form of great interest is f. *lutescens,* in which the red colouring is replaced by yellow. In some regions particular colour variations have acquired a more permanent character and, on this basis, several geographical races have been described. The single generation flies from June to August. These moths are remarkable for their nocturnal flight rhythm: they are not attracted to light until about midnight, but then, all of a sudden, they come swarming in great numbers. For much of the time they sit among grasses and herbs, and, despite their bright colouration, they usually escape discovery. The caterpillar (2b) which is polyphagous, hibernates in a half-developed stage, and is most voracious in spring. It is regarded as an occasional pest, and it does sometimes cause damage to vegetables in gardens and fields — but its economic impact is trivial.

3 *Arctia villica* (L.) — Cream-spot Tiger. 45—60mm. A species distributed in the warmer regions of Europe and Asia, approximately as far east as Armenia, it is very abundant in its haunts and is often attracted to light. The Cream-spot shows similar variability to the Garden Tiger. A great many individual forms and several geographical races have been described. These include f. *radiata,* where the individual spots merge into continuous bands, and f. *paucimacula,* where the markings on the forewings tend to become completely obsolete. This species is single-brooded, the moths being on the wing in May and June in warm steppe and forest-steppe biotopes. The caterpillars (3b) hibernate in very much the same way as in other tiger moths, and are polyphagous, feeding on various low-growing plants. The pupal stage, which occurs in spring, lasts for a short time only.

144

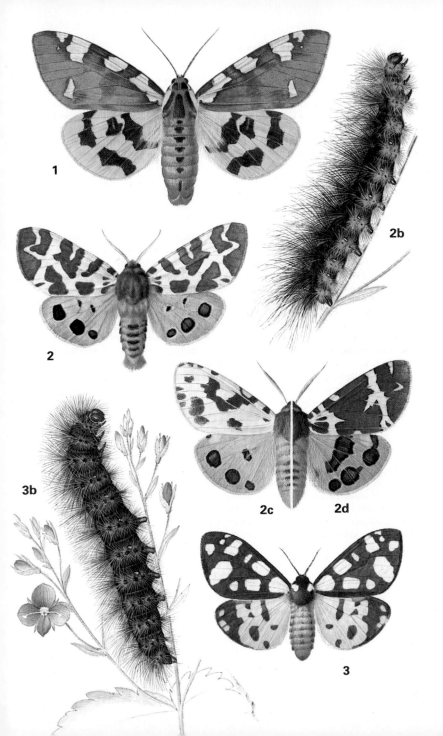

Family: **Arctiidae — tiger and footman moths**

1 *Ammobiota festiva* (Hfn.) (= *hebe* L.). 45—60mm. A thermophilic species occurring in sandy and limestone localities, on sunny slopes and in arid wastelands of central and southern Europe. Eastwards it occurs in the warm regions of Asia, to Manchuria. It is very variable in its colour pattern and produces innumerable forms (including transitional ones), some of which evidently represent true geographical races. For example, in southern Europe the moths are marked vivid red and black (1c) while in central Europe they are most often merely grey or pink (1). The moths of the single generation fly in May. The caterpillars (1b) are polyphagous, growing to full size in summer. After completing their development they overwinter and pupate in spring, immediately after emerging from hibernation. The mature larvae can be collected easily on sunny spring days, when they lie on the ground basking. This attractive moth has become extinct lately in many central European localities. Evidently it fails to tolerate agricultural processes, or any interference with its natural habitats. A great number of the caterpillars perish when grass is burnt in the spring.

2 *Callimorpha dominula* (L.) — Scarlet Tiger. 45—55mm. The distribution area of this species corresponds to the temperate regions of Europe — the Caucasus is its eastern limit. Together with the following species it belongs among those few tiger moths having well-developed mouthparts, which they use to obtain nectar from flowering plants. The Scarlet Tiger has a particular liking for damp forests and woodland clearings overgrown with nettles and raspberries. It also frequents pastures and land in the neighbourhood of settlements where the soil is enriched with nitrogen, and lush valleys. Along such valleys the moth may gain access to the mountains, and may even occur above the timberline. It can often be disturbed, darting from the rank vegetation bordering mountain streams. Both nocturnal and diurnal in habit, it is extremely wary. Annually it produces only one generation, which flies from May to July. The caterpillar hibernates while young and completes its development next spring (2b), living on a variety of plants, frequently nettles. The moth exhibits a great number of variations and produces many forms. One of the more notable is f. *flavia,* in which the red colour is all replaced by yellow. Some forms have the character of subspecies, for example ssp. *pompalis* Nitsche inhabiting southern Alpine valleys, which has reduced pale spots on its forewings and a more complex black pattern on the hindwings.

3 *Euplagia quadripunctaria* (Poda) — Jersey Tiger. 42—52mm. In comparison with the above species, this moth is distributed more to the south. Nevertheless, it can be found in mountains at quite high elevations, which it attains by way of deep valleys. It occurs most abundantly in forest-steppe regions, favouring those on a limestone substrate. Moths assemble in moist places where they suck nectar from hemp agrimony, thistles and other plants blooming in late summer. This moth is a feature of late summer, the single generation being on the wing from July to September. The valleys of southern Europe are often the scene of mass concentrations of these moths: they literally cover the vegetation, one of the most famous places where this phenomenon can be witnessed being the so-called 'Valley of Butterflies' on Rhodes. The caterpillars emerge from the eggs in autumn, hibernate, and wake up in spring to complete their development. They are polyphagous.

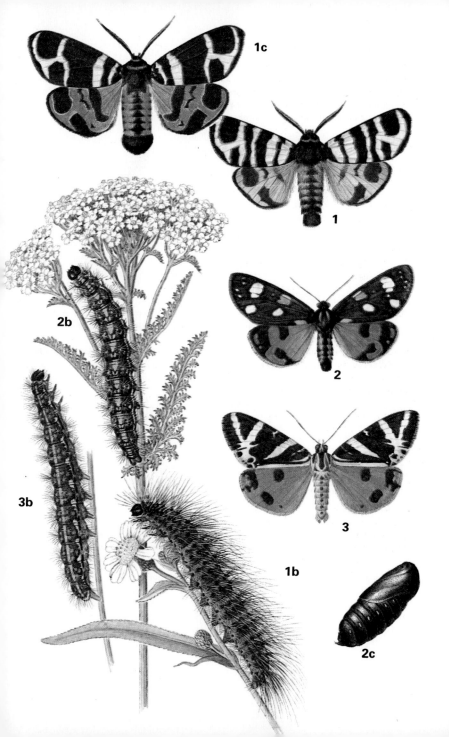

Family: **Ctenuchidae — ctenuchids**

1 *Syntomis phegea* (L.) — Nine-spotted. 35—40mm. This moth is distributed in the warmer regions of Europe (especially in the south), in Asia Minor and across Armenia to the Altai. The single generation is on the wing from June to August. The adults can be seen flying on sun-warmed, flowery slopes and in woodland margins. They like to settle on flowering wild marjoram. The caterpillar (1b) lives on various herbs, and hibernates.

2 *Dysauxes ancilla* (L.) — Handmaid. 22—25mm. Confined to Europe where it can sporadically be found in open, warm woods and forest steppes, usually at lower elevations, this moth produces only one generation in the year. It is diurnal, sometimes also nocturnal, and on the wing in July and August. The caterpillars, which feed on mosses, young tree leaves and herbs, hibernate when quite young.

3 *Dysauxes punctata* (F.). 18—23mm. A thermophilous species peculiar to oak forests and forest-steppes, which occurs in southern Europe, the Balkan Peninsula, and Asia Minor, Armenia forming the eastern limit of its distribution. It is highly variable, and many individual forms and geographical races have been described. The moth may be found on the wing in May and June. The caterpillar, which hibernates, lives on lichens attached to trees, and (reputedly) on flowers.

Family: **Arctiidae — tiger and footman moths**

4 *Thumatha senex* (Hb.) — Round-winged Muslin. 15—20mm. Widespread throughout central and northern Europe, eastwards as far as the Urals, its distribution being continuous in the north but discontinuous in the south. This moth may be found in cold, or at least damp, peaty biotopes from June to August, being abundant in appropriate situations. The caterpillar, which hibernates, often eats lichen and moss growing amongst grass, but prefers a diet of liverworts.

5 *Endrosa roscida* (D. & S.). 23—27mm. This thermophilous species is scattered in the warmer regions of Europe and Asia as far as the Altai. The two generations may be found flying about in dry, grassy places, from May to June and again in August. The caterpillar hibernates. Its usual food is various lichens attached to trees and stones, or growing on the ground.

6 *Setina irrorella* (L.) — Dew. 27—33mm. A species of central and northern Europe, ascending to about 1,500m in the mountains. Eastwards it extends to eastern Asia. The single generation flies from June to August in woodland clearings, submontane meadows and forest margins. The caterpillar feeds on lichen, and hibernates.

7 *Pelosia muscerda* (Hfn.) — Dotted Footman. 24—28mm. This footman is distributed in scattered localities throughout Europe and Asia, but is rare in all its haunts. This is exacerbated by the continuing loss of appropriate biotopes. It is found in damp and swampy meadows and in moist woodland clearings. The single generation flies from the end of June to the beginning of August. The caterpillars live on lichen, and hibernate.

8 *Pelosia obtusa* (H. S.) — Small Dotted Footman. 24—28mm. A rare species locally distributed in central and eastern Europe, and in Asia, where it reaches to the southern parts of the Ussuri Basin. It is a familiar sight in reed-beds and damp meadows, yet its biology so far remains almost unknown. The time of flight is so protracted that two generations might easily be involved. Not even the food-plant of the caterpillars has been discovered; it might be one of the reeds.

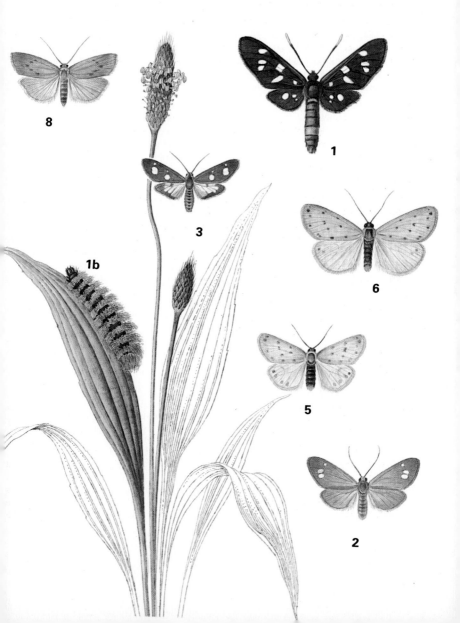

Family: **Lymantriidae — tussock moths**

1 *Dasychira fascelina* (L.) — Dark Tussock. 35—45mm. Widespread in northern and central Europe, it ranges eastwards to central Asia. In the mountains this moth occurs up to 1,000m. It gives rise to various geographical forms. Northern Germany is the home of ssp. *callunae* Peets, which is paler and bears a sharply outlined design, whereas the alpine ssp. *alpina* Kitt is darker. The single generation is on the wing from June to mid August. The caterpillar, which hibernates, is polyphagous, feeding on the leaves of various shrubs and herbs.

2 *Dasychira abietis* (D. & S.). 43—45mm. To be found in submontane regions of central and northern Europe, in the mountains up to the spruce-tree line, and at higher elevations further east (for example in the Carpathians). A local species, it must be considered quite rare. The adult flies in June and July. The caterpillar, to be found at the end of summer, hibernates while half-grown and completes its development in spring, feeding on the needles of spruces and firs.

3 *Dasychira pudibunda* (L.) — Pale Tussock Moth. 40—60mm. One of the common and widespread species, occurring throughout the temperate parts of Europe and Asia as far as Japan. It is characteristic of deciduous forests, parks and gardens, where it flies in May and June; occasionally a second brood appears in September. It is a variable species; f. *concolor*, which is grey and has no pattern whatsoever, appears very frequently. The caterpillar (3b) lives from summer till autumn on various deciduous trees and shrubs. The pupa hibernates.

4 *Orgyia antiqua* (L.) — Vapourer. 25—30mm. An inhabitant of forests and forest-steppes in the northern and temperate Palaearctic, it is absent from the warmest regions only. In the mountains it has been reported to ascend to an elevation of about 2,000m. One generation is produced in the north and in the mountains, while elsewhere there may be two or three generations annually, which fly from June till the end of October. The egg hibernates. The caterpillar is polyphagous (4b) and considered as a pest of fruit and forest trees. Sexual dimorphism is very marked: the male flies in a darting zigzag fashion both day and night; the female has vestigial wings and is consequently incapable of flight, being little more than a small, egg-filled barrel. She is usually fertilized immediately after eclosion, close to her flimsy pupal cocoon, on which she lays her whole ample batch of yellowish-grey eggs.

5 *Penthophera morio* (L.). 20—25mm. Widespread in central and eastern Europe, this moth occurs locally but in fair numbers in grassy, dry places. If the weather is sunny, males may be seen in the morning flitting about close above the undergrowth, in search of females, which, because of their degenerate wings, cannot fly. The single generation of moths lives from May to July. The caterpillars (5b) hibernate within grassy turfs, their favourite food being grasses. They are extremely voracious, and sometimes cause damage to meadows.

6 *Arctornis l-nigrum* (Müll.) — Black V. 35—45mm. A species distributed in the deciduous forest belt of the whole Palaearctic. Colouration of the wings is the same in both sexes but the female differs from the male by having pectinate antennae with short rami and a considerably stouter abdomen. The single generation flies in June and July. The caterpillar hibernates in the fourth instar and grows to full size in spring (6b), living on a variety of trees, especially on beeches, birches, poplars, etc.

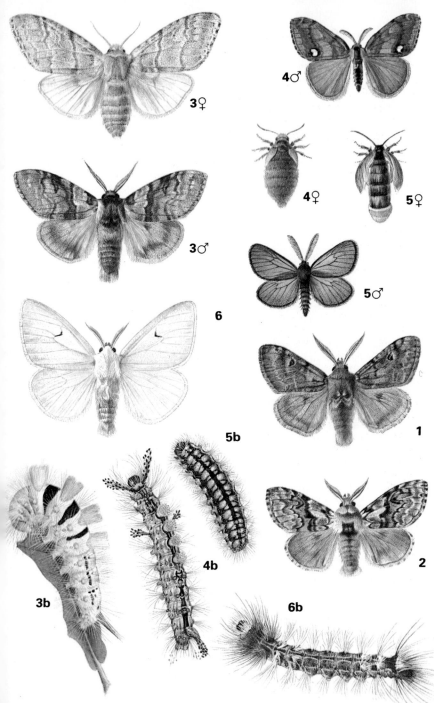

Family: **Lymantriidae − tussock moths**

1 *Leucoma salicis* (L.) − White Satin. 37−50mm. Distributed throughout Europe, this species ranges to eastern Asia and is associated particularly with warmer lowland elevations. The single brood flies in June and July. The caterpillars (1b), which hibernate while young, are most voracious in spring, feeding on willows, poplars and other trees which they often completely defoliate − hence their significance as forest pests. Although not a particularly variable species, several interesting forms have been described. The nominate form has transparent wings sparsely covered with scales; f. *candida* has the wings invested with dense white scales; and f. *nigrociliata* has a black outer margin to the wings.

2 *Lymantria dispar* (L.) − Gypsy. 32−55mm. A dangerous pest of deciduous trees all over the northern hemisphere. In 1869 it was taken to America for experimental purposes, but escaped from captivity and rapidly established itself in the wild. In outbreak years tree trunks are often strewn with clutches of eggs covered with pale hairs from the females' abdomens − these are visible from a distance as light spots. This species is not only characterized by conspicuous sexual dimorphism, but is also variable in pattern and colouration. The males are active in the daytime: they fly in an erratic, zigzag manner; the females are extremely cumbersome. There is only one brood in the year, on the wing from June to August. The eggs hibernate, and the caterpillars (2b) live in spring on the foliage of oaks, poplars and other trees.

3 *Lymantria monacha* (L.) − Black Arches. 30−50mm. Widespread throughout the temperate zone of Europe and Asia, ranging far eastwards. In comparison with the foregoing species, its range occurs more to the north and at higher elevations. At the beginning of this century the Black Arches Moth caused catastrophic damage in the spruce monocultures of central Europe, even though the caterpillar is polyphagous and can thrive on deciduous trees. The female differs from the male both in size and in colouration. The markings are highly variable, and darkly coloured specimens are frequently found (f. *atra* − 3c). There is but one generation a year, the moths being active at night, and on the wing from July to September. The eggs hibernate, and the caterpillars develop during the spring.

4 *Euproctis chrysorrhoea* (L.) − Brown-tail. 28−38mm. Widespread in the warmer regions of Europe and across Asia Minor to Transcaucasia, this species, peculiar to deciduous forests, has become well adapted even to agricultural landscapes. Its only generation is on the wing from June to August. The female possesses a robust abdomen covered with yellowish-brown hairs at the tip − these she uses to cover her clutch of eggs. In autumn the young caterpillars spin a pear-shaped nest in the branches of a tree, hibernate therein, and complete their development in spring (4b). They live gregariously, in great numbers. Among forest trees this moth favours the oak as food, while fruit trees such as cherry, pear and plum are also attacked. Because they strip all leaves from the branches, they are serious pests in forests and orchards.

5 *Euproctis similis* (Fssl.) − Yellow-tail. 28−35mm. Less widely distributed than the Brown-tail, being more abundant in cooler regions only. One, sometimes two, generations are produced, flying from June to September. The young caterpillars hibernate and can be found in spring, scattered singly on various deciduous trees and shrubs.

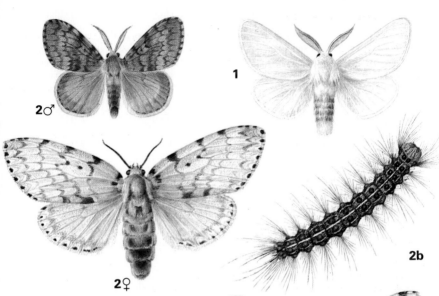

2♂

1

2♀

2b

3c

3♀

4♂

4♀

4b

1b

5♂

Family: **Noctuidae** — **noctuids (owlet moths, millers)**

1 *Euxoa obelisca* (D. & S.) — Square-spot Dart. 30—40mm. Belongs to a group of cutworms so similar to each other that many of them were long regarded as one species, and their differentiation remains difficult even now. This species is distributed in the temperate and warmer regions of Europe, eastwards as far as central Asia. Moths of the single generation fly in August and September in dry, mostly sandy and limestone biotopes. The caterpillars develop in spring, and are polyphagous.

2 *Euxoa nigricans* (L.) — Garden Dart. 28—35mm. Distributed throughout the temperate zone of Europe and Asia as far as the Amur, up to elevations of about 1,000m, this species has one generation per year. The moths are on the wing from July to the beginning of September. The eggs hibernate and the polyphagous caterpillars live in spring.

3 *Euxoa aquilina* (D. & S.). 30—35mm. Abundantly distributed in fields and steppes, from lowlands to submontane elevations, in Europe and in Asia, the single generation of this moth is on the wing in July and August. The eggs hibernate; the caterpillars develop in spring and are polyphagous. At times they are pests of corn.

4 *Agrotis vestigialis* (Hfn.) — Archer's Dart. 30—35mm. Locally distributed in all non-polar Europe, reaching to southern Russia, this species is confined to biotopes with a sandy substrate. The moths, which fly in July and August, are extremely variable in pattern and colouration. The caterpillars feed on the roots of grass and tree seedlings.

5 *Agrotis segetum* (D. & S.) — Turnip Moth. 27—40mm. Widespread in agricultural and steppe areas of Europe and Asia, reported also from South Africa. There are one or two generations of this moth, depending on climate. Adults are on the wing from May to July and August to October. Their colouration shows innumerable variations. The polyphagous caterpillars (5b), which overwinter, are classed among the most destructive agricultural pests.

6 *Agrotis exclamationis* (L.) — Heart and Dart. 30—40mm. One of the most common moths in the temperate and warm parts of the entire Palaearctic. There is one brood in the year, flying from June to September; in the warmest localities a partial second brood may appear occasionally in the autumn. The caterpillars are polyphagous and hibernate when full-grown. In spite of its great abundance, it is of little agricultural significance, since it prefers to feed on wild plants.

7 *Agrotis ipsilon* (Hfn.) — Dark Sword Grass. 35—50mm. The worldwide distribution of this moth is attributable to its migratory habits. It does not hibernate in central Europe but migrates to Europe each year during April to July. In the summer the caterpillars develop at a rapid rate, and the pupal stage is also brief, thus the moths are able to emerge in August, and remain on the wing till late autumn. Then they gradually disappear — probably there is a return migration to the south. The caterpillars cause considerable damage in fields and vegetable gardens situated in relatively damp localities.

8 *Ochropleura praecox* (L.) — Portland Moth. 35—40mm. A local and rather rare moth found in sandy regions throughout Europe and Asia. Its only generation is on the wing from July to September. The polyphagous caterpillars hibernate.

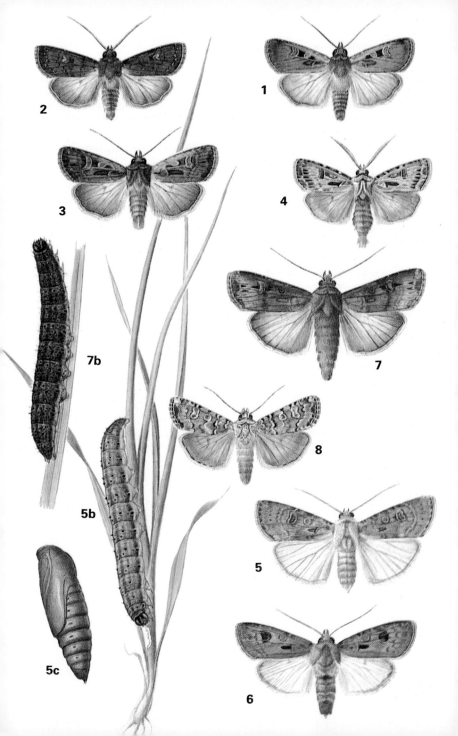

Family: **Noctuidae — noctuids (owlet moths, millers)**

1 *Ochropleura plecta* (L.) — Flame Shoulder. 25—30mm. The transportation of familiar European vegetables to all parts of the world has contributed to the worldwide distribution of this moth. It produces two generations, flying from May to July and July to September, in lowland and submontane localities, in agricultural areas and in meadows, and has a particular liking for damp biotopes overgrown with lush plants. The pupa hibernates. The caterpillar is polyphagous.

2 *Eugnorisma depuncta* (L.) — Plain Clay. 30—35mm. Widespread in northern and central Europe, this moth extends eastwards to central Asia. It can be found in lowlands, but is more abundant in submontane elevations to about 1,000m. This inhabitant of grassy woodland biotopes and upland meadows is on the wing in July and August. The caterpillar hibernates, and is polyphagous.

3 *Chersotis cuprea* (D. & S.). 28—35mm. Distributed in the hills and mountains of central and northern Europe, and the whole of temperate Asia to the Kamchatka Peninsula. Adult moths appear in July and August, and sometimes may be seen flitting around flowers even in daytime. The young caterpillar hibernates; it feeds on a variety of meadow plants.

4 *Noctua pronuba* (L.) — Large Yellow Underwing. 45—55mm. Together with the following species it belongs to a group of moths with bright yellow hindwings. The forewings are very varied in hue, generally darker in males and paler in females. With the exception of northern regions, this abundant species is distributed throughout the Palaearctic. In Europe there is only one generation, which has an exceptionally long flight period — from June till autumn. Reports of two generations produced in central Europe are incorrect. Aestivating females spend the summer in a state of dormancy and eggs do not start developing in their ovaries until August, when the length of the day falls below a critical level — about 15 hours. The caterpillars (4b), which hibernate, are polyphagous and occasionally cause some damage to vegetables.

5 *Noctua comes* (Hb.) — Lesser Yellow Underwing. 37—45mm. Occurs through central and southern Europe, eastwards into Asia Minor and Armenia. The most abundant of a complex of three very similar species (*N. orbona* (Hfn.), *N. interposita* (Hb.)). The females aestivate, oviposit towards the end of summer, and the polyphagous caterpillars hibernate. This moderately abundant species is at home in agricultural countryside, and in low-lying and submontane meadows.

6 *Noctua fimbriata* (Schreb.) — Broad-bordered Yellow Underwing. 45—55mm. Very abundant in central and southern Europe, rather rare in the north, this species ranges eastwards across the northern parts of Asia Minor, reaching its eastern limit in the Caucasus and adjacent areas. The Broad-bordered Yellow Underwing produces but one generation, flying from June to September. The young caterpillars hibernate — these can be reared continuously to pupation if exposed to artificial illumination to give more than fifteen hours daily light. Males and females have differently coloured forewings, which is rather unusual in moths. Furthermore, the forewings of males exhibit a wide range of hues — reddish, green, or brown (6♂) while the females' wings are yellowish-grey in colour.

7 *Noctua janthina* (D. & S.) — Lesser Broad-bordered Yellow Underwing. 30—40mm. This thermophilic species is distributed in warmer European lowland regions and penetrates to Asia in the southeast. It does not occur in mountains. The single generation is on the wing from July to September. The caterpillars are polyphagous and hibernate when half-grown.

4c

4♀

2

3

6♀

6♂

5

7

1

4b

Family: **Noctuidae — noctuids (owlet moths, millers)**

1 *Opigena polygona* (D. & S.). 35—40mm. Widespread throughout continental Europe, except the polar regions, and ranging eastwards to Siberia, this migratory species is evidently a permanent resident in the warm regions of the south, while in the north it develops only during the summer. This view is supported by the occurrence of two generations: the first from April to June, the second from August till late autumn. The caterpillar is polyphagous.

2 *Graphiphora augur* (F.) — Double Dart. 35—42mm. The range of this species extends from Europe to Japan. It penetrates also to North America but is absent from the warmest parts of the Palaearctic. The single generation flies from the end of June till the beginning of August. It is abundant in lower-lying, isolated localities, but can also be found at higher elevations. The caterpillar (2b) hibernates and is polyphagous.

3 *Lycophotia porphyrea* (D. & S.) — True Lover's Knot. 25—30mm. Locally distributed throughout the Palaearctic, from Europe to Japan, and from lowlands to about 2,000m. The caterpillar (3b) feeds on heather, the distribution of the species being closely determined by this. It is on the wing in June and July; the caterpillar hibernates.

4 *Diarsia mendica* (F.) — Ingrailed Clay. 28—35mm. Widespread in the forest belt of Europe and Asia as far as Mongolia and Kamchatka, this is an extremely variable species, many individual forms and geographical races having been described. The single generation flies from June to August — appearing first in lowlands, and later in the mountains. The caterpillar hibernates; it can be found in open woods and meadows, on cowslip and other broad-leaved herbs.

5 *Diarsia brunnea* (D. & S.) — Purple Clay. 35—38mm. Distributed in northern and central Europe, it ranges eastwards across the Urals and the Altai to eastern China. The single generation is on the wing from mid June to August, both in lowlands and mountains up to about 1,500m. The caterpillar hibernates and feeds on various herbs and shrubs. On spring evenings it can be found feeding on the new growth of leaves.

6 *Diarsia rubi* (View.) — Small Square-spot. 28—33mm. An inconspicuous moth inhabiting meadows and open woodland. Though it may also occur sporadically in relatively dry, warm localities, it is most abundant in damp submontane habitats and in mountains up to about 2,000m. It is distributed in non-polar Europe and in Asia, ranging far eastwards. The similar ssp. *florida* Schmidt, sometimes regarded as an independent species, represents an unresolved point. Depending on the climate, *D. rubi* has one or two generations: one flying in May and June, the other in August and September. The polyphagous caterpillar hibernates.

7 *Xestia speciosa* (Hb.). 37—45mm. Besides its circumpolar distribution in the northern tundra, it can be found in scattered localities in the mountains of central Europe and Asia, in the natural spruce-forest belt from 1,000—2,000m. In favourable situations it is relatively abundant. The species has several geographical races, including ssp. *arctica* Zett. in the north, and ssp. *obscura* Frey in the high Alps. It also presents an extraordinarily wide range of individual variations. The dark f. *millieri* is particularly notable, appearing almost like a negative of the normal colouration. The caterpillars hibernate when very young. In spring and at the beginning of summer they may be found feeding, often on bilberry. Adult moths are on the wing in July and August.

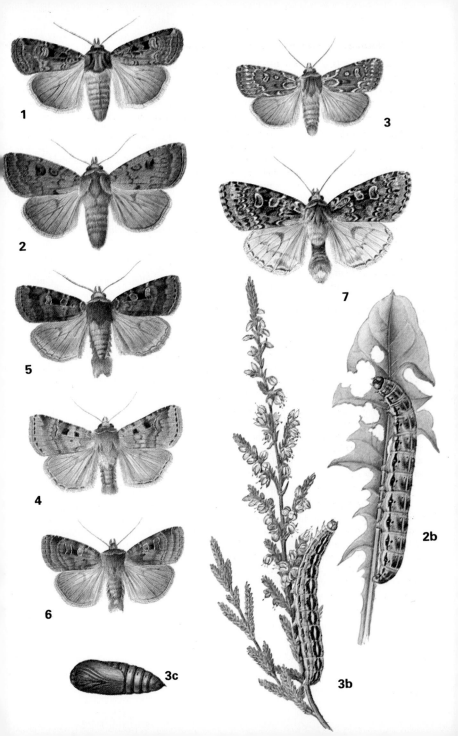

Family: **Noctuidae — noctuids (owlet moths, millers)**

1 *Xestia c-nigrum* (L.) — Setaceous Hebrew Character. 35—42mm. This is perhaps the most abundant noctuid in general — at least in open lowland habitats across the whole northern hemisphere. It has adapted excellently to agricultural environments, and in Europe often represents about 80% of all the lepidopterous insects captured in light traps. Except for a short inter-generation period in summer, it is on the wing continuously from May till October in two generations. The caterpillar (1b) is polyphagous and hibernates when half-grown, that is in the third or fourth instar.

2 *Xestia ditrapezium* (D. & S.) — Triple-spotted Clay. 35—42mm. A species which ranges across the temperate zone of Europe and Asia to the Amur. It is abundant in the lowlands, in the mountains ascending to the timberline. At home in steppes and forest-steppes, in submontane meadows, on cultivated ground near woods, etc., moths of the single generation are on the wing from June till the beginning of August. The polyphagous caterpillars hibernate.

3 *Xestia baja* (D. & S.) — Dotted Clay. 35—40mm. A typical inhabitant of the forest and forest-steppe belt, this species ranges from Europe across the whole of Asia to North America. An extremely variable insect, the basic colour varies from grey to reddish-brown, and the pattern from very bold to almost obsolete. The single generation flies in July and August. The caterpillars live on bilberry, raspberry, and a variety of other plants, from autumn till spring.

4 *Xestia xanthographa* (D. & S.) — Square-spot Rustic. 32—35mm. Distributed in the warmer regions of central Europe, in southern Europe, Asia Minor and Iran, it frequents steppes and forest-steppes, where the moth may be seen flying in August and September. The polyphagous caterpillar does not hatch until spring, and grows to full size by early summer.

5 *Naenia typica* (L.) — Gothic. 33—40mm. A rather rare species which of late has been substantially decreasing in numbers. It can be found in damp localities, mostly at submontane elevations, but also in lowlands. The single generation is on the wing from June to August. The polyphagous caterpillar lives on various herbs, from autumn till spring.

6 *Eurois occulta* (L.) — Great Brocade. 50—60mm. Widespread in the north of Europe and the whole of Asia, confined to scattered localities in the mountains and foothills of regions situated more to the south, this moth inhabits the taiga and reaches the borders of the tundra. Alaska and northern Canada are included in its range. In central Europe it keeps to spruce forests with an undergrowth of bilberry. The polyphagous caterpillar hibernates while young and after reawakening in spring is to be found feeding on the young leaves of bilberry, birch, etc.

7 *Anaplectoides prasina* (D. & S.) — Green Arches. 40—50mm. This inhabitant of wooded regions is widespread at submontane elevations in Europe, Asia and North America. It is associated with taiga and penetrates into the tundra, but also occurs in forest-steppes and mountains, where it ascends up to 2,000m. A variable species as regards colouration, its typical greenish colour is sometimes replaced by red; sometimes the moths may be greyish-brown, as is the case with the northern f. *lugubris*. The single generation flies from June to August; the polyphagous caterpillar lives from autumn to spring.

8 *Mesogona acetosellae* (D. & S.) — Pale Stigma. 35—40mm. This moth inhabits the warmer regions of Europe and Asia as far as the Altai, occurring in deciduous forests and forest-steppes. The adults fly in August and September. The egg hibernates, and the caterpillar lives in spring on blackthorn, oak, and other shrubs and deciduous trees.

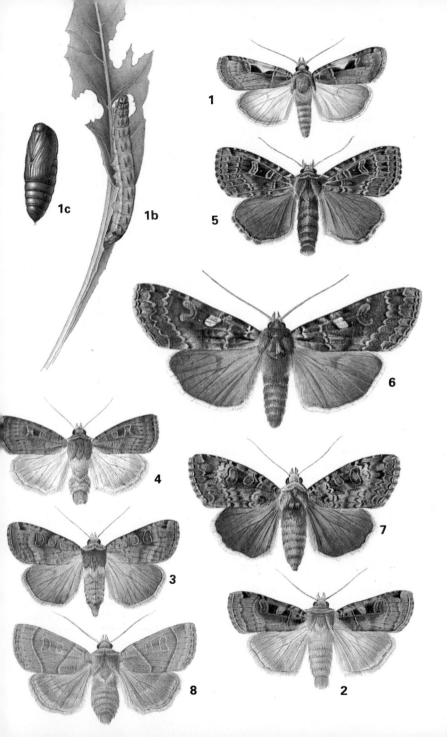

Family: **Noctuidae — noctuids (owlet moths, millers)**

1 *Anarta myrtilli* (L.) — Beautiful Yellow Underwing. 20—22mm. The range of this moth in Europe is restricted by the distribution of heather. It is absent from polar regions, but is otherwise generally distributed in both warm and cold areas. Depending on local climate, it has one or two generations. Peat-bogs are favourable habitats for the species, even though it produces only one generation in such situations. This swift day-flier is on the wing on sunny days only. The well-camouflaged caterpillars (1b) can be found towards the end of summer on heather; they are frequently parasitized. The pupa hibernates.

2 *Anarta cordigera* (Thbg.) — Small Dark Yellow Underwing. 20—25mm. A species with a Boreo-Alpine distribution, continuous in the northern tundra, but local farther south, it occurs in Europe, Asia and North America. In central Europe it can be found in high mountains or on peat-bogs. The single generation flies on sunny days from May to July. The caterpillar lives in summer on *Vaccinium uliginosum,* and probably on several other bog plants.

3 *Discestra trifolii* (Hfn.) — Nutmeg. 30—35mm. Distributed throughout the temperate zone of Europe and Asia, also reported from North America, this species occurs neither in the extreme north or south, nor in high mountains. Characteristic of meadows and steppes, it has adapted excellently to cultivated land, where it causes damage from time to time. There are two or three generations annually, from May to October. The caterpillar (3b) is polyphagous; the pupa hibernates.

4 *Hada nana* (Hfn.) — Shears. 30—35mm. Widespread in both Europe and Asia, this moth ranges to the Far East. It can be found in both warmer and colder localities, where it flies in one or two generations, from May to September. In mountains it ascends to high altitudes, sometimes to situations above the timberline. The species is given to great variation. The caterpillar lives in summer and in autumn and is polyphagous. The pupa hibernates.

5 *Polia bombycina* (Hfn.) — Pale Shining Brown. 40—50mm. This species ranges from Europe as far as North America but is confined to the temperate zone. It inhabits deciduous forests and forest-steppes but is also common on arable land. The single generation flies in June and July. The polyphagous caterpillar hibernates and pupates in spring.

6 *Polia nebulosa* (Hfn.) — Grey Arches. 45—55mm. With a distribution similar to that of the preceding species, this moth is found even in the mountains, where it ascends to considerable altitudes. It is at home in steppes, open woods, shrubby slopes, or in valleys overgrown with lush vegetation. The single generation is on the wing from the end of May till July. The caterpillar (6b) lives on various plants. After hibernation it completes its development and then pupates.

7 *Pachetra sagittigera* (Hfn.) — Feathered Ear. 35—45mm. A moth which inhabits the warm regions of Europe east as far as southern Siberia. It can be found in steppes and forest-steppes where it annually produces one, exceptionally two generations, flying in May and June: if there is a second generation it appears in August. The polyphagous caterpillar often shows a particular liking for milfoil. The pupa hibernates.

8 *Heliophobus reticulata* (Gz.) — Bordered Gothic. 32—37mm. Found in the warmer regions of Europe, this moth ranges in the east to central Asia. It produces one generation, on the wing during June and July in meadows, low-lying woods, and wasteland in the vicinity of human settlements. The caterpillars live on unripe seeds as well as leaves of plants of the pink family, particularly on soapwort, catchflies, and others. The pupa hibernates.

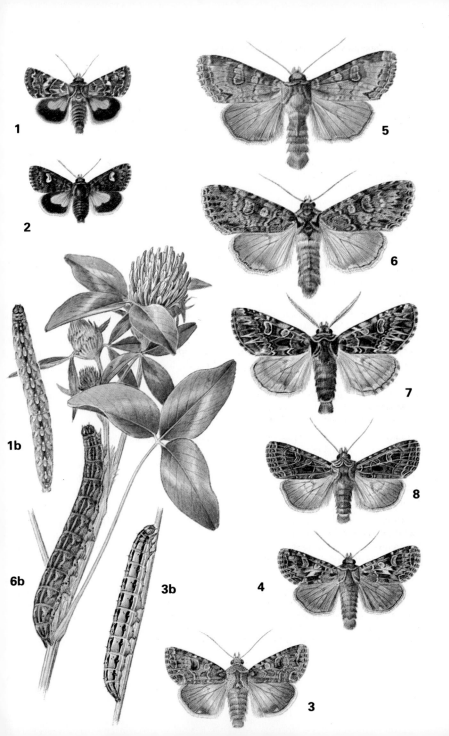

Family: **Noctuidae — noctuids (owlet moths, millers)**

1 *Mamestra brassicae* (L.) — Cabbage. 37—45mm. The distribution of this moth is Palaearctic, from western Europe to Japan; it also occurs in North America. Though most abundant in lowlands, it also lives in mountains up to 2,000m. One of the commonest agricultural pests, especially of vegetables, in cool climates it produces one generation, in warm climates two or three — these are on the wing from May to October. The caterpillar (1b) is polyphagous; the pupa hibernates.

2 *Melanchra persicariae* (L.) — Dot. 37—40mm. Generally distributed in the mild zone of the Palaearctic subregion, the only generation of this moth flies from May to August. There is considerable variability in the colour of the kidney-shaped spot on the black wings. In f. *accipitrina* this spot is reddish-brown, while in f. *unicolor* it is black in the middle. The caterpillars, to be found in July and August, are polyphagous and occasionally attack vegetables; the pupae hibernate.

3 *Lacanobia thalassina* (Hfn.) — Pale-shouldered Brocade. 35—38mm. An extremely variable species as regards both colour and pattern. It is widespread in the forest belt of the whole of temperate Europe and Asia, and ascends high in the mountains. Annually it usually produces one generation, but in the south there are two. It flies from May to July. The caterpillars are polyphagous, living on herbs but also on shrubs and trees. The pupa hibernates.

4 *Lacanobia suasa* (D. & S.) — Dog's Tooth. 32—37mm. This noctuid ranges from Europe to North America. It is found in meadows, forest-steppes and open woods, mostly in lowlands, and has adapted well to the agricultural environment of fields, gardens and wastelands. The Dog's Tooth is often a significant pest. This highly variable moth has two generations: one flies in May and June, the other in August and September. The caterpillar completes its development in autumn, and the pupa hibernates.

5 *Lacanobia oleracea* (L.) — Bright-line Brown-eye. 32—37mm. A species whose distribution is Palaearctic, according to climatic conditions it produces one to three generations, flying from May to September. The caterpillars are polyphagous, and the pupae hibernate. A species which can be a pest, it is closely monitored for agricultural purposes.

6 *Ceramica pisi* (L.) — Broom. 32—37mm. Peculiar to submontane habitats in central and northern Europe and Asia, from where it ranges to the Far East, this species is decreasing in numbers. The flight of its single brood is of short duration, but depending largely on elevation, it can take place at any time between May and July. The polyphagous caterpillars occur in two forms: brown (6b) or green, striped with yellow. In summer they may frequently be found on weeds growing amongst stubble, on clover, peas and in flax fields. The pupae hibernate.

7 *Hadena rivularis* (F.) — Campion. 27—30mm. Distributed in lowlands and submontane elevations of the temperate zone, from Europe to eastern Asia, this species is fond of meadows and slopes where the caterpillars live in the pericarps of plants of the pink family. One or two generations develop during the year, flying from May to August. The pupa hibernates.

8 *Hadena compta* (D. & S.) — Varied Coronet. 25—30mm. Distributed throughout the temperate Palaearctic as far as Japan, it is not an abundant species anywhere. The size of the white markings on the wings varies. The single generation flies from May to July. The caterpillars live in the pericarps of catchflies and pinks; hibernation occurs in the pupal stage.

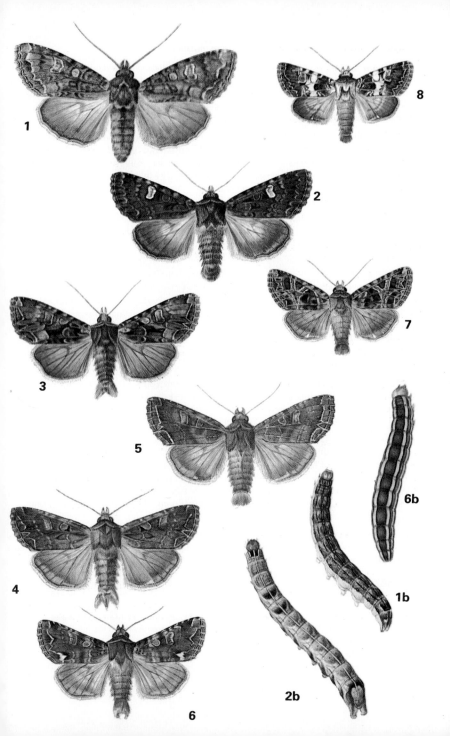

Family: **Noctuidae — noctuids (owlet moths, millers)**

1 *Eriopygodes imbecilla* (F.) — Silurian. 22—28mm. A locally abundant submontane and montane species, inhabiting wet meadows and peaty biotopes, often close to streams and springs. It is locally distributed in central and northern Europe, ranging eastwards across the Urals and Siberia to Mongolia. The single generation flies in June and July, and the caterpillars hibernate.

2 *Tholera decimalis* (Poda) — Feathered Gothic. 32—45mm. A species associated with meadows and steppes throughout the temperate zone of Europe and Asia. It flies in August and September. The caterpillars hatch in autumn and hibernate while very young; they feed on a variety of grasses. This moth is one of the very few species of the family Noctuidae in which the male has pectinate antennae.

3 *Panolis flammea* (D. & S.) — Pine Beauty. 30—33mm. Widespread in non-polar Europe and Asia, as far as Japan, it occurs in coniferous forests in both the south and the north, in lowlands and in highlands, having only one generation everywhere. Adult moths are on the wing in April and May; the caterpillars (3b) live gregariously on pines and other conifers in summer, and often cause calamitous damage to forests. The pupae hibernate amongst moss and litter.

4 *Egira conspicillaris* (L.) — Silver Cloud. 33—37mm. Distributed throughout temperate and warm Europe, in Asia this species ranges eastwards to the Altai. Recently this characteristic species of forests and forest-steppes has shifted to urban parks, gardens and orchards. The moths are exceedingly variable. The f. *melaleuca* (4c) is marked with contrasting colours, and the variegated f. *intermedia* appear in great numbers. This single-brooded species flies in April and May. The caterpillar develops during summer, and the pupa hibernates.

5 *Orthosia cruda* (D. & S.) — Small Quaker. 25—30mm. One of the most abundant moths of early spring, it can be beaten off flowering sallow catkins as early as March or April. It exhibits a wide range of variation. The ground colour ranges from grey through yellowish to reddish. Males have comb-like antennae. Suitable habitats include lowlands and highlands, damp woods situated at low elevations, and deciduous forests; it occurs all over Europe, extending east as far as the Volga basin and Armenia. The caterpillar completes its development on deciduous trees by the end of spring; the pupa hibernates.

6 *Orthosia incerta* (Hfn.) — Clouded Drab. 35—40mm. This abundant species starts to fly in the first warm days of March; its flight ends at the beginning of May. With the exception of polar regions, it occurs throughout Europe, Asia and America. Its colouration is extremely variable (for example, f. *obscura* 6c): it would be difficult to find two identical specimens. The caterpillars live in spring on deciduous trees; the pupae spend the winter in diapause, the moth developing and emerging early in the spring.

7 *Orthosia gothica* (L.) — Hebrew Character. 30—35mm. Inhabits all mild regions of the Palaearctic, and though most abundant in lowlands, this moth is frequently also found at high mountain altitudes. It appears on the wing early in spring, from March to May. Males possess pectinate antennae, while the females have a somewhat more conspicuous design. The caterpillars (7b) develop in spring and live on various herbaceous plants. The pupa hibernates. There is but one generation a year.

8 *Orthosia gracilis* (D. & S.) — Powdered Quaker. 35—40mm. Even though it is also a spring species, it is the last of the *Orthosia* group to start flying — from April till the beginning of June. It exhibits many variations, pinkish specimens being fairly common; there is also some sexual dimorphism. The caterpillars (8b) develop in spring between spun-up leaves of various herbs, including clover and wormwood. The pupae hibernate in the ground.

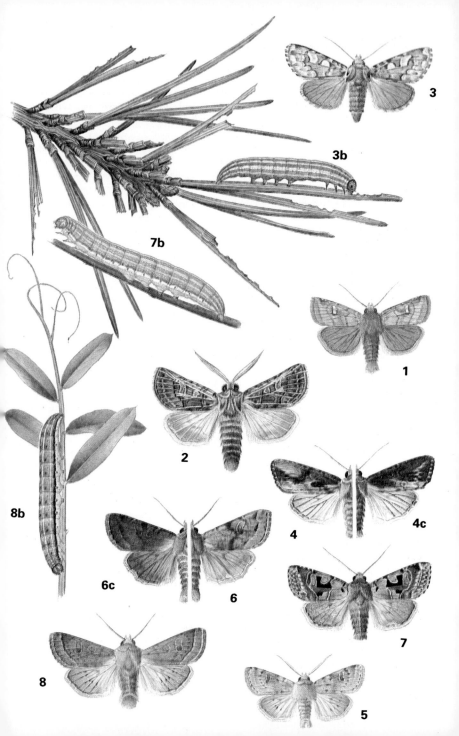

Family: **Noctuidae — noctuids (owlet moths, millers)**

1 *Mythimna turca* (L.) — Double Line. 37—45mm. A species distributed throughout the temperate zone of the Palaearctic subregion, it occurs more abundantly in the north and in regions with a humid and cool climate. Its one generation (or two in more southern habitats) can be seen on the wing from June to the beginning of August. Its main haunts are peat-bog margins, damp meadows and heather moors. The caterpillar, which hibernates, feeds on various grasses.

2 *Mythimna conigera* (D. & S.) — Brown-line Bright-eye. 30—35mm. Inhabiting the whole mild belt of the Palaearctic, ranging from western Europe to Japan, this moth may be seen flying from June to August in forest clearings and glades, along woodland margins and meadows covered with profuse vegetation. The caterpillar is polyphagous. It pupates in spring.

3 *Mythimna ferrago* (F.) — Clay. 35—40mm. Ranging throughout Europe and eastwards to central Asia, this species is only absent from the extreme north and south. It is particularly abundant in the warmer regions of central Europe. The moth is on the wing from the end of July till mid August, in various biotopes, but is not found in large forests. The caterpillar hibernates. It feeds on a variety of soft grasses.

4 *Mythimna albipuncta* (D. & S.) — White-point. 30—35mm. In the dry, grassy biotopes of central Europe this is one of the most abundant moth species. Eastwards it ranges to central Asia. It can be found at elevations up to 1,000m but at higher altitudes it is less abundant. There are two generations, the first of which flies from May to July, the second from August to September. The species is given to considerable variation. The caterpillar of the second generation hibernates. Various kinds of grasses constitute its diet.

5 *Mythimna pudorina* (D. & S.) — Striped Wainscot. 35—38mm. An inhabitant of central and northern Europe (absent from southernmost parts), it extends eastwards into Asia as far as the Amur and Ussuri basins. The single generation flies from the end of May till July, but is never abundant. It shows a preference for moist biotopes, riversides and pond margins, damp meadows and peat-bogs. The caterpillar lives from autumn till spring on reeds and other marsh grasses.

6 *Mythimna pallens* (L.) — Common Wainscot. 30—35mm. A plain and common moth peculiar to meadow biotopes, including both dry steppe meadows and damp ones. It ascends the mountains to considerable elevations, although it may be replaced high up by another, similar species. It has a Palaearctic distribution and also ranges to North America. In cooler regions there is a single brood in July and August; in warmer areas two generations appear on the wing from May till October. The caterpillars of the second generation hibernate; they are polyphagous, but may show a preference for various kinds of grasses (6b).

7 *Mythimna l-album* (L.) — L-album Wainscot. 30—35mm. A migrant, arriving annually in the north from the subtropics of Africa and western and eastern Asia. It never hibernates in central Europe or further to the north. The immigration lasts from May to July; one generation develops during the summer, the adults of which appear on the wing in the autumn until frosts set in, and then gradually disappear. Sometimes they find refuge in glasshouses, where they can cause much damage to produce.

8 *Mythimna comma* (L.) — Shoulder-striped Wainscot. 32—37mm. Distributed in non-polar temperate Europe and Asia, spreading as far as the Amur. It prefers damp localities, especially meadows, slopes and open, grassy woods. The moths are on the wing from May to July; occasionally a second brood makes its appearance from August to October. The caterpillars, which eat various kinds of grass, hibernate.

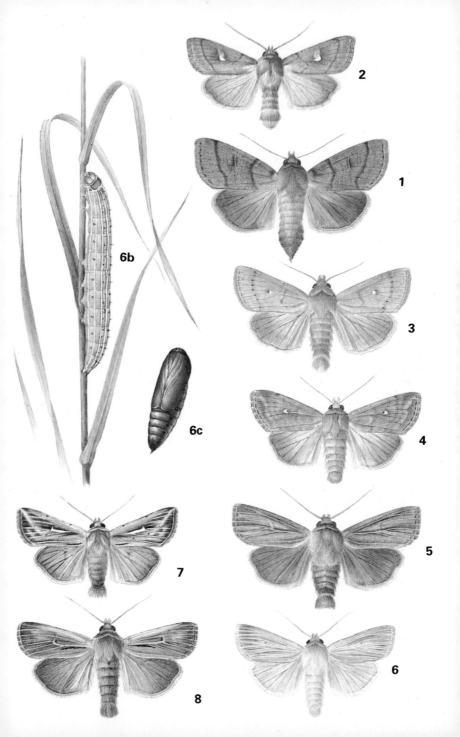

Family: **Noctuidae — noctuids (owlet moths, millers)**

1 *Cucullia fraudatrix* Ev. 30—35mm. A thermophilic species ranging from central and southern Europe far eastwards into Asia, to the Amur. There is but one generation, flying from the end of July till mid August. The caterpillars develop towards the end of summer, on wormwood; the pupa hibernates. In the last few decades this moth has extended its range northwards considerably — it seems to profit from agricultural changes which are conducive to the growth of wasteland plants.

2 *Cucullia artemisiae* (Hfn.) — Scarce Wormwood. 37—42mm. This moth occurs in localities on sandy ground in the mild regions of Europe and Asia, spreading east to the Amur basin. Its one generation flies in June and July; the caterpillars are found towards the end of August and in September on flowering wormwood. Their protective colouration is most effective (2b). The pupae hibernate in the ground in firm cocoons constructed of earth and plant particles.

3 *Cucullia absinthii* (L.) — Wormwood. 32—40mm. With a range and biology similar to that of the preceding species, the adults of this moth are on the wing in June and July. The caterpillars develop on wormwood towards the end of summer, and the pupae hibernate. The caterpillar also shows a well-developed cryptic colouration (3b). Both species are locally abundant, but otherwise extremely rare in many areas.

4 *Cucullia chamomillae* (D. & S.) — Chamomile Shark. 40—42mm. Distributed in the warmer regions of Europe and ranging across Asia Minor to the east, this is one of the species appearing very early in the year: its time of flight begins as early as April and ends at the beginning of June. In early July the caterpillars can be found on chamomiles and mayweeds, etc. The pupa hibernates.

5 *Cucullia umbratica* (L.) — Shark. 42—52mm. Ranges across Europe to central Asia and is the most abundant species of this large genus. It is on the wing from May to August. The caterpillar develops towards the end of summer and feeds on various low plants; the pupa hibernates.

6 *Cucullia verbasci* (L.) — Mullein. 45—50mm. This species inhabits a limited range of localities in Europe, and expands eastwards to the Volga, Armenia and Syria. It flies very early in the year, in April and May. The caterpillars (6b) live in May and June on various mulleins. The pupa hibernates.

7 *Brachionycha nubeculosa* (Esp.) — Rannoch Sprawler. 45—48mm. Ranging from central and northern Europe eastwards to the Amur, this is one of the earliest moths to emerge in spring, flying in March and in April. It is at home in mixed forests and low-lying woodlands, particularly in damp places, on riversides, etc. The caterpillars feed on the foliage of various deciduous trees in May and June; the pupae hibernate.

8 *Dasypolia templi* (Thbg.) — Brindled Ochre. 35—40mm. Widespread in mountainous areas of central and northern Europe as well as in some mountains of Asia. The moth is very abundant in a limited range of localities in the Alps and the Sudetes. It is on the wing in autumn, from September onward, and hibernates. After emerging from hibernation it continues to fly till May. The caterpillars develop in summer on the roots and stalks of umbelliferous plants, most often on cow-parsnip. This moth has a markedly discontinuous distribution, and several clearly defined geographical races have been described.

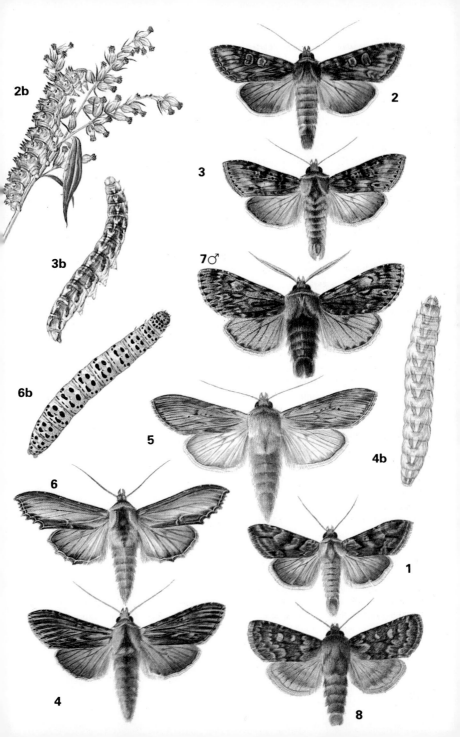

Family: **Noctuidae — noctuids (owlet moths, millers)**

1 *Calliergis ramosa* (Esp.). 28—32mm. A moth characteristic of European uplands where it lives in valleys, and thin mixed and coniferous forests up to an altitude of about 1,000m. There is only one brood in the year, on the wing in May and June. The caterpillar lives in July and August on various kinds of honeysuckle.

2 *Lithomoia solidaginis* (Hb.) — Goldenrod Brindle. 40—45mm. Widely distributed through the northern and mild parts of the Palaearctic, and also in North America. It is strictly confined to specific biotopes, mostly in sparse pine forests with an undergrowth of heather, in outskirts of woods and clearings within them, and in peat-bogs. The moth lives from August till autumn, the egg hibernates, and the caterpillar feeds on *Vaccinium*, willow, etc. from May to July. It is a local species.

3 *Lithophane socia* (Hfn.) — Pale Pinion. 38—42mm. Within its Palaearctic range it extends to the north and quite far to the south. It can be found in various biotopes rich in deciduous trees and shrubs, also in gardens, orchards and urban parks to which it has become adapted. Nowhere, however, is it abundant. The moth starts flying in August, and, after emerging from its winter sleep, it reassumes its flight till May. The caterpillar develops in early summer on various deciduous trees (including fruit trees).

4 *Lithophane ornitopus* (Hfn.) — Grey Shoulder-knot. 32—38mm. Widespread in the temperate and warm zones of the whole Europe and Asia, as far as Japan, this species is relatively common in deciduous forests and forest-steppes. The moth lives from August to May (hibernating in the winter); the caterpillar feeds on oak, willow, etc., and is full-fed by the beginning of summer.

5 *Xylena vetusta* (Hb.) — Red Sword-grass. 50—57mm. Generally distributed throughout Europe, Asia and North America, this moth tolerates various biotopes — open woodland, meadows, fields, forest margins and peat-bogs. Though it emerges at the end of summer, it becomes most active only after hibernation, from April till June. The fully developed caterpillar forms a little cell in the ground in which to pupate — before doing so, however, it rests in this cell for a long time. The adult moth emerges soon after pupation. The caterpillars (5b) are polyphagous and can frequently be found on crops.

6 *Xylena exsoleta* (L.) — Sword-grass. 55—65mm. Widespread in the temperate regions of Europe as far as the Caucasus, the bionomics and annual cycle of this moth are similar to those of the preceding species. Its caterpillars have frequently been found on flax, beet and vegetables; they are polyphagous. The adult moths hibernate, and during warm spells in the winter they sometimes appear on snow.

7 *Allophyes oxyacanthae* (L.) — Green-brindled Crescent. 35—45mm. Inhabiting deciduous forests and forest-steppes of Europe and Asia, the moths are on the wing in autumn, during September and October. They are easily lured with bait and come swarming in great numbers. The eggs hibernate, and the caterpillars live in spring on blackthorn, apple trees, hawthorn, etc. In some regions the species shows a tendency to melanism.

8 *Dichonia aprilina* (L.) — Merveille du Jour. 35—40mm. Distributed in the temperate and warm regions of Europe and Asia Minor, this species is associated with deciduous forests and forest-steppes. It flies late in autumn, from August to October. The eggs hibernate, and the caterpillars develop in spring, in May and June, feeding on the foliage of oaks, hornbeams, limes, apple trees, etc. It is a local and rather rare species.

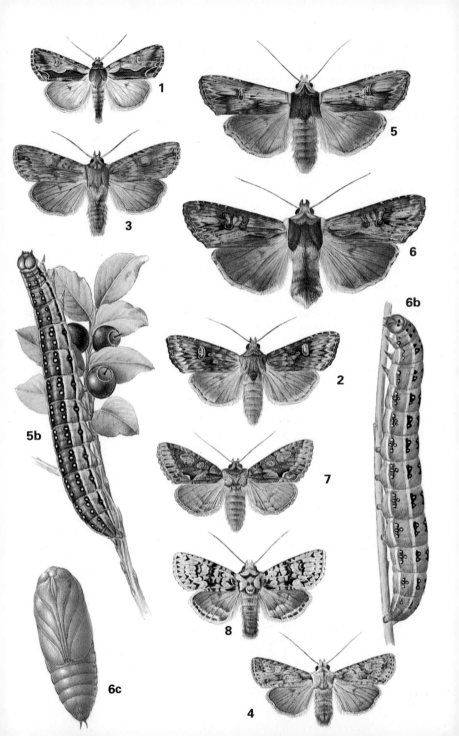

Family: Noctuidae — noctuids (owlet moths, millers)

1 *Blepharita satura* (D. & S.) — Beautiful Arches. 40—45mm. Distributed in the temperate zone throughout the Palaearctic subregion, this moth lives in mixed and coniferous forests, on shrubby slopes and in lowland woods. It is found both at low elevations and high up in the mountains. A herald of autumn, the single generation takes wing in mid August and continues flying as late as October. The eggs hibernate; the caterpillars live in May and June on a variety of plants.

2 *Antitype chi* (L.) — Grey Chi. 32—37mm. A species widespread in the temperate zone of Europe, stretching eastwards to the Altai. This moth is characteristic of dry and sparse mixed forests and their margins, forest-steppes, and valleys, through which it penetrates into the mountains — to about 1,000m. The single generation flies from August to October. The eggs hibernate, and the polyphagous caterpillar develops in spring. This species shows a wide range of variation.

3 *Ammoconia caecimacula* (D. & S.). 40—45mm. Widespread in non-polar Europe as far as the Urals, in Asia Minor, and far into Asia, this moth is on the wing in autumn — from the end of August to October — and is often easily attracted to bait or to light. It is found both in lowlands and in highlands. The egg hibernates; the caterpillar lives in spring and is polyphagous.

4 *Eupsilia transversa* (Hfn.) — Satellite. 32—42mm. Distributed practically throughout the entire Palaearctic, from lowlands to high altitudes, especially in deciduous forests and forest-steppes, this moth has become well adapted to urban parks and orchards. The adult is polymorphic. The nominate grey-brown form is rare. Forms *rufescens* (yellowish-brown — 4) and *rufosatellitia* (with orange spot — 4d) are frequent. The moth, which hibernates, is on the wing from September to May and often appears even in winter, if there is a sudden spell of warmer weather. The caterpillars (4b) live in spring on various deciduous trees. Being predatory, they eat, in addition to foliage, caterpillars of leaf rollers, ermine moths and other moths

5 *Conistra vaccinii* (L.) — Chestnut. 28—35mm. Living in the belt of deciduous forests and forest-steppes, this species ranges through the whole Palaearctic subregion — from western Europe to Japan. The adult moth, which hibernates, is on the wing in September, and continues until the arrival of the first frosts. It oviposits in the following spring, until May — at higher elevations even later on. The caterpillar (5b) emerges in spring and eats the leaves of various herbs and shrubs. This species is characterized by extraordinary variability, even among specimens from the same locality occurring at the same season.

6 *Conistra rubiginosa* (Scop.). 30—35mm. This moth occurs in the warmer parts of Europe, predominantly in forest-steppes. The adult does not start flying before October and hibernates, as with other species of the genus *Conistra*. The females lay their eggs in spring, and the caterpillars live from April to June — initially on blackthorn, later on a variety of low-growing plants.

7 *Conistra rubiginea* (D. & S.) — Dotted Chestnut. 30—35mm. Widespread all over the temperate parts of the Palaearctic as far as Japan, this moth is associated with various biotopes, being found in mixed and deciduous forests, on warm slopes, and on heather-covered moors. The adults appear in autumn (about September) but they show little activity at this time. On emerging from hibernation in spring they come to flowering sallows, from which they can be collected in the evenings. The caterpillar (7b) lives from May to July on oak, willow, and other trees, frequently on low-growing plants also.

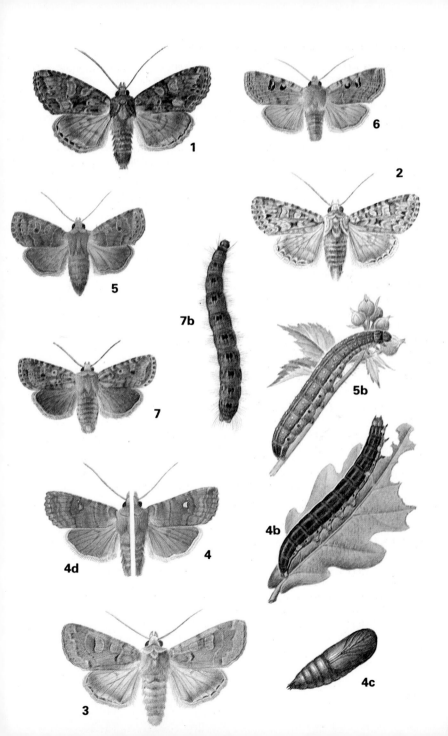

Family: **Noctuidae — noctuids (owlet moths, millers)**

1 *Agrochola circellaris* (Hfn.) — Brick. 33—38mm. Very widely distributed in the temperate zone of Europe and Asia, and also in North America, this moth is found in lowlands and in the mountains, in forest-steppes, deciduous forests, lowland woods, and also in peat-bogs. There is but one brood in the year, and this is on the wing from mid August till October. The eggs hibernate, and caterpillars emerge in spring to eat the foliage of various shrubs and trees, later on also herbs.

2 *Agrochola helvola* (L.) — Flounced Chestnut. 30—35mm. A species which occurs all over Europe, ranging eastwards to central Asia. It inhabits deciduous or mixed forests having abundant undergrowth, watersides, sandy pine forests, and often peat-bogs, from lowlands to high mountain elevations. The adults fly from the end of August to October, the eggs hibernate, the caterpillars live in spring on deciduous trees, later on low-growing plants.

3 *Agrochola litura* (L.) — Brown-spot Pinion. 28—35mm. Widespread in the whole of non-polar Europe, eastwards to Armenia and Asia Minor, the only generation of this moth appears on the wing from August to October. The eggs hibernate, and the polyphagous caterpillars live in spring until June, on a variety of low plants.

4 *Agrochola lychnidis* (D. & S.) — Beaded Chestnut. 30—35mm. Although it is the most abundant species of the genus *Agrochola,* it is confined to the warmer biotopes of Europe and Asia Minor, as far as Syria. Its most usual habitats are thin deciduous forests with profuse undergrowth, forest-steppes, and various types of grassy biotopes. This extremely variable species includes dozens of individual forms. The moth is on the wing from August till the end of autumn. The eggs hibernate, and the caterpillars (4b) develop in spring on various trees until June, transferring to various herbs later on.

5 *Xanthia aurago* (D. & S.) — Barred Sallow. 27—32mm. Widespread in warm deciduous forests of Europe, this species is absent from higher elevations. It presents a wide range of individual pattern variations, in addition to sexual dimorphism. The time of flight is from the end of August till October. The eggs hibernate and the caterpillars live in spring on oak, lime, poplar, etc.

6 *Xanthia togata* (Esp.) — Pink-barred Sallow. 27—30mm. Frequent in the temperate and northern parts of the whole Palaearctic and in North America, this moth is distributed in lowlands as well as in the mountains, where it reaches the deciduous forest line. The time of flight of its single generation begins towards the end of August and continues until October. The eggs hibernate and in spring the caterpillars feed on sallow catkins; at a later time they live near the ground, eating a variety of plants.

7 *Xanthia icteritia* (Hfn.) — Sallow. 27—35mm. An abundant species distributed throughout the deciduous-forest belt of the entire Palaearctic, favouring damp localities rich in sallows. There is one generation in the year, on the wing from August to October. The eggs hibernate, and in spring the caterpillars (7b) eat sallow catkins; when larger in size, they take to the ground to feed on various herbs. Subsequently they enter the soil and pupate (7c) in tough earthen cells reinforced by silk.

8 *Xanthia citrago* (L.) — Orange Sallow. 28—33mm. A species widespread all over Europe, with the exception of the extreme south. It occurs in damp deciduous forests, woodland margins, clearings and glades, and on slopes overgrown with vegetation. The moths are on the wing from August to October. The eggs hibernate, and the caterpillars may be found by day during spring amongst undergrowth at the base of lime trees; at night the larvae ascend the trunk to feed on the leaves.

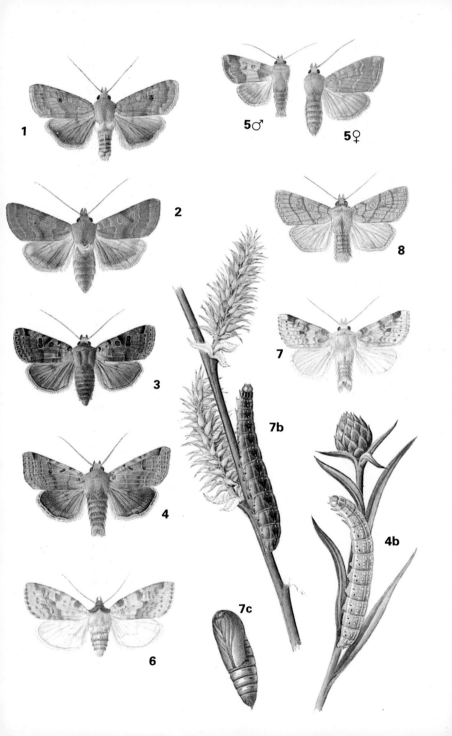

Family: **Noctuidae** — **noctuids (owlet moths, millers)**

1 *Moma alpium* (Osb.) — Scarce Merveille du Jour. 30—35mm. Occurring in non-polar Europe, in the east as far as central Asia, this species is to be found in deciduous forests or heather-covered peat-bogs. The moth is on the wing from May to August. The caterpillar lives from July to September on oak, beech, birch and other deciduous trees; the pupa hibernates.

2 *Acronicta aceris* (L.) — Sycamore. 35—45mm. Distributed in the mild zone of Europe, ranging in the east to central Asia, this moth is characteristic of deciduous forests in warmer situations, but has become equally at home in urban parks. It may be seen flying from May to August. The caterpillar completes its development at the beginning of autumn; it lives on various deciduous trees, particularly horse chestnut, apple, hazel, etc. The pupa hibernates in a flimsy cocoon.

3 *Acronicta leporina* (L.) — Miller. 35—42mm. An inhabitant of cooler and mild regions of Europe, spreading eastwards far into Asia, it often occurs in the mountains. According to elevation and climatic conditions, it flies from May to August in various scattered localities. In warmer regions a partial second brood may emerge. The caterpillar (3b) lives from July to September, showing a particular preference for birches, but also eating willow, poplar, etc. The pupa hibernates.

4 *Acronicta alni* (L.) — Alder. 33—38mm. A species widely distributed throughout Europe, except the extreme south; eastwards it ranges to Armenia and the Amur basin. The moth flies in damp deciduous forests, in valleys and on watersides in May and June. The caterpillar lives on various deciduous trees — especially willow, oak, and alder — from June to September. It is noteworthy for its colouration and clubbed hairs (4b). The pupa hibernates.

5 *Acronicta psi* (L.) — Grey Dagger. 30—40mm. The most abundant of three exceedingly similar species (*A. tridens* (D. & S.) and *A. cuspis* (Hb.)) which, however, can easily be distinguished by the caterpillars. It does not occur in cool situations. Usually there is only one brood in the year, but a partial second brood may appear in the south. The moth is on the wing from May to August. The caterpillar lives from June to August on a variety of trees and shrubs. The pupa hibernates.

6 *Acronicta rumicis* (L.) — Knot Grass. 30—35mm. With the exception of polar regions, this moth has a Palaearctic distribution and, depending on climatic conditions, produces one to three generations. In central Europe there are usually two generations, flying from April to September. The polyphagous caterpillar (6b), feeding on a variety of herbs, may be an occasional pest of cultivated plants. The pupa (6c) hibernates in a flimsy cocoon.

7 *Craniophora ligustri* (D. & S.) — Coronet. 30—35mm. Widespread in the temperate zone of the whole Palaearctic, it is a characteristic species of deciduous or mixed forests and of forest-steppes. There are two broods of this moth annually: one is on the wing from May to July, the other in August and September. The caterpillar lives on ash, privet and lilac. The pupa hibernates. In areas where the atmosphere is polluted by industry, these moths show a tendency to melanism, producing dark forms such as f. *nigra* (7c).

8 *Cryphia domestica* (Hfn.) — Marbled Beauty. 20—25mm. A variable species, distributed in all the warmer parts of Europe as far as the Caucasus. Its single generation flies in July and August. The caterpillar, which hibernates, lives on various lichens and mosses growing on walls and tree trunks.

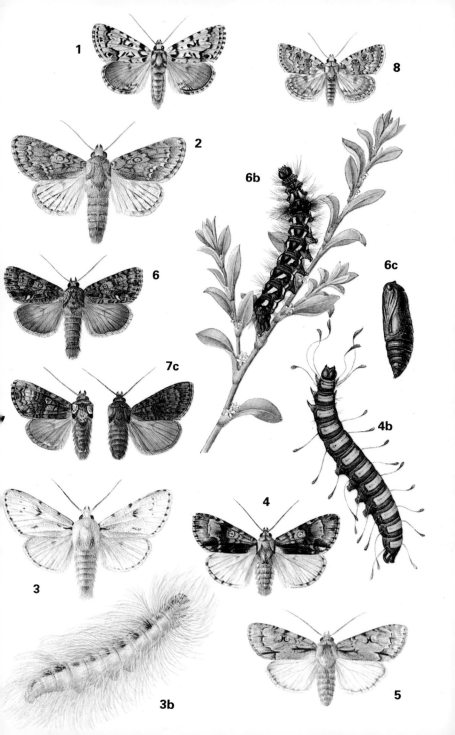

Family: **Noctuidae — noctuids (owlet moths, millers)**

1 *Amphipyra pyramidea* (L.) — Copper Underwing. 40—52mm. Widespread in the belt of deciduous forests ranging across Europe and Asia to Japan, this moth produces a single generation, on the wing from mid July to the end of September. The egg hibernates, and the polyphagous caterpillar (1b) develops in spring. This species does not show much general variation — nevertheless, several interesting forms have been described. Among these a very similar but separate species has recently been recognised, named *A. berbera* Rungs (Svensson's Copper Underwing). So far, little is known about its distribution, but it is also to be found in Europe.

2 *Amphipyra tragopogonis* (Cl.) — Mouse. 33—38mm. Widely and abundantly distributed in the whole of temperate Europe and Asia, this species can be found in mountains, but its main haunts are meadows and woodland margins, in shrubs bordering streams, etc. This single-brooded moth is on the wing from July to October. The eggs hibernate unhatched, and the polyphagous caterpillars develop in spring. The adult moths are interesting for their habit of hiding in crevices, under the bark of trees, and so on.

3 *Mormo maura* (L.) — Old Lady. 55—65mm. With a range which extends throughout Europe and Asia and further southeastwards, this moth is at home in damp biotopes, especially along the banks of brooks and rivers, where it can be seen on the wing in July and August. In urban areas it often roosts in out-buildings, porches, etc. The caterpillar lives from autumn until the following spring, on alder, sallow, and a variety of herbs.

4 *Dypterygia scabriuscula* (L.) — Bird's Wing. 32—37mm. Generally distributed in Europe, this species reaches far to the north, and is also found in Asia as far as Japan, and in North America. However, it is never abundant in any of its habitats. One or two generations emerge in the year, which remain on the wing practically continuously from May to September. Caterpillars of the winter brood hibernate; they are polyphagous.

5 *Trachea atriplicis* (L.) — Orache Moth. 38—42mm. A Palaearctic species occurring as far east as Japan. It is found in varied open-country habitats, chiefly in meadows, heaths and peat-bogs in lowlands, also in fields and wasteland. The time of flight of the two annual generations lasts from May up to October. The caterpillars live in the summer and autumn on various low-growing herbs, showing a preference for orache and knotgrass. The pupa hibernates. Of recent years, this species has become exceedingly rare in central Europe.

6 *Euplexia lucipara* (L.) — Small Angle Shades. 27—32mm. Ranging from Europe across Asia to North America, this moth mostly inhabits rather damp biotopes with abundant vegetation, meadows, riverbanks, valleys, etc. According to climate, it produces one or two broods, which emerge from May to August. The caterpillars are polyphagous but have a definite preference for common nettle. The pupa hibernates.

7 *Phlogophora meticulosa* (L.) — Angle Shades. 45—50mm. A migratory species native to the European and African parts of the Mediterranean region, ranging east to the Caucasus. The moths arrive in the north from April to July and the new generation flies from August until late autumn, when they probably set out on a return migration to the south. The polyphagous caterpillars live only in summer; being unable to bear frost, the second generation emerging in the northern autumn is doomed to extinction.

8 *Ipimorpha subtusa* (D. & S.) — Olive. 27—30mm. Widespread in the temperate parts of the Palaearctic, this moth has but one generation a year, on the wing from July to September. The eggs hibernate, and the caterpillars live in spring on poplars.

Family: **Noctuidae** — **noctuids (owlet moths, millers)**

1 *Enargia paleacea* (Esp.) — Angle-striped Sallow. 35—42mm. Distributed in northern and central Europe, also in central and eastern Asia and in North America, this species is at home in damp meadows, heather moors, grasslands and peat-bogs. A relatively scarce moth, flying from July to September. The egg hibernates, and the caterpillar develops in spring, eating foliage of birches, aspens, alders, etc.

2 *Cosmia trapezina* (L.) — Dun-bar. 25—33mm. With the exception of polar regions, this is a moth abundantly distributed throughout the Palaearctic; it is associated with deciduous and mixed forests, also with urban parks and gardens. The species exhibits an extraordinarily wide range of variations — including almost black forms. It flies in one generation, from the end of June till September. The egg hibernates. The caterpillar develops in spring (2b), living on oaks, hornbeams, birches, etc. It is also predacious, and attacks other caterpillars.

3 *Actinotia polyodon* (Cl.) — Purple Cloud. 23—30mm. Generally distributed in the Palaearctic, but more abundant in the warmer parts, this species has one or two generations, emerging from May to August. The caterpillar lives in autumn on *Hypericum* and milk-vetch; the pupa hibernates.

4 *Apamea monoglypha* (Hfn.) — Dark Arches. 45—55mm. A very abundant species to be found in all types of meadows and ascending the mountains to high elevations. It occurs in Europe and Asia — with the exception of the southernmost regions where it is replaced by some similar species. The one annual generation is on the wing from July to August. The caterpillars feed on the subterranean parts of a variety of grasses. There are innumerable variations of this moth, one of the most interesting being the black f. *aethiops*.

5 *Apamea lithoxylaea* (D. & S.) — Light Arches. 43—50mm. This species, more thermophilic than the Dark Arches, is common through the temperate and warm regions of Europe and Asia, as far as the Altai. It appears on the wing in grassy and dry biotopes, more often in lowlands, from June to August. The caterpillar hibernates, and feeds on various grasses.

6 *Apamea anceps* (D. & S.) — Large Nutmeg. 35—40mm. Found in temperate Europe, this species extends to southeastern Asia and eastern Siberia. It flies from May to July. The caterpillar, which hibernates, lives on grasses and is also regarded as a corn pest.

7 *Oligia strigilis* (L.) — Marbled Minor. 22—25mm. Widespread in northern and central Europe, in Asia and in North America, this moth occurs in mountains to high altitudes. In cultivated areas this extremely variable species shows a tendency to produce dark, melanic forms similar in appearance to 8c. It flies in various biotopes, particularly grassy places, from May to July. The caterpillar hibernates, and feeds on grasses.

8 *Oligia latruncula* (D. & S.) — Tawny Marbled Minor. 20—24mm. With the exception of North America, the distribution of this moth is similar to that of the foregoing species. Forests, peat-bogs and steppes are its favourite haunts. In areas affected by air pollution this moth also tends to produce melanic forms such as f. *aethiops* (8c). The caterpillar's life-cycle is similar to that of the Marbled Minor.

9 *Mesapamea secalis* (L.) — Common Rustic. 27—30mm. Widely distributed from Europe to North America, this species becomes progressively less abundant at higher elevations. It flies in one generation, from July to September. The caterpillar hibernates; it lives on grasses and is often a pest of corn. This species is given to great variation (9, 9c), presenting innumerable forms, from pale to quite black.

Family: **Noctuidae — noctuids (owlet moths, millers)**

1 *Photedes minima* (Hw.) — Small Dotted Buff. 20—23mm. Continuously distributed in northern and central Europe. It inhabits damp meadows and peat-bogs, frequently situated high up in the mountains around the sources of streams. The moth is on the wing from June to August, but the females do not fly well. The caterpillar hibernates, and feeds on grasses.

2 *Photedes fluxa* (Hb.) — Mere Wainscot. 22—25mm. Distributed over mild and more northern parts of Europe, extending eastwards across the Urals into central Asia, this species is associated with meadows and other grassy biotopes. The moth is on the wing from July to September. The caterpillar, which hibernates, lives in bushgrass stalks. The female differs from the male in being more yellow; the male's colouring is usually reddish.

3 *Luperina testacea* (D. & S.) — Flounced Rustic. 30—35mm. Confined in Europe to the mild zone, eastwards it spreads across Asia Minor to Armenia. This moth has innumerable variations in pattern. It flies from July to September, in grassy, dry biotopes, steppes, forest-steppes, etc. The caterpillar lives from autumn to spring — at first in the stalks of various grasses, later on in turfs.

4 *Amphipoea fucosa* (Frr.) — Saltern Ear. 30—35mm. Belonging to a complex of several species closely similar in appearance, the present insect is widely distributed and abundant. It occurs over practically the whole Palaearctic, being common in both damp and dry meadow biotopes. The moth is on the wing in July and August, and its colouring is exceedingly variable. Many forms have been described, making the distinction from other species seem all the more difficult. The caterpillar lives in spring (possibly it hibernates), eating various kinds of grasses and dicotyledonous plants.

5 *Hydraecia micacea* (Esp.) — Rosy Rustic. 28—45mm. Occurring generally throughout Europe and Asia, this insect favours damp, treeless biotopes overgrown with lush vegetation — in valleys, along brooks, in fields and on wasteground. The moth is on the wing from the end of July to October. The egg hibernates. The caterpillar develops from spring to summer, inside pulpy stalks and roots of various plants. Occasionally it can be a pest of hops, asparagus, beet, etc. Several similar species of this genus can be found in Europe, one being *H. ultima* Holst, discovered as late as 1965.

6 *Gortyna flavago* (D. & S.) — Frosted Orange. 35—40mm. With the exception of the extreme south, this moth is generally distributed over temperate Europe, and further across Asia Minor to Armenia. There is one generation in the year, on the wing from August to October. The egg hibernates, and the caterpillar develops (6b) during spring and summer inside the pulpy stalks of burdocks, groundsels, thistles, and other plants.

7 *Calamia tridens* (Hfn.) — Burren Green. 32—42mm. An inhabitant of steppe and grassy biotopes, it can often be found on wasteground, such as railway banks, etc. Generally distributed throughout temperate Europe, recently, however, it has become exceedingly rare. The moth is on the wing from July to August and is diurnal in habit. It passes the winter in the egg stage, and the caterpillar develops in spring, on various grasses.

8 *Staurophora celsia* (L.). 37—42mm. Distributed over central and northern Europe and spreading across the steppes of eastern Europe and central Asia to eastern Siberia, this species occurs on sandy soils, sometimes also on limestone. Local and rare (only very seldom can it be found in abundance at some localities) it flies in September and October. The caterpillar develops from June to August on bushgrass and the turfs of several other grass species.

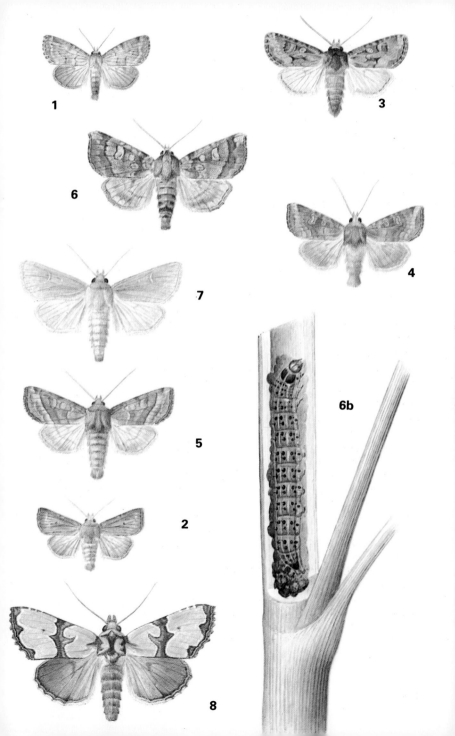

Family: **Noctuidae — noctuids (owlet moths, millers)**

1 *Nonagria typhae* (Thbg.) — Bulrush Wainscot. 45—50mm. Widespread in northern and central Europe, ranging eastwards to central Asia, this moth is associated with damp and peaty biotopes situated by riversides, near ponds, lakes, peat-bogs, etc. On the wing from July to October; it is nowhere abundant. The caterpillar lives in the stalks of certain aquatic plants, including cat's-tail and rush.

2 *Archanara geminipuncta* (Hw.) — Twin-spotted Wainscot. 27—32mm. Distributed throughout temperate Europe as far as central and southern Russia. The moth flies in June and August, in rushes and along watersides, and is locally abundant. The caterpillar develops from autumn till spring in reed stems (2b). The moth shows many variations of pattern, e. g. the well-known f. *nigricans,* with almost black wings, and f. *obsoleta* without the white dot, have been described.

3 *Archanara sparganii* (Esp.) — Webb's Wainscot. 32—40mm. Distributed in the temperate zone of the Palaearctic. Like all the other species of this genus, it is associated with damp biotopes near water, particularly stagnant ponds. There is a single generation of this moth, on the wing from August to October. The caterpillar passes the winter and spring, until July of the following year, in the pulpy stalks of various aquatic plants.

4 *Rhizedra lutosa* (Hb.) — Large Wainscot. 42—50mm. Widely distributed over the greater part of the temperate Palaearctic, this moth ranges eastwards to the Ussuri basin. On the wing from August to November, it passes the winter in the egg stage, and the caterpillar lives in spring and summer within reed stems. These moths are very variable and a number of forms have been described, including f. *rufescens* with reddish wings, and f. *strigata* with rather conspicuous dark cross-lines.

5 *Charanyca trigrammica* (Hfn.) — Treble Lines. 35—40mm. Associated with the warmer regions of Europe and Asia Minor, this species extends eastwards as far as Armenia, and may be found in mountains, where it reaches considerable altitudes. It shows a preference for areas having abundant vegetation: meadows and woodland margins, clearings in forests, etc. Usually there is one generation in the year, which flies from May to July; occasionally a second brood may emerge in September. It passes the winter as caterpillars; these feed on various low-growing plants. Great variability is a characteristic of this species. Notable are forms *brunnea* and *bilinea,* the wings of which have a dark cell.

6 *Hoplodrina alsines* (Brahm) — Uncertain Moth. 28—34mm. This species is widespread and very common in central to northern Europe, ranging eastward to Siberia. It appears to be native to forest-steppe biotopes, but it has adapted to treeless wastelands and agricultural land. The one generation is on the wing from June to August. The polyphagous caterpillar hibernates.

7 *Hoplodrina ambigua* (D. & S.) — Vine's Rustic. 28—30mm. The species inhabits treeless biotopes in Europe and central Asia. It has become well adapted to life in cultivated areas, where wastelands provide it with suitable living conditions. This moth has two generations in the year — flying from May to July and August to September. The caterpillars are polyphagous.

8 *Athetis pallustris* (Hb.) — Marsh Moth. 27—32mm. Confined to cooler areas of northern and central Europe, this insect occurs in damp meadows, frequently also in mountains (particularly in areas situated more to the south), living in swamps, peat-bogs, along streams, etc. Moths of the single generation fly from May to July. The caterpillar, which hibernates, eats various grasses and low, succulent herbs.

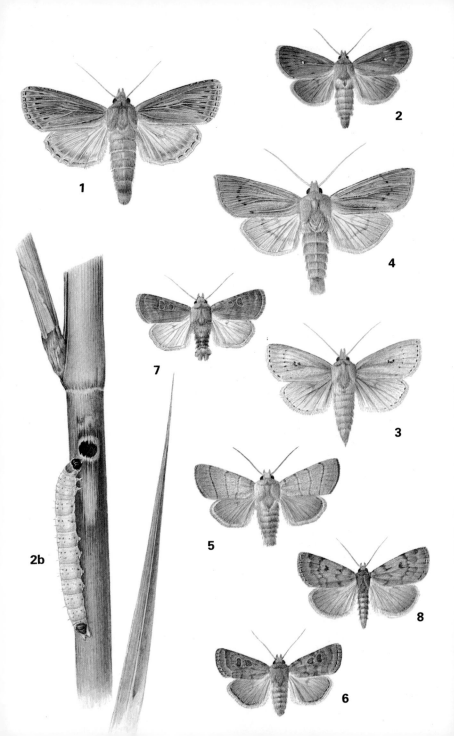

Family: **Noctuidae — noctuids (owlet moths, millers)**

1 *Heliothis maritima* (Grasl.) — Shoulder-striped Clover. 28—35mm. This Atlantic-Mediterranean species occurs in the coastal areas of western and southern Europe and in southeastern Europe, and ranges east across steppe regions to central Asia. In areas near the edge of its range it tends to be migratory, temporarily colonising suitable localities. Its one or two generations emerge in June and August to September. Any second brood is partial, some of the pupae (1c) overwintering to emerge the following year. The caterpillars (1b) live in the summertime in the flowers of various plants, and cause damage to cultivated lucerne.

2 *Heliothis viriplaca* (Hfn.) (= *dipsacea* L.) — Marbled Clover. 25—30mm. Widely distributed over the steppe areas of Europe and Asia, ranging eastward to Japan, this species is also a migrant. In Europe there are two generations, the first flies in May to June, the second in July to August. The caterpillars are polyphagous; winter is passed in the pupal stage.

3 *Protoschinia scutosa* (D. & S.) — Spotted Clover. 30—35mm. Widespread in the warmer regions of Europe and Asia as far as Korea, this migrant also appears from time to time in localities which it does not ordinarily inhabit. It produces two generations and winters in the pupal stage. The caterpillar is polyphagous, showing a preference for flowers of various plants, such as wormwood, goosefoot, etc.

4 *Pyrrhia umbra* (Hfn.) — Bordered Sallow. 27—35mm. A moth with a Palaearctic distribution, closely related species occur in North America. It inhabits the deciduous forest zone, mainly in warmer situations and lowlands. There is a single generation per year, on the wing from May to July. The caterpillars develop in summer months on various deciduous trees or low plants.

5 *Axylia putris* (L.) — Flame. 27—32mm. Formerly classed with the cutworms, but this is incorrect. This species is distributed throughout the temperate Palaearctic and annually produces a single generation, flying from May to August. Occasionally a partial second brood appears during August. The caterpillars are polyphagous, feeding on low-growing plants; it goes through the winter as pupae.

6 *Lithacodia deceptoria* (Sc.) — Pretty Marbled Moth. 20—22mm. Ranging from Europe across the Urals to northern China, but absent from extreme situations in the north and south, it is a species characteristic of grassy biotopes, mainly damp meadows. Its single generation flies from May to July. The caterpillars develop towards the end of summer on various grasses; the pupae hibernate.

7 *Lithacodia pygarga* (Hfn.) — Marbled White Spot. 20—22mm. Its distribution coincides with that of the previous species; however, it is found chiefly in open forests with grassy clearings and lush vegetation, or hillsides overgrown with plants of all kinds, etc. Sometimes it ascends to high mountain elevations. It produces one generation, flying from May to August. The caterpillar feeds on grasses; the pupa hibernates.

8 *Eustrotia uncula* (Cl.) — Silver Hook. 20—22mm. Widespread throughout the cooler Palaearctic in wet meadows, swamps, peat-bogs, and so on. It produces one, occasionally two generations, on the wing from May to August. The caterpillar lives from June to September on various sedges and rushes.

9 *Emmelia trabealis* (Sc.) — Spotted Sulphur. 18—20mm. Except for polar regions, this moth is distributed over the entire Palaearctic in treeless areas, such as meadows and steppes. The two generations that emerge in the year fly from May to June and July to August. They can be found in sunny biotopes, even in arid areas, but also in fields. The caterpillar is polyphagous and lives on low plants. The pupa hibernates.

Family: **Noctuidae — noctuids (owlet moths, millers)**

1 *Tyta luctuosa* (D. & S.) — Four-spotted. 22—25mm. Generally distributed over the Palaearctic as far as eastern Siberia, this moth is to be found on grassy hillsides and in steppes. By night it is attracted to light but it also can be seen flying on sunny days. It has two generations in the year, which fly from May to August.

2 *Aegle koekeritziana* (Hb.). 23—25mm. A rare inhabitant of all the warm territories of Europe, spreading across Asia Minor to the Caucasus. The single generation flies during June. The caterpillars live in July and August on *Consolida segetum;* winter is passed in the pupal stage.

3 *Nycteola revayana* (Sc.) — Oak Nycteoline. 20—25mm. Distributed all over Europe, this moth spreads eastward across Asia Minor to Syria, and across the Altai as far as Japan. It produces an extraordinarily wide range of variations and presents innumerable forms, many of which (3, 3c) it would seem almost impossible to belong to a single species. Forms of great interest include f. *ramosana,* in which the wings bear a black longitudinal shade, and f. *ilicana,* in which the relatively pale ground colour is spotted with black. Annually there are two generations; the adults of the second hibernate. The caterpillars develop in May and June, and then again in August and September, on oak.

4 *Earias clorana* (L.) — Cream-bordered Green Pea. 16—20mm. This moth occurs in deciduous forests, particularly in those bordering streams and rivers, over the non-polar parts of the entire Palaearctic subregion. There are two generations per year, flying from May to August. Winter is passed in the pupal stage. The caterpillar feeds on the leaves of various kinds of willows.

5 *Pseudoips fagana* (F.) — Green Silver-lines. 30—35mm. Distributed throughout the Palaearctic, this moth ascends to high altitudes in the mountains, approximately coinciding with the beech-forest line. The single generation is on the wing from May to July. The colour of the wings is orange-yellow in males and white in females. Caterpillars live until September on beech, oak, hornbeam, etc. The winter is passed in the pupal stage.

6 *Bena prasinana* (L.) — Scarce Silver-lines. 40—45mm. A thermophilic species widely distributed in deciduous and mixed forests and forest-steppes of Europe and Asia Minor, as far as the Caucasus. There is but one annual generation, which flies from May to July. The caterpillar lives from August throughout winter until the following spring on oak, and pupates in a tough yellow cocoon.

7 *Panthea coenobita* (Esp.) 40—50mm. Occurring in northern and northeastern Europe, this species ranges eastwards to Siberia, being confined to the zone of coniferous, pine and spruce forests. The single brood flies from May to August. The caterpillars (7b) live from summer till autumn on spruce, pine, and other coniferous trees. The winter is passed in the pupal stage (7c) in a firm cocoon.

8 *Trichosea ludifica* (L.). 35—45mm. A species peculiar to montane and submontane elevations, widespread in the temperate parts of Europe. Moths are on the wing in May and June. The caterpillars live towards the end of summer, mostly on mountain ash but also on other trees; the pupae hibernate.

9 *Colocasia coryli* (L.) — Nut-tree Tussock. 27—35mm. This species ranges from Europe to eastern Asia, southwards also to Asia Minor and Armenia; it is confined to the deciduous-forest zone. In the greater part of its range it produces one generation which emerges from April to June; occasionally a second brood appears on the wing in August. The caterpillars (9b) live on oak, beech, hazel, birch, etc. The species overwinters in the pupal stage.

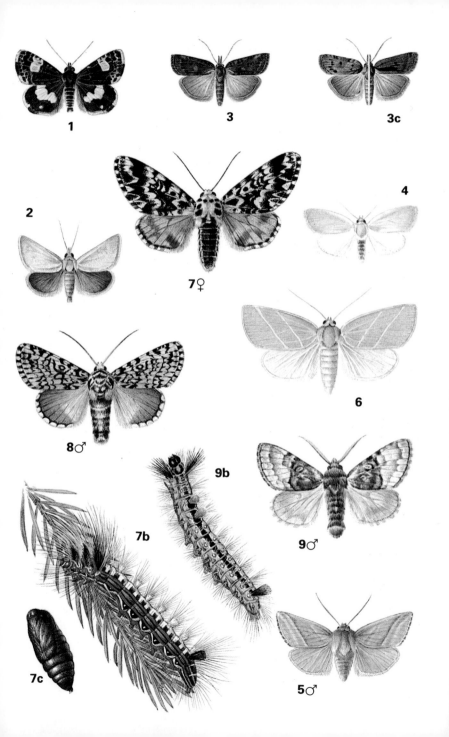

1 **2** **3** **3c** **4** **7♀** **8♂** **7b** **9b** **9♂** **7c** **5♂**

Family: **Noctuidae — noctuids (owlet moths, millers)**

1 *Syngrapha interrogationis* (L.) — Scarce Silver Y. 30—35mm. A Boreo-Alpine species with a continuous distribution in the northern polar regions of the Palaearctic; further south, its occurrence is confined to mountains and peat-bogs. The moth flies from the end of June to August. The caterpillar hibernates in the third or fourth instar, and pupates in spring in a flimsy white cocoon. The larval food-plant is *Vaccinium uliginosum* — less frequently, bilberry and nettle.

2 *Syngrapha ain* (Hochw.). 30—35mm. Central Europe represents the western limit of this moth; eastwards it extends to the Altai and the Amur. This single-brooded species is on the wing in July and August. The young caterpillars pass the winter. The range of the species depends on the distribution of the larch, the food-plant of the caterpillars.

3 *Euchalcia variabilis* (Pill.) — Purple-shaded Gem. 33—38mm. Commonly distributed in northern and central Europe (more to the south only in mountains), this rather scarce moth can be found in lowland localities where its foodplant occurs. In the east this, or a closely related species, extends to Mongolia and the Amur basin. The adults are on the wing from May to July. The caterpillars hibernate when very young and grow to full size by the end of spring. Their food-plants are aconite and larkspur.

4 *Euchalcia consona* (F.). 27—32mm. A species which ranges over the warmer part of central and southeastern Europe, the Balkan Peninsula, Asia Minor and Armenia. It prefers warm hillsides, forest-steppes and woodland margins. The moth flies from June to September, in two generations. In spring after the hibernation of the egg, the caterpillar (4b) emerges to feed on *Nonea pulla*.

5 *Autographa gamma* (L.) — Silver Y. 35—40mm. Generally distributed throughout the Palaearctic, this is a most important migrant which, year by year, penetrates from into subtropics into regions situated in the far north. There it produces one or two generations over the summer, and in autumn there is a return migration to the south. In addition, the lowlands of central Europe are inhabited by a population hibernating there in the larval stage (5b). However, the presence of the moth in mountainous regions is due to immigration from the south or from lowlands only. The larvae eat a wide range of low-growing plants, and can become pests in outbreak years. The adults can often be seen by day, visiting flowers.

6 *Autographa pulchrina* (Hw.) — Beautiful Golden Y. 35—40mm. Occurs mostly in the mountains and in northern Europe; in Asia it extends from the Urals to the Amur. The moths are on the wing in one generation, from July to August. The caterpillars, which live on low plants, overwinter in the third or fourth instar. A species given to great variation, sometimes it is very difficult to distinguish it from the similar *A. jota* (L.), distributed mainly in eastern Europe.

7 *Autographa bractea* (D. & S.) — Gold Spangle. 37—42mm. Generally distributed over the northern parts of the Palaearctic (more to the south only in mountains), this moth flies from June to August in one generation. The caterpillars, whose food is provided by nettles, hawkweed, plantain, and other plants, hibernate. Occasionally the moths migrate from the mountains to the lowlands.

8 *Plusia festucae* (L.) — Gold Spot. 30—35mm. Widespread throughout the non-polar Palaearctic as far as Japan, this species is associated with wet meadows, swamps, and other watery habitats along both running and stagnant waters. There are one or two generations, flying from May to September. The winter is passed as a caterpillar, which feeds on various marsh grasses.

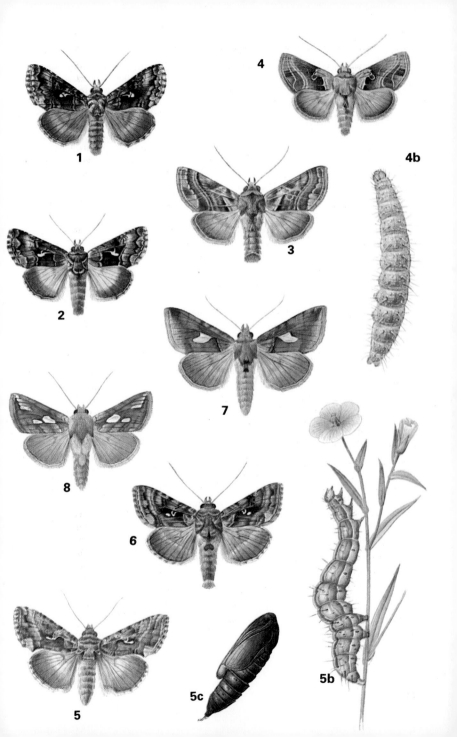

1

4

4b

2

3

7

8

6

5

5c

5b

Family: **Noctuidae** — **noctuids (owlet moths, millers)**

1 *Polychrysia moneta* (F.) — Golden Plusia. 32—37mm. Ranging over northern and central Europe, and further to the southeast across Asia Minor to Armenia, this moth is found mostly in mountains. A single generation emerges in June and July. The caterpillars hibernate while very young and grow to full size in spring. They live on aconite, larkspur and globeflower.

2 *Diachrysia chrysitis* (L.) — Burnished Brass. 28—35mm. Distributed throughout the Palaearctic, except polar regions. Even though this moth may be found at high mountain elevations, it occurs most abundantly in lowlands, especially localities overgrown with new vegetation. This species is abundant even in towns. Two generations emerge in the year, during May to June and August to September. The winter is passed as a half-grown caterpillar, which feeds on a variety of plants, having a special liking for dead nettle, nettle, woundwort, etc.

3 *Diachrysia zosimi* (Hb.). 28—32mm. Abundant in southeastern Europe, this moth has spread during the present century to many localities in central Europe. Eastwards it extends to the Altai and the Amur basin. It is a species peculiar to damp meadows and lowlands. Two generations occur in the year — one flying in May, the other in July and August. The caterpillars hibernate while very young; their food-plant is wild burnet.

4 *Macdunnoughia confusa* (Steph.) — Dewick's Plusia. 27—35mm. Distributed mainly in southern areas of the Palaearctic, where it is fairly abundant, this migrant species has apparently spread to the north during the second half of this century. Two or three merging generations are on the wing from May to June and again from August to the end of autumn. The caterpillars of the summer brood develop quickly (about 3 weeks); those of later generations hibernate, but they do not tolerate hard frosts. They live on nettle, mint, etc.

5 *Abrostola triplasia* (L.) (= *tripartita* Hfn.) — Spectacle. 27—30mm. One of a group of exceedingly similar species. Distributed throughout the temperate zone of Europe and Asia as far as eastern Siberia, it may be found even at high mountain altitudes, reaching the upper limit of deciduous forests. Damp habitats in woodland margins and valleys, and wasteground in the neighbourhood of towns and cities, are its favourite haunts. There are two generations in the year, flying from May to September. The caterpillars live on nettles; winter is passed as pupae.

6 *Abrostola trigemina* (Wernb.) — Dark Spectacle. 28—32mm. Bears great resemblance to the preceding species with respect to colouration of the adult moth, distribution and ecological requirements, including foodplant. Two generations develop in the year; the pupa hibernates. This species, being slightly more thermophilic than *A. triplasia,* does not ascend to quite such high elevations in mountains.

7 *Catocala sponsa* (L.) — Dark Crimson Underwing. 60—70mm. A thermophilic species distributed in northern Africa, in temperate Europe as far as the Urals, and Asia Minor. It inhabits oak and mixed forests. There is but one generation in the year, on the wing from July to September. It overwinters in the egg stage; the caterpillar lives in spring, feeding on oaks.

8 *Catocala fraxini* (L.) — Clifden Nonpareil. 75—95mm. Because of its colouration and size this beautiful moth is well-known and much sought after. Widespread in deciduous forests of the entire Palaearctic subregion, with the exception of the extreme south, and also in North America, there is one generation which flies, according to climatic conditions, from July to October. It passes the winter in the egg stage. The caterpillars develop in spring; they favour poplars but also feed on birch, ash, oak, etc. The dark brown, blue-dusted pupa lies in a flimsy cocoon spun among leaves. The moth is rather variable, in response to differing climatic conditions. Form *moerens*, with dark forewings, is more common in the north, while in warmer lowland regions the light f. *gaudens* prevails.

Family: **Noctuidae — noctuids (owlet moths, millers)**

1 *Catocala nupta* (L.) — Red Underwing. 65—75mm. Of the red-coloured moths of the genus *Catocala*, this one is the most abundant. It is widely distributed throughout non-polar Europe, with the exception of the extreme south, and spreads to eastern Asia. An inhabitant of moist deciduous forests, most often to be found near water, it is also fairly common in urban parks and avenues. There is only one generation, on the wing from July to as late as October. The moths like to settle on the ledges of houses, or on tree trunks, where they are barely visible due to the cryptic colouration of their forewings, which conceal the brightly coloured hindwings. If the moth is disturbed, it darts away in a zigzag flight. Like all the moths of this group, it may easily be lured to bait or fallen fermenting fruits (chiefly pears and plums) to suck the juices. The eggs overwinter; the caterpillars (1b) develop in spring on various species of willows and poplars. The pupa (1c) is hidden among leaves spun together. Although the range of variation exhibited by this species is not very great, several forms have been described, the most remarkable of which is f. *flava* in which the red colouring is replaced by yellow. The very dark f. *atra* is also notable.

2 *Catocala elocata* (Esp.). 65—80mm. A common species, more thermophilic than the preceding one. It occurs in central and southern Europe, Asia Minor, Syria, and penetrates eastwards to northern India. This moth is associated with damp biotopes, such as humid forests in coastal areas, or shrubs bordering banks of streams and rivers. It is often abundant in urban parks. The single generation is on the wing from July to September. After the egg has passed the winter, the caterpillar (2b) develops on poplars and willows. The pupal stage occurs in summer and lasts for a very short time. The pupa is formed among spun-up leaves and is dusted with blue, as is the case with all species of the genus *Catocala*. The most notable individual form is the yellow f. *flava*.

3 *Catocala electa* (View.) — Rosy Underwing. 60—70mm. A very rare species which, moreover, seems to be disappearing rapidly in nature. It is a thermophilic insect, inhabiting deciduous forests of central and southern Europe, and ranging eastwards across the warmer regions of Asia to Korea and Japan. The moth is on the wing from July to September. The egg hibernates; the caterpillar lives in spring and completes its development in summer, preferring a diet of willow leaves. The yellow form of this species is called f. *lugdunensis*.

4 *Catocala promissa* (D. & S.) — Light Crimson Underwing. 60—65mm. Widespread in the deciduous forests of temperate Europe and Asia Minor, as far as Armenia. Of the whole genus *Catocala*, this species is one of the earliest to appear — it sometimes emerges as early as the end of June and remains on the wing until August. Just like in the other species, the egg overwinters, and the caterpillar, which feeds on the foliage of oaks, develops in spring. This moth resembles *C. sponsa* (L.) which also has rich crimson hindwing bands. Yellow individuals may occur instead of red ones (f. *ochracea*), but these are quite rare.

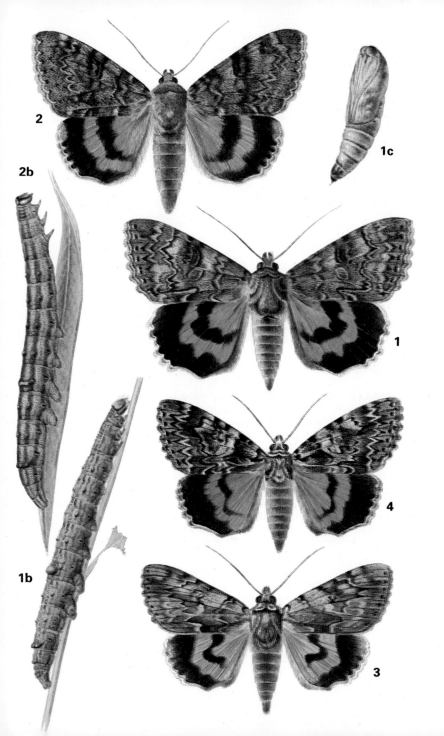

Family: **Noctuidae — noctuids (owlet moths, millers)**

1 *Catocala nymphagoga* (Esp.). 35—43mm. A thermophilic species, distributed over central and southern Europe, Asia Minor, Armenia and Syria, it can be found flying in oak forests and forest-steppes from the end of June to August. The caterpillar (1b) lives from March to the end of May or June on oaks. The winter is passed in the egg stage. In appropriate localities this species occurs in quite large numbers, and is the most abundant of the yellow-coloured representatives of the genus *Catocala* in Europe.

2 *Ephesia fulminea* (Sc.). 45—52mm. Widely distributed throughout the warmer regions of Europe and Asia, in the east this species ranges as far as Japan. It lives in steppes and forest-steppes, and is one of the earliest moths of the catocalid group to emerge, being on the wing from June to August. It is easily attracted to bait. The egg overwinters; the caterpillar (2b) develops in spring, feeding on blackthorn and plum trees, exceptionally also on hawthorn, pear trees and oak. This moth has now become almost extinct in many localities, apparently due to changes in agricultural practice.

3 *Minucia lunaris* (D. & S.) — Lunar Double-stripe. 50—60mm. This thermophilic species is restricted to limited areas in central Europe; it also extends from southern Europe eastwards through Asia Minor to the Caucasus. The moth can be seen on the wing early in spring, from April to June, favouring oak forests and forest-steppes. On sunny days it can easily be flushed from undergrowth. The caterpillar develops from June to August, living on young oak shoots. The winter is passed in the pupal stage.

4 *Callistege mi* (Cl.) — Mother Shipton. 25—30mm. With the exception of polar regions, this species ranges over the whole of Europe, across Asia Minor and Armenia to central Asia, eastwards as far as the Amur. In Europe there are two broods, flying from April to June and July to August. The caterpillar lives on clover, lucerne, vetch, etc. Winter is passed in the pupal stage.

5 *Euclidia glyphica* (L.) — Burnet Companion. 25—30mm. The range of this moth is almost the same as that of the previous species, except that it spreads further eastwards to Japan. Also there are usually two generations, flying from April to August, but at higher elevations, however, there is only one. The caterpillar enjoys a mixed diet including lucerne, clover, vetch, and numerous other plants. The pupa hibernates. Both the Burnet Companion and the Mother Shipton are diurnal in habit.

6 *Scoliopteryx libatrix* (L.) — Herald. 40—45mm. Generally distributed throughout the Palaearctic, ranging from northern Africa to Asia, this species also lives in North America. In the mountains it ascends up to 2,000m. It shows a distinct preference for those damp, waterside biotopes where the food-plants of the caterpillar (6b), willows and poplars, grow. One or two broods appear annually. It overwinters in the adult stage. Moths may often be found hibernating in cellars and caves, sometimes assembled in great numbers.

7 *Lygephila pastinum* (Tr.) — Blackneck. 37—42mm. Widely distributed throughout Europe to the Volga, and in Asia to the Amur; there are two annual generations of this species, appearing in May and June, and again in August and September. It can be found in steppes and forest-steppes, open woods, on hillsides, etc. Winter is passed in the caterpillar stage, which feeds on vetches of various kinds.

Family: **Noctuidae — noctuids (owlet moths, millers)**

1 *Catephia alchymista* (D. & S.) — Alchymist. 35—40mm. Inhabits the warmer regions of Europe and passes across Asia Minor to the Caucasus; elsewhere this species occurs only sporadically. There is but one generation, which flies from May to July, in oak and mixed forests, and also in warm forest-steppe localities. The caterpillar develops in July and August on oak, mainly on young shoots or saplings. Winter is passed in the pupal stage.

2 *Aedia funesta* (Esp.). 28—33mm. Spreads over much the same territory in both Europe and Asia as the preceding species, but this more abundant moth has somewhat different ecological requirements. The single generation flies in June and July in rather damp forests, coastal and lowland woods, and often also in fields, particularly those adjacent to vineyards. The caterpillar, which lives from July throughout the winter until the following spring, feeds on larger bindweed.

3 *Laspeyria flexula* (D. & S.) — Beautiful Hook-tip. 23—27mm. Distributed in temperate Europe and Asia as far as the Ussuri, this moth also reaches quite far to the north. The single annual generation flies from June to August. It passes the winter as a caterpillar. This feeds on a variety of lichens growing on the trunks of both deciduous and coniferous trees.

4 *Parascotia fuliginaria* (L.) — Waved Black. 18—28mm. Distributed over the whole of temperate Europe, this is another species whose larvae do not live on flowering plants, eating instead lichens, mushrooms (particularly polypores) and rotten wood. The moth has a single generation emerging over the period June to September. The male has pectinate antennae and is superficially more like a geometrid than a noctuid. The caterpillar overwinters. This species is frequently found around buildings, where it lives in lofts, mossy roofs and decaying timbers.

5 *Epizeuxis calvaria* (D. & S.). 25—32mm. Ranging from warmer central and southern Europe eastwards across Asia Minor to Armenia and Iran, this moth produces one, exceptionally two generations, flying from June to September. The winter is passed in the form of caterpillars: these feed on withered and decaying leaves of trees and various plants.

6 *Rivula sericealis* (Sc.) — Straw Dot. 18—22mm. Widespread throughout the entire Palaearctic subregion in damp meadows, occurring from lowlands well up into the mountains, this moth produces one or two generations, on the wing from May to September. The caterpillars, which feed on various grasses, overwinter.

7 *Polypogon tentacularia* (L.). 22—28mm. This moth ranges over temperate and northern Europe eastwards across the Urals to the Altai and eastern Siberia. It is common in all moist, grassy localities, showing a preference for woodland clearings. Its only generation flies from June to August. The polyphagous caterpillar hibernates.

8 *Hypena crassalis* (F.) — Beautiful Snout. 25—30mm. Widely distributed in northern and central Europe as far as the Caucasus, this moth occurs in wetlands, peat-bogs and coniferous forests, where it flies from May to July. The caterpillar's diet consists of bilberry and heather. Winter is passed in the pupal stage.

9 *Hypena proboscidalis* (L.) — Snout. 25—38mm. This extremely abundant species is characteristic of both lowland and mountain forests. It produces two generations, emerging from May to September, and passes the winter in the caterpillar stage. Larval food is provided by nettles and other plants.

1

4

2

5

3

7

8

9

6

Family: **Dilobidae**

1 *Diloba caeruleocephala* (L.) − Figure-of-Eight. 30−40mm. Distributed in the warmer parts of Europe, particularly in regions bordering the Mediterranean, this species extends over the steppes and forest-steppes of southeastern Europe to the Caucasus. 1,000m is the highest elevation reached by this species in mountains. As its time of flight is limited to October and caterpillars live in May and June on hawthorn, blackthorn, apple trees, etc. Occasionally it becomes destructive in orchards. The Figure-of-Eight was formerly placed in the family Noctuidae, where it was continually transferred from one subfamily to another, but none of them was really appropriate for it. This is why an independent family has recently been established to receive this single species.

Family: **Notodontidae − prominents (puss moths)**

2 *Furcula bicuspis* (Bkh.) − Alder Kitten. 30−35mm. Ranging over Europe and Asia as far as the Ussuri basin, this moth is peculiar to mixed and deciduous forests where birch grows, and also to certain types of peat-bogs. There is only one annual generation, flying from May to July. The caterpillar can be found at the end of summer on birch and alder. Winter is passed in the form of a pupa enclosed in a tough cocoon, as is the case with all species of this genus.

3 *Furcula furcula* (Cl.) − Sallow Kitten. 27−35mm. Generally distributed over the whole of non-polar Europe and Asia, as well as in North America, the Sallow Kitten is found in peat-bogs, heather moors, deciduous and mixed forests, overgrown clearings, etc. The moth is on the wing from May to July. The caterpillar lives from July to September on birch, beech, oak, etc.; the pupa overwinters.

4 *Furcula bifida* (Brahm) − Poplar Kitten. 35−45mm. Occurs in Europe and Asia, the Altai being the eastern limit of this species. The moths can be found in damp deciduous forests, mixed woods and peat-bogs, by running water, and occasionally also in urban parks, from April till July. The caterpillar lives in July and August on poplars and willows; the pupa hibernates.

5 *Cerura vinula* (L.) − Puss. 45−70mm. Widespread throughout the entire temperate Palaearctic, including mountains up to the altitude of 2,500m, this species is typical of damp biotopes and vegetation by watersides, in valleys and woodland margins. A single generation flies from April to July, depending on climatic conditions. The caterpillars (5b) live towards the end of summer on poplars and willows. The pupa overwinters (5c) in a hard cocoon attached to a tree trunk or in the fork of a branch.

6 *Stauropus fagi* (L.) − Lobster. 45−60mm. Commonly found in the deciduous forest zone of Europe and Asia, this moth is more or less confined to warmer situations. Occasional outbreaks causing destruction of forest trees are reported from southern Asia. In Europe, however, the moth only occurs in widely scattered localities, although it is far from rare. It is on the wing from April to July. The caterpillar, remarkable for its long legs and appearing somewhat like a large spider, lives from June to September, feeding on beech, oak, lime, and other trees.

7 *Harpyia milhauseri* (F.). 40−50mm. A rare thermophilic species ranging over central and southern Europe and Asia Minor, as far as eastern Asia. It may be seen on the wing in deciduous forests in May and June. The caterpillar lives from June to August on oak, hornbeam and birch. The winter is passed in the form of a pupa encased in a hard cocoon.

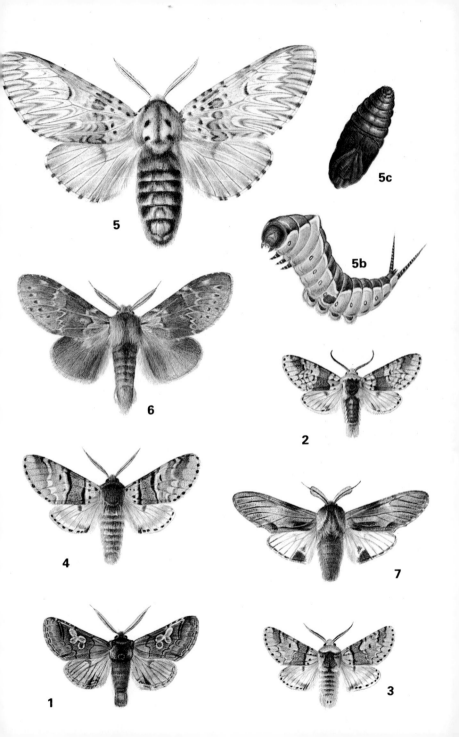

Family: **Notodontidae — prominents (puss moths)**

1 *Drymonia querna* (F.). 35—40mm. Confined to scattered localities in central, southern and western Europe, this species occurs in warm deciduous forests, most often in oak or mixed forests, in wooded steppes, or on hillsides exposed to sunshine. Though in central Europe it is a local and rare species, its abundance increases southeastwards. There is one generation which flies from May to June; in warmer regions a second brood of moths appears on the wing in July and August. The caterpillars live on oak from July to September. Winter is passed as a pupa concealed in the uppermost layer of the soil or forest litter.

2 *Drymonia dodonaea* (D. & S) — Marbled Brown. 33—38mm. In Europe this is the most abundant species of the genus. It occurs in deciduous and mixed forests all over Europe, ranging eastwards to the Caucasus, its eastern limit; however, it is absent from the southern-most parts of Europe. The moth flies in a single generation from May to July. The caterpillar lives from June to August on oak, beech and birch, and the pupa overwinters. Subspecies *trimacula* Esp. is native to western Europe, while the populations of central and southeastern Europe constitute the darker coloured, nominate ssp. *dodonaea*.

3 *Drymonia ruficornis* (Hfn.) (= *chaonia* D. & S.) — Lunar Marbled Brown. 35—40mm. Also an abundant species, but far more local, it ranges more to the east, as far as Japan. The moth appears on the wing early in spring, in April and May. The caterpillar (3b) lives in June and July on oak; winter is passed in the pupal stage.

4 *Peridea anceps* (Gz.) — Great Prominent. 50—65mm. Distributed throughout the temperate zone of Europe to the east as far as the Caucasus and Armenia, this species inhabits deciduous and mixed forests on warm hillsides, and in lowlands. The moth is on the wing from April to June. The caterpillar lives during summer on oak, and pupates in leaf-litter.

5 *Pheosia tremula* (Cl.) — Swallow Prominent. 45—55mm. Ranges over temperate and warmer Europe eastwards to southern Siberia. This moth is associated with damp vegetation bordering rivers and brooks, in lowland woods and in open deciduous forests. It produces two genera-tions, the first of which flies from April to June, the second from July to August. The caterpillars (5b) manage to complete their development during autumn, so that the pupae hibernate. The caterpillars feed on poplars, willows and birches.

6 *Pheosia gnoma* (F.) — Lesser Swallow Prominent. 45—50mm. Distributed over very much the same territory as the preceding species, in Asia it ranges to the Far East. There are two generations of this moth having the same flight period as the Swallow Prominent, and also the caterpillars develop at the same time of year. They live on birch. Winter is passed in the pupal stage.

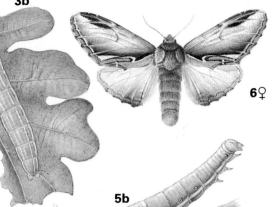

1

2

3

4

5♂

3b

5b

6♀

Family: **Notodontidae — prominents (puss moths)**

1 *Tritophia tritophus* (D. & S.) (= *phoebe* Sieb.) — Three-humped Prominent. 45—55 mm. Distributed throughout temperate Europe, eastwards as far as the Caucasus. Annually this moth produces two generations, one of which flies from April to June, the other in July and August. The species inhabits diverse biotopes overgrown with a variety of trees and shrubs, preferring lush habitats. In mountains it ascends to quite high elevations, but is not abundant in any locality. The caterpillar lives from June to September, depending on the brood it belongs to. Poplars, willows and birches provide its diet. The hibernating pupa is formed on the ground in an earthen cocoon, usually near the trunk of the tree.

2 *Notodonta torva* (Hb.) — Large Dark Prominent. 40—50mm. Distributed more abundantly in the north of Europe than in the south, where it reaches to central Italy, there are some localities from which the moth is altogether absent. Eastwards it spreads to eastern Asia. It occurs in damp woodland biotopes with deciduous trees and abundant clearings, in peat-bogs etc. However, being rare in all its habitats, data concerning the ecology and distribution of this species are often rather contradictory. In the mountains it has been caught as high as the upper limit of deciduous trees. Two generations usually develop in the year, flying from May to August. The caterpillars, which feed on poplar, live somewhat later, from June to October. Winter is passed in the pupal stage.

3 *Notodonta dromedarius* (L.) — Iron Prominent. 35—40mm. Distributed in the northern and southern parts of central Europe and in the east to the Amur, this moth flies abundantly in deciduous and mixed woods where birches grow, also in peat-bogs and their margins. It also occurs commonly in urban parks. Two generations are produced in the year, flying from May to August. The caterpillars (3b) live from June to September on birch, willow, poplar, hazel, etc; the pupae hibernate. The species is variable in colour, and sometimes tends to be melanic.

4 *Eligmodonta ziczac* (L.) — Pebble Prominent. 40—45mm. Generally distributed throughout Europe and Asia, this moth can be found at up to 2,500m in mountains as well as in lowlands. Typical biotopes are damp deciduous forests and stream-filled valleys, riverine woods, overgrown hillsides, etc., but it has also become well adapted to urban parks. The two annual generations (only one in the mountains) are on the wing from April to August; the moths are very variable in colour. The caterpillars (4b), which feed on the leaves of willows and poplars, appear from June to September.

5 *Spatalia argentina* (D. & S.). 30—35mm. A thermophilic species of oriental origin, to be found in central, southern and southeastern Europe, in the eastern Mediterranean regions. Two generations appear during the year, the first in May to June, the second in August. The caterpillars live on oaks, poplars, willows — but predominantly on shrubs. Typical habitats are open and warm deciduous woods, forest-steppes and sunny hillsides.

6 *Leucodonta bicoloria* (D. & S.) — White Prominent. 30—37mm. Locally distributed in birch and mixed forests of the temperate zone of the entire Palaearctic, this insect can also be found in peat-bogs at lower or medium elevations up to about 1,000m. Never abundant, the moth has but one generation in the year which flies in May and June. The caterpillars live from June to August, mostly on birch, less often on oak.

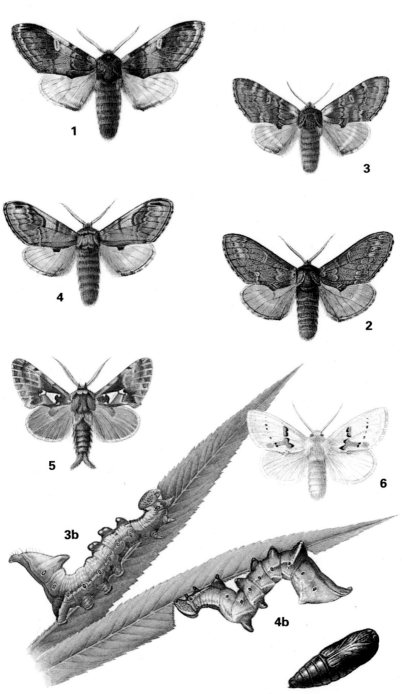

Family: **Notodontidae — prominents (puss moths)**

1 *Ochrostigma velitaris* (Hfn.). 35—40mm. Distributed over the warmer parts of central Europe, this species is locally scattered elsewhere in Europe (with the exception of the British Isles), spreading eastwards to Galicia, southwards as far as central Italy, and across Asia Minor to the Caucasus. The moth may be seen on the wing from May to July in warm oak woods and on shrubby, forest-steppe hillsides. The caterpillar lives towards the end of summer, mainly on oak, but also on poplar.

2 *Ochrostigma melagona* (Bkh.). 32—36mm. An exceedingly rare species, limited in range from western Europe to the more southern parts of central Europe. It inhabits open mixed and deciduous forests having a lush undergrowth, particularly those in which oak is dominant. The moth is on the wing from the end of May to August, in one or two generations. The caterpillar lives from July to September, the leaves of oak, beech, and small shrubs being its food.

3 *Odontosia carmelita* (Esp.) — Scarce Prominent. 38—45mm. A moth confined to scattered localities in Europe, especially in its northern and eastern parts, notably southern Scandinavia and northeastern Russia, southwestern Germany, northern Italy, and in the eastern Carpathians, inhabiting birch woods and peat-bogs situated in lowlands and submontane elevations up to about 900m. The moth can be seen on the wing from the end of April to May; the caterpillar lives from June to August, feeding on birch and alder leaves. Winter is passed in the pupal stage. Central Europe, approximately where the Carpathians begin, is the western limit of the similar species *O. sieversi* Men., which extends as far as eastern Asia. Somewhat paler in colour, this moth flies at the beginning of April, somewhat earlier than the Scarce Prominent.

4 *Ptilodon capucina* (L.) (= *camelina* L.) — Coxcomb Prominent. 35—40mm. Generally distributed throughout the temperate zone of almost the whole Palaearctic as far as Korea, this moth can be found in mixed and deciduous forests, also in urban parks, to which it has become adapted. There are two generations in the year, the first flies in July and the second in August to September. The pupa overwinters. The moth exhibits colour variations; the male and the female also show some sexual dimorphism. It is one of the most abundant species of the family Notodontidae. The caterpillars are polyphagous, feeding on the leaves of various deciduous trees and bushes, but mainly oak, birch, hazel, willow and beech.

5 *Ptilodontella cucullina* (D. & S.) (= *cuculla* Esp.) — Maple Prominent. 35—40mm. The distribution of this species is very restricted, and it does not occur abundantly in any of the scattered localities in central and eastern Europe to which it is confined. The moth lives from May to June, the caterpillar from June to August (5b). It passes the winter as a pupa. Maple is the foodplant of the caterpillar.

6 *Pterostoma palpina* (Cl.) — Pale Prominent. 35—55mm. The anal margins of the forewings of this moth are provided with two conspicuous projections. Also remarkable are its long labial palps, jutting out in front. The male has pectinate antennae. When at rest the moth has an interesting elongate form, resembling a dry, rolled-up leaf. It is distributed over Europe and generally throughout the warmer parts of the Palaearctic as far as southern Siberia. It is known to ascend to mountain altitudes, its upper limit being about 1,500m. There are one or two generations per year on the wing from the end of April to August. The caterpillar (6b) lives from summer till autumn, and winter is passed in the pupal stage (6c). The caterpillars feed on the leaves of willows, poplars, alders, oaks, etc.

3

1

4

2

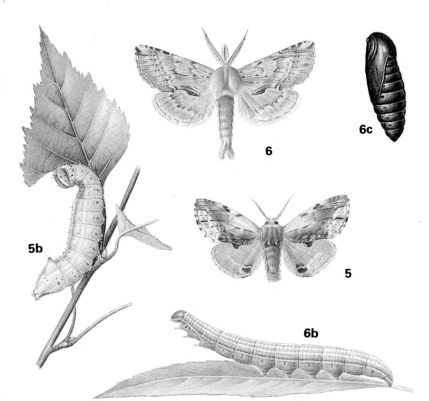

6

6c

5b

5

6b

Family: **Notodontidae — prominents (puss moths)**

1 *_Ptilophora plumigera_ (D. & S.) — Plumed Prominent. 32—40mm. Ranges over the belt of deciduous and mixed forests in Europe and Asia as far as Japan. In Europe this species is abundant in many localities, usually at submontane elevations, but from Asia — with the exception of Japan — very little data is available. This moth is one of the latest to appear on the wing, flying after the onset of frosts in October and November. If the autumn weather is bad, the moths may be seen in wintertime, in occasional spells of warm weather, until March. The caterpillar (1b) lives in spring on maples. The moth shows a wide range of variation as regards colouring. Conspicuous variations include the variegated f. _variegata,_ and the almost black f. _obscura._

2 *_Phalera bucephala_ (L.) — Buff-tip. 42—55mm. An abundant inhabitant of deciduous forests all over Europe, and being well adapted to living in cultivated areas, it can be found in avenues and urban parks. In Asia it ranges to the Far East. There is but one generation, which flies from May till July. The caterpillars (2b) appear in July and August. They live gregariously when young, stripping all leaves from the branches of limes, oaks, hazels, willows and other trees. When shaken by the wind they fall to the ground, particularly at the time immediately preceding pupation. Winter is passed in the form of the black, immobile pupae, which are found in the soil (2c).

3 *_Clostera curtula_ (L.) — Chocolate-tip. 27—35mm. Abundantly distributed in the deciduous-forest zone throughout the Palaearctic, the favourite haunts of this moth are damp riverside localities, wooded hillsides with an abundant vegetation, etc. The two annual generations appear from April to August. The caterpillar lives on poplars and willows until September; the pupa hibernates. The moth's forewings vary in hue, ranging form grey to reddish.

4 *_Clostera anachoreta_ (D. & S.) — Scarce Chocolate-tip. 30—35mm. Its distribution in the Palaearctic from west to east is very much the same as in the preceding species, but it is absent from the extreme north and south. In the mountains it ascends to about 1,600m. There are two broods in the year. Willows and poplars are the caterpillars' (4b) foodplants; the winter is passed in the pupal stage.

5 _Clostera anastomosis_ (L.) 25—40mm. Distributed over central and northern Europe, and eastwards across the whole of Siberia as far as Japan, this moth shows a preference for damp valleys, sunny hillsides overgrown with lush vegetation, stream and river sides, etc. Two or three broods appear annually. The caterpillars (5b) live gregariously on poplars and willows. Damage caused to woodland trees by this species has often been reported but for quite a number of years it may be rare. Winter is passed in the pupal stage.

6 *_Clostera pigra_ (Hfn.) — Small Chocolate-tip. 22—27mm. Widespread in non-polar Europe, primarily in the mountains, where it occurs in abundance and ascends to an altitude of 2,500m. The moth has two generations, on the wing from May to August. The caterpillar continues developing until October; the pupa overwinters. The moth has a very characteristic resting position: it sits with wings closely clasped and a tuft of hairs situated on the posterior part of the abdomen projecting upwards between them. The moth is not often seen, but the caterpillars are very abundant, living among spun-up leaves on sallow or other willows, or on aspen; they are especially common on low trees growing near springs, damp hillsides, and boggy places overgrown with bushes, where their foodplants may be found abundantly.

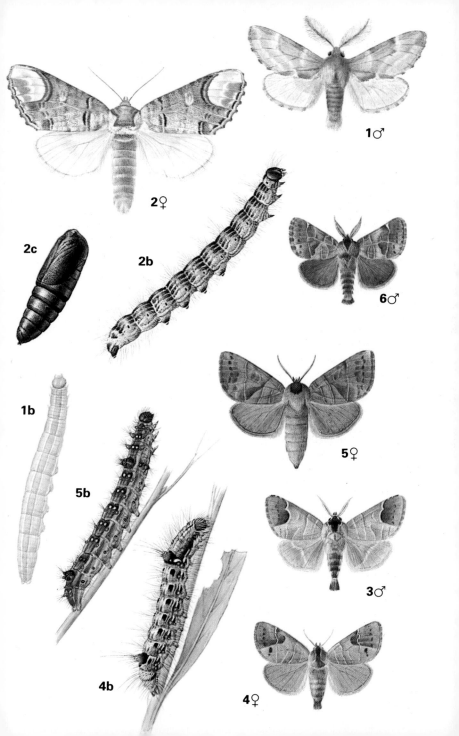

1♂ **1b** **2**♀ **2b** **2c** **3**♂ **4**♀ **4b** **5**♀ **5b** **6**♂

Family: **Sphingidae — hawkmoths**

1 *Mimas tiliae* (L.) — Lime Hawkmoth. 55—70mm. Occurring in Europe and Asia, associated with the belt of deciduous forests, this hawkmoth is absent from polar regions and the southernmost parts of the Palaearctic. The Lime Hawk is common in urban parks, flying from May to July; in warmer regions a second brood may exceptionally appear on the wing in autumn. The caterpillars can be found from July to September on various deciduous trees, such as birches, elms, oaks and alders, but the most favoured foodplant is lime. It is quite common to find the stout larvae lying on the ground under old lime trees after a strong wind. Winter is passed in the pupal stage. This species shows a wide range of colour variation. The most common forms include the well-known reddish-brown f. *brunnea,* and f. *transversa,* in which the median markings on the forewings are coalescent.

2 *Laothoe populi* (L.) — Poplar Hawkmoth. 65—90mm. A species abundant in lowlands but also penetrating in the mountains up to about 1,500m. It is generally distributed throughout Europe, from where it ranges across the Urals and Caucasus to the Altai. Depending on climatic conditions it produces one or two generations in the year. The time of flight of this moth is very long, from May to August, the second generation merging with the first. Caterpillars (2b) may be found from July to September on poplars, willows, and very often on low shrubs. The hibernating pupae (2c) can easily be unearthed by digging at the foot of trees; they often fall victim to moles and other insectivores burrowing for food. The most usual habitats of this species are damp deciduous forests, trees beside running waters, scrublands, peat-bog margins, etc.

3 *Marumba quercus* (D. & S.) 90—100mm. A thermophilic hawkmoth whose range reaches its northern limit in the warmer areas of central Europe, in the steppe and forest-steppe zone. It is more abundant in southern Europe, and extends east across Asia Minor to Armenia. There is but one annual generation which may appear on the wing as early as May but also as late as August. The caterpillars (3b) live towards the end of summer, feeding on oak leaves, especially those of small trees and saplings. Winter is passed in the pupal stage.

4 *Smerinthus ocellata* (L.) — Eyed Hawkmoth. 70—80mm. A species generally distributed in Europe and in the western parts of Asia. There are several species of this genus in the northern hemisphere (particularly in eastern Asia), but this is the only one that lives in Europe. Abundant wherever it occurs, in the mountains it ascends to an altitude of about 2,000m above sea level. A night-flier, like the three preceding hawkmoths, all four species have wings with sinuate outer margins, which they hold in a horizontal position when at rest; in this they differ from the other hawkmoths, which clasp their wings over their bodies in a roof-like manner. The Eyed Hawk produces one generation in the year, flying from May to July; the proboscis is degenerate. The caterpillars live at the end of summer till September, feeding on various deciduous trees, including fruit trees. However, they prefer willows and poplars, and may frequently be found on weeping willows in urban parks.

Family: **Sphingidae — hawkmoths**

1 *Acherontia atropos* (L.) — Death's-head Hawkmoth. 80—120mm. A native of Africa and southwestern Asia, from where it migrates, year by year, far to the north. It arrives from May till June, to give rise, in appropriate localities, to a summer generation. The caterpillars are full-grown by the end of summer and pupate in the soil in a large earthen cell. The pupa is stout, blackish-red in colour, and with a distinct sheen. If the autumn weather is warm the adult moth may emerge and can be found as late as the beginning of December: such individuals are doomed to die without reproducing. And even if the moth does not hatch in autumn, the pupae usually perish during the winter, being incapable of bearing cold or even frosty weather. Only in the warmer parts of central Europe the pupae may, exceptionally, survive a mild winter and the moths emerge in spring. Hibernation in southern Europe is usually more successful. Caterpillars of the Death's-head live on leaves of potato, woody nightshade, thorn-apple, etc. In the past it was possible to find these larvae in potato fields with the aid of a telescope, looking for stripped plants. Nowadays, however, this method would rarely prove successful, because of the abundance of the Colorado Beetle — but the caterpillars may easily be seen on thorn-apple. It frequently happens that the moths are lured by the smell of honey and enter beehives. The bees sometimes kill the intruder and the beekeeper then finds the Hawkmoth's mummified body in his hive. The moth acquired its name from the weird design on its thorax, reminiscent of a skull or death-mask.

2 *Agrius convolvuli* (L.) — Convolvulus Hawkmoth. 80—120mm. This is another visitor arriving from the warm south. Its home is in the tropics of Africa, Asia and Australia, and also North America. Every year it journeys thousands of kilometres to the temperate zone, where it produces a summer generation. Migration occurs from May to July; the caterpillars (2b) live in summer on bindweed. The moths emerge in autumn and, in some years, fly in abundance about deep, tubular flowers, such as *Phlox*. Towards the end of summer the new generation seems to be augmented by further immigrants coming from the south. This species has quite a number of interesting features. First there is the very long proboscis (approximately 10cm) which enables it to suck nectar from even very deep flowers (tobacco for example). The pupa is about 6cm in length and has a very large proboscis sheath in the form of a spiral (2c). Formed in the soil within an earthen cell, the pupa can sometimes be unearthed while digging in the garden, or when ploughing fields or lifting potatoes — this is because bindweed (the foodplant of the caterpillars) is a common weed in fields.

3 *Daphnis nerii* (L.) — Oleander Hawkmoth. 90—130mm. Widely distributed in southern Europe, Africa, Asia Minor and India, this species occurs in most places where the caterpillars' foodplant, *Nerium oleander*, is distributed. In central Europe it occasionally appears as an extremely rare migrant from the south, being unable to survive the European winter. Sometimes it lays eggs on oleanders cultivated as ornamental plants, but the voracious caterpillars soon come to the attention of the gardeners, who usually kill them. This species, like other large hawkmoths, is very rewarding to breed. The large and impressive caterpillars have a little horn at the posterior end (3b) and the newly emerged, immaculate moths are exquisitely coloured — excellent subjects for photography.

Family: **Sphingidae — hawkmoths**

1 *Sphinx ligustri* L. — Privet Hawkmoth. 90—120mm. Distributed throughout the Palaearctic as far as Japan, this fine moth is absent only from northern regions: these it visits, however, without hibernating there. The moths may be seen flying about on warm evenings in May, sometimes still in daylight, using their long proboscides to suck nectar from various deep flowers (mainly from ornamental shrubs in parks). They often lay their eggs in parks and garden situations, even though in nature they inhabit shrubby hillsides and open deciduous woodland with lush undergrowth. Moths are on the wing from May to July; the caterpillars (1b) live in August and September on lilac, common privet, *Spiraea*, and other shrubs. While resting, the larvae sit on a twig in a characteristic position, holding the anterior part of the body erect. The pupa, which hibernates in the ground, is dark reddish-brown, and has a short and smooth proboscis sheath.

2 *Hyloicus pinastri* (L.) — Pine Hawkmoth. 65—80mm. A common species of coniferous forests, particularly in drier biotopes. It is most abundant in warm lowlands and in pine forests on a sandy substrate, but can also be found in mountains nearly to the upper limit of spruce forests. It ranges throughout Europe (with the exception of the south), eastwards across the Urals to Lake Baikal, and has been reported from Japan. One, exceptionally two generations are produced in the year; it flies from May to July, any second generation being on the wing in August. In late evening it can be seen fluttering around blossom, but it also flies late at night, when it can easily be lured to light. The caterpillars live towards the end of summer on pine, spruce, and sometimes also on larch — mostly in young plantations or sunny clearings. The pupae overwinter in moss and pine needles at the foot of the trees. This species seems to undergo local migrations, since the moths can be attracted to light in places where they could not possibly breed. Melanic individuals (f. *unicolor*) sometimes appear in polluted areas.

3 *Deilephila elpenor* (L.) — Elephant Hawkmoth. 45—60mm. Absent from the northernmost regions, otherwise this is one of the more common European hawkmoths species; it also ranges across Asia as far as Japan. Most abundant at medium and submontane elevations, it also ascends to high altitudes in the mountains — approximately 1,500m. In effect it is contained by the distribution of two plants: *Epilobium hirsutum* and *Chamaenerion angustifolium*, on which, towards the end of summer, the caterpillars are most frequently to be found. These are polymorphic, being coloured either green or dark brown (3b). Pupation takes place among plant debris on the ground. Winter is passed in the pupal stage (3c). There is one generation of this moth, flying from May to July; sometimes a second generation appears in August and September.

4 *Deilephila porcellus* (L.) — Small Elephant Hawkmoth. 40—45mm. One of the smaller hawkmoths, it is generally distributed throughout Europe and Asia as far as the Altai. The moth is on the wing from May to June, another generation sometimes appears in August. It is abundant in all grassy localities rich in flowering herbs. In late evening it sucks nectar from flowering catchflies, lychnises, *Viscaria* and other flowers; in the night hours it will come to light. Occurring most abundantly in lowlands, in the mountains it ascends to an elevation of about 1,600m. The caterpillars live in July and August on bedstraw and willow-herb. They resemble the caterpillars of the Elephant Hawkmoth, but they are smaller and have no horn on the abdomen (4b) — the horn is replaced by a double wart. The winter is passed in the pupal stage (4c) on the ground.

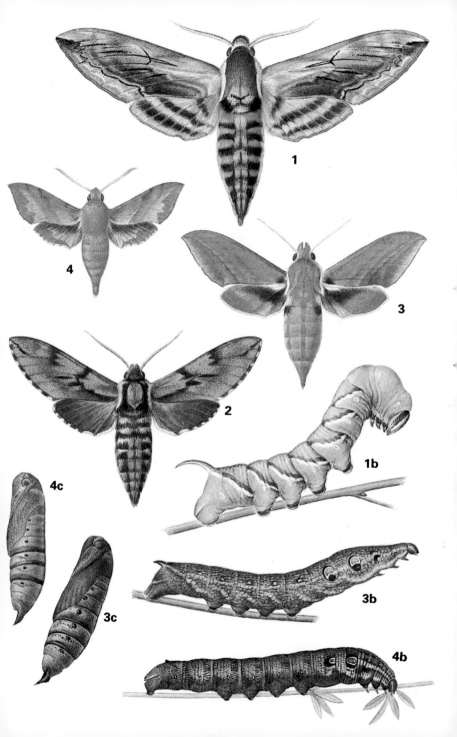

Family: **Sphingidae — hawkmoths**

1 *Hyles euphorbiae* (L.) — Spurge Hawkmoth. 55—75mm. Occurs in central and southern Europe and ranges from western Asia to northern India. Formerly it was one of the most abundant hawkmoths. At harvest time its caterpillars could be found everywhere on wasteground and at the edges of fields where cypress spurge was growing, but in many localities it has now become almost extinct, and, apparently, it comes to the northern parts of central Europe only as a migrant from the south. Only in the warmer regions does it still occur in numbers. There some individuals hibernate, while the populations are also reinforced by immigration from the subtropics. One or two broods are produced in the year, on the wing from May to August. The caterpillars (1b) develop in summer, and again in September and October, many perishing with the onset of early frosts if they have not yet managed to pupate. Various spurge species constitute their diet. The winter is passed in the form of the greyish-ochreous pupae. The moth exhibits a number of variations in pattern and colouration, one of the most frequent being the adoption of a reddish hue (f. *rubescens*).

2 *Hyles vespertilio* (Esp.). 55—75mm. A Mediterranean hawkmoth ranging across Asia Minor to Armenia, it sometimes migrates northwards and may then appear in central Europe, including the Danube basin. In the north it is, of course, an extraordinarily rare visitor. There are two generations: one flies in May and June, the other in August and September. The caterpillar lives from June to October on willow-herb, loosestrife and bedstraw.

3 *Hyles gallii* (Rott.) — Bedstraw Hawkmoth. 60—80mm. With the exception of polar areas this moth inhabits all Europe and Asia, and also North America. It is found from lowlands to high altitudes in the mountains (to about 2,000m), but is most abundant at submontane elevations. Here it flies about in the late evenings, sometimes (mainly in the mountains) even in daytime, visiting flowers in woodland clearings, on flowery hillsides, in outskirts of forests, etc. It has one, sometimes two generations, flying from May to September. The caterpillars can mostly be found towards the end of summer on fireweed (willow-herb) and bedstraw. They pupate in flimsy cocoons among plant debris on the ground. The pupa hibernates.

4 *Hyles lineata* (F.) — Striped Hawkmoth. 60—80mm. Widespread in the subtropics and tropics throughout the world, the nominate ssp. *lineata* (F.) was described from North America, while the European populations are classified as ssp. *livornica* (Esp.) (4). This subspecies extends further to Africa, southern Asia and Australia. This moth is an excellent flier, migrating to great distances, and in years when exceedingly abundant in its breeding areas, it flies far to the north. Such an invasion occurred in 1952, when innumerable individuals were caught at various localities in central Europe. In the late evenings they fluttered about flowering *Phlox* and assembled to light. The species usually produces two generations, one flying in May and June, the other in August and September. The caterpillars live in the intervening period, feeding on bedstraw, willow-herb or other plants. The pupae of the second generation overwinter.

5 *Hippotion celerio* (L.) — Silver-striped Hawkmoth. 70—80mm. A tropical to subtropical species which, in addition to parts of Europe, also inhabits Africa, Asia, Indonesia and Australia, and is found in great abundance everywhere. Several generations are produced, from May to September, which merge into each other. In the Mediterranean region of Europe it has two generations. From there it often flies far to the north — it has been caught in Scotland. Migrations take place most frequently in August and September. The caterpillar lives from June to October on bedstraw, grapevine, and other plants.

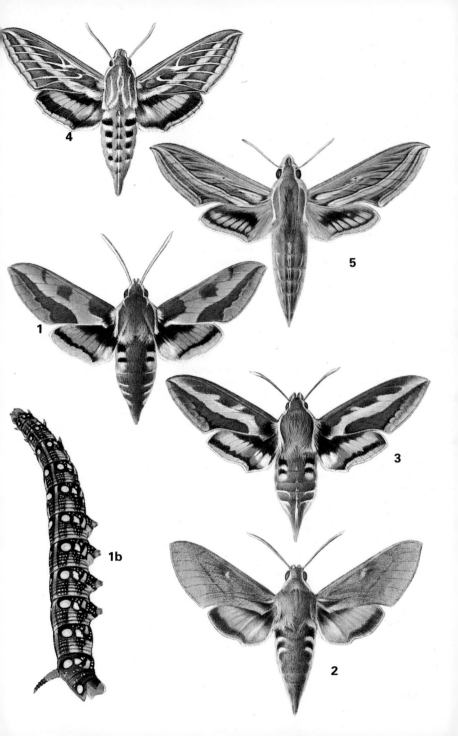

Family: **Sphingidae — hawkmoths**

1 *Proserpinus proserpina* (Pall.) — Willow-herb Hawkmoth. 37—42mm. This hawkmoth occurs predominantly in lowlands, and is to be found by rivers or ponds, or on sandy ground and wastelands, such as old tow-paths or railway banks. In all such localities its foodplants tend to abound. This rare species of oriental origin has penetrated to the warmer parts of Europe, across western Asia. Recently, however, it seems to be rapidly disappearing from central Europe. The moth's single generation is on the wing in May and June; the caterpillars (1b) live in July and August on *Oenothera* and willow-herb. Winter is passed in the pupal stage.

2 **Macroglossum stellatarum* (L.) — Hummingbird Hawkmoth. 40—50mm. An inhabitant of the warmer parts of the Palaearctic subregion, only a short time ago this hawkmoth also spread to North America. It is an outstanding migrant, visiting regions in the far north, polar areas and high mountain elevations, where it can be found at the upper limit of vegetation. These moths come to central Europe at the beginning of summer, sometimes in great numbers. They are diurnal, and may be seen fluttering about in meadows and on field margins, in flower-beds in towns and cities, towards the end of June, and especially from August through autumn, when progeny of the spring immigrants are on the wing. They suck nectar while flying; moving their wings at very high speed they hover in one spot, extending their long proboscis into the flowers. Then they move on to another flower at lightning speed. The caterpillars (2b) live from June to October on bedstraw. In a mild climate the winter is passed in the pupal stage (2c), but in regions with winter frosts the pupae survive the winter only occasionally.

3 **Hemaris tityus* (L.) — Narrow-bordered Bee Hawkmoth. 37—42mm. Distributed throughout temperate Europe and Asia as far as the Altai, this moth lives in flowery meadows and on grassy hillsides, appearing on the wing during bright sunshine in May and June. They are not particularly rare, but being very shy they are frightened away by any attempt to approach them. They also escape attention due to their inconspicuous colouration and vitreous wings. The caterpillar (3b) may be found in July and August on *Knautia, Scabiosa, Succisa*, etc. The pupa hibernates.

4 **Hemaris fuciformis* (L.) — Broad-bordered Bee Hawkmoth. 40—47mm. Ranges over very much the same area as the preceding species, and also flies on bright, sunny days in May and June, in flowery meadows and overgrown forest clearings. It also occurs up to high altitudes in mountains. Its usual haunts are sparse mixed and coniferous woods in whose undergrowth the foodplant of the caterpillars, honeysuckle, can be found growing. *Symphoricarpos* is also a foodplant. The larvae occur in July and August; the pupae overwinter.

5 *Haemorrhagia croatica* (Esp.). 37—42mm. A southern European hawkmoth spreading across Asia Minor to Kurdistan, it is rare in all its habitats. The two generations of the moth are on the wing in June and August. The caterpillar appears from June to October, feeding on scabious. Winter is passed in the pupal stage.

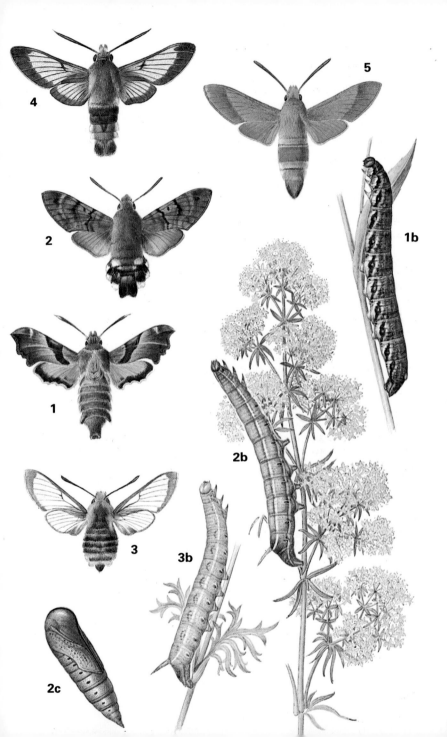

Family: **Saturniidae — emperor moths**

1 *Saturnia pyri* (D. & S.) — Greater or Viennese Emperor. 100—130mm. The largest European moth, widespread in the Mediterranean region both in its European and African parts; from here it ranges eastwards across Asia Minor over the Caucasus to Transcaucasia and the Near East. Central Europe is the northern limit of its European range. This thermophilic moth naturally occurs in forest-steppe areas overgrown with shrubby vegetation, but in agricultural regions it has been able to survive in gardens and orchards. There is but one generation a year, which flies early in spring, from the end of April till the beginning of June (at latest). It is exclusively nocturnal in habit and can easily be lured to light, especially by ultraviolet. Often can be seen whirling about street-lamps and, due to its size, is more suggestive of a bird or a bat than of an insect. By day it may be found sitting, with slightly opened wings, on walls or tree trunks. Since it does not take any food the adult can only survive while its fat reserves last, but usually this is time enough to fulfil its reproductive function. The female lays large, oval, reddish-coloured eggs, slightly flattened at both ends. The young caterpillars are black and invested with red tubercles; when older they are yellowish-green, with coloured tubercles and tough starlike bristles, and are 10—12cm in length (1b). They are polyphagous, but can be found most frequently on fruit trees. The food consumption of so large a caterpillar is considerable, and they can cause damage in a fruit tree nursery. Apart from this these insects do no harm, and their size and beauty justify regarding them as amongst the most remarkable Lepidoptera, to be protected for this reason alone. At about the beginning of August the caterpillar searches for a suitable pupation site. Usually it is a tree trunk about 1m above the ground, or the fork of a branch. Here the caterpillar spins a large pear-shaped cocoon of rough brown or greyish-white silk (1c) and pupates inside. The pupa, which is sturdily built, and brown with black wing sheaths (1d), hibernates.

The Greater Emperor is only one of approximately 1,200 moths of the family Saturniidae that have been described (chiefly from the tropics). The Palaearctic subregion is inhabited by only a few of these gigantic species, which include some of the largest Lepidoptera in the world, attaining a wingspan of more than 200mm. The European species are shown in the following plates. Characteristic of emperor moths are the broad wings adorned with markings suggestive of eyes. Their role is almost certainly protective — to discourage birds from attacking. The mouth-parts are usually degenerate. Males have broad, pectinate antennae. The emperor moths include several species which, in eastern Asia, are bred for silk production. However, they are relatively unimportant compared with the Silkworm, the production of silk from these species being small.

1

1b

1c

1d

Family: **Saturniidae — emperor moths**

1 *Saturnia pavonia* (L.) — Emperor. 40—60mm. Ranges all over Europe; in Asia it reaches the Far East. Having a broad ecological tolerance, this moth can inhabit biotopes of various types, being found in forest-steppes at lower and medium elevations, as well as at high mountain altitudes where it ascends to the upper limit of conifers, at about 1,500—2,000m above sea level. This species shows conspicuous sexual dimorphism. Males differ from the females not only in the shape of their antennae but also in the colouration of the wings. The ground colour of the females' wings is uniform grey all over, while in the males it is orange-brown on the hindwings. Females are also larger than males and have a very stout abdomen. There are also differences in behaviour. While the females remain quietly sitting in daytime and fly only at night, the males are diurnal in habit: in a zigzag flight they dash about at top speed in the afternoon on sunny days in April and May. The basic pattern is the same in all the individual moths, variation affecting only minor details, but more marked differences occur in the colouring of the caterpillars. When young they are black, later on they bear orange-coloured, wart-like protuberances laterally, while the full-grown caterpillars are green, and marked with a black pattern in the form of spots or transverse bands (1b). It is of interest that in caterpillars from lowlands only limited zones of black colour may be observed; sometimes they may even be of a uniform green. In contrast, caterpillars from mountain regions show a tendency to melanism, the green giving way to extensive areas of black. At lower elevations the caterpillars may be found chiefly on blackthorn; at higher elevations they live on bilberry, sallows and other kinds of willows, birches, heather, etc. The pear-shaped cocoon (1c) is spun of brown silk, and, inside, there is a massive violet-brown pupa (1d). This is the overwintering stage, and sometimes two or more winters may pass in dormancy before the moths finally emerge.

2 *Aglia tau* (L.) — Tau Emperor. 50—65mm. Being somewhat different from true emperor moths in certain morphological features, this insect is sometimes classed in a separate family, the Syssphingidae. Living in deciduous forests over the entire Palaearctic as far as Japan, being absent only from the British Isles, it is primarily associated with the distribution of beech, ascending with it to its highest elevations, more than 1,000m. The Tau Emperor has only one generation in the year. Its time of flight coincides with the period when the beeches are budding, appearing on the wing in April; in the mountains this may be postponed until July. The day-flying males may be seen fluttering on bright, sunny mornings. Although there is plenty of opportunity to see them, their capture is extremely difficult because of their darting, zigzag flight. The female is slightly larger and paler than the male. From time to time she may come to light during the night; by day the female rests. In some places, particularly at higher elevations, different individuals sometimes occur in which a dark colouring prevails (2c). The form *ferenigra* has wings with an almost black underside, while in f. *melaina* they are almost black even on their upperside. Most common, however, are intermediately coloured, transitional forms. The caterpillars (2b) live from May to August and, in the course of their development, undergo considerable changes both in shape and colour. The furcular appendages of young caterpillars gradually vanish. Food is provided by beech, oak, birch, hornbeam, lime, and other deciduous trees. The full-fed caterpillar is transformed, in a rough cocoon formed from leaves and a few silken fibres, into an almost black pupa, in which stage the insect overwinters.

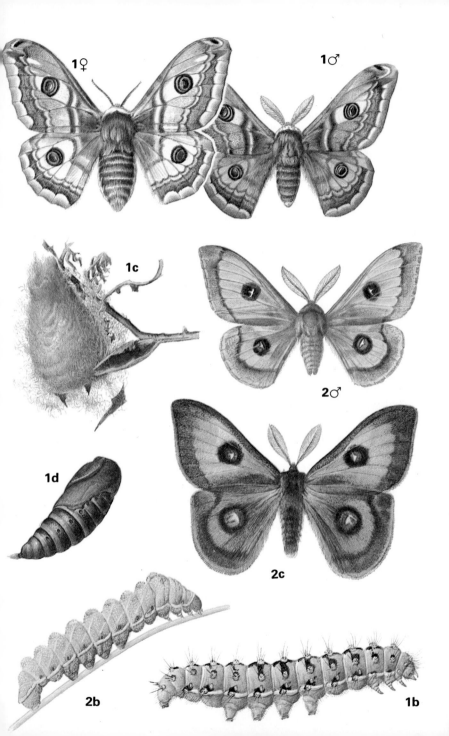

Family: **Lasiocampidae — eggars (lappet moths, lackey moths)**

1 *Malacosoma neustria* (L.) — Lackey. 25—35mm. A common species distributed throughout Europe and Asia. About 1,600m is the highest elevation reached by this species in mountains, but at this level it is scarce. Fundamentally an inhabitant of sparse deciduous forests and forest-steppes, it has adapted to agricultural conditions quite well. It has a particular liking for copses and fruit trees bordering roads. Population explosions often take place in such situations, and it can then become a pest of orchards. Annually there is but one generation, on the wing from June to August. The females oviposit in characteristic ringlets around twigs. Winter is passed in the form of eggs which, in spring, hatch into brightly coloured larvae (1b) which live gregariously in nests. They are largely polyphagous and eat the leaves not only of various fruit trees but also of oaks, willows, etc. The caterpillars pupate in sparse cocoons dusted with yellow, and located in the tree tops, amongst the leaves (1c, d). The Lackey shows much variation, ranging from quite pale specimens of a sandy yellow with barely distinguishable markings, to dark brown moths with a conspicuous transverse band.

2 *Malacosoma castrensis* (L.) — Ground Lackey. 25—35mm. Ranges all over Europe, except for the polar regions; nowhere, however, is this moth abundant. In the east it spreads to central Asia. A local species showing a preference for sunny biotopes, especially those with a sandy substrate, it has but one generation in the year, flying in July and August. Winter is passed as an egg and the caterpillar (2b) develops in late spring, during May and June. It can be found in grassy localities, on slopes exposed to the sun or in dry meadows, feeding on cypress spurge, wormwood, cornflowers, etc. The caterpillar pupates in the grass, wrapped in a whitish cocoon. This somewhat sexually dimorphic species is moderately variable in colour and pattern.

3 *Trichiura crataegi* (L.) — Pale Eggar. 25—30mm. Ranging over northern and central Europe, the northern parts of Asia Minor, and Armenia, in central Europe this insect occurs quite abundantly at submontane elevations, but is rather scarce elsewhere. Its usual haunts are woodland margins, areas with scattered copses, also peaty meadows and heaths, and other such biotopes. There is but one generation a year, on the wing from August to October. The eggs hibernate, and the caterpillars develop in spring. Foodplants include blackthorn, birch, sallow, and other trees and shrubs.

4 *Poecilocampa populi* (L.) — December Moth. 30—45mm. Widespread in Europe, with the exception of the extreme south, spreading further throughout Asia as far as the Amur. This cold-loving species can be found most abundantly at submontane elevations, occurring in lowlands only sporadically. One of the last moths to appear in the year, it does not fly before the onset of the first autumn frosts in October and November. In appropriate localities it may be very abundant, and often comes to light. The range of colour variations is not great, and the female may be distinguished from the male by the antennae. The eggs hibernate, and the caterpillars live in late spring and summer, from May to July, feeding on the leaves of poplars, willows, ashes, alders, but sometimes also on fruit trees.

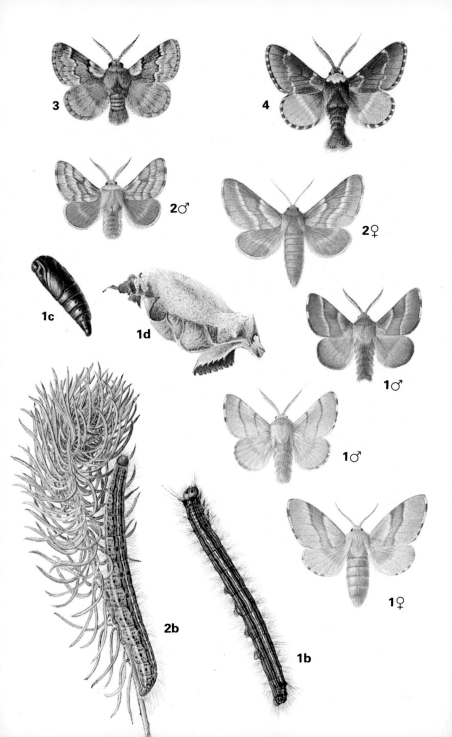

Family: **Lasiocampidae — eggars (lappet moths, lackey moths)**

1 *Eriogaster catax* (L.). 30—40mm. Confined to central, southern and southeastern Europe, to the east of Switzerland and France, this moth favours deciduous forests and forest-steppes, woodland outskirts, shrubby slopes and overgrown meadows. There is only one brood in the year, on the wing in September and October; the caterpillar (1b) lives from May to July on blackthorn, sallow, birch, hawthorn, etc. The pupae, enclosed in an egg-shaped parchment cocoon, often remain dormant until the second or even third year. This species is rather rare in all its localities.

2 *Eriogaster lanestris* (L.) — Small Eggar. 30—40mm. Inhabits almost the whole of Europe, its northern as well as southern regions, and extends eastwards into Asia as far as the Amur. This single-brooded species flies early in spring, sometimes as early as March, and is difficult to catch in nature. Material for collections is more frequently obtained from reared stocks, in which the moths may sometimes hatch in autumn. Under natural conditions the caterpillars (2b) live from May to July, pupating (2c) in a brown, parchment-like cocoon. They feed on a variety of deciduous trees, including blackthorn, hawthorn, birches and willows. The caterpillars are notable for living in large pear-shaped nests which they spin amongst the twigs. Such a nest can be seen from a considerable distance since it is so overloaded with a multitude of caterpillars and frass as to make the supporting branch bend down, out of the crown of the tree or shrub.

3 *Eriogaster rimicola* (D. & S.). 30—35mm. One of the rarer species, it is confined to various circumscribed localities in Europe, mainly in the warmer regions, and displays a marked preference for dry oak forests. Here the moth can be seen on the wing during September and October. The caterpillars hatch in spring, after the eggs have passed through hibernation, and develop in May and June, feeding on oak leaves — chiefly on those of the turkey oak *(Quercus cerris)*.

4 *Lasiocampa quercus* (L.) — Oak Eggar. 45—75mm. Widely distributed all over Europe and Asia, this moth is never abundant in any locality, although in the mountains it ranges up to the elevation of dwarf mountain-firs, where it can be found rather more plentifully. Its bright colouration, particularly that of the males, makes it one of the most beautiful eggars. The female is larger and rather inconspicuously patterned. The day-flying male can be seen on sunny days, darting about in a zigzag flight. Females start being active late in the afternoon, and at night they occasionally come to light. The moth is on the wing from June to August. The caterpillars develop very slowly in autumn and spring, often overwintering twice at higher elevations. They are polyphagous and can be found most frequently on oaks, bilberry, sallows, heather, etc. They pupate in a firm cocoon made of rough brown silk, formed amongst grass. As with the majority of eggars, rearing is not difficult, but rather lengthy.

5 *Lasiocampa trifolii* (D. & S.) — Grass Eggar. 40—55mm. Widely distributed in temperate Europe, mainly in the warmer regions, it extends eastwards across Asia Minor to Armenia. This species, typical of grassy biotopes, steppes and forest-steppes, can be found on sunny hillsides, but also in lucerne and clover fields and on uncultivated wasteground, such as railway banks, etc. It produces one generation a year, on the wing from July to September. The male flies swiftly in early evening; the female is nocturnal in habit. The polyphagous caterpillar (5b) develops in May and June on various low-growing plants. Winter is passed in the egg stage.

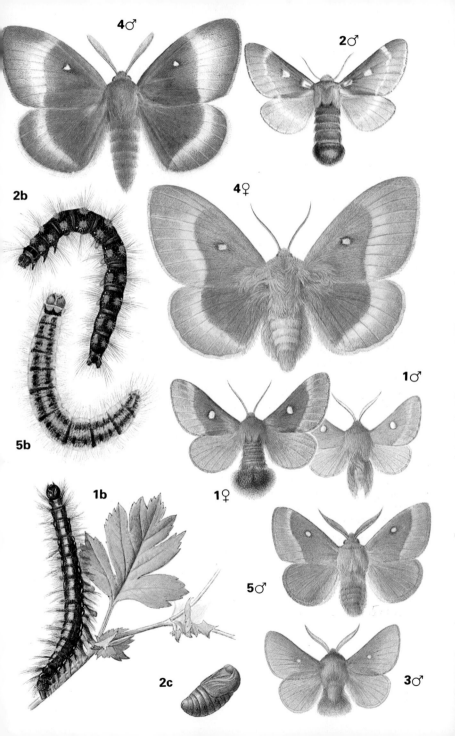

Family: **Lasiocampidae — eggars (lappet moths, lackey moths)**

1 *Macrothylacia rubi* (L.) — Fox. 40–65mm. Widely distributed over the whole of Europe, except for the extreme south and north, and throughout Asia to the Far East, the Fox is at home in grassy biotopes (predominantly at lower elevations) but is also found in the mountains up to an altitude of 1,500m. It occurs most abundantly in steppes, dry meadows and grassy woodland clearings. The single annual brood flies from May to July, the males being conspicuous for their crepuscular activity and swift, darting flight. The females, in contrast, come to light in the night hours. Clutches of the eggs may often be discovered amongst grass; from these emerge hairy caterpillars which, later on, bear golden-yellow dorsal stripes between each segment (1b). The full-grown caterpillars are almost black, with their dorsal parts invested with brownish hairs. The caterpillars are quite large when they hibernate, but continue to feed in spring. In appropriate biotopes they are sometimes extremely abundant, feeding on various low-growing plants, mostly preferring strawberry, bramble, medick, clover, etc. The pupae are formed in brownish cocoons, to be found amongst grass.

2 *Philudoria potatoria* (L.) — Drinker. 45–65mm. Ranging over the whole temperate Palaearctic, from western Europe to Japan, this moth inhabits warm, grassy localities, preferring sandy biotopes. Recently the Drinker has become rare. One generation is produced in the year, on the wing from June to August. The caterpillar (2b) overwinters and, in spring, continues to develop until June. Its diet consists of a variety of grasses. The male differs slightly from the female in colour, but the species also shows much individual variation.

3 *Cosmotriche lunigera* (Esp.). 35–40mm. Widely distributed in both Europe and Asia, but nowhere abundant, this species is associated with the belt of coniferous forests of northern and central Europe, and ranges further to the east. It is of interest that the pale nominate form is, at present, very rare indeed in all localities, while the darkly coloured f. *lobulina* has become prevalent. The time of flight of this single-brooded moth is in May and June. The caterpillar, which hibernates, lives on spruce, rarely on other conifers.

4 *Phyllodesma ilicifolia* (L.) — Small Lappet. 35–40mm. A rare species appearing locally in central and northern Europe, and in the colder parts of Asia as far as the Amur and Japan. It inhabits heather-covered moors, peat-bogs and sparse forests where bilberry is abundant. There is one generation in the year, flying from April to May. The caterpillars live in summer on bilberry, willows, aspens, oaks, etc. Winter is passed in the pupal stage. This species has lately rapidly declined in numbers.

5 *Phyllodesma tremulifolia* (Hb.). 35–45mm. A more thermophilic species, distributed throughout central and more southern Europe, whence it ranges eastwards across southern Russia and Armenia to Central Asia. It also produces only one annual generation, which flies from April to June. The caterpillar lives in July and August, feeding on the leaves of oak, poplar, birch, rose, bilberry, and other shrubs and trees. Winter is passed as a pupa. This is another rare species, although it does not seem to be endangered to the same extent as the Small Lappet.

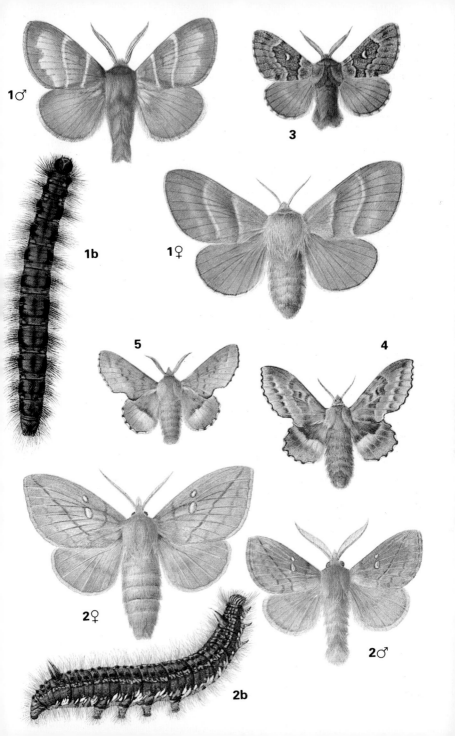

1♂

1b

1♀

3

5

4

2♀

2♂

2b

Family: **Lasiocampidae** — **eggars (lappet moths, lackey moths)**

1 *Gastropacha quercifolia* (L.) — Lappet. 50—90mm. One of the largest European Lepidoptera. Besides Europe, it is distributed throughout Asia to the Far East and Japan. This species, peculiar to forest-steppes and open, warm deciduous forests, has also become well adapted to gardens and orchards, and can be found in many agricultural areas. Of late, however, pesticides and probably also other factors have contributed to its disappearance from orchards, and to it becoming a rather rare species in many places. The Lappet exhibits a very wide range of colour variations. Northern Europe is the home of the darker-coloured form *alnifolia*. In the south, where this species produces two generations a year, there occurs a lighter-coloured summer generation, f. *meridionalis*. In the greater part of its range there is a single generation in the year, on the wing in July and August. The caterpillars hibernate while relatively young and develop very quickly in May and June. They prefer to live on various fruit trees of the genus *Prunus*, but may also be found on apple trees, hazels, etc. In the past, fruit tree branches completely stripped by these larvae could often be observed. When this happened the dark grey cocoons of the pupae were conspicuous among the naked branches. The adult moths emerge about ten days after pupation.

2 *Odonestis pruni* (L.). 40—65mm. Ranging from central Italy and the Balkan Peninsula across Asia Minor further to the east, this species produces but one generation a year. The moths are on the wing from June to August and are, for the most part, rather rare. The caterpillars (2b) develop towards the end of summer and hibernate (probably) in the third instar. They grow to full size in spring. Their food is provided by various species of the genus *Prunus*, and by oak, birch, alder, elm, etc.

3 *Dendrolimus pini* (L.) — Pine-tree Lappet. 45—70mm. Widespread in the temperate zone throughout the Palaearctic subregion, the occurrence of this moth is largely circumscribed by the distribution of pine *(Pinus silvestris)*, and is absent from the British Isles, southern Europe and northern Africa. The species is given to great variation as regards colouring, there also being some difference in size and colouration between the male and the female; many forms have been described. The most interesting of these are the brightly coloured f. *montana* which occurs in mountains, and the small and dark f. *obscura* to be found on peat-bogs. Paler and rather large specimens (f. *grisescens*) are often found at warm, lower elevations. The Pine-tree Lappet has one generation in the year, on the wing from June to August. The caterpillar passes the winter when almost full-grown. Some caterpillars develop rather slowly and may hibernate twice. They live on the pine, rarely on spruce or fir, and pupate (3c) in a grey web amongst pine needles. This moth is a forest pest, outbreaks occurring at long, irregular intervals, but on these occasions it can cause devastation to pine plantations (mostly in the lowlands).

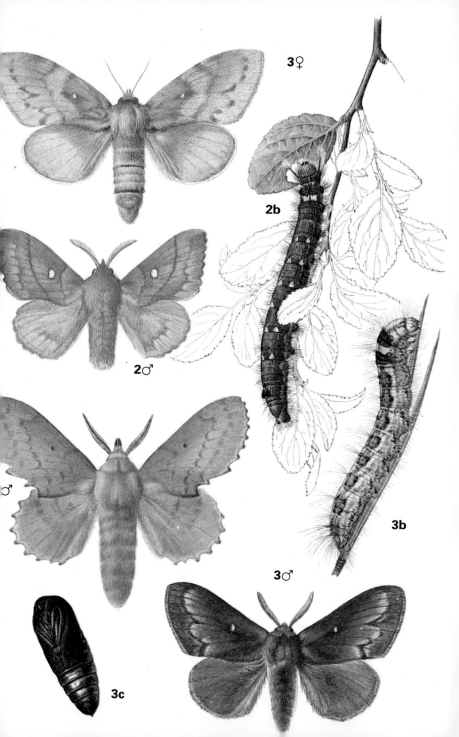

3♀

2b

3b

2♂

♂

3♂

3c

Family: **Lemoniidae**

1 *Lemonia taraxaci* (Esp.). 45—55mm. One of a family whose few species are strictly confined to the Palaearctic subregion. Central Europe is the home of only the two species included here: they are very local and usually rather rare. *Lemonia taraxaci* haunts warm, grassy slopes in hills and mountains, 2,000m being the highest altitude attained. Its range extends from France to southern Russia, and is limited to warmer areas. There is one brood in the year, which appears on the wing from August to October and is nocturnal in habit. The polyphagous caterpillars emerge in spring, after the eggs have passed the winter, and live from May to July on a variety of low plants — primarily hawkweed and dandelion.

2 *Lemonia dumi* (L.) 50—65mm. Distributed over the temperate zone of Europe from temperate Scandinavia to the Balkans, this *Lemonia* extends east to the Urals. Its haunts are confined to damp meadows overgrown with profuse herbaceous vegetation, at low and moderate elevations. It also favours peat-bogs. There is a single generation of this day-flying moth, on the wing on bright days from September to November. Winter is passed in the egg stage. The caterpillars (2b) develop in spring, in May and June, on low plants, also showing a preference for hawkweed and dandelion.

Family: **Thaumetopoeidae — processionary moths**

3 *Thaumetopoea processionea* (L.) — Oak Processionary Moth. 25—35mm. Widespread in central and southern Europe, in western Europe this moth inhabits Portugal. Confined to warm oak forests and forest-steppes, it is extremely abundant in its haunts. There is but one generation a year, flying in July and August. The eggs hibernate and the caterpillars develop in late spring, during May and June, living gregariously in nests made on old oak trees. The larvae have long tufted hairs which easily break off when touched, and can cause unpleasant dermatitis. The caterpillars often develop in such multitudes that they cause considerable damage to forests by stripping the leaves from whole branches. Their interesting behaviour involves marching in columns in head-to-tail contact, which habit is the basis of the name for this species.

4 *Thaumetopoea pinivora* (Tr.). 25—45mm. As with the previous species, the geographical distribution of this moth is not very extensive either, being limited to eastern and central Europe. It occurs in dry pine forests growing on sandy soil. One generation is produced in the year, on the wing in July and August. Winter is passed in the egg stage; the caterpillar develops in spring, from April to July, and feeds on pine. The moths bear a close resemblance to the preceding species, with which they are commonly confused: the only obvious difference is the more conspicuous markings on the pale, greyish-white wings.

Family: **Endromidae**

5 *Endromis versicolora* (L.) — Kentish Glory. 50—65mm. This locally abundant species haunts the birch forests of Europe, including the mountains. Eastwards it ranges over the forest and forest-steppe zone of Asia as far as southern Siberia and the Far East. A large-sized spring moth, on the wing from March to May, the males can be seen flying about on sunny mornings in birch woods, at a time when the leaves have not yet opened. They also fly at night. The caterpillar (5b) develops from May to July, and is usually to be found on birch; the pupa (5c) spends the winter in the ground until the following spring.

3♂

5♂

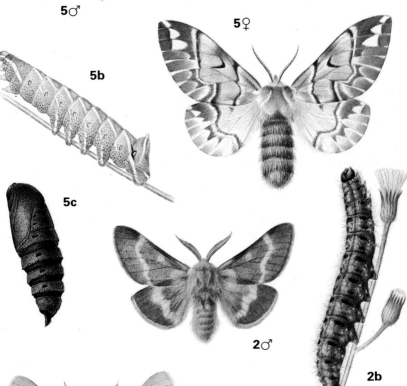

5♀

5b

5c

2♂

2b

1♂

4♂

Family: **Drepanidae — hook-tips**

1 *Drepana falcataria* (L.) — Pebble Hook-tip. 27–35mm. Distributed over central and northern Europe, this moth occurs in great numbers in deciduous forests, shrubby biotopes, and in the parks of towns and cities. The first of the two generations produced in the year flies from April to June, the second from July to August. The caterpillars (1b) live in June, and again from August to October, feeding on birch and alder, showing a particular affection for young saplings. Winter is passed in the pupal stage (1c).

2 *Sabre harpagula* (Esp.) — Scarce Hook-tip. 25–35mm. Ranges from central and northern Europe eastwards over the whole of Asia to the Far East. The favourite habitats of this moth are deciduous forests or forest-steppes. Two broods develop in the year: one flying from May to June, the other in August. The caterpillars live in July, and again in autumn, the second generation producing pupae which hibernate. The caterpillar's foodplants are alder, birch, oak and lime. This species is relatively rare. Both caterpillars and pupae can be found among spun-up leaves.

3 *Falcaria lacertinaria* (L.) — Scalloped Hook-tip. 27–35mm. Occurs throughout northern and central Europe, in the east extending across the Urals to Siberia and the Far East. In the more southern parts of Europe it can be found only in the mountains. There are two generations in the year, flying from April to August — their caterpillars develop in June and in September, and live among spun-up leaves of birches or alders, where they also pupate. Winter is passed in the pupal stage. The second generation is somewhat different from the first, being larger in size and paler in colour.

4 *Drepana binaria* (Hfn.) — Oak Hook-tip. 18–30mm. A species peculiar to warm deciduous forests (mostly oak and mixed woodland), distributed over the warmer parts of Europe, and southeastwards across Asia Minor to Armenia. Annually two broods are produced, which are sometimes partial, on the wing from May to August. The caterpillars develop towards the beginning of summer and again in September, their foodplants being oak, beech and alder. The pupa hibernates among leaves spun together. The male is considerably smaller than the female, and there are also slight differences in the markings.

5 *Drepana cultraria* (F.) — Barred Hook-tip. 20–28mm. The distribution of this hook-tip is limited to central and southeastern Europe, the northern parts of Asia Minor being its eastern limit. In addition, it can be found sporadically in southern Europe. It accompanies beech forests to the upper limit of their distribution (approximately 1,000m). Two generations emerge in the year, the second of which may be partial; at higher altitudes there is only one generation. In nature the moths are in evidence from April to August. The caterpillars live at the beginning of summer and in September, feeding on the leaves of beeches, and probably oaks. Winter is passed in the pupal stage.

6 *Cilix glaucata* (Sc.) — Chinese Character. 18–22 mm. In colouration and shape this moth is rather different from the other species of this family, being mostly white and the wings lacking the concavity typical of the other species. The Chinese Character also has a much wider distribution area, occurring in central and southern Europe, and in the east in the forest and forest-steppe parts of Asia as far as the Amur. It has also been reported from North America. In warm localities exposed to sunshine it usually occurs in great abundance. There are two generations annually, on the wing from April to August. The caterpillars live from May to September on blackthorn, plum trees, and hawthorn. Winter is passed in the form of pupae.

Family: **Thyatiridae**

1 *Habrosyne pyritoides* (Hfn.) — Buff Arches. 35—40mm. Ranges over temperate Europe eastwards across Armenia and northern India to eastern Asia. This common species occurs in all forests having an abundant herbaceous and shrubby undergrowth, on overgrown slopes and clearings, and in urban parks and gardens. It is a single-brooded species appearing on the wing from May to August; caterpillars live towards the end of summer, feeding on raspberry canes and bramble; the pupae overwinter.

2 *Thyatira batis* (L.) — Peach Blossom. 32—38mm. Widely distributed throughout temperate Europe and Asia to the Far East and Japan, this beautiful species is characteristic of deciduous and coniferous forests with dense undergrowth. One or two generations develop in the year, according to climatic conditions, and can be seen on the wing from May to August. The biology of the caterpillars (2b) and their foodplants are similar to the preceding species.

3 *Tetheella fluctuosa* (Hb.) — Satin Lutestring. 35—40mm. Confined to temperate Europe only, in the south this moth is more common in the mountains. Its occurrence depends largely on the distribution of birch forests, but it is also at home in peat-bogs and in mixed forests. The single generation is on the wing from June to August. The caterpillars live towards the end of summer on birch; winter is passed as pupae. In the southern part of the range, a second generation may occasionally develop.

4 *Ochropacha duplaris* (L.) — Common Lutestring. 27—32mm. The range of this species extends from central and northern Europe over the forest belt of Asia to southern Siberia. It is found in damp biotopes, including deciduous forests and shrubby clearings, also in the parks of towns and cities. There is one generation of the moth at higher elevations, two in the lowlands; they are on the wing from May to September. The caterpillar lives from June to October on poplar, alder and birch.

5 *Tethea or* (D.& S.) — Poplar Lutestring. 35—42mm. Inhabits the forest zone of the whole of Europe and Asia and reaches to the Far East, northern Japan and Korea. This moth is most common in regions covered with deciduous and coniferous forests, but has also become adapted to urban gardens and parks. The time of flight of the two annual generations is from April to August. The caterpillars live on poplars and sallows. Winter is passed in the pupal stage. This species exhibits tendencies to melanism. The almost black f. *albingensis* is abundant in cultivated areas (5c).

6 *Tethea ocularis* (L.) — Figure of Eighty. 32—38mm. Though also generally distributed throughout Europe and Asia, it is somewhat rarer and more thermophilic than the previous species. It haunts damp localities, water meadows, and banks of brooks and rivers. Two generations occur, flying from May to August. The caterpillar lives on various kinds of poplars until September. The pupa hibernates.

7 *Achlya flavicornis* (L.) — Yellow Horned. 35—40mm. Ranges throughout northern and temperate Europe, across the whole of Asia to eastern Siberia. As one of the first Lepidoptera of spring, it appears on the wing as early as March and April, at a time when sallows are in bloom. Its favourite haunts are birch and mixed woods. There is but one generation a year. The caterpillars live in May and June on birch.

8 *Polyploca ridens* (F.) — Frosted Green. 30—35mm. Widespread throughout the warmer parts of central Europe, as well as in southern and southeastern Europe, the single generation of this moth resembles the above species in appearing on the wing very early in the year. The caterpillars (8b) live in May and June on oak. They pupate among spun-up leaves or in litter on the ground, the pupae lying dormant until the next spring. The species is rather abundant.

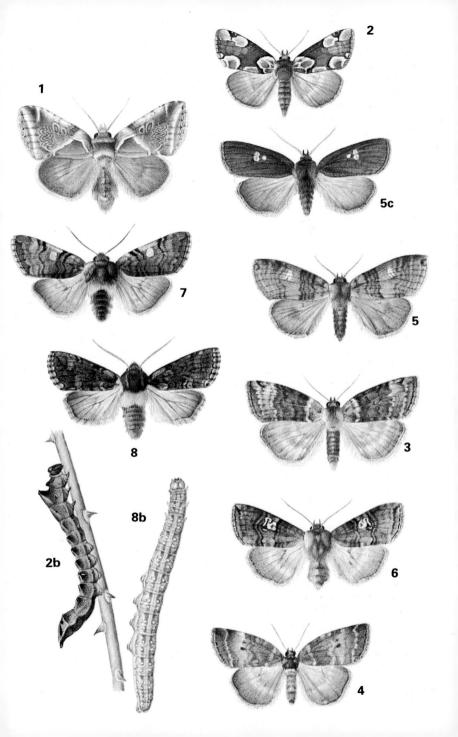

Family: **Geometridae** — **geometrids (inchworms, loopers)**

1 *Archiearis parthenias* (L.) — Orange Underwing. 30—40mm. Distributed throughout the temperate and colder regions of Europe and Asia as far as Japan, in the mountains this moth ascends up to the treeline. On sunny days, it can be seen on the wing as early as March and April, and has a special liking for settling on wet ground to suck water. On frosty mornings it can easily be beaten from trees. The caterpillar lives in spring, feeding on birches.

2 *Archiearis notha* (Hb.) — Light Orange Underwing. 28—35mm. Closely resembles the preceding moth in appearance, but in this species the males have pectinate antennae. It inhabits moist deciduous forests in Europe and Asia. The moths are on the wing in March and April, when the weather is sunny. The caterpillar lives on aspen, birch and sallow.

3 *Alsophila aescularia* (D. & S.) — March Moth. 25—35mm. An abundant early spring species widely distributed over all Europe and Asia, associated with deciduous and mixed forests, forest-steppes and orchards. Moths appear from February to May, but only males may be seen flying: the females are wingless. The caterpillars live in spring on various deciduous trees. Winter is passed in the pupal stage.

4 *Asthena albulata* (Hfn.) — Small White Wave. 14—18mm. Ranges from Europe eastwards to the Caucasus and Kazakhstan. This moth produces one generation a year which flies from May to July. The caterpillar feeds on oak, birch, hazel, etc. The pupa hibernates.

5 *Hydrelia flammeolaria* (Hfn.) — Small Yellow Wave. 14—20mm. Distributed over Europe and Asia as far as Japan, the favourite habitats of this moth are damp biotopes on the outskirts of deciduous forests, valleys, and water meadows. It flies in one generation, from May to August. The caterpillars live in summer on alder, maple, lime, birch, etc.; winter is passed as a pupa.

6 *Spargania luctuata* (D.& S.) — White-banded Carpet. 22—28mm. Occurs in central and northern Europe; in the south it is more common in the mountains. The species is also widespread throughout Asia and North America, so that its distribution is circumpolar. One or two generations emerge during the year — from May to August. The caterpillars live from summer till autumn and feed on various kinds of willow-herbs and *Vaccinium*. Winter is passed in the pupal stage.

7 *Minoa murinata* (Sc.) — Drab Looper. 14—18mm. An inconspicuous geometrid distributed over central and southern Europe, and in western and central Asia — predominantly in hilly regions. The two generations it produces in the year can be seen on the wing from April to September, fluttering about in grassy places in woodland margins and forest-steppes. The caterpillar, living until October, is peculiar to cypress and other spurges. The moth has no markings whatsoever but the basic colouration is variable: yellowish, pink or grey-brown.

8 *Epirrita autumnata* (Bkh.) — Autumnal Moth. 25—35mm. Distributed throughout central and northern Europe and the colder regions of Asia to the Far East. In the mountains this moth ascends to the treeline; otherwise it displays a preference for peat-bogs, birch or mixed woodlands on peaty grounds, and cool valleys. The moths are on the wing until late autumn, from September to November. Winter is passed in the egg stage. The caterpillar feeds on willow, birch, maple, etc.

9 *Operophtera brumata* (L.) — Winter Moth. 22—28mm. Generally distributed in central and northern Europe, in Asia as far as the Amur, the single generation of this moth flies in late autumn and winter — from September till December and even January and February. The caterpillars (9b) are polyphagous, and, in spring, can become pests of deciduous trees in forests and orchards. The female moth has degenerate wings.

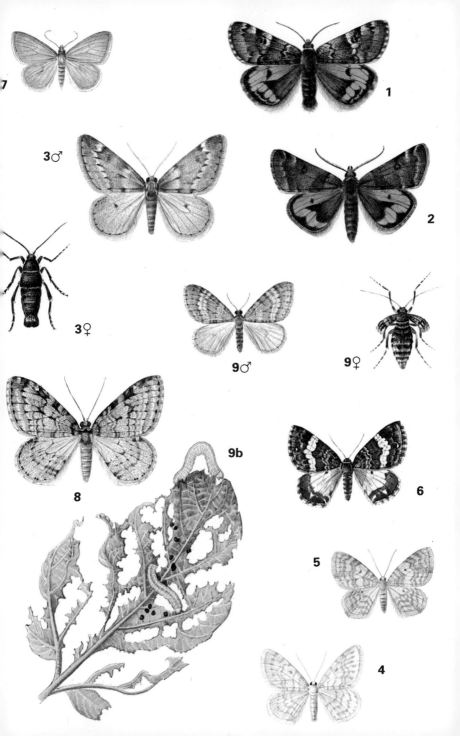

Family: **Geometridae** — **geometrids (inchworms, loopers)**

1 *Entephria caesiata* (D.& S.) — Grey Mountain Carpet. 30—35mm. A species peculiar to northern and mountainous regions, known from central and northern Europe and northern Asia as far as Kamchatka. The single annual generation flies from June to August, and is very abundant in mountain localities. The moths are given to great variation — dark, melanic specimens may frequently be seen. Geographical forms have also been described, which probably arose in consequence of long-term separation of isolated populations (in Iceland, for example). The caterpillar feeds on bilberry, and overwinters.

2 *Anticlea badiata* (D.& S.) — Shoulder Stripe. 25—30 mm. Widespread throughout temperate Europe, this species ranges across the northern parts of Asia Minor to central Asia and Japan. Lowlands and warm, forested hillsides are its principal habitats. There is but one generation a year which can be seen on the wing early in spring, from March to May. The caterpillar lives from May to July and feeds only on dog rose. The moth overwinters in the pupal stage.

3 *Pelurga comitata* (L.) — Dark Spinach. 25—30mm. Distributed over temperate Europe and eastwards as far as eastern Asia, this moth is common in open country, steppes, forest-steppes, fields, and wasteground. The flight period of this moth is very long, from June to September, yet it probably has only one generation. The caterpillars live towards the end of summer on orache, goosefoot, and wormwood. Winter is passed in the pupal stage.

4 *Mesoleuca albicillata* (L.) — Beautiful Carpet. 27—32mm. Widely distributed in Europe and Asia as far as Siberia, this rather scarce species inhabits open, damp, but warm forests and sunny overgrown hillsides. Moths are on the wing from May to August; the caterpillars live towards the end of summer on raspberry canes and bramble. The pupae hibernate.

5 *Colostygia olivata* (D.& S.) — Beech-green Carpet. 22—27mm. Ranges over the temperate zone of Europe across the Urals and the Caucasus eastwards to the Altai. A moth more abundant in the mountains, it occurs in sparse deciduous and coniferous forests. There is one generation, on the wing in July and August. The caterpillar lives from autumn till spring, inclusive of its winter sleep, feeding on bedstraw, sorrel, and other herbs.

6 *Colostygia pectinataria* (Kn.) — Green Carpet. 22—27mm. Distributed over central and northern Europe, in Asia this species extends to the Altai. In the south it is more or less confined to the mountains, its usual habitats being deciduous and coniferous forests, reaching to the upper limit of deciduous trees. The single generation flies from May to July. The caterpillars live from autumn till spring, hibernating through the wintertime. Their diet consists of various kinds of bedstraw and nettle. Locally this species is very abundant. A few days after emergence the moths tend to lose their green colour.

7 *Lampropteryx suffumata* (D.& S.) — Water Carpet. 25—32mm. One of the spring geometrids, occurring from April to July. It inhabits beech, spruce and mixed forests, from lowlands up to high mountain altitudes in temperate Europe, and ranging east into central Asia. The caterpillar lives at the beginning of summer, feeding on various kinds of bedstraw and goosegrass.

8 *Cosmorhoe ocellata* (L.) — Purple Bar. 20—25mm. An abundant geometrid species widespread in Europe, with the exception of polar regions, and extending in Asia as far as the Altai. There are two annual generations, the first of which flies from May to July, the second overlaps and continues until September. The caterpillars feed on bedstraw of various kinds, where they can be found from June until autumn. The full-fed caterpillars hibernate, each wrapped in a finely spun web, wherein they pupate immediately after the onset of spring.

8

3

1

4

2

7

5

6

Family: **Geometridae — geometrids (inchworms, loopers)**

1 *Eulithis prunata* (L.) — Phoenix. 30—35mm. Distributed throughout Europe, Asia and North America, this moth is peculiar to the margins of deciduous forests and forest-steppes, and ascends to quite high mountain elevations. Annually there is one generation, on the wing from June to September. Hibernation takes place in the egg stage, and the caterpillars emerge in spring to develop during May and June, feeding on various species of the genus *Prunus* — mainly blackthorn, but also hawthorn, gooseberry and currant. The moth exhibits much variation in markings.

2 *Eulithis testata* (L.) — Chevron. 25—35mm. The distribution of this species in central Europe is discontinuous, but in the north of Europe and Asia, in the Urals and in Siberia, and also in North America it is continuous. It inhabits damp meadows, peat-bogs, and deciduous and coniferous forests growing on peaty soil. There is one generation in the year, the flight period being July to September. The egg hibernates; the caterpillar develops in spring on heather, bilberry, aspen, willow, etc.

3 *Eulithis populata* (L.) — Northern Spinach. 25—32mm. Also distributed over the whole Palaearctic and in North America, the Northern Spinach occurs in greatest abundance in mountains, where it ascends up to the belt of dwarf pines: the dark forms it produces here are most interesting. The species has but one generation a year, which emerges over a rather long period — from June to September, depending primarily on the climate of the particular locality. The egg overwinters. The caterpillars (3b) feed mainly on bilberry and certain trees, such as willow and aspen. The species is variable, and there are a number of geographical races.

4 *Eulithis mellinata* (F.) — Spinach. 27—30mm. Distributed over the whole Palaearctic to the Far East, but only locally, this moth is associated with open woods where the undergrowth includes gooseberries and currants, the foodplants of the caterpillars. The species also occurs on cultivated plants in the neighbourhood of towns and cities. It is single-brooded, flying during June and July. The caterpillar develops in spring, after the egg has hibernated.

5 *Eulithis pyraliata* (D.& S.) — Barred Straw. 28—33mm. Distributed over Europe and Asia as far as the Amur, this moth tolerates a wide range of ecological conditions. It is often found in grassy biotopes in lowlands and steppes, as well as in mountains at rather high altitudes, and is on the wing from June to August. The caterpillars live in spring (as is the case with all species of this genus), feeding on bedstraw of various kinds and on several other plants.

6 *Ecliptopera silaceata* (D.& S.) — Small Phoenix. 23—27mm. Found in open woods, mainly those situated by water, throughout Europe, Asia and North America. The species produces a number of clearly defined forms. Two broods develop during the year, flying during April to August. The caterpillar lives from June to September on willow-herb, touch-me-not, etc. Winter is passed in the pupal stage.

7 *Chloroclysta citrata* (L.) — Dark Marbled Carpet. 25—30mm. An extremely abundant and variable species, widespread in central and northern Europe and Asia, predominantly in the mountains. One or two generations are produced, flying from July to August. Hibernation takes place in the egg stage. The polyphagous caterpillars live in spring.

8 *Chloroclysta truncata* (Hfn.) — Common Marbled Carpet. 24—30mm. The distribution of this moth is similar to that of the preceding species, although it extends further to the south and descends to lower altitudes. Annually there are one or two generations, on the wing from May to September. The polyphagous caterpillar (8b) hibernates. This species presents innumerable variations. Moreover, it is so similar to the preceding species that certain differentiation is often dependent on examination of the genitalia.

Family: **Geometridae — geometrids (inchworms, loopers)**

1 *Cidaria fulvata* (Forst.) — Barred Yellow. 20—25mm. Ranging over temperate Europe and Asia to the Altai, this species, an inhabitant of steppes and forest-steppes to arid grassy and shrubby biotopes, produces only one generation in the year: this flies from June to August. It is also common in fields and gardens, particularly in lowlands. Winter is passed in the egg stage; the caterpillar lives in spring both on dog rose and on cultivated roses.

2 *Thera variata* (D.& S.) — Spruce Carpet. 18—25mm. Widely distributed throughout Europe and Asia, wherever spruce forests are to be found, this moth ascends to high elevations in mountains (reaching the timberline) and occurs in the polar regions of the north. One or two generations are produced in the year: these are on the wing from May to September. When only one generation develops, the caterpillars grow very slowly, feeding on spruce, fir, and (exceptionally) on other conifers (2b). In this larval form the species hibernates.

3 *Eustroma reticulata* (D.& S.) — Netted Carpet. 20—25mm. Locally distributed in the forest belt of Europe (but more abundant in Asia), this species has a special liking for shady localities, damp valleys, and waterside biotopes rich in the caterpillars' foodplant, the touch-me-not. The moth flies from June to August, mostly in one generation, but sometimes in two. It is to be found in lowlands as well as in the mountains up to 1,000m. The caterpillar develops towards the end of summer, and the pupa hibernates. The species is extremely variable in its markings.

4 *Electrophaes corylata* (Thbg.) — Broken-barred Carpet. 22—30mm. Widely distributed in non-polar Europe and Asia, crossing the Urals and extending over Siberia to the Amur, this moth is found in deciduous forests and damp woods at low elevations, but also in mixed forests in the mountains. Its only generation flies from May to July. The caterpillar develops towards the end of summer, feeding on the leaves of birch, blackthorn, hawthorn, hazel, etc. Winter is passed in the pupal stage.

5 *Hydriomena furcata* (Thbg.) — July Highflier. 23—30mm. An extraordinarily variable species (5,5c) occurring in northern and central Europe, the whole of Asia and in North America. It flies from June to September and may be extremely abundant in circumscribed localities, particularly in the mountains, where it ascends above the timberline. The eggs hibernate and the caterpillars develop in spring, eating various kinds of willow and blueberry.

6 *Melanthia procellata* (D.& S.) — Pretty Chalk Carpet. 27—32mm. A thermophilic species ranging over central and southern Europe, across Asia Minor and Transcaucasia to southern Siberia, Korea and Japan. Two generations appear on the wing from May to September. The caterpillar develops in the summertime, feeding on *Clematis vitalba*; the pupa hibernates. The species is confined to low-lying, moist woods and deciduous forests, warm lowland valleys and river basins, where the foodplant occurs.

7 *Rheumaptera subhastata* (Nlck.). 23—28mm. An immensely variable species flying in the north and in the high mountains of the Holarctic region. It is rather rare at lower elevations. One brood produced per year, on the wing from May to July. The caterpillar lives from July to September, feeding on bilberry. Winter is passed in the pupal stage.

8 *Rheumaptera undulata* (L.) — Scallop Shell. 25—30mm. Occurs locally in the temperate zone of Europe, as well as in all Asia, reaching to the Far East. This moth is only sporadic in mountains, preferring open mixed or pine forests interspersed with deciduous trees where the forest floor is covered with bilberry. There is only one generation, which flies from May to August; caterpillars develop towards the end of summer and feed on sallow, aspen, alder and bilberry. Winter is passed in the form of pupae.

246

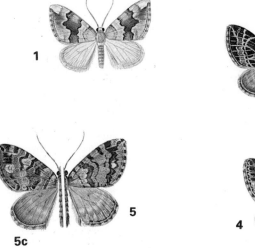

Family: **Geometridae** — **geometrids (inchworms, loopers)**

1 *Eupithecia abietaria* (Gz.) — Cloaked Pug. 20—25mm. A moth belonging to the very abundant genus *Eupithecia*, represented by more than 100 species in Europe alone, most of them being very similar in appearance. Their identification requires much experience, or else recourse to genitalic preparations must be made. Distinctively coloured species are exceptional. However, the species differ considerably in their larvae, foodplants and bionomics. *E. abietaria* is distributed over central and northern Europe and ranges into Asia as far as southern Siberia. A single generation appears from May to July. The caterpillars live in summer on young spruce, pine and fir cones.

2 *Eupithecia linariata* (D.& S.) — Toadflax Pug. 11—16mm. Occurs in Europe and western Asia. Two generations emerge annually, flying from May to September. The caterpillar lives from July to October on the flowers of toadflax. The pupa hibernates. Very similar in colouration is *E. pyreneata* Mab., a species living in the flowers of foxglove (*Digitalis lutea* and *D. grandiflora*).

3 *Eupithecia venosata* (F.) — Netted Pug. 17—22mm. Distributed over Europe and eastwards to central Asia, this pug lives both in lowlands and mountains, and flies from May to July. The caterpillar occurs in July and August on various plants of the pink family. The pupa overwinters.

4 *Eupithecia centaureata* (D.& S.) — Lime-speck Pug. 16—20mm. Ranges from northern Africa across the whole of Europe to central Asia, and is abundant everywhere. Two generations of the moth fly practically continuously from May to September. The caterpillar occurs from June till autumn, feeding on the flowers of various plants. This species is an inhabitant of various biotopes, including sparse forests, forest-steppes and fields.

5 *Eupithecia vulgata* (Hw.) — Common Pug. 15—18mm. An extremely abundant species ranging from Europe to eastern Asia. It is a brownish, uniformly coloured species, typical of the majority in the genus *Eupithecia*. Its single generation is on the wing from May to July, in mixed forests and fields. The caterpillar is polyphagous and occurs during July and August. Winter is passed in the pupal stage.

6 *Eupithecia icterata* (Vill.) — Tawny Speckled Pug. 20—23mm. Distributed throughout Europe and east into central Asia, this pug lives in both wooded and treeless areas, from lowlands to the mountains. The species produces innumerable variations, a conspicuous and frequently occurring form being the yellowish f. *subfulvata*. The moth flies from June to September; the caterpillar lives in the autumn on milfoil and common tansy.

7 *Eupithecia succenturiata* (L.) — Bordered Pug. 20—23mm. Widespread in Europe and in central Asia, this moth haunts both wooded and treeless areas. An extremely variable species, it flies from May to September. The caterpillar lives towards the end of summer on wormwood, milfoil and common tansy. The pupa hibernates.

8 *Eupithecia nanata* (Hb.) — Narrow-winged Pug. 13—17mm. Found all over Europe wherever the foodplant of the caterpillar, heather, is found. Far from rare on heaths and peat-bogs, the wings of this pug are markedly pointed. There are two generations in the year, flying from May to August. The caterpillar lives from June to October; the pupa overwinters.

9 *Chloroclystis rectangulata* (L.) — Green Pug. 15—20mm. Widely distributed over the whole of Europe and Asia as far as Japan, it is a species characteristic of forest-steppes and forests where its foodplants, pears and apples, grow. The caterpillars (9b) eat the blossom during spring. The moth is on the wing from June to August, and is abundant in gardens and orchards.

Family: **Geometridae — geometrids (inchworms, loopers)**

1 *Perizoma alchemillata* (L.) — Small Rivulet. 14—18mm. Distributed over temperate Europe and Asia as far as the Amur, this moth lives in a variety of wooded and treeless biotopes, ranging from lowlands to high elevations in the mountains. The time of flight of the single generation is very long — from May till September. The caterpillar, which lives from July to September, feeds mainly on flowers and seeds of labiate plants.

2 *Perizoma blandiata* (D.& S.) — Pretty Pinion. 15—18mm. Widespread throughout northern and central Europe, Asia Minor, Armenia, extending as far as Mongolia, this species favours damp, grassy biotopes, mostly in submontane elevations. It flies from May to August. The caterpillar lives from July to September on eyebright.

3 *Perizoma didymata* (L.) — Twin-spot Carpet. 18—23mm. Distributed over central and northern Europe, with the exception of polar regions; the Urals represent its eastern limit. In the south this moth is found in mountains, where it ascends to the treeline. One generation flies from June to September in moist deciduous and coniferous forests. The egg passes the winter. The caterpillar lives in spring; although polyphagous it prefers anemone, groundsel, etc.

4 *Coenotephria verberata* (Sc.). 22—25mm. Occurs over much of Europe except southern regions. A moth which can be found everywhere in the mountains, it flies up to the treeline and frequents damp, grassy localities and woodland clearings, flying from June to August. The caterpillar lives in spring and is polyphagous.

5 *Euphyia biangulata* (Hw.) — Cloaked Carpet. 25—30mm. Ranges from temperate Europe eastwards to the Urals and the Caucasus. A moth peculiar to natural beech woods, which it accompanies to their highest elevations. The two generations are on the wing from June to August; the caterpillars live on starwort and other plants of the pink family.

6 *Euphyia frustata* (Tr.). 25—30mm. A thermophilic and local species inhabiting southern Europe and extending across Asia Minor to northern Iran. It flies, in a single generation, from June to August, on stony and rocky hillsides exposed to sunshine. The caterpillar lives from summer to the following spring on mouse-ear chickweed, saxifrage, starwort, bedstraw, etc.

7 *Xanthorhoe biriviata* (Bkh.) — Balsam Carpet. 18—22mm. Ranging throughout the deciduous-forest belt from Europe to eastern Asia, there are two generations in the year — flying from April to August. The caterpillar lives until September, feeding on touch-me-not and other balsams. Winter is passed in the pupal stage.

8 *Xanthorhoe ferrugata* (Cl.) — Dark-barred Twin-spot Carpet. 18—22mm. Distributed over Europe and Asia as far as the Amur, this moth shows a preference for lowlands; in the mountains it is replaced by the very similar *X. spadicearia* (D.& S.). There are two generations appearing from April to September. The caterpillar is polyphagous, the pupa hibernates.

9 *Xanthorhoe montanata* (D.& S.) — Silver-ground Carpet. 24—28mm. This moth has a wide distribution in Europe and Asia as far as the Altai, displaying a preference for mountains, where it is extremely abundant in forests. It can be seen on the wing from May to July. The caterpillar lives from summer until the following spring (inclusive of hibernation); it is polyphagous and frequents low-growing plants.

10 *Xanthorhoe fluctuata* (L.) — Garden Carpet. 18—25mm. One of the most abundant geometrids, this species is chiefly an inhabitant of lowlands, where it haunts forests as well as areas outside them. It ranges from Europe across Asia to North America. In the mountains it occurs more rarely. The two generations can be seen on the wing from April to October. The caterpillar occurs on crucifers. Winter is passed in the pupal stage.

Family: **Geometridae** — **geometrids (inchworms, loopers)**

1 *Scotopteryx chenopodiata* (L.) — Shaded Broad-bar. 25—30mm. Occurs in all grassy biotopes and over both Europe and Asia to the Far East. This moth is extremely abundant in all its habitats. On the wing from July to September, the caterpillar develops from August to June. It prefers papilionaceous plants.

2 *Catarhoe cuculata* (Hfn.) — Royal Mantle. 22—27mm. Distributed over temperate Europe and Asia to the Amur, it is a species rare in all localities. The two generations fly from May to September. The caterpillar lives throughout the summer until October, feeding on various kinds of bedstraw. The insect passes the winter in the pupal stage.

3 *Epirrhoe tristata* (L.) — Small Argent and Sable. 20—23mm. This extremely variable species inhabits lowlands and mountains of temperate Europe and Asia, extending to the Far East. It is found abundantly in damp grassy biotopes or in forest clearings. The two generations can be seen on the wing from April to September. The caterpillar occurs from June until autumn and is restricted to bedstraw.

4 *Epirrhoe alternata* (Müll.) — Common Carpet. 20—25mm. One of the abundant geometrids of all — only in the mountains is it more scarce. It occurs throughout the deciduous-forest belt of the whole of Europe and Asia, and has become well adapted to cultivated areas. Two annual generations develop, on the wing from April to September. Caterpillars, dependent on bedstraw, can be found from June till autumn. This species produces innumerable variations both in markings and colour.

5 *Camptogramma bilineata* (L.) — Yellow Shell. 20—25mm. Another very abundant species, it ranges from North America across Europe and Asia to Siberia. It produces one or two generations, flying from May to August, occurring in lowlands as well as in mountains, favouring damp, shrubby situations, stream banks, etc. The caterpillars, which hibernate, eat a number of plants, including nettle, cinquefoil, and sorrel.

6 *Chesias legatella* (D.& S.) — Streak. 30—35mm. A local species widespread in the warmer regions of Europe, it inhabits open pine forests on sandy soils, and stony and sunny hillsides rich in the foodplant of caterpillars — broom. In September and October it may be seen on the wing. The caterpillar develops during spring and early summer.

7 *Chesias rufata* (F.) — Broom-tip. 28—32mm. Occurs over much the same territory as the preceding species, and also inhabits biotopes of the same kind, but takes the wing early in spring — from April to June; a second generation occasionally appears in July and August. Winter is passed in the form of pupae. The caterpillars live in summer on broom.

8 *Carsia sororiata* (Hb.) — Manchester Treble-bar. 20—23mm. Mostly confined to scattered peat-bog localities of central Europe, it is also found in northern Europe and Asia. Related species occur in North America. The flight period is from June to August. The egg hibernates, and the caterpillar lives in spring on bilberry, cranberry and cowberry.

9 *Aplocera praeformata* (Hb.) — Purple Treble-bar. 33—38mm. A predominantly montane species distributed in temperate Europe, and in the east to the Caucasus. The moth appears on the wing from June to August. The caterpillar hibernates and completes its development in spring, feeding only on *Hypericum*. This species is often very abundant.

10 *Aplocera plagiata* (L.) — Treble-bar. 27—40mm. The distribution of this moth is Palaearctic. Being more thermophilic than the preceding species, it shows a preference for lowlands. Two broods develop making their appearance from May to October. Caterpillars of the winter generation hibernate; they also feed on *Hypericum*.

9

5

1

6

7

2

3

4

10

8

Family: **Geometridae — geometrids (inchworms, loopers)**

1 *Odezia atrata* (L.) — Chimney Sweeper. 23—27mm. Distributed over central and northern Europe and into eastern Asia, the favourite haunts of this species are grassy submontane and montane localities up to the treeline. On the wing from May to July. Locally it is abundant. The caterpillar grows to full size during spring, feeding on chervil and bulbous chervil.

2 *Lithostege farinata* (Hfn.). 25—32mm. Widespread in the warmer regions of Europe and western and central Asia, this moth can be seen on the wing from May to July, haunting steppes and other grassy localities. The caterpillars live in summer on umbelliferous and cruciferous plants. Winter is passed in the pupal stage.

3 *Lobophora halterata* (Hfn.) — Seraphim. 20—25mm. Distributed over central and northern Europe, and Asia as far as the Amur, this moth inhabits deciduous forests in lowlands and mountains, also margins of peat-bogs, watersides, etc. It flies from April to June. The caterpillar lives on poplar, willow, birch, etc.; the pupa hibernates.

4 *Idaea serpentata* (Hfn.) — Ochraceous Wave. 15—20mm. Rather abundant and distributed throughout Europe and Asia in dry places overgrown with grass, the single generation of this species flies from June to August. The caterpillar is polyphagous and develops from summer throughout winter, until the following May.

5 *Idaea rusticata* (D.& S.). 15—17mm. Widespread throughout the temperate zone of Europe, this species occurs eastwards into central Asia. Grassy, arid slopes and steppes are its most usual habitat. The moth flies in a single generation, from June to August; the caterpillar hatches in summer, spends the winter in hibernation, and reawakens the following spring. Its diet consists of withered or decaying leaves and moss.

6 *Idaea biselata* (Hfn.) — Small Fan-footed Wave. 15—20mm. Occurs in Europe, predominantly in the warmer parts, and in Asia Minor. Found in deciduous forests having luxuriant undergrowth, on shrubby hillsides, in forest margins, etc., this moth has but one generation per year, on the wing from June to September. The caterpillars hibernate, and then grow to full size in spring. They feed on fallen and decaying leaves, but also eat grass and other low plants.

7 *Idaea inquinata* (Sc.) — Rusty Wave. 12—17mm. The way of life of this insect is similar to that of the preceding species. It appears abundantly in buildings in places where dry plants are stored. Thus it has become a common store pest. The moth produces at least two generations (from May to September). The caterpillars of the last generation overwinter.

8 *Idaea dimidiata* (Hfn.) — Single-dotted Wave. 13—18mm. Distributed over the whole of temperate Europe and Asia Minor as far as Syria, this moth is chiefly an inhabitant of woodlands and damp localities on the banks of streams. A single-brooded species, flying from June to August; the caterpillar develops over winter until the following spring. Like other members of the genus, it eats dry and withered leaves.

9 *Idaea aversata* (L.) — Riband Wave. 23—30mm. Distributed over the whole of non-polar Europe and extending across Asia Minor to Syria, this moth is abundant in deciduous forests, throughout the whole season, producing two merging generations. The caterpillars live in summer; those of the second generation hibernate. The species is very variable — individuals having broad dark bands across their wings are frequently encountered.

10 *Idaea deversaria* (H. S.). 23—27mm. Widespread throughout the warmer regions of Europe and extending across Asia Minor and Asia as far as the Altai, this is a moth of deciduous forests. On the wing at the beginning of summer, it overwinters in the larval stage. The diet is much the same as in the previous species. The moth is locally abundant.

9

1

10

2

7

6

3

5

8

4

Family: **Geometridae** — **geometrids (inchworms, loopers)**

1 *Cyclophora albipunctata* (Hfn.) — Birch Mocha. 20—25mm. Distributed over Europe and Asia as far as southern and eastern Siberia, this is an inhabitant of deciduous and mixed forests, mainly those with scattered birches. There are two annual generations — the first of these takes wing as early as April, the second in July. The caterpillars can be found from June to September on birch, but also on oak and alder. Winter is passed in the pupal stage.

2 *Cyclophora annulata* (Schulze) — Mocha. 18—22mm. Ranges over temperate Europe, Asia Minor and Transcaucasia. A moth of deciduous and mixed forests, but never abundant anywhere. Its two generations fly between April and August. The caterpillar develops in June and, if there is a second brood, again towards the end of summer and in autumn, until October. The larvae feed on the leaves of maple species, also on birch and hornbeam.

3 *Cyclophora punctaria* (L.) — Maiden's Blush. 18—25mm. A very variable species distributed throughout the belt of deciduous forests in Europe; from here it ranges across Asia Minor to Iran. It is abundant everywhere. Two broods emerge, flying from April to August. The caterpillars live from June to September on oak, and less frequently on birch.

4 *Timandra griseata* (Petersen) (= *amata* auctt.) — Blood-vein. 23—28mm. Distributed throughout Europe and Asia as far as Japan, this moth has been reported even from Ceylon (Sri Lanka). It is abundant in all localities overgrown with lush grass and on wasteground. Annually two merging generations appear on the wing, from May to October. The caterpillars live in summer; those that develop later hibernate. Their diet consists of various species of sorrel and knotgrass. The intensity of the wing markings is extremely variable.

5 *Scopula immorata* (L.) — Lewes Wave. 20—27mm. Distributed over temperate Europe (with the exception of its southernmost parts) and Asia, far to the east, this moth is found in grassy, dry biotopes in the lowlands, but also high up in the mountains where it haunts forest clearings overgrown with grass. Depending on climatic conditions it produces one or two generations a year — these emerge from May to August. The polyphagous caterpillar hibernates.

6 *Scopula ornata* (Sc.) — Lace Border. 18—25mm. Found throughout temperate Europe and Asia as far as the Amur basin, the favourite haunts of this species are dry, grassy places, forest margins and sunny slopes overgrown with shrubs. Annually it produces two, perhaps even three merging generations, seen on the wing from May to September. The caterpillars live in summer; late developing individuals hibernate. The larvae feed on a variety of plants, chiefly thyme, speedwell and wild marjoram. Of recent years this moth has become rather rare.

7 *Scopula rubiginata* (Hfn.) — Tawny Wave. 15—20mm. Occurring in Europe, Asia Minor and throughout Siberia, it is common in dry, grassy habitats, on hillsides, pastures, and other warm biotopes. The moth has two generations a year which merge into each other, the flight period being from May to September. The caterpillars live in summer, those of the second generation hibernating. Being polyphagous, they feed on a variety of plants.

8 *Rhodostrophia calabra* (Pet.). 30—35mm. Ranges from central Europe to the south, and to the southeast into western Asia. This moth can be seen in June and July. The caterpillar hibernates. It thrives on broom and related plants. The species shows great variation.

9 *Rhodostrophia vibicaria* (Cl.). 25—30mm. With the exception of the polar regions, this species is generally distributed over much of Europe and Asia; it ascends to high altitudes in the mountains. There is one generation, flying from June to August; sometimes there is a second brood. Winter is passed in the larval stage. The caterpillar lives on various papilionaceous plants but also feeds on other herbs. This species is also very variable.

1

2

3

7

6

4

9

8

5

Family: **Geometridae — geometrids (inchworms, loopers)**

1 *Abraxas grossulariata* (L.) — Magpie. 35—40mm. Formerly this was an abundant species whose caterpillars caused much damage to cultivated gooseberries and currants. During the present century, however, the Magpie has been decreasing rapidly in numbers and is now rare in many localities. It is only in the warmer parts of central Europe that it still continues to be plentiful. The moth has a Palaearctic distribution, ranging as far as Japan. There is only one annual generation, on the wing from June to August, the exact date depending on climate and elevation above sea-level. The caterpillar hibernates and grows to full size in the following spring. Besides the plants mentioned above, it also feeds on blackthorn, peach, hazel, etc.

2 *Abraxas sylvata* (Sc.) — Clouded Magpie. 30—38mm. Distributed throughout the forest zone of the Palaearctic, this moth may be seen on the wing in shady and damp forests, such as old beech woods with herbaceous undergrowth. The single generation flies from May to August. The caterpillar lives towards the end of summer, feeding on a variety of deciduous trees.

3 *Lomaspilis marginata* (L.) — Clouded Border. 20—25mm. Occurring abundantly throughout the forest zone of the entire Palaearctic, there are two generations of this moth, on the wing from April to August. The caterpillar lives until autumn on various deciduous trees. Winter is passed in the pupal stage. The species exhibits a considerable range of variation.

4 *Ligdia adustata* (D.& S.) — Scorched Carpet. 20—25mm. Reported from Europe, western and central Asia, and also from Japan, this is also a typical forest species, but more thermophilic than the preceding one. Both the two generations and the other stages of the moth appear at the same time as the previous species; the larvae feed on spindle-tree.

5 *Semiothisa alternaria* (Hb.) — Sharp-angled Peacock. 22—27mm. Ranges over almost the whole of Europe, and in Asia it extends as far as Siberia. This species is found in open, deciduous woods from lowlands to the mountains, and in various shrubby biotopes. Its two generations fly from May to August. The caterpillars feed on various deciduous trees.

6 *Semiothisa liturata* (Cl.) — Tawny-barred Angle. 22—27mm. A species typical of coniferous forests (chiefly pine forests) throughout the entire Palaearctic. It develops one or two generations, which can be seen flying from April to August. The caterpillar can be found from summer till autumn on pine, spruce, etc. Winter is passed as a pupa.

7 *Semiothisa clathrata* (L.) — Latticed Heath. 20—25mm. An extremely variable species distributed throughout the Palaearctic, it is very abundant in fields and other grassy situations. Two broods appear, flying from April to August. The caterpillars develop until September on clover and medick; the pupae hibernate.

8 *Isturgia roraria* (F.). 20—25mm. Distributed over the warmer parts of Europe, in the east this species extends to Armenia. 2,000m is the highest elevation it reaches in mountains. It is double-brooded. The caterpillars live on broom; winter is passed in the pupal stage.

9 *Semiothisa wauaria* (L.) — The V-moth. 25—30mm. Occurring in Europe, Asia and North America, this species is to be found in damp, shrubby woods, and has also adapted to cultivated areas. The moth flies in June and July. The eggs hibernate; the caterpillars eclose in spring to feed on gooseberries and currants.

10 *Semiothisa brunneata* (Thnbg.) (= *fulvaria* Vill.) — Rannoch Looper. 20—27mm. Ranges over central and northern Europe, elsewhere it may be found in the mountains only; in Asia it extends as far as Japan. In mountains the moth may be seen flying above the timberline. Associated with bilberry, on which the caterpillars are largely dependent for food, this species may be seen on the wing between June and August. The caterpillar develops in spring.

Family: **Geometridae** — **geometrids (inchworms, loopers)**

1 *Cepphis advenaria* (Hb.) — Little Thorn. 23—26m. This moth ranges from Europe to Japan, but is confined to appropriate localities, inhabiting forests with an undergrowth of bilberry, peat-bogs, heather moors and lowland woods. It has but one annual generation, which flies from May to July. The caterpillar develops towards the end of summer on bilberry, cow-wheat *(Melampyrum)* and hare's ear *(Bupleurum)*. The winter is passed as a pupa.

2 *Plagodis pulveraria* (L.) — Barred Umber. 28—33mm. Occurs widely in Europe except the polar regions and the extreme south; in the east it ranges over the whole of Asia from the Urals across the Altai to Japan and Korea. This species is characteristic of open deciduous and mixed forests — primarily at low and submontane elevations. There is only one generation, which flies from April to July. The caterpillar can be found from June to September on willow, birch, oak, alder, hazel, etc.

3 *Plagodis dolabraria* (L.) — Scorched Wing. 28—32mm. Distributed over the whole Palaearctic from Europe to Japan, this is a moth commonly found in warm deciduous and mixed forests, and on shrubby hillsides (generally at low elevations), yet it is never abundant anywhere. Over the major part of the territory it has one generation only; in warmer localities two generations may emerge, flying from April to August. The caterpillar lives towards the end of summer on oak, lime, blackthorn, etc. Winter is passed in the pupal stage.

4 *Opisthograptis luteolata* (L.) — Brimstone Moth. 32—37mm. The bright yellow colour of this moth precludes confusion with any other species. It ranges over Europe and Asia to eastern Siberia. Most common in lowlands, in forest steppes and shrubby biotopes, it has also become adapted to urban parks and gardens. The moth is on the wing from the end of April to July; the caterpillar (4b) lives until August, feeding on hawthorn, blackthorn, woodbine, willow, etc.

5 *Epione repandaria* (Hfn.) — Bordered Beauty. 25—30mm. Ranges throughout the temperate zone of Europe and Asia across the Urals to the Amur basin and southern Siberia. This moth occurs in damp biotopes, and in lowland forests and wet meadows overgrown with scrub. There are two generations in the year, the first of which takes wing in June, the second continues until late autumn. Winter is passed in the egg stage. The caterpillars develop in spring, and those of the second generation, in August. They feed on willow, poplar, alder and blackthorn.

6 *Epione paralellaria* (D.& S.) (= *vespertaria* auctt.) — Dark Bordered Beauty. 25—30mm. This moth has a distribution similar to that of the preceding species, inhabiting localities of a similar kind, yet it is much rarer. The single annual generation flies from June to August. The female lays eggs which remain unhatched during winter, the caterpillars not emerging until spring. They then feed on the leaves of aspen, birch, hazel, etc.

7 *Pseudopanthera macularia* (L.) — Speckled Yellow. 23—28mm. Inhabiting the whole of Europe, with the exception of polar regions, it is more abundant in the south, yet it may also be found in the mountains at high altitudes. This geometrid takes wing early in spring, sometimes as early as April, and can be seen until July. The caterpillar develops during summer; the pupa hibernates. Various low-growing plants constitute the caterpillar's diet. This species exhibits a wide range of colour variation.

8 *Epirranthis diversata* (D.& S.). 30—40mm. A rare species occurring in northern and central Europe, eastern Europe and Siberia. There is only one generation, which flies early in spring, from March till May at latest (at higher elevations). Its haunts include damp deciduous forests, overgrown clearings, and woodland margins where low aspen bushes grow amidst grass. The caterpillar, living in May and June, is only found on young aspens. Winter is passed in the pupal stage.

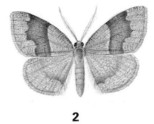

2

1

8

3

5

4

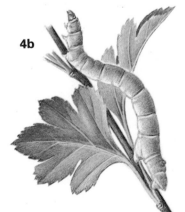

4b

6

7

Family: **Geometridae** — **geometrids (inchworms, loopers)**

1 *Ennomos autumnaria* (Wernb.) — Large Thorn. 40−50mm. Widespread over the whole Palaearctic and in North America. Abundant in all its haunts (in deciduous forests, particularly in the lowlands), it ascends with deciduous forests to their upper limit in the mountains. The one generation produced per year is on the wing from August to October. Winter is passed in the egg stage. The caterpillars (1b) emerge in spring to feed on the leaves of a variety of trees and shrubs. This species presents innumerable variations. Most interesting is the rare, dark brown f. *schultzi*.

2 *Ennomos fuscantaria* (Hw.) — Dusky Thorn. 35−40mm. A species with a limited distribution, practically known only from central Europe and the southern parts of northern Europe. It is seen from July to September in deciduous woods and their margins, and in other shrubby biotopes. The caterpillar hatches in spring from the egg, and develops from May to July. It feeds on ash and common privet. The species shows much variation in colour.

3 *Ennomos erosaria* (D.& S.) — September Thorn. 30−35mm. Distributed over temperate Europe and eastwards to the Caucasus. This moth is found in deciduous, predominantly oak forests, but also in mixed forests, ranging to relatively high altitudes in the mountains. The flight period is June to September. The eggs hibernate and the caterpillars live in spring, feeding on oak, birch, lime, and other trees.

4 *Selenia dentaria* (F.) (= *bilunaria* Esp.) — Early Thorn. 28−40mm. Ranges throughout the whole of Europe and Asia as far as Kamchatka, inhabiting open deciduous woodlands, and plantations, even in the neighbourhood of towns and cities. This species is found both in lowlands and high up in the mountains. The two annual generations are on the wing from April to August practically continuously, with only a short interval in June. The caterpillars (4b) enjoy a mixed diet including lime, hawthorn, birch, elm, woodbine, and many other shrubs and trees, on which they can be found from May to September. The moth is extremely variable, and those of the second brood are considerably smaller than the first.

5 *Selenia lunularia* (Hb.) (= *lunaria* D.& S.) — Lunar Thorn. 28−40mm. Spreads in Europe over very much the same territory as the preceding species, but is somewhat rarer. In the east it reaches only to central Asia. It also inhabits similar biotopes and the time of occurrence is the same in both species. Winter is passed in the pupal stage.

6 *Selenia tetralunaria* (Hfn.) — Purple Thorn. 30−38mm. Widely distributed over Europe and the whole of Asia as far as Japan, this species is more thermophilic than those preceding. Its normal haunts include deciduous, mainly oak forests, and lowland forest-steppes. There are two annual generations of this moth, flying from April to August. The two caterpillar broods develop from May to September, leaving the pupa to hibernate. The caterpillar is polyphagous on trees and shrubs. Moths of the variable second generation are smaller than the first.

7 *Artiora evonymaria* (D. & S.). 30−35mm. Occurs in the warmer parts of central and southeastern Europe, the Crimea being its eastern limit. Annually there is one generation of this moth, on the wing from July to September. It passes the winter as an egg. The caterpillar lives in spring until June, feeding on spindle-tree. A very local species, only found on stony hillsides and in open woods where spindle-tree forms a part of the undergrowth.

8 *Odontopera bidentata* (Cl.) — Scalloped Hazel. 32−40mm. Ranges over the whole of Europe and Asia to the Far East. This abundant species is common in deciduous forests, peat-bogs, heaths, and various shrubby biotopes, mostly at submontane elevations. The moth flies in May and June; the caterpillar develops from June to August on various trees and shrubs. A moth given to great variation in colour and pattern.

Family: **Geometridae** — **geometrids (inchworms, loopers)**

1 *Crocallis elinguaria* (L.) — Scalloped Oak. 32—42mm. Widespread throughout the Palaearctic, except the coldest, polar regions. In mountains this species occurs up to 1,500m. It inhabits diverse damp biotopes, such as shrubby areas or woods with a rich undergrowth including bilberry. The moth is on the wing from May to August. The caterpillar lives during summer, hibernates, and then grows to full size in spring. It feeds on the leaves of bilberry, willow, hawthorn, etc.

2 *Ourapteryx sambucaria* (L.) — Swallow-tailed Moth. 40—50mm. One of the largest European geometrids, it inhabits the western part of the Palaearctic subregion — eastwards it ranges no further than central Asia. In Europe it is common in lowlands and in warmer areas; in Asia it occurs only locally. The moth flies in July and August. The caterpillar, which hibernates, lives on common elder, clematis, alder, currant, gooseberry, and other shrubs.

3 *Colotois pennaria* (L.) — Feathered Thorn. 35—45mm. Distributed over Europe and eastwards into central Asia, this species occurs in deciduous forests and in forest-steppes, and is abundant in all its habitats. The moth flies from September to November; the caterpillar develops in spring. The egg is the hibernating stage. Foodplants include various trees. The moth presents a wide range of variation; the sexes are also slightly different.

4 *Angerona prunaria* (L.) — Orange Moth. 35—45mm. Generally distributed throughout temperate Europe and Asia, extending to the Far East. This species haunts various shrubby biotopes and scattered woodlands with rich undergrowth. There is one generation per year, which flies from May to August. The caterpillar (4b) lives in winter on various shrubs. This species is of interest for its immense variability. Some forms are so surprisingly different that they would not appear to belong to the same species at all, for example the dark forms *pickettaria* and *fuscaria*.

5 *Agriopis leucophaearia* (D. & S.) — Spring Usher. 23—28mm. The range of this species extends over the warmer parts of Europe, across Asia Minor and Syria, and continues eastwards — it has been reported from Japan. This early moth appears with the first warm spell of weather in spring. The caterpillar feeds on the leaves of oak in April and May, and the pupa remains in the ground, dormant until the following year. The female has vestigial wings.

6 *Agriopis aurantiaria* (Hb.) — Scarce Umber. 27—35mm. Distributed in the deciduous forests of Europe, this moth also ranges across Asia Minor to the Caucasus. Its abundance oscillates greatly from year to year. The single generation is on the wing in late autumn, during October and November. The egg overwinters, and the caterpillars live in spring on a variety of deciduous trees. The female is wingless.

7 *Agriopis marginaria* (F.) — Dotted Border. 27—32mm. A thermophilic moth having a similar distribution to that of the preceding species. Displaying a preference for oak forests, it flies very early in spring, sometimes from February, but not later than May. The caterpillar develops until June; the pupa hibernates. Foodplants include oak, blackthorn, and various fruit trees. The female has degenerate wings.

8 *Erannis defoliaria* (Cl.) — Mottled Umber. 30—40mm. Occurs in deciduous forests and forest-steppes of Europe as far as the Caucasus. In the east this moth is replaced by the related species *E. sichotenaria* Kurenzov. The Mottled Umber is a serious forest pest. The male moths fly very abundantly in late autumn, while the females, having stunted wings, only crawl about on the trees. Winter is passed in the egg stage. The caterpillars are polyphagous and often wreak havoc in extensive wooded areas, since they strip off all the leaves from oak, hornbeam, birch, and other trees. The moth is very variable.

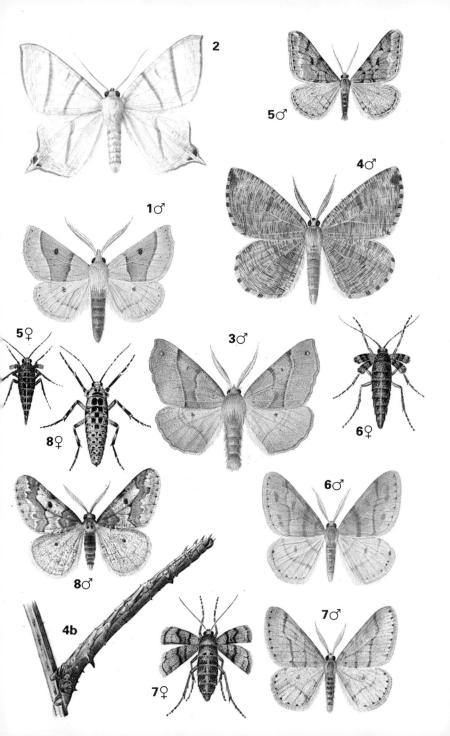

Family: **Geometridae — geometrids (inchworms, loopers)**

1 *Apocheima pilosaria* (D. & S.) — Pale Brindled Beauty. 35—40mm. Distributed over the temperate regions of Europe and Asia to the Far East, this is a species found in deciduous and mixed forests, forest-steppes, and also in orchards. It is one of the first moths to appear in spring — it may be seen on the wing from February to April, and a sudden spell of warm weather may cause it to appear even in January. The female is apterous. The caterpillars live from April to July on oak, birch, pear, etc. Winter is passed in the pupal stage.

2 *Apocheima hispidaria* (D. & S.) — Small Brindled Beauty. 28—35mm. Extends over the same range as the above species, and is found in deciduous forests, also in scrubby fields. The flight period of the one generation is from March to May. The caterpillars live from May to July, on oak, elm, and other trees. The pupae hibernate. Females of this species are wingless.

3 *Poecilopsis pomonaria* (Hb.). 25—30mm. Occurring in the warmer regions of Europe, ranging eastwards approximately to the Urals, this moth inhabits light and warm deciduous forests and forest-steppes, frequently also orchards. The adults of the single generation appear as soon as the sun begins to shine in spring — in March and April. Only the male is capable of flight; the colouration of his wings is very variable even though the markings are rather simple. The female, with stunted wings, crawls about on tree trunks. Caterpillars can be found from May to July, on various deciduous trees, including oak and birch.

4 *Poecilopsis isabellae* Hesl. — Harr. 27—32mm. This species bears a close resemblance to that preceding, but the male is more gray. Its distribution is poorly known; it occurs in the eastern parts of central Europe. Moths appear in March and April; the caterpillars live on larch. The pupae overwinter.

5 *Lycia zonaria* (D. & S.) — Belted Beauty. 27—30mm. Distributed over the warm lowlands of Europe, this species extends eastwards to central Asia. The moth flies in spring, during March and April, haunting grassy biotopes and fields. The female is similar in appearance to the preceding two species. The caterpillar feeds on grasses and herbs.

6 *Lycia hirtaria* (Cl.) — Brindled Beauty. 35—45mm. Generally distributed over temperate Europe and Asia to the Far East, this insect inhabits similar biotopes to the preceding species, and flies from March to May. The female has wings. The caterpillars can be found from May to August, on deciduous trees.

7 *Biston strataria* (Hfn.) — Oak Beauty. 40—50mm. A highly variable species which, in developed areas, manifests tendencies to melanism. Widespread in the western part of the Palaearctic, including northern Africa, it flies from March to May in deciduous woods and parks. The caterpillar develops at the end of spring and during early summer; it is polyphagous, feeding on a number of deciduous trees. The pupa hibernates.

8 *Biston betularia* (L.) — Peppered Moth. 35—60mm. Peculiar to the deciduous-tree zone of Europe and Asia; the related species *B. cognataria* Guen., inhabiting North America, is often considered to be merely a geographical race of *betularia*. The Peppered Moth is polymorphic, and famous for its hereditary black form (f. *carbonaria* — 8c) which has become common in the industrial areas of England in the last 150 years; in many localities it has superseded the original variegated or 'peppered' form (8). A connection exists between melanism of this kind and air pollution caused by industrial fumes (particularly sulphur dioxide), but the precise nature of the relationship is complex. However, the greater crypsis of f. *carbonaria* on smoke-blackened tree trunks seems undoubtedly to be a factor involved. There is one generation of this moth per year, flying from May to July. The caterpillar (8b) develops towards the end of summer on a variety of deciduous trees. Winter is passed in the pupal stage (8d).

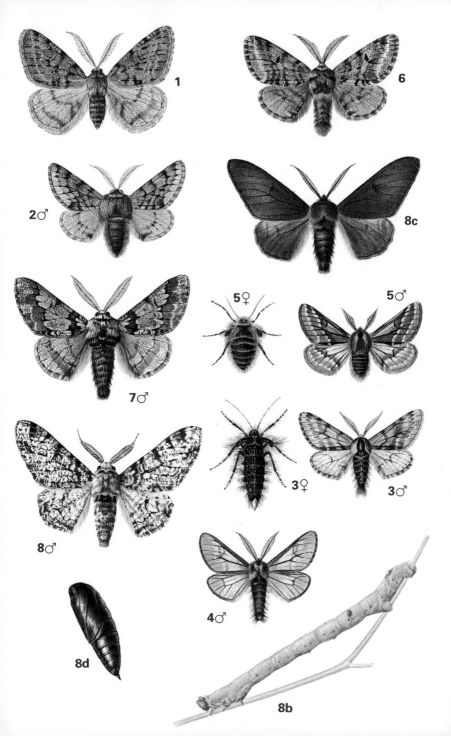

1

6

2♂

8c

7♂

5♀

5♂

3♀

3♂

8♂

4♂

8d

8b

Family: **Geometridae — geometrids (inchworms, loopers)**

1 *Peribatodes rhomboidaria* (D. & S.) — Willow Beauty. 30—38mm. A former representative of the originally large group *Boarmia,* which genus has more recently been divided into a number of separate genera. It ranges over Europe and western Asia, and can be seen on the wing from June to September; rarely it has two generations. The polyphagous caterpillar overwinters.

2 *Cleora cinctaria* (D. & S.) — Ringed Carpet. 28—35mm. Distributed in temperate and more northerly parts all over the Palaearctic, this moth flies in one generation early in spring, when it can be seen in forests and fields. The caterpillars (2b) live from May to July on various low-growing plants. Winter is passed as a pupa.

3 *Deileptenia ribeata* (Cl.) — Satin Beauty. 30—40mm. Distributed over Europe and Asia, this species is mostly confined to spruce and mixed forests. The single generation flies in abundance during July and August. Although the caterpillar, which hibernates, has a special liking for spruce and fir, it also feeds on certain deciduous trees.

4 *Alcis repandata* (L.) — Mottled Beauty. 30—45mm. Widespread throughout Europe but absent from southernmost parts, in Asia this moth extends far to the east. The flight period of its one brood is between May and August. The caterpillar (4b) overwinters, and feeds on coniferous and deciduous trees and shrubs, also on low plants. This abundant species shows great variation and tends to melanism. Almost black individuals occur.

5 *Arichanna melanaria* (L.). 35—40mm. Distributed throughout the northern regions of Europe and Asia as far as Japan. In more southerly areas this species is confined to peat-bogs, or peaty biotopes in mountains. The moths are evidently migrants, since they have often been captured in localities where they could not possibly develop. The moth remains on the wing throughout summer. Winter is passed as caterpillars, which live until May on *Vaccinium uliginosum* and several other plants peculiar to peat-bogs.

6 *Boarmia roboraria* (D. & S.) — Great Oak Beauty. 40—50mm. Widespread in the deciduous forests of the whole Palaearctic (but absent from the southernmost areas), this is a moth found in abundance only in scattered localities. Two generations occur, on the wing from May to August. The caterpillar passes the winter; it thrives on deciduous trees. The colouration of the moth is very variable.

7 *Fagivorina arenaria* (Hfn.) — Speckled Beauty. 25—30mm. Occurs only in central Europe and adjacent parts, and is peculiar to old oak forests — only rarely does this species appear in other habitats. Due to much felling of old forests, it has of late been rapidly disappearing and has, for example, become extinct in Britain. The moth is on the wing from May to July; the caterpillar lives towards the end of summer on oak, beech, birch, and other trees.

8 *Ascotis selenaria* (D. & S.). 35—45mm. A more thermophilic species, distributed throughout the temperate Palaearctic as far as eastern Asia. Forest and open steppes are its favourite haunts, but it has also become adapted to man-dominated landscapes. Two (in some places only one) generations develop between April and August. The caterpillars are polyphagous and can be found until autumn. The species passes the winter as a pupa.

9 *Ectropis bistortata* (Gz.) — Engrailed. 30—40mm. An abundant species peculiar to Europe and eastern regions, reaching far into Asia. In view of its easy confusion with the similar *E. crepuscularia* (D. & S.), much remains to be discovered concerning the precise distribution of this species. There are two broods in the year, often to be found flying from March till autumn. The pupae hibernate. The caterpillars live on low plants and many deciduous trees and shrubs. The moths show tendencies to melanism.

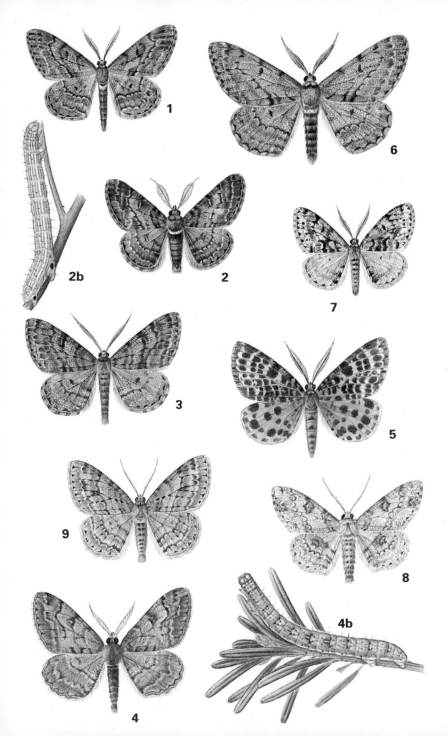

Family: **Geometridae** — **geometrids (inchworms, loopers)**

1 *Ematurga atomaria* (L.) — Common Heath. 22—30mm. An extremely variable species distributed throughout Europe and Asia, with the exception of the south. It inhabits heaths, peat-bogs, alpine meadows and clearings, and ascends in the mountains to altitudes high above the timberline. The female is paler than the male. Two merging generations are on the wing from April to September. The caterpillar develops until autumn, feeding on heather, wormwood, etc.

2 *Bupalus piniaria* (L.) — Bordered White. 28—35mm. Abundant throughout Europe and Asia, absent only from the far north; the sexual dimorphism of this insect is conspicuous. The moth flies in spring, from April to July, while the caterpillar lives towards the end of summer. The larvae, although largely restricted to pine, can sometimes be found on other conifers. The pupa hibernates in the ground. The species can occur in huge numbers in pine woods, leading to complete defoliation.

3 *Cabera pusaria* (L.) — Common White Wave. 25—28mm. Found in the temperate zone of Europe and Asia, from where it extends far to the east. Seen on the wing from spring till autumn, this moth is common in lowlands and mountains, occurring in forests or open country, and in meadows overgrown with scrub or in waterside habitats. Depending on climatic conditions, it produces one or two generations. The caterpillar develops until autumn and feeds on willow, birch, elm, alder, etc. Winter is passed in the pupal stage.

4 *Lomographa bimaculata* (F.) — White-pinioned Spotted. 22—26mm. Distributed throughout the entire temperate Palaearctic, this species has one or two generations in the year, to be seen on the wing from April to August. The caterpillar lives during the summer or until late autumn, on a variety of deciduous trees. Overwintering is achieved by the pupal stage.

5 *Lomographa temerata* (D. & S.) — Clouded Silver. 22—26mm. The range of this moth is similar to that of the preceding species, although it possibly ascends to higher elevations in mountains. The flight period is April to July, there being only one generation. The caterpillar lives in summer; the pupa hibernates. The larval foodplants are various deciduous trees and shrubs.

6 *Campaea margaritata* (L.) — Light Emerald. 30—40mm. Occurs in the belt of deciduous forests over Europe and Asia Minor as far as the Caucasus, beech and mixed forests being the usual habitats of this emerald moth. One generation develops per year, flying in June and July. A partial second generation may appear in August. The caterpillar either develops during the summer, or hibernates. It is commonly found on beech, hornbeam, oak and birch, even in town and city parks.

7 *Puengeleria capreolaria* (D. & S.). 27—35mm. Confined to the fir and spruce forests of central Europe, this is a species characteristic of submontane and montane forests up to the highest altitudes reached by them. There is one brood, on the wing for a rather long time, from June to September. This moth shows a wide range of variation. The caterpillars (7b) overwinter at various stages of development. They gradually complete their development in late spring and early summer, feeding on fir and spruce.

8 *Hylaea fasciaria* (L.) — Barred Red. 27—40mm. Widespread throughout coniferous forests in the temperate and northern zones of Palaearctic Europe and Asia, this species shows interesting colour polymorphism. In low-lying pine forests the pink f. *fasciaria* (8) is found; at higher elevations, in spruce and fir forests, the green f. *prasinaria* (8c) occurs. The moth produces one generation, flying from May to August. The caterpillar lives from summer until the following spring, feeding on spruce, fir, pine, etc.

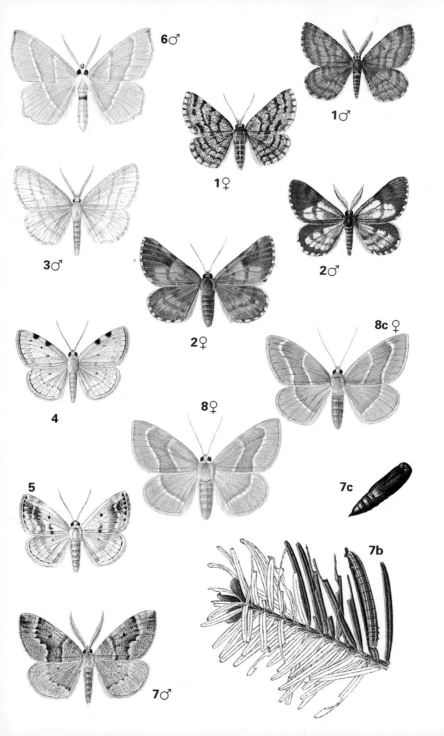

Family: **Geometridae** — **geometrids (inchworms, loopers)**

1 *Gnophos furvata* (D. & S.). 40—50mm. A thermophilic species occurring in central, southern and southeastern Europe. It is peculiar to dry, even arid, localities, including steppes and rocky hillsides — particularly those with a limestone substrate. The moth has one generation which flies in midsummer; it passes the winter in the larval stage. The caterpillar feeds on a variety of plants such as plantain, vetch, and cinquefoil. This species is the largest of the genus *Gnophos*.

2 **Gnophos obscuratus* (D. & S.) — Annulet. 27—32mm. Ranges over much the same territory as the preceding species, but is absent from the extreme south and extends further northwards. This moth is also found in dry localities, woodland margins, slopes and heaths, where it flies from July to September. The caterpillar, which hibernates, feeds on a variety of herbs. This species is very variable.

3 *Gnophos dilucidaria* (D. & S.). 28—35mm. A moth restricted in central Europe to the mountains, but in the north of Europe, and also in parts of Asia, it has a continuous distribution (a Boreo-Alpine species). In central Europe it is probably an ice-age relict. This extremely variable species lives above the timberline; at lower elevations it is mostly restricted to peat-bogs. The moth is on the wing from June to September, depending on elevation above sea level. The caterpillars, which overwinter, feed on a variety of herbs and grasses.

4 *Psodos quadrifaria* (Sulz.). 18—23mm. One of a group of geometrids ('mountain moths') locally distributed in European and Asian mountains. In consequence of their discontinuous distribution a number of geographical races can be recognised. The present species is the most brightly coloured, most of the others being grey or black. *P. quadrifaria* lives in the dwarf pine and alpine-meadow zone of the Alps, the Sudetes and the Carpathians. It is on the wing from June to August; the polyphagous caterpillars hibernate.

5 *Psodos alpinata* (Sc.). 20—25mm. Largely confined to European mountains, from the Pyrenees over the Alps and the Sudetes to the Carpathians, this moth has also been reported from Siberia. It inhabits alpine meadows, where it ascends to the perpetual snowline, and is one of the most abundant representatives of the genus *Psodos* in high mountains. The flight period of the single generation is from June to August. Its habits are diurnal, as with the other species in this genus. The caterpillar, which overwinters, feeds on various low-growing plants.

6 *Psodos canaliculata* (Hochw.). 20—25mm. A relatively abundant species in the higher parts of the Alps. In the Carpathians it occurs as the more variegated ssp. *schwingenschussi* Wehrli (6). The moth flies about in alpine meadows and among rock and scree during July and August. The caterpillar, which hibernates, feeds on low plants, as do almost all the other mountain geometrids.

7 **Siona lineata* (Sc.) — Black-veined Moth. 35—40mm. Distributed over temperate Europe and Asia as far as the Amur, this moth occurs abundantly in grassy biotopes and submontane meadows, along stream banks, etc., flying from May to July. The caterpillar lives from summer to the following spring on a variety of plants.

8 **Aspitates gilvaria* (D. & S.) — Straw Belle. 25—30mm. A thermophilic species locally occurring in the drier biotopes of central Europe and ranging eastwards over southeastern Europe and Asia Minor as far as Siberia. In July and August it may be seen flying in steppes and fields. The caterpillar overwinters, and feeds upon milfoil, *Hypericum*, wormwood, etc.

Family: **Geometridae** — **geometrids (inchworms, loopers)**

1 *Pseudoterpna pruinata* (Hfn.) — Grass Emerald. 30—35mm. Distributed in central and southern Europe whence it ranges eastwards across Asia Minor to the Caucasus and central Asia. There is one generation of the moth per year, which flies from June to August. The caterpillars live at the end of summer, and hibernate. They are restricted to broom (*Sarothamnus*) and *Genista*. This species occurs at various elevations in dry localities, including sandy areas or stony slopes where the larval foodplants can be found.

2 *Geometra papilionaria* L. — Large Emerald. 40—50mm. An inhabitant of deciduous forests throughout Europe and Asia, the moths of this single-brooded species can be seen on the wing from June to August, flying mostly in damp forests, scrubby meadows, along the banks of brooks and rivers, and in the mountains up to the deciduous treeline. The caterpillar (Fig. 2b) hibernates, and feeds on birch, alder, willow, hazel, lime, etc.

3 *Comibaena bajularia* (D. & S.) (= *pustulata* Hfn.) — Blotched Emerald. 23—27mm. Its distribution in the warmer regions of central Europe is only local, but from southern Europe to Asia Minor it is more continuous. The single generation of this species can be seen on the wing in June and July. The caterpillar is restricted to oak leaves. Winter is passed in the larval stage. In nature specimens are usually only captured when the beautiful malachite-green colour has faded. The species flies in warm oak forests and wooded hillsides.

4 *Thetidia smaragdaria* (F.) — Essex Emerald. 25—30mm. Occurs in the warmer regions of central Europe, southern Europe, and in the steppes, forest-steppes, and stony, shrubby slopes of Palaearctic Asia. There are two generations in the year: the first flies in June and July, the second immediately after, in August and September. The caterpillars of the second brood hibernate; they feed on wormwood, groundsel, milfoil and tansy.

5 *Hemithea aestivaria* (Hb.) — Common Emerald. 24—27mm. Ranges over temperate Europe eastwards across the Caucasus to eastern Asia. Found in deciduous forests and shrubby biotopes in woodland margins, there is one generation of the moth per year, on the wing from May to August. It passes the winter as a caterpillar. This feeds on various deciduous trees and shrubs, and will also eat bramble and raspberry. It is a local species.

6 *Thalera fimbrialis* (Sc.) — Sussex Emerald. 25—30mm. Widespread in the whole of temperate Europe, this moth penetrates eastwards into central Asia. It has one or two generations in the year, which may be seen flying at any time between May and September. The caterpillar overwinters. Various low plants constitute its diet. This species favours dry localities overgrown with grass, but also heather moors, peat-bogs, fields and wastelands.

7 *Hemistola chrysoprasaria* (Esp.) — Small Emerald. 28—32mm. A more thermophilic species distributed over central and southern Europe, and further eastwards over the warmer parts of the Palaearctic as far as Japan. It is single-brooded, the moths being on the wing from June to August. The caterpillars develop from the end of summer onwards, and again in spring after hibernation. *Clematis* (traveller's-joy, or old man's beard) is their foodplant.

8 *Jodis putata* (L.). 20—22mm. Distributed practically throughout the Palaearctic in woodlands with a luxuriant undergrowth of bilberry, also in peat-bogs and in mountains up to the timberline, this moth is on the wing from May to June. The caterpillar lives on bilberry during July and August. Winter is passed in the pupal stage. The moths soon lose their original greenish colour and become white; their markings also are rarely discernible.

Family: **Pterophoridae — plume moths**

1 *Agdistis adactyla* (Hb.) 20—25mm. Ranging over warmer regions from Morocco across southern and central Europe to southeastern Europe, this moth is seen on the wing from June to August in dry and warm, usually sandy biotopes. The caterpillar, which probably overwinters, develops until June, feeding on wormwood and *Teucrium*.

2 *Platyptilia gonodactyla* (D. & S.). 24—30mm. Widespread in Europe and Asia Minor, this species inhabits damp, treeless localities, wastegrounds and fields, and especially habitats by running water. There are two generations — the first flies in May and June, the second from July to September. Caterpillars develop in June and July; those of the second generation hibernate. The larvae feed on coltsfoot.

3 *Platyptilia nemoralis* (Z.) 30—32mm. The largest of all European 'plumes', occurring in central and southern Europe, mainly in submontane regions or in damp biotopes. It produces one annual generation, on the wing in July and August. The caterpillar develops in spring, feeding on the stalks of groundsels (*Senecio fuchsii, S. nemorensis, S. fluviatilis*).

4 *Stenoptilia pterodactyla* (L.). 20—25mm. Occurs throughout the whole of temperate Europe, and in Asia Minor and North America. There are two generations, the first of which is seen on the wing in June and July, the second appears from August onwards, hibernating until April. The caterpillar lives in spring and again in summer, feeding on germander speedwell *(Veronica chamaedrys)*. This species is abundant in wet meadows and shady places in forest margins and open woods.

5 *Stenoptilia pelidnodactyla* (Stein). 20—25mm. In Europe this species is abundant at low and medium elevations. The adult moth is on the wing from May to July in grassy localities, on field margins and forest edges. The caterpillars (5b) develop in April and May, eating *Saxifraga granulata*, pupating on the stalks of the host plant (5c).

6 *Cnaemidophorus rhododactyla* (D. & S.). 20—25mm. Distributed over the whole of Europe and Asia to the Far East, also in North America, this moth flies from May to August and is abundant on shrubby slopes. The caterpillar lives from autumn till spring, feeding on roses.

7 *Capperia trichodactyla* (D. & S.). 18—20mm. Reported from northern and central Europe, this moth develops two generations — one flying in June, the other in July and August. The caterpillars live in summer, those of the second generation hibernating on motherwort. A local species, it can be found in woodland margins and on rough ground where motherwort *(Leonurus)* occurs.

8 *Pterophorus pentadactyla* (L.) — White Plume Moth. 28—35mm. This moth is widely distributed in the Palaearctic. In Europe it can be found everywhere except in Spain. Found in grassy and shrubby biotopes, but also common in fields and gardens, the single generation flies from May to September; the caterpillar lives from autumn till spring on bindweeds (*Convolvulus arvensis* and *Calystegia sepium*).

9 *Pterophorus tridactyla* (L.). 13—22mm. Widespread in northern Africa and Europe as far as Asia Minor, this species is found in abundance in dry woodland clearings, and on slopes and wasteland overgrown with thyme. The moth is on the wing throughout the summer, from May to September. The caterpillar probably hibernates; it grows in May and June, feeding on thyme, lungwort and marjoram.

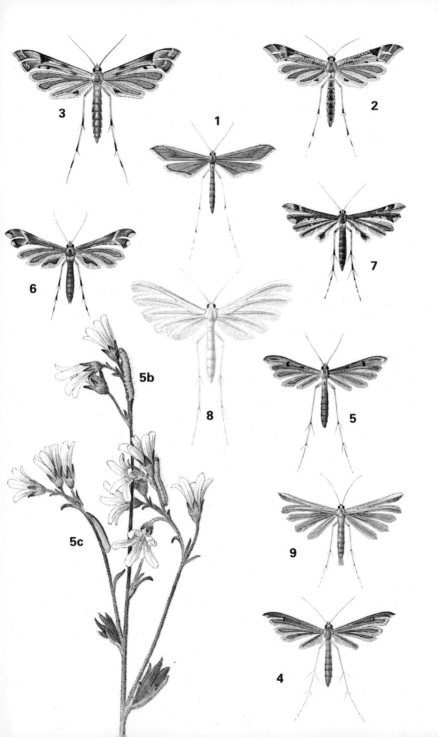

Family: **Pyralidae — pyralids**

1 *Crambus ericella* (Hb.). 22−24mm. Distributed over northern and central Europe, this species inhabits dry woods and heaths. Its single generation appears on the wing from June to August. The caterpillar (which is probably the overwintering stage) lives on grasses, as do the larvae of the majority of members of this group.

2 *Crambus nemorella* (Hb.). 19−22mm. One of the most common members of this group, appearing in great abundance in meadows and grassy localities both in lowlands and high up in the mountains. In older literature it is often known under the misapplied name *C. pratellus* (L.). The adult moth occurs throughout summer; the caterpillar lives from August until spring on various grasses.

3 *Crambus alienellus* (Germ. & Klfs.). 17−20mm. The distribution of this species is local, only in the north, tundra or mountains, it is continuous. It is on the wing from May to July. No information concerning the life of the caterpillar is available.

4 *Crambus perlella* (Sc.). 21−24mm. Another abundant species, occurring in Europe in meadows and pastures (or other biotopes covered with grass), both in lowlands and in the mountains. It flies from June to August; the caterpillar lives from summer over the winter until spring, feeding on low grasses, especially *Deschampsia* and *Festuca*.

5 *Agriphila tristella* (D. & S.). 23−26mm. A variable species abundant in the lowlands and mountains of Europe, inhabiting drier biotopes. This moth flies from June to September, but is most common in late summer. The caterpillar is a grass feeder, and hibernates.

6 *Thisanotia chrysonuchella* (Sc.). 22−25mm. Widespread in central and southern Europe, this species is seen on the wing in grassy, dry or even arid biotopes. The flight period is May to June. The caterpillar starts its development in summer, overwinters, and becomes active again in early spring; it stays close to the ground, feeding on fescues, including *Festuca ovina*.

7 *Chrysocrambus craterella* (Sc.). 23−27mm. Known from central and southern Europe, where it inhabits dry meadows and steppe localities. The moth flies from May to July; no information is available concerning the early stages.

8 *Catoptria permutatella* (H.S.). 20−25mm. Distributed over central Europe, this moth is very similar to two other species, from which it can be distinguished only with certainty on the basis of the copulatory organs. The moth is abundant in damp, partly wooded meadows, both in submontane regions and in the mountains. It is on the wing from June to August; the caterpillar hibernates and has been reported to feed on moss.

9 *Catoptria margaritella* (D. & S.). 20−23mm. Widespread in northern Africa and Europe in damp localities, peat-bogs, heaths, and in damp places within pine woods, this species flies from June to August. Nothing is known about the life-history of the early stages.

10 *Platytes alpinella* (Hb.). 19−22mm. Ranges over central and southeastern Europe, inhabiting dry localities, predominantly those with a sandy substrate. The moth appears on the wing from July to September. The caterpillar has been found in spring and is reported to live on certain kinds of moss.

11 *Chilo phragmitella* (Hb.). 28−35mm. Reported from Britain, Scandinavia and central Europe, but certainly has a far more extensive distribution. This species can be found near ponds and reed-choked streams. The male is considerably different from the female: the latter is larger and has pointed wings. The flight period is from June to August. The caterpillar lives inside reed stems.

Family: **Pyralidae — pyralids**

1 *Galleria mellonella* (L.) — Wax Moth. 20—30mm. Distributed all over the world, it is better known as a laboratory animal or as a pest of commercial beehives rather than in nature. Naturally it occurs in the nests of wild bees or bumble-bees. It takes wing in spring when the weather gets warmer, and flies until autumn, producing several generations. The caterpillar overwinters in a strong silken cocoon in the comb; it feeds on bees' wax from the honeycombs.

2 *Achroia grisella* (F.) — Lesser Wax Moth. 13—25mm. Another unwelcome beehive parasite, also having a worldwide distribution due to transportation of honeybee colonies to all parts of the world. Several broods of the moth are produced in the year. The caterpillars cover the honeycombs with silken webs, frequently preventing emerging bees from making their way out. The moth larvae feed on wax and pollen; often they can be found in food stores eating sweet substances of various kinds.

3 *Acrobasis repandana* (F.) (= *tumidella* Zinck.). 17—22mm. Found abundantly in the oak forests of central Europe, this species flies about the tree tops. Moths can be found in June and July; the caterpillars occur in spring, when they feed on the oak.

4 *Catacrobasis obtusella* (Hb.). 17—22mm. Widespread all over Europe on bushy slopes, in dry deciduous woods, in gardens and orchards, this species flies in June and July. The eggs hibernate. The caterpillars develop in spring on blackthorn, plum trees, and other species of the genus *Prunus,* smothering the young shoots with silken webbing, and eating the tender leaves within this protective covering.

5 *Oncocera palumbella* (D. & S.). 20—25mm. Distributed over central and southern Europe, where it flies in clearings within open deciduous forests and on heaths, from June to August. In daytime the moths are easily flushed out of heather. The caterpillars live from autumn till spring on heather, but they will also eat rockrose and thyme.

6 *Oncocera semirubella* (Sc.). 25—30mm. Distributed throughout the Palaearctic, where it lives in lowlands and also high up in mountains, favouring dry meadows and pastures, this moth is locally abundant. The adults occur in a great number of colour variations. On the wing in July and August, winter is passed in the larval stage. The foodplants are clover, medick, restharrow *(Ononis),* bird's-foot trefoil *(Lotus corniculatus),* etc.

7 *Etiella zinckenella* (Tr.). 22—25mm. Widely distributed over the tropics and the subtropics of Africa, Europe, Asia and North America, this species has evidently extended its range through the transportation of agricultural products. The moth is on the wing from June to August; the caterpillar lives inside the pods of various leguminous plants — such as peas, beans, and vetch. From two up to seven generations develop during the year, depending on the climate.

8 *Dioryctria abietella* (D. & S.). 25—32mm. Widespread in the belt of coniferous forests in Europe, Asia and North America, there are one or two generations of this moth per year — the first flies in June and the second in August and September. The caterpillars, which live in the cones of *Pinus silvestris* and other coniferous trees, grow to full size in autumn, and hibernate in flimsy cocoons on the ground. The species is abundant, occurring from lowlands to high altitudes in the mountains.

9 *Assara terebrella* (Zinck.). 20—25mm. Occurring in Europe and Asia in the areas of fir forests, there is but one generation of this species in the year. From June to August the moth can be seen on the wing in fir forests at dusk — it is thus a species of montane and submontane regions. The caterpillars overwinter in fir cones.

1

2

8

3

4

6

7

5

9

Family: **Pyralidae — pyralids**

1 *Ephestia kuehniella* Z. — Mediterranean Flour Moth. 20—25mm. Carried with stored and manufactured foods, this species has been introduced to all parts of the world. It can be found in mills and food stores, where the caterpillars cause immense damage, but in nature it is very rare. With the exception of winter, the moth flies throughout the year. There are two to five generations depending on local conditions.

2 *Plodia interpunctella* (Hb.) — Indian Meal Moth. 15—20mm. Another cosmopolitan species, the adult moths fly from May to September (although in storehouses they can be found throughout the year). The caterpillars of the several generations can also be found throughout the year, feeding on various seeds, nuts, dried fruit, corn, pastry, etc., and are serious storehouse pests.

3 *Pyralis farinalis* (L.) — Meal Moth. 18—30mm. A common species in mills, flour-product stores and households, its distribution is worldwide. In central Europe there are one or more generations of this moth, on the wing from June to August; often it comes to light. Living naturally on a variety of seeds and plant detritus, the caterpillars overwinter in flimsy tubular cocoons.

4 *Pyralis regalis* D. & S. 18—23mm. Ranges over central and southern Europe eastwards to Asia Minor and eastern Asia. This moth inhabits warm deciduous forests and forest-steppes, and produces just one generation per year, on the wing from June to August. The caterpillars develop from September throughout the winter until May, feeding on withered and dry leaves.

5 *Orthopygia glaucinalis* (L.). 22—27mm. With the exception of northernmost regions, this species is distributed over almost all Europe and Asia, tolerating most diverse habitats, but preferring grassy ones. The moth can be seen on the wing from June to August. The caterpillar probably hibernates and is most active in spring. It feeds on various dry plant material, and can be found in hay-lofts, barns, stacks, birds'nests, etc.

6 *Endotricha flammealis* (D. & S.). 16—20mm. Widespread over the warmer regions of Europe, northern Africa and western Asia, this species is confined to deciduous oak forests. The moth flies in June und July. The caterpillar lives in autumn on the leaves of various shrubs and plants, and overwinters in a cocoon, to pupate in the following spring.

7 *Eudonia truncicolella* (Stt.). 20—22mm. This insect belongs to a very large genus comprising many extremely similar species, and is one of the most abundant. It occurs in central Europe, where it can be seen on the wing at the beginning of summer. The caterpillar lives from autumn till spring on moss, in which it also pupates.

8 *Eudonia sudetica* (Z.). 18—24mm. One of the larger species of this group, it is locally distributed in the mountains of central and northern Europe, but is not abundant. It differs somewhat from the other species in markings. The single generation flies in summer; the hibernating caterpillars live on mosses growing on tree trunks.

9 *Scoparia pyralella* (D. & S.) (= *arundinata* Thbg.). 16—20mm. Widespread in central and southern Europe, this is an abundant species in all grassy biotopes. The moth flies at the beginning of summer; the caterpillar lives on moss in grass growing on marshes and in water-meadows. The genus *Scoparia* differs from the genus *Eudonia* (= *Witlesia*) primarily in the structure of the sexual organs, the moths looking outwardly very much alike.

2

1

5

4

3

6

9

7

8

Family: **Pyralidae** — **pyralids**

1 *Nymphula nymphaeata (L.) — Brown China-mark. 22—30mm. Distributed throughout Europe (absent only from the extreme north), this moth is abundant where found. Like the other species of this group, it is dependent on aquatic plants. In June and July it flies at night in the vicinity of stagnant or slowly flowing waters, hiding by day in the vegetation growing along the banks. In the night the moths will frequently come to light. From August until the following spring, the caterpillars feed on water lily, pond lily and semi-aquatic knotgrass. Occasionally the species is a pest of waterlilies growing in park or garden pools. The larvae live entirely under water, breathing dissolved oxygen with the aid of an air bubble trapped by silk.

2 *Parapoynx stagnata (Don.) — Beautiful China-mark. 18—22mm. Distributed throughout the warmer parts of Europe and Asia Minor, spreading to eastern Asia, this moth inhabits very similar biotopes to the preceding species. The adults fly at the beginning of summer. The aquatic caterpillars hibernate, to complete their development the following May, feeding on *Sparganium*.

3 *Cataclysta lemnata (L.) — Small China-mark. 15—22mm. This species, which has a most interesting sexual dimorphism (the male is much smaller than the female and almost white, while the female is brownish), occurs in Europe. The moths can be seen flying throughout the summer, near stagnant waters. The caterpillar develops in water from August until the next May in a little chamber spun from duckweed, wherein it also pupates.

4 *Parapoynx stratiotata (L.) — Ringed China-mark. 20—23mm. With the exception of regions where a poor climate prevails, this species is distributed over the whole of Europe, and is to be found close by stagnant and slowly flowing waters. There is but one annual generation, flying from June to August. By day this night-flying moth, which produces a great number of colour variations, hides in the vegetation at the waterside. The caterpillar is well adapted to aquatic life, the tracheae, protruding from the body, having been modified to form 'tracheal gills' — which the caterpillar uses to absorb oxygen directly from water, as do the majority of truly aquatic animals. These larvae live from summer to spring on a variety of aquatic plants, including *Stratiotes*, *Potamogeton*, and *Alisma*.

5 *Schoenobius gigantella (D. & S.). 25—40mm. A very variable species, ranging from Europe to eastern Asia, it may be seen on the wing from June to August, being quite abundant in reed beds on the banks of stagnant waters. The caterpillars develop in spring, within new reed shoots. Before the larvae reach full size the reeds grow, so the caterpillars subsequently live inside the stalks. There they also pupate, after having each gnawed an opening in the stem wall barely discernible from outside, through which the adult moths will emerge.

6 *Schoenobius forficella (Thbg.). 25—30mm. The distribution and life cycle of this moth are rather similar to the preceding species. The caterpillar, when very young, mines the leaves of *Glyceria*. Later it cuts out a part of the leaf to construct a case wherein it drifts in the water in search of new food. Nothing is known about the way in which it overwinters. The caterpillars can be found in spring.

7 *Donacaula mucronellus (D. & S.). 25—30mm. Recorded from Britain, Scandinavia and central Europe, where it flies during June and July in damp biotopes, such as meadows and ditches. The female is larger than the male, somewhat paler, and possesses long, pointed wings. The caterpillar hibernates. It is reported to live inside the stalks of *Glyceria*, sedges and reeds, close to the ground; here it also pupates.

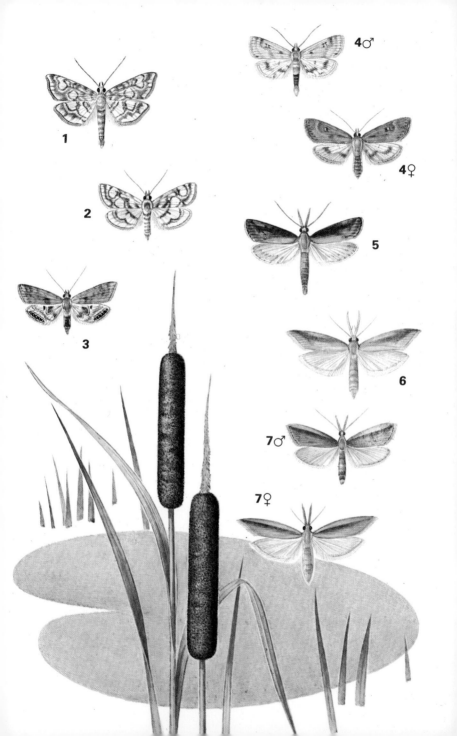

Family: **Pyralidae — pyralids**

1 *Evergestis limbata* (L). 18—23mm. Ranges over central, southeastern and part of southern Europe. This is a fairly abundant species in warm, dry localities, where it flies in July and August after dusk. The caterpillar lives in late summer on hedge-mustard and woad.

2 *Evergestis frumentalis* (L.). 22—30mm. Distributed throughout central Europe as far as Finland, but absent from the British Isles and Holland, this species ranges eastwards into western Asia. One brood is produced annually to be seen on the wing in May and June, the moths being fairly common in fields and on wasteground. The caterpillar develops at the end of summer, feeding on various cruciferous plants. It overwinters in the ground, enclosed in a cocoon, in which it pupates during spring.

3 *Evergestis forficalis* (L.) — Garden Pebble. 25—28mm. Widely distributed in the whole of temperate Europe and Asia, and also in North America, this species prefers habitats with lush vegetation, being most common in overgrown fields and gardens. Two generations are produced, flying from May to September. The caterpillars live at the beginning of summer and again during autumn in a web spun on the undersides of the leaves of various crucifers, including vegetables. The full-grown caterpillar hibernates in a flimsy cocoon formed in the ground, and pupates in spring.

4 *Evergestis extimalis* (Sc.). 20—25mm. Ranging over temperate Europe and Asia, being common in all warm localities, the single generation of this moth is seen on the wing from June to August. The caterpillars develop in autumn on the seeds of cruciferous plants. Pupation takes place in the spring.

5 *Titanio pollinalis* (D. & S.). 20—22mm. Widespread in central and southern Europe and in Asia Minor, this moth is at home in dry localities within and outside forests, and produces two annual generations. The caterpillar is found in autumn, most often on broom and *Ononis*. Winter is passed in the pupal stage.

6 *Metaxmeste phrygialis* (Hb.). 20—22mm. A species characteristic of higher European mountains, occurring eastwards as far as the Urals, and also found in the mountains of northern Europe. The adults, which are very variable, fly at various elevations ranging up to the zone of perpetual snow, where they are to be seen from the moment spring sets in, from June to August; they particularly like to settle on scree. The caterpillars are polyphagous, but little else is known about the bionomics of this moth.

7 *Cynaeda dentalis* (D. & S.). 22—28mm. Distributed over central and southern Europe, and eastwards into western Asia, this moth flies in July and August, but never abundantly. Occasionally it appears at quite high elevations. The caterpillar lives from summer to spring, and is found only on bugloss.

8 *Diasemia litterata* (Sc.). 18—22mm. Ranges over the warm parts of Europe and Asia, far to the east. This moth inhabits dry, grássy localities, forest-steppes and steppes (probably in two generations), flying from April to September. The caterpillar lives early in spring and summer, feeding from beneath the lowest leaves of various low-growing plants.

9 *Nomophila noctuella* (D. & S.) — Rush Veneer. 24—28mm. Due to its migratory tendencies, this moth has a cosmopolitan distribution, penetrating year after year into places it does not normally inhabit, including the highest mountains. Generally it is most common in fields and other grassy biotopes, flying from June to October, but it is not equally abundant every year. The caterpillar lives during summer, and is sometimes considered a pest of clover, lucerne and wheat. Winter is passed in the adult or pupal stage — depending on circumstances.

Family: **Pyralidae — pyralids**

1 *Agrotera nemoralis* (Sc.). 18—22mm. Distributed over Europe and the whole of Asia. In June and July moths of the single generation may be seen on the wing in deciduous forests, flying round hornbeam, aspen and hazel. The caterpillars live in summer among spun-up leaves of these trees.

2 *Pleuroptya ruralis* (Sc.) — Mother of Pearl. 25—40mm. Very abundantly distributed over the whole Palaearctic, this species is found in lowland forests, damp overgrown wastelands, and in fields. The moths are on the wing in June and July. The caterpillar (2b) lives from August until spring in little tubes rolled from the leaves of nettle, hop, and several other plants (2c), within which it also pupates (2d).

3 *Mecyna trinalis* (D. & S.). 24—27mm. Widespread in the warmer parts of central Europe, southern Europe and northern Africa, extending eastwards to central Asia, this species haunts dry meadows, stony hillsides, and other biotopes of a steppe character. The moth flies in July and August; the caterpillar lives in May, on rockrose.

4 *Udea ferrugalis* (Hb.). 18—22mm. Distributed over the warmer parts of the Palaearctic, this migratory species also flies in northern Europe. The adults are on the wing from May to August. The caterpillars feed on a great number of low plants and shrubs. Two generations apparently emerge during the year.

5 *Udea alpinalis* (D. & S.). 24—28mm. Confined to European mountains, alpine meadows are the favourite haunts of this species. The moth's flight period lasts from June to August; the caterpillars can be found in spring among spun-up leaves of groundsel, cornflower or wormwood.

6 *Udea lutealis* (Hb.). 22—28mm. A very abundant species distributed in meadows of submontane and montane regions of Europe, east as far as the Caucasus. The moth is on the wing in July and August, the caterpillar lives in spring on various herbs.

7 *Udea olivalis* (D. & S.). 24—28mm. Reported from temperate Europe and various localities in Asia, this is a single-brooded species; the moths fly in July and August in both lowland and mountain forest. The polyphagous caterpillars feed on a variety of low plants.

8 *Udea prunalis* (D. & S.). 20—24mm. Occurs in central and northern Europe and in western Asia, except the coldest regions. A single generation of moths is on the wing from June to August. The caterpillar lives from summer to spring, on a great variety of plants.

9 *Eurrhypara hortulata* (L.) — Small Magpie. 24—28mm. Found in scattered localities all over the Palaearctic, recently in North America, favouring damp biotopes, forests, areas overgrown with shrubs, and gardens. This species flies from June to August. The caterpillar lives in spring in folded or spun-up leaves of nettle, mint, woundwort, etc.

10 *Eurrhypara lancealis* (D. & S.). 26—34mm. This species ranges from Europe as far as eastern Asia. The moths fly from May to July in damp biotopes, mostly in open woodlands, and are conspicuous for their narrow wings. The caterpillar lives from summer to spring in tubes spun from leaves of woundwort, hemp agrimony or groundsel. Pupation takes place in a firm cocoon on the ground, covered by leaves.

11 *Eurrhypara coronata* (Hfn.). 22—25mm. This moth has a Palaearctic distribution. Two generations are on the wing between May and August. The caterpillar lives in summer in a flimsy, cocoon-like nest on the underside of leaves of elder, lilac, ash, etc.

Family: **Pyralidae — pyralids**

1 *Ostrinia palustralis* (Hb.). 32—40mm. Reported mostly from the more eastern parts of central Europe, and from southeastern Europe, this is a local species, rather rare everywhere — but conspicuous for its colouration. It flies, in a single generation, during June and July, in damp localities where waterdock, the foodplant of the caterpillars, can be found.

2 **Ostrinia nubilalis* (Hb.) — European Corn-borer. 26—30mm. A native European species introduced with maize to all parts of the world, it is one of the most serious agricultural pests. In temperate areas there are one or two generations, but in the tropics there may be as many as six. The moths are on the wing from May to September. The caterpillar (2b) lives in the stalks of maize, sunflower, hemp, etc. There it hibernates when full-grown, and pupates in spring. The male is smaller and more brightly coloured than the female.

3 **Anania funebris* (Ström) (= *octomaculata* L.). 18—22mm. Locally distributed over central, northern and southern Europe, this moth flies in dry steppe and forest-steppe biotopes from May to July. The caterpillar lives at the end of summer on goldenrod and broom.

4 **Anania stachydalis* (Germ.). 20—23mm. Lives in central and southern Europe. Two generations of the moth emerge between May and August. The caterpillars develop in summer and again in autumn, spending the winter enclosed in a web; pupation takes place in spring. The foodplants are various species of woundwort.

5 **Pyrausta cingulata* (L.). 14—18mm. Distributed in almost the whole of Europe and Asia Minor, there are two generations of this moth per year, the first on the wing in May and June, the second in July and August. On sunny days the moths can be seen flying over sunny hillsides or pastures, but they are also active at night. The caterpillar hatches in autumn and lives on thyme and sage; as winter approaches it enters the soil, wraps itself in silken webbing, and pupates in spring.

6 **Pyrausta aurata* (Sc.). 16—18mm. Distributed in Africa, Europe and Asia, this species occurs on the wing from April to September, in two merging generations. It is fairly abundant in dry meadows and grassy localities exposed to sunshine. The caterpillar lives on various labiate plants and, before pupating, hibernates in the ground inside a flimsy cocoon.

7 **Pyrausta sanguinalis* (L.). 16—18mm. Widespread in northern Africa, in Europe and in western Asia, showing a preference for warmer localities, this moth can be found on the wing on bright, sunny days in warm and dry localities overgrown with grass. The two generations fly from May to August. The caterpillar, like the preceding species, feeds solely on thyme or sage.

8 **Sitochroa verticalis* (L.). 24—28mm. Ranges over the whole temperate Palaearctic. This single-brooded moth is on the wing in June and July, and can be found in various treeless biotopes. The caterpillars live at the end of summer on *Teucrium, Cirsium, Atriplex* and other plants, but do not pupate before spring.

9 **Margaritia sticticalis* (L). 22—27mm. Occurring throughout Europe, Asia and North America, this is a species characteristic of steppes — but it has also become adapted to fields, and is now a rather notorious sugar-beet pest. At various times it appears in vast numbers as a migrant; then it can be found even at high mountain altitudes up to 3,000m. There are two generations in the year, flying from June to September. In autumn the polyphagous caterpillar (9b) encloses itself within a firm cocoon; pupation takes place in spring.

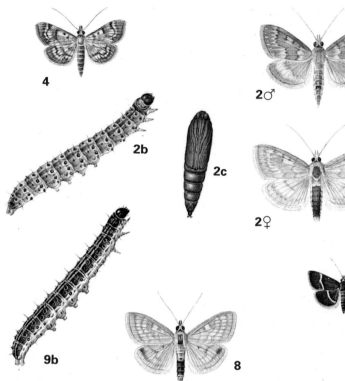

4

2♂

2b

2c

2♀

9b

8

5

9

6

3

1

7

Family: **Pyralidae — pyralids**

1 *Acentria nivea* (Oliv.) — Water Veneer. 10—12mm. Facts about the distribution of this peculiar species are rather scarce, but it appears in relatively great abundance in some localities in central and eastern Europe. Due to its way of life it is dependent on freshwater habitats. The flight period is protracted, lasting from May to September, yet only one generation seems to be involved. The caterpillar lives in deep water within the aquatic plants *Elodea canadensis* and *Ceratophyllum demersum* during the autumn, and continues its development in spring. It pupates under the water inside an air-filled cocoon. This species is sexually dimorphic; furthermore, the females are polymorphic, some of them being winged while others have degenerate wings. Immediately after copulation, both kinds of females oviposit on the water plants and die. (Note this species, together with those placed in *Schoenobius* and *Donacaula,* are sometimes placed in a separate family, the Schoenobiidae.)

Family: **Thyrididae — leaf moths**

2 *Thyris fenestrella* (Sc.). 14—18mm. Ranges over central and southern Europe, eastwards across Asia Minor to the Amur basin, northern China and Korea. This is a local species, scarce throughout its range. It inhabits waterside biotopes and other damp places in limestone areas, the home of its foodplant, *Clematis vitalba.* This day-flying moth can be seen on the wing from May to July. The caterpillar hatches at the end of summer; the pupa hibernates.

Family: **Limacodidae — slug-caterpillar moths**

3 *Apoda limacodes* (Hfn.) — Festoon. 20—30mm. Distributed in the belt of warm deciduous forests of Europe, and further eastwards to the southern Urals, the Near East, and the southern parts of the Far East. There is one generation per year, flying from the end of May to the beginning of August, at low elevations, and showing a distinct preference for oak forests. The male is smaller and bears more conspicuous markings than the female; occasionally he may be seen flying by day in sunny weather. The caterpillar (3b) lives until autumn on oak, hornbeam, and other deciduous trees and shrubs. The pupa hibernates, sometimes overwintering twice, lying concealed in the soil.

4 *Heterogenea asella* (D. & S.) — Triangle. 15—20mm. Distributed in the deciduous woodlands of the Palaearctic like the preceding species, but very rare. The moths of the single annual generation fly in June and July, favouring warm oak and hornbeam forests at low elevations. The caterpillar develops at the end of summer and during autumn, usually on hornbeam, less frequently on other trees. Winter is passed in the pupal stage.

Family: **Alucitidae — many-plume moths**

5 *Alucita hexadactyla* (L.) — Twenty-plume. 12—14mm. The distribution of this generally rather scarce European species is local. One generation is produced annually. The night-flying moth takes wing in August, and flies again in spring, after hibernation, until May. The caterpillar develops from May to July in the flower buds and leaves of honeysuckle.

6 *Alucita grammodactyla* (Z.). 12—14mm. Known from central and southern Europe and Asia Minor, where it inhabits dry steppe localities, this species flies in two generations, from May to June and August to September. The caterpillars (6b) feed on *Scabiosa ochroleuca* (and probably other kinds of scabious), those of the first generation developing from April to May in thickened basal buds, while those of the second generation develop during June to July within galls on the stalks (6c). This night-flying moth is both rare and local.

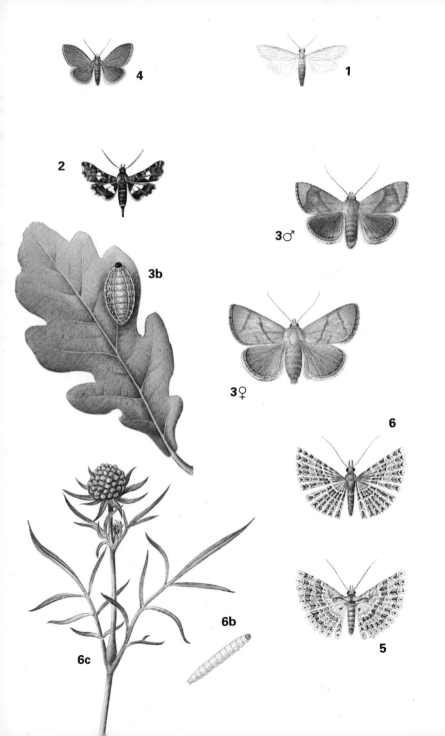

Family: **Zygaenidae — burnets and foresters**

1 *Rhagades pruni* (D. & S.). 20—25mm. In northern and western Europe confined to numerous circumscribed localities from Finland to Italy, this moth has a more continuous distribution in southeastern Europe, western Asia, and the Far East. A relatively thermophilic species, on the wing in July, it is at home in forest-steppes overgrown with blackthorn. However, the heather moors of northern Europe are inhabited by ssp. *callunae* — but this is often regarded as an independent species. The caterpillars, which normally feed on blackthorn leaves, hibernate and grow to full size in May.

2 *Adscita statices* (L.) — Forester. 22—28mm. Ranging throughout Europe and eastwards as far as the Urals, this species is abundant in damp meadows, on flowery hillsides or in forest clearings. It can also be found high up in the mountains, above the timberline. The moths fly from May to August, depending on climatic conditions. The caterpillar hibernates, and feeds on various common species of sorrel.

3 *Adscita chloros* (Hb.). 18—23mm. A thermophilic species distributed in southern parts of central Europe, in southern and southeastern Europe, also in Asia Minor and in the USSR, as far as the Volga basin. The moths are found in grassy steppe biotopes during June and July. The caterpillar (as with other species in this group) hibernates; it lives on cornflower and globe-daisy.

4 *Zygaena purpuralis* (Brünnich) — Transparent Burnet. 28—35mm. This is one of the larger and more abundant species; as with most burnets and foresters, it produces many individual forms. Distributed all over Europe (except Spain), it extends across Asia Minor to eastern Siberia, and occurs from lowlands to mountains, wherever thyme, the caterpillar's foodplant, can be found. The moths fly from June to August, depending on the elevation of the locality.

5 *Zygaena punctum* (O). 22—25mm. A thermophilic species extending from the more southern parts of central Europe to the southeast, across Asia Minor to Armenia. The single generation flies in June and July in warm steppe localities. In spring, after hibernation, the caterpillar feeds on field eryngo until summer. The pupal stage lasts several days only, but is still enclosed within a whitish, papery, spindle-shaped cocoon characteristic of burnets and foresters.

6 *Zygaena scabiosae* (Schev.). 28—32mm. Distributed in steppe and forest-steppe regions of Europe and Asia, this very local species frequents open woodland or neighbouring flowery slopes. The moths are very variable, with the result that many individual and geographical forms have been described; the single generation is on the wing during June and July. The caterpillar lives from summer till spring on various species of vetchling; the pupal cocoon is white and shiny.

7 *Zygaena loti* (D. & S.) (= *achilleae* Esp.). 27—30mm. Inhabits most of temperate and southern Europe, extending to the southeast, Asia Minor and Syria, across the Caucasus to the Altai. An abundant species seen on the wing in grassy steppe localities from June to August. Like all burnets and foresters it is diurnal in habit. The caterpillar lives from summer till the following spring on *Coronilla* and horseshoe vetch; the pupal cocoon is brownish.

8 *Zygaena laeta* (Hb.) — Bloodwort Burnet. 25—27mm. A thermophilic species ranging from central Europe to the southeast, as far as Asia Minor. There is a single generation per year, seen on the wing from June to August. The caterpillar (8b) hibernates; it can be found towards the end of spring on eryngo. The cocoon is yellowish-white and shiny (8c). This species formerly inhabited mild localities in central Europe (for example, in the neighbourhood of Prague), but has become extinct in this area during the present century.

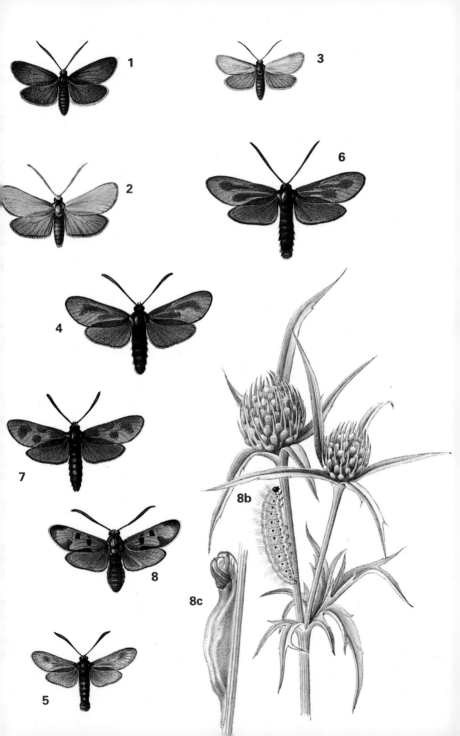

Family: Zygaenidae — burnets and foresters

1 *Zygaena carniolica* (Sc.). 25—32mm. The range of this thermophilic species extends across Asia Minor and Iran to the Altai. The moths, which exhibit many colour variations, fly from June to August only at lower elevations, mostly on limestone. The caterpillar (1b) lives from summer throughout winter until spring, feeding on trefoil *(Lotus)* and sainfoin. It pupates on the ground in a yellow, spindle-shaped cocoon (1c). This moth used to be abundant in many localities but has vanished from many of them of late, mostly from biotopes affected by agricultural activities involving the application of fertilizers and insecticides.

2 *Zygaena filipendulae* (L.) — Six-spot Burnet. 30—38mm. The most common burnet in lowlands and mountains up to 2,000m, it is distributed throughout Europe (except a few regions) eastwards to central Asia. Though not exhibiting great variation in comparison with other species, many forms have been described. The moth flies from June to September in grassy, rather damp and fresh biotopes, but also in steppes, forest margins, or clearings and glades within them, and is abundant everywhere. The caterpillar (2b) lives from end of summer till next spring; foodplants are *Coronilla* and trefoils. Pupation takes place inside the oblong, white and yellow cocoon, attached to stalks (2c).

3 *Zygaena trifolii* (Esp.) — Five-spot Burnet. 28—33mm. One of the earliest burnets to emerge, appearing in some years as early as the end of May, it ranges over northern Africa, Europe and eastwards to central Asia. A species peculiar to damp, flowery meadows, at low and medium elevations, where it remains on the wing till the end of August. The caterpillar lives from summer to the following spring on scorpion's tail; it pupates in an oblong yellow cocoon attached to grass stalks. An extremely variable species, in which the red patches on the hindwings often fuse to form diverse patterns; many forms have been described, including f. *minoides* (3c).

4 *Zygaena angelicae* (O.). 30—33mm. More comnon in the east and southeast of Europe, this moth inhabits warm, mostly limestone localities, but also occurs up to almost 2,000m in the mountains. An abundant species, it is on the wing from June to August. The caterpillar lives from August until the next May on *Lotus* and *Coronilla;* it pupates in a spindle-like yellow cocoon attached to grass stalks.

5 *Zygaena ephialtes* (L.). 30—40mm. Widespread throughout temperate Europe and Asia, this species is relatively abundant in open woodlands and their margins, and on warm slopes and forest-steppes — chiefly those with a limestone substrate. It exhibits an extraordinarily wide range of variation, some forms having a clearly delimited geographical distribution. Besides typical, white-spotted individuals, the red-coloured f. *peucedani* (5c) may commonly be found, while the yellow-coloured f. *icterica* (5d) is rather rare. Most numerous are various transitional forms, many of which have their own names (for example, f. *coronillae* — 5e). The moth flies from June to August. The caterpillar lives from summer to spring, on *Coronilla;* pupation takes place in a silvery-white cocoon formed on grass stalks.

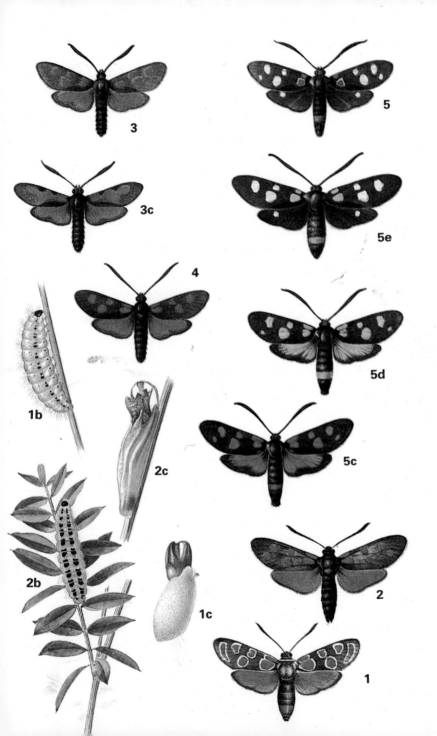

Family: **Gelechiidae — gelechiid moths**

1 *Anarsia lineatella* (Z.) — Peach Twig Borer. 12—14mm. Distributed in the Palaearctic as far as central Asia, it also occurs in North America, where it was introduced. The moths fly in June and July; the caterpillars, which hibernate, are pests of fruit-tree buds and blossoms.

2 *Acompsia cinerella* (Cl.). 16—18mm. Widespread in Europe and Asia Minor. One generation of this typically forest-dwelling species is on the wing in June and July. The larvae feed on moss.

3 *Sophronia semicostella* (Hb.). 15—16mm. A single-brooded European species flying from May to July, it is abundant in dry localities. The caterpillar lives in a flimsy cocoon attached to low-growing leaves of various plants.

4 *Nothris verbascella* (Hb.). 18—20mm. Reported from Europe, Asia Minor and central Asia. Two generations of this moth, which occurs on dry hillsides and wastelands where its foodplant is found, develop between May and August. The caterpillars are found in June and again in autumn, feeding on the cordate leaves of mullein. Being gregarious, they are capable of completely destroying the plant's meristem.

5 *Scrobipalpa ocellatella* (Boyd) — Beet Moth. 11—13mm. The distribution of this moth is associated with that of its original foodplant *(Beta maritima)* in all coastal areas of western Europe, ranging over regions bordering the Mediterranean in Europe and Africa, as far as Asia Minor and the Black Sea coast, whence it spreads to warmer parts of central Europe. There are two or more generations per year. In agricultural areas this species has adapted to cultivated sugar-beet, where the caterpillar lives in the vegetative apex, causing putrefaction. The caterpillars, found throughout the summer, overwinter.

6 *Gelechia turpella* (D. & S.) (= *pinguinella* Tr.). 18—22mm. Distributed over central and southern Europe, there is one annual generation of this abundant moth flying in June and July. The caterpillar develops during spring on the leaves of black poplar.

7 *Lita virgella* (Thbg.). 14—16mm. Distributed in mountains and peat-bogs of central and northern Europe and further to the east, this moth is associated with the occurrence of the caterpillar's foodplant — heather. On the wing in May and June.

8 *Teleiodes luculella* (Hb.). 10mm. This abundant species occurs in deciduous forests, evidently all over Europe. There is one generation, flying from May to July; the caterpillar lives until autumn among oak or birch leaves joined together by silk.

9 *Recurvaria leucatella* (Cl.). 13—15mm. Widespread throughout temperate Europe, this moth produces one brood, on the wing in June and July. The caterpillar lives in spring among spun-up leaves of deciduous trees, and may cause damage in orchards.

10 *Chrysoesthia drurella* (F.) (= *hermannella* auctt.). 8mm. Distributed over Europe and Asia Minor, this is a common species in fields and steppes. The two broods fly from May to August. The caterpillars mine orache and goosefoot leaves.

11 *Metzneria lappella* (L.). 18—22mm. Ranging over Europe and western Asia, this moth is on the wing from May to August. The caterpillar lives from summer till spring in burdock seeds. Waterside and wasteland habitats are its favourite haunts.

1

2

4

3

5

7

11

8

9

10

6

8

Family: **Oecophoridae**

1 *Schiffermuelleria schaefferella* (L.). 11−17mm. Ranging over Europe and Asia, this species occurs in deciduous forests from lowlands to mountains. There is one annual generation, flying in May and June. The caterpillar lives until spring under the bark of various deciduous trees, chiefly oak, lime, beech, poplar, etc.

2 *Dafa formosella* (D. & S.). 11−15mm. Distributed over central and southern Europe, also in northern Africa, this moth has a single generation per year, on the wing from May to August. The caterpillar lives from autumn till spring under the bark of deciduous trees.

3 *Endrosis sarcitrella* (L.) − White-shouldered House-moth. 15−21mm. A cosmopolitan storehouse pest introduced with agricultural products to all parts of the world. Adult moths appear for the whole season, from May to October. The caterpillars can be found all year, feeding on seeds and decaying plant remains, or in storehouses, where outbreaks frequently occur.

4 *Hofmannophila pseudospretella* (Stt.) − Brown House-moth. 16−25mm. A cosmopolitan species generally distributed throughout the world in the same way as that preceding. The moth flies from spring to autumn; the caterpillar lives all year round on plant and animal remains, or on agricultural and food-stuff products in storehouses.

5 *Oecophora bractella* (L.). 12−16mm. A relatively rare species from Europe and Asia Minor, where it inhabits damp, shady localities in deciduous forests. The moths are on the wing in May and June; the caterpillars live from autumn till spring under the bark and on the wood of decaying trees − mainly oaks, beeches and hornbeams.

6 *Harpella forficella* (Sc.). 21−27mm. Ranges over Europe and Asia Minor in the deciduous-forest zone, mainly in old and damp forests in both lowlands and mountains: here the species reaches the upper limit of deciduous trees. The moth, which is quite abundant, flies in June and July; caterpillars live from summer till spring on decaying wood and under the bark of old stumps.

7 *Oecophora staintoniella* (Z.). 12−20mm. Distributed throughout Europe and Asia Minor in deciduous forests over much the same area as the preceding species, it is abundant in warmer forests with a rich undergrowth of shrubs. The single brood of this day-flying moth is seen in May and June; the caterpillar lives until spring in rotting wood of deciduous trees.

8 *Topeutis barbella* (F.). 16−22mm. Known from warmer regions of Europe and Asia Minor, this moth flies in grassy and steppe biotopes. On the wing from May to July, nothing is known about the early stages of this relatively rare species.

9 *Topeutis criella* (Tr.). 18−22mm. Recorded from central Europe and Yugoslavia, this rather rare species flies in grassy localities and steppes in lowlands and mild areas, even in mountains, from June to August. The caterpillar is supposed to live in June on hairy greenweed.

10 *Hypercallia citrinalis* (Sc.). 15−20mm. A species inhabiting dry, warm, flowery and grassy biotopes situated mostly in lowlands, but also in the warmer mountain ranges. The moths fly in June and July. Little is known about the caterpillar, which has been found in May on alpine milkwort *(Chamaebuxus);* in Britain common milkwort *(Polygala vulgaris)* and chalk milkwort *(P. calcarea)* are known to be foodplants.

Family: **Oecophoridae**

1 *Carcina quercana* (F.). 16—20mm. Distributed in Europe, northern Africa, Asia Minor, and also in North America, the single annual generation of this moth flies in July and August. The caterpillar lives in May and June on oak, beech and pear-tree leaves.

2 *Exaeretia allisella* (Stt.). 20—23mm. Occurs locally in northern and central Europe. The one generation per year flies from July to August. The caterpillar lives on wormwood, but not much is known about the life cycle of this species.

3 *Agonopterix alstroemeriana* (Cl.). 17—19mm. Belonging to a large genus of mostly very similar species, the present moth is an exception, being more brightly coloured than the others. Widespread throughout Europe south to Morocco, and eastwards to Siberia, it flies in July and August. The caterpillar lives during June and July among hemlock leaves spun together with silk.

4 *Agonopterix arenella* (D. & S.). 19—23mm. Distributed in northern Africa, the whole of Europe, and in North America, this moth takes wing in August, overwinters and reproduces in spring. The caterpillars develop during June and July on burdock, various thistles, etc.

5 *Agonopterix furvella* (Tr.). 20—25mm. Known from central and southern Europe as well as from Asia Minor, the distribution of this moth is restricted by that of its foodplant. It flies predominantly in warm situations, notably forest-steppe localities, in June and July. The caterpillar (5b) lives in spring on *Dictamnus,* among leaves spun together.

6 *Depressaria chaerophylli* (Z.). 18—21mm. A representative of a similar genus to *Agonopterix,* also involving many barely distinguishable species: genital preparations are usually essential for accurate identification. The range of this species extends over Europe as far as the Caucasus. The moths fly in August and hibernate until May; the caterpillars live in July in chervil umbels.

7 *Depressaria pastinacella* (Dup.) (= *heracliana* auctt.) — Parsnip Moth. 23—28mm. Common in meadows and by running water in the more northern parts of Europe and Asia, as well as in North America. The moth flies in August and September, and, after hibernation, until June. The caterpillar spins together and eats away the umbels of parsnip or cow-parsnip.

8 *Semioscopis avellanella* (Hb.). 20—28mm. Distributed in deciduous forests of Europe, primarily at lower elevations, and in damp biotopes by running water. There is a single generation per year, on the wing in March and April. Females are much smaller than the males. The caterpillar lives in July and August on hornbeam, hazel, birch, and other shrubs and trees.

9 *Diurnea fagella* (D. & S.). 19—29mm. Confined to the deciduous forests and forest-steppes of Europe, Asia Minor and central Asia, this single-brooded species flies from March to May, ascending in the mountains to the upper limit of deciduous trees. The caterpillars (9b) develop on various deciduous trees during summer. In industrial regions this very variable species shows a tendency to melanism; the females have stunted wings.

10 *Diurnea phryganella* (Hb.). 18—24mm. Distributed throughout Europe, the females of this species also have degenerate wings — but in contrast to the previous insect this is a late-autumn moth, on the wing in October and November. The caterpillar develops during spring on trees and shrubs.

Family: **Ethmiidae**

1 *Ethmia pusiella* (L.). 22—30mm. Distributed all over Europe and Asia Minor, this rare and local species haunts grassy forest clearings abounding in herbs, and shrubby hillsides. The moths are on the wing from July to September. The caterpillars (1b) develop in spring on a variety of plants, including forget-me-not, lungwort and *Symphytum*.

2 *Ethmia funerella* (F.). 16—20mm. Confined to the belt of deciduous forests of Europe and Asia Minor as far as the Caucasus, this moth is found in shady deciduous forests with profuse herbaceous undergrowth, also in mountains at high altitudes. On the wing from June to September, the caterpillars develop in autumn on various rough-leaved forest plants, for example lungwort, forget-me-not and gromwell.

3 *Ethmia terminella* Fletch. 14—22mm. A thermophilic species found in central and southern Europe, and Asia Minor, in steppe and forest-steppe localities, and also on wastelands where similar conditions prevail. It is restricted by the distribution of its foodplant, viper's bugloss. There is one annual generation, on the wing in June and July. The caterpillar lives from midsummer till autumn.

4 *Ethmia bipunctella* (F.). 20—28mm. With a range and biotopes very similar to the preceding species, the caterpillar of this moth is also dependent on viper's bugloss. Two generations occur, flying from April to June and August to October. The caterpillars develop in spring, and again in midsummer.

Family: **Scythrididae**

5 *Scythris obscurella* (Sc.). 14—22mm. Though found in mountains and hills of central and southeastern Europe and Asia Minor, this species is largely restricted to warm valleys and exposed submontane and montane meadows overgrown with lush vegetation. Annually there is one generation, flying from May to July. The caterpillars occur in spring, and are thought to feed on various Papilionaceae or various grasses.

o *Scythris cuspidella* (D. & S.). 14—15mm. Reported from central and southern Europe, but the exact distribution of this relatively rare species is not known. The moths fly in June and July in dry, grassy localities. The life cycle is largely unknown, but the larvae are presumed to feed on thyme.

Family: **Elachistidae**

7 *Cosmiotes freyerella* (Hb.). 7—9mm. Inhabits lowlands and mountains of all non-polar Europe. Annually there are two broods, the first flies in spring (April to May), the second in summer (July to August). The caterpillars live from March to June, mining grasses. This is a rather abundant species, with a wide range of variation.

8 *Elachista nobilella* (Z.). 7—8mm. This is a representative of another large genus of minute, systematically extremely difficult Lepidoptera. There is one annual generation, which flies in July. The caterpillar develops in spring, mining a variety of tough woodrush and grasses such as *Luzula, Festuca, Aira,* etc. It has been recorded from various parts of central and southern Europe.

Family: **Coleophoridae** — **case bearers**

1 *Coleophora frischella* (L.) (= *alcyonipennella* auctt.) — Small Clover Case-bearer. 10—13mm. Distributed in Europe, Asia Minor and Afghanistan, this abundant, single-brooded moth flies from June to September. The caterpillar, which hibernates, lives from October till May in a tubular case on thistles, cornflower, scabious, and several other Compositae or plants of the genus *Dipsacus*.

2 *Coleophora hemerobiella* (Sc.). 12—14mm. Ranges over greater part of Europe and Asia Minor. The moth flies in June and August in deciduous forests, forest-steppes and orchards, and is abundant in warmer regions. Its caterpillar takes two years to develop, living chiefly on fruit trees and various shrubs of the family Rosaceae (probably also on oak). Case of caterpillar is at first crescent-shaped; later it becomes straight and is attached to the support almost at a right angle (2c).

3 *Coleophora onosmella* (Brahm). 14—20mm. Distributed over Europe, the moths fly in June and July, in steppes and grassy biotopes. The caterpillars live from autumn till May, each in a case (3c) made from a piece of leaf, feeding on plants such as *Nonea*, bugloss, and viper's bugloss.

4 *Coleophora vibicella* (Hb.). 16—24mm. Widespread in central and southern Europe, and in Asia Minor, this rather local species inhabits dry biotopes, favouring woodland margins and sandy localities. A single-brooded moth, flying in July and August, the caterpillar lives in a black, pistol-shaped case (4c) on greenweed *(Genista)* from autumn till the following spring.

5 *Coleophora ornatipennella* (Hb.). 18—25mm. Occurs in central and southern Europe, confined to steppe localities, grassy slopes and field boundaries. The moth has one generation, on the wing in June. Caterpillars occur from summer to May in a case (5c) made from a piece of leaf, feeding at first on sage flowers and seeds, later, in spring, on a variety of soft grasses.

6 *Coleophora laricella* (Hb.) — Larch Case Bearer. 8—10mm. Distributed over Europe and Asia as far as Japan, predominantly in submontane regions and the taiga zone in the north. One of the smallest, inconspicuously coloured species, it is on the wing in June and July. Most commonly found is the caterpillar form, living in a tiny tubular case (6c) and mining larch, leaving behind dessicated, empty, white needles. Occasionally the species completely strips all needles from larch trees.

7 *Coleophora leucapennella* (Hb.). 16—20mm. Flies in warm steppe and forest-steppe localities of Europe and western Asia, producing one generation per year. The moths fly in May and June. The caterpillars live until autumn in the pericarps of catchflies *(Silene, Viscaria)* and each uses several small pericarps to construct a case. Pupation takes place in spring.

8 *Coleophora anatipennella* (Hb.) — Pistol Case Bearer. 12—16mm. Sparsely distributed in the British Isles, northern and central Europe, this moth extends eastwards to Iran. One generation occurs annually, on the wing in June and July. The caterpillar lives in a pistol-shaped case (8c), feeding on leaves of fruit trees, lime, oak, hawthorn, etc.

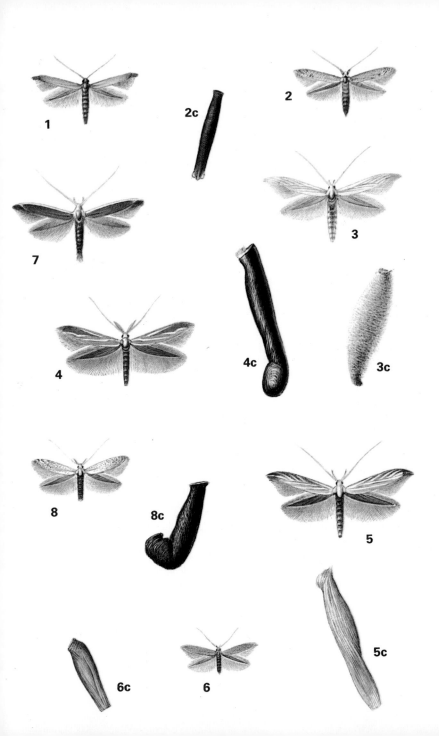

Family: **Yponomeutidae** — **ermine moths**

1 *Yponomeuta vigintipunctata* (Retz.). 16—18mm. Common in steppes, forest-steppes and on stony slopes all over Europe, eastwards as far as the Ussuri basin, always associated with its foodplant. Two generations of the moth emerge in the year, the first in April and May, the second in July and August. The caterpillars live gregariously on several species of the genus *Sedum*, especially *S. telephium* (orpine), covering each plant with a fine grey web (1b). Winter is passed in the pupal stage.

2 *Yponomeuta evonymella* (L.) — Bird-cherry Ermine. 22—24mm. An abundant species, differing from several very similar ones by having five rows of black dots on the white wings. It has a Palaearctic distribution, and ranges from lowlands up to the deciduous tree line in mountains. Moths are on the wing in July and August. The caterpillars live gregariously on bird-cherry in spring, spinning whitish webs on the trees, over which they can move rapidly; they often seriously injure trees by stripping all the leaves.

3 *Yponomeuta cagnatella* (Hb.) — Spindle Ermine. 20—25mm. Abundantly distributed all over Europe, this moth flies in June and July in sparse deciduous forests with shrubby undergrowth, or on shrubby hillsides; common also on wastelands and overgrown patches among fields, along roads, etc. The caterpillars (3b) live gregariously in May and June on spindle-trees, completely stripping all leaves from the shrubs, which become enwrapped in white webbing; they pupate in large numbers at the foot of the trees. This species greatly resembles several others which live on apple, blackthorn, willow, etc., the principal differences being the life cycle and foodplant.

4 *Yponomeuta plumbella* (D & S.). 16—18mm. Differs from the white species in bearing a marked black patch on its forewings. Distributed over Europe and central Asia, this moth flies in July and August. The caterpillar lives in spring on spindle-tree, most often individually, mixing with the preceding species, but sometimes also gregariously.

Family: **Plutellidae**

5 *Prays fraxinella* (Bjerk.) (= *curtisella* Don.) — Ash Bud Moth. 14—18mm. Ranges over Europe and the forest zone of Asia to the Far East. The moths fly from June to September, in two generations. The caterpillar hibernates, but much is uncertain about its bionomics; it feeds on ash and alder. This and other species of the family Plutellidae are often classified among the more extensive family Yponomeutidae.

6 *Eidophasia messingiella* (F. v. R.). 12—14mm. Distributed over northern and central Europe, across Asia Minor to Turkestan, this species favours meadows, chiefly damp ones. Moths are on the wing in June and July. The caterpillar lives among spun-up leaves of bitter cardamine *(Cardamine amara)* and spring cress *(C. impatiens)*.

7 *Plutella xylostella* (L.) (= *maculipennis* Curt.) — Diamond-back Moth. 13—15mm. This well known insect has a cosmopolitan distribution. Originally a steppe species, it has become well adapted to agricultural areas, and been introduced to all parts of the world as a pest of vegetables. Its considerable migratory capacities have also helped to extend its range. Found in nature from May to September, in 2—5 generations. The caterpillar mines leaves when young; later on it lives under a slight web spun of silken fibres on the underside of leaves of cruciferous vegetables, as well as wild plants and weeds. Here it also pupates, and passes the winter in this form (or, exceptionally, as an adult).

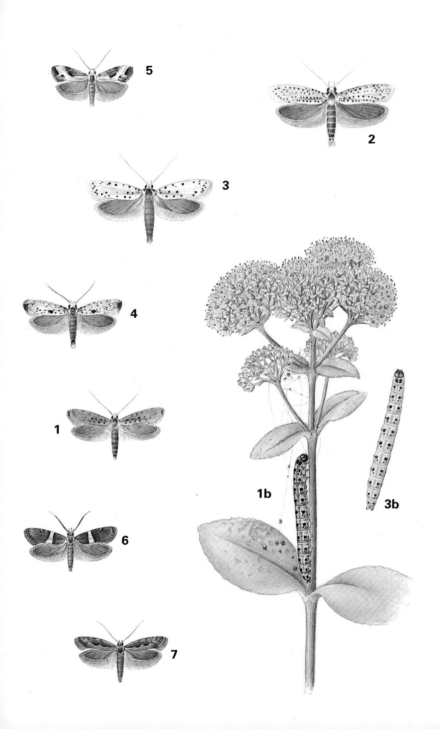

Family: **Plutellidae**

1 *Ypsolopha dentella* (F.) (= *xylostella* auctt.) — Honeysuckle Moth. 18—22mm. Distributed throughout Europe and eastwards to Armenia, inhabiting damp deciduous forests, or even urban parks where honeysuckle can be found, on which the caterpillar depends for food. A single-brooded species, the flight period is June to August. The caterpillar (1b) develops from May to July, depending on climate and elevation above sea-level.

2 *Ypsolopha falcella* (Hb.). 16—18mm. Confined to the zone of deciduous forests in Europe, this insect is much rarer than the preceding species. There is one generation per year, moths being on the wing from June to August. The caterpillars develop in spring, feeding on honeysuckle.

3 *Ypsolopha sequella* (Cl.). 16—20mm. Distributed throughout temperate Europe and Asia Minor in deciduous forests, gardens and parks, this species flies from June to August, but only sporadically. In daytime the moths like to settle on tree trunks, and are visible from afar. The caterpillar lives in spring on sallow and lime, but also thrives on other deciduous trees. A species given to great variation of the wing patterning.

4 *Ypsolopha parenthesella* (L.). 16—20mm. Widespread in deciduous forests all over Europe, extending eastwards to central Asia, this moth is on the wing from June to October, here and there possibly having two generations. The caterpillar develops in spring on hornbeam, oak, beech and hawthorn, favouring low shrubs and the suckers of larger trees. This species manifests an extraordinarily wide range of colour variation.

5 *Ypsolopha sylvella* (L.). 18—20mm. In Europe the distribution of this species is restricted by that of the oak; it is abundant in warmer regions. The single annual generation flies from July to September. Caterpillars develop towards the end of spring in webs fastened to the underside of oak leaves.

6 *Ypsolopha lucella* (F.). 18—20mm. Widespread throughout Europe as far as the Caucasus, the moth is on the wing from June to September. The caterpillar develops towards the end of spring on various oaks, feeding on the leaves, in a slight web.

7 *Ypsolopha alpella* (D. & S.). 16—20mm. The distributional range and bionomics of this moth are much the same as those of the preceding species (7b caterpillar, 7c cocoon).

8 *Ypsolopha persicella* (F.). 18—24mm. A thermophilic species ranging over warmer parts of all Europe, Asia Minor, and eastwards to Transcaucasia, it is single-brooded, having a greatly extended flight period: from June to September. Overwintering in the egg stage, the caterpillars develop during spring in rolled-up young leaves of peach, apricot, and sometimes plum trees.

9 *Ypsolopha asperella* (L.). 18—21mm. Ranges over the whole of temperate Europe, eastwards across Asia Minor as far as southern Siberia. A rather rare species, it favours deciduous forests, shrubby hillsides, forest-steppes and also orchards. It passes the winter in the adult stage, which exists from July to May. The caterpillar is found in spring, feeding on apple and other fruit trees, but also on oak or hawthorn.

10 *Ypsolopha scabrella* (L.). 20—22mm. Reported from various parts of Europe, but nowhere abundant, there is one generation of this moth per year, flying in June and July. The caterpillar develops in spring on apple, pear and plum trees, also on hawthorn. Found in deciduous forests, on shrubby slopes and orchards.

Family: **Argyresthiidae**

1 *Argyresthia pruniella* (Cl.) − Cherry Fruit Moth. 10−12mm. Belongs to a group of extremely similar species in the extensive genus *Argyresthia*. Generally distributed in Europe and Asia Minor, there is one annual generation with a considerably extended flight period, from May to September; the moths are most abundant in early summer. The eggs hibernate, and the caterpillars (1b) emerge in spring to eat their way into sprouting leaf and flower buds (1c). A notorious and serious pest of cherry, plum, apricot and peach trees, it also occurs on rowan, hawthorn and hazel.

2 *Argyresthia goedartella* (L.). 10−11mm. Widespread chiefly in central and northern Europe, this moth haunts mixed and deciduous forests. Annually there is one generation, flying from June to August. The caterpillars start developing in autumn, overwinter, and can be found in spring in catkins and buds, later on under the bark of birches and alders.

3 *Argyresthia ivella* (Hw.) (= *andereggiella* Dup.). 10−12mm. A thermophilic species more common in southern parts of central Europe. The single generation produced in the year flies from June to August. The caterpillars develop in spring, inside buds of apple trees and hazel.

4 *Argyresthia conjugella* (Z.) − Apple Fruit Moth. 10−12mm. Abundantly distributed throughout Europe and Asia, also in North America, this moth is confined to the deciduous forest zone, from lowlands to the upper altitudinal limit of deciduous trees. There is one brood per year, on the wing from May to July. The caterpillars live towards the end of summer until autumn, feeding inside fruits of rowan and apple trees. Pupation takes place on the soil surface in a firm cocoon.

Family: **Glyphipterigidae**

5 *Glyphipterix thrasonella* (Sc.). 10−13mm. Distributed over the whole of Europe and Asia Minor, the moths of the single annual generation are on the wing in June and July. The caterpillars develop from autumn till spring on various rush and sundew species.

6 *Glyphipterix bergstraesserella* (F.). 11−14mm. Ranging over central and northern Europe, mostly confined to mountains, this moth has a single brood with a similar time of occurrence to the previous species. The caterpillar lives from summer till the following spring, feeding on woodrush.

7 *Tebenna bjerkandrella* (Thbg.). 11−15mm. This species has a vast range, including the mountains of northern Africa, most of Europe and the Asiatic region. In central Europe it is found in the Alps, Sudetes and Carpathians, being rare everywhere. A single brood is produced, on the wing in July and August. The caterpillars live gregariously, under fine webbing, on leaves of carline thistle.

8 *Anthophila fabriciana* (L.). 11−16mm. Widely distributed throughout Europe, Asia, and North America, this moth occurs abundantly in damp deciduous forests, river valleys and wasteground. There are two generations, flying from May to September. The caterpillars feed mainly on nettle.

9 *Eutromula pariana* (Cl.) − Apple Leaf Skeletonizer. 11−13mm. Known from all Europe and Asia, the moths appear on the wing in two partial generations during May and at the end of summer. These adults overwinter. The caterpillars (9b) characteristically bite off the surface of leaves of various trees of the Rosaceae family, chiefly apple (9c).

Family: **Sesiidae** — **clearwings**

1 *Sesia apiformis* (Cl.) — Hornet Moth. 30—40mm. Distributed throughout the warmer regions of Europe, central Asia, Siberia, and also North America, this spectacular hornet mimic is usually found in lowlands, in damp waterside habitats. The moth, which is diurnal in habit, flies from May to August. The caterpillar lives for two years, boring in roots of poplars and sallows.

2 *Paranthrene tabaniformis* (Rott.) — Dusky Clearwing. 25—40mm. Distributed over Europe and almost the whole of Asia, this species has also been recorded from the Caucasus, central Asia, Siberia and Mongolia. A day-flying moth, on the wing from May to August, its caterpillar lives for two years in poplar wood.

3 *Pennisetia hylaeiformis* Lasp. 20—25mm. Widespread in Europe, Asia Minor and central Asia, this day-flying moth is on the wing from June to August. Often found sitting on leaves of raspberry canes. The caterpillars (3b) develop from August throughout winter until May, feeding in the roots of raspberry (3c), from which they can be collected easily in spring and reared to the adult stage.

4 *Synanthedon scoliaeformis* (Borkh.) — Welsh Clearwing. 24—32mm. Occurs in central and eastern Europe in deciduous forests where birches are found. The moth flies in June and July; the caterpillar takes two years to develop, feeding in birch trunks close to the ground. Not rare where old trees occur, it rapidly becomes locally extinct if they are felled.

5 *Synanthedon tipuliformis* (Cl.) — Currant Clearwing. 16—18mm. Distributed over Europe, Asia, North America, Australia and New Zealand, having been spread with consignments of currant bushes. The single generation flies, in sunny weather, from June to August. The caterpillar (5b) lives from August over the winter until spring, feeding in the twigs of red currant, black currant or gooseberry (5c), often causing serious damage in plantations.

6 *Synanthedon conopiformis* (Esp.). 16—20mm. Distributed over the warmer regions of Europe and the Near East, it is to be found in oak forests. Moths of the single generation are on the wing on bright days, in May and June. The caterpillars develop for two years in oak branches, mostly in the crowns of old trees.

7 *Synanthedon vespiformis* (L.) — Yellow-legged Clearwing. 18—20mm. A thermophilic species, ranging over the more southern parts of central Europe, regions bordering the Mediterranean, across Asia Minor to the Caucasus. There is one annual brood, which flies in deciduous forests from May to July. The caterpillar lives for two years under the bark of oak and beech trunks and stumps.

8 *Synanthedon myopaeformis* (Brkh.) — Red-belted Clearwing. 16—20mm. Occurs in northern Africa, at lower and warmer elevations of Europe, also in Asia Minor as far as the Caucasus. Moths of the single annual generation are on the wing from May to August; the caterpillars live from August until the following spring under the bark of apple trees, mostly where branches have been broken or cut off. Often a pest of apple orchards, other fruit trees are attacked less frequently.

9 *Chamaesphecia tenthridiniformis* (D. & S.) (= *empiformis* Esp.). 14—18mm. Reported from central and southern Europe, Asia Minor and Armenia, this clearwing is confined to dry steppe and forest-steppe localities where its foodplant, cypress spurge, grows. A day-flying moth on the wing from May to August, the caterpillars pass the winter in spurge roots.

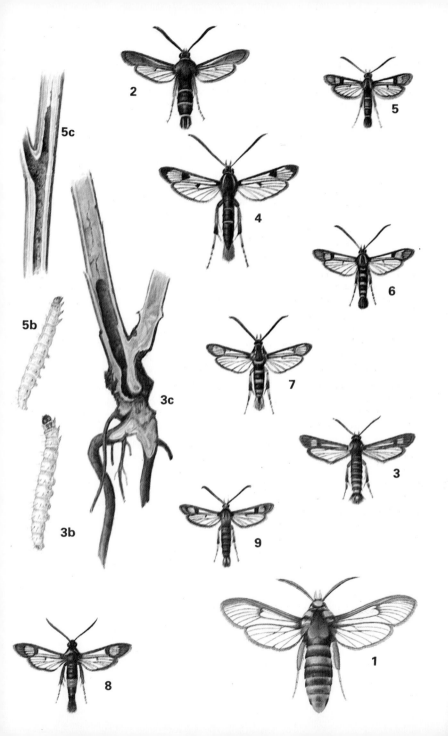

Family: **Lyonetiidae — ribbed case bearers**

1 *Lyonetia clerkella* (L.) — Apple Leaf Miner. 7—9mm. Distributed over the whole of Europe and northern Africa, from lowlands to the upper limit of deciduous forests. There are one to three annual generations, depending on climatic conditions, the moths being found throughout the year — the last generation hibernates from September till April. The caterpillars mine in leaves, marking them with characteristic patterns (1c). Most commonly found on cherry and other trees of the family Rosaceae, including apple.

Family: **Gracillariidae — narrow-winged leaf miners (blotch miners)**

2 *Phyllonorycter sylvella* (Hw.) (= *acerifoliella* Z.). 6—8mm. Occurs in northern and central Europe in deciduous forests. Two broods are produced in the year, the moths flying in May and August. The caterpillar occurs in June and in autumn, hibernating in mines on fallen leaves.

3 *Phyllonorycter roboris* (Z.). 8mm. Very abundant in oak forests of central and southern Europe, this moth has two generations, on the wing in April to May and July. The caterpillar mines the undersurface of leaves; in autumn it encloses itself with silk and then pupates after hibernation.

4 *Phyllonorycter nigrescentella* (Log.). 7—9mm. Found in meadows, steppes, and fields, the moths fly in two generations during May and July. The caterpillars produce inflated blister-like mines in leaves of clover, medick or vetchling.

5 *Phyllonorycter cerasicolella* (H. S.). 7—8mm. Distributed in northern and central Europe, where it inhabits deciduous forests and shrubby hillsides, this moth is also abundant in orchards. Two annual generations occur, flying in May and July. The caterpillars develop at the beginning of summer and again in autumn, overwintering in oblong, blister-like mines on the underside of leaves of cherry and plum trees, or blackthorn bushes.

6 *Phyllonorycter blancardella* (F.). 6—8mm. Occurring in deciduous forests and orchards throughout the Palaearctic, the life-cycle of this moth is similar to that of the preceding species. The caterpillar gnaws mines on the undersurface of apple leaves (6c), in which the winter generation hibernates and pupates in spring.

7 *Phyllonorycter kleemannella* (F.). 8mm. Found in deciduous forests of Europe, this species is abundant wherever alders grow. There is thought to be one generation, on the wing during May. The caterpillars hibernate in blister-mines and pupate therein in spring.

8 *Parornix devoniella* (Stt.) (= *avellanella* Stt.). 9mm. An inhabitant of woodlands and forest-steppes of Europe, its distribution elsewhere is unknown. The generations occur from April to August. The caterpillars live and overwinter in mines formed from the folded margins of hazel leaves.

9 *Callisto denticulella* (Thbg.). 10—12mm. Distributed all over Europe and eastwards to central Asia, this species occurs in woods, forest-steppes and apple orchards. The moths fly in two generations, from May to August. The caterpillars live in mines formed by folding the edge of apple leaves (9c); here they also pupate.

10 *Caloptilia syringella* (F.) — Lilac Leaf Miner. 12—14mm. Occurs throughout Europe in deciduous forests with shrubby undergrowth, also in urban parks. Two annual generations of this moth develop, flying from April to August. The larvae are gregarious, living in large blister-mines (10c), or in rolled-up leaves of lilac, ash, privet or spindle-tree. Pupation takes place in the ground.

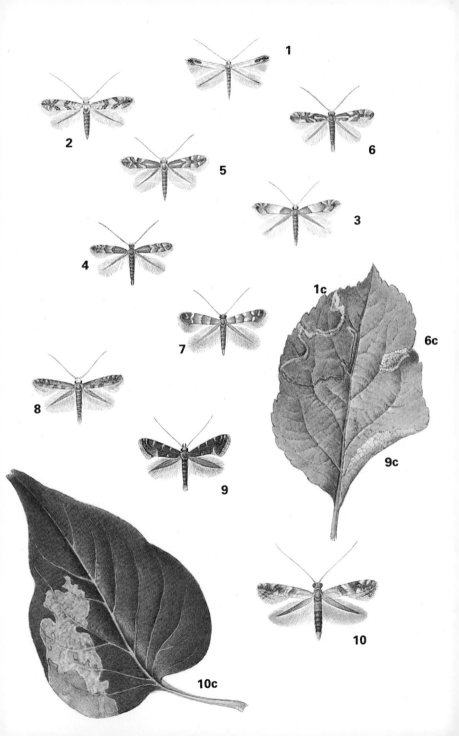

Family: **Tineidae — tineid moths (clothes and scavenger moths)**

1 *Nemapogon granella* (L.) — Corn Moth. 8—12mm. The cosmopolitan distribution of this species is due to its introduction to all parts of the world with corn. In nature there are two generations of this nocturnal moth, the first flying in April and May, the second in July and August. The caterpillars (1b) can be found practically all year round, feeding on plant remains, seeds, dry fruits and fungi (1c), often causing considerable economic damage.

2 *Nemapogon clematella* (F.) (= *arcella* auctt.). 10—15mm. Distributed in Europe, eastwards as far as the Caucasus, this moth is on the wing in a single generation during June and August. The caterpillar lives from spring onwards, feeding on fungi growing under bark and on twigs of elm or oak, also on polyporus.

3 *Trichophaga tapetzella* (L.) — Tapestry Moth. 12—22mm. This species has a cosmopolitan distribution, as is the case with many storehouse pests. The moth flies from May to August; the caterpillars live from autumn till spring, feeding on detritus in birds' nests and the lairs of mammals. Occasionally it appears in great numbers, the larvae feeding in old woollen fabrics and clothes in storehouses or lofts. Of late this species has somewhat decreased in numbers.

4 *Tineola bisselliella* (Hum.) — Common Clothes Moth. 10—16mm. An inconspicuous, yellow-ish moth whose caterpillars are notorious for damaging woollen clothes and fabrics (4b, 4c). Introduced to all parts of the world, the moths fly outdoors from May to September, in households all the year round. In nature they eat animal remains in birds' nests and in lairs and dens of mammals.

5 *Tinea semifulvella* (Hw.). 12—20mm. Widespread in northern, central and eastern Europe, the single generation of this moth is on the wing from May to August. The caterpillar passes the winter in nature in similar places to the preceding two species.

6 *Tinea trinotella* (Thbg.). 12—18mm. Reported from Europe only, the two generations fly from May to August. The caterpillar lives from autumn till spring in the nests of birds, where it feeds on food remains. A night-flier, its favourite haunts are deciduous forests.

7 *Monopis monachella* (Hb.). 12—16mm. Distributed over Europe, Africa, the Near East, southeastern Asia and the Hawaiian Islands. Moths of this species are on the wing from June to August; the caterpillars develop from autumn till spring. Similar to preceding species in way of life.

8 *Morophaga choragella* (D. & S.) (= *boleti* F.). 18—30mm. Widespread in Europe, Asia Minor, central and eastern Asia, the single annual generation of this fairly abundant moth flies from June to August, in old, usually deciduous forests. The caterpillars live from autumn until spring, feeding on various species of tree polypores and decaying wood.

9 Euplocamus anthracinalis (Sc.). 26—32mm. This species has a scattered distribution in the deciduous-forest belt of warmer Europe (especially in the southeast), extending eastwards to the Caucasus. The flight period of the single generation is from May to August. Found in sparse but damp deciduous forests, this day-flier is on the wing on sunny days. The caterpillar lives from autumn till spring in polypores attached to decaying oak, beech, hornbeam, and other trees.

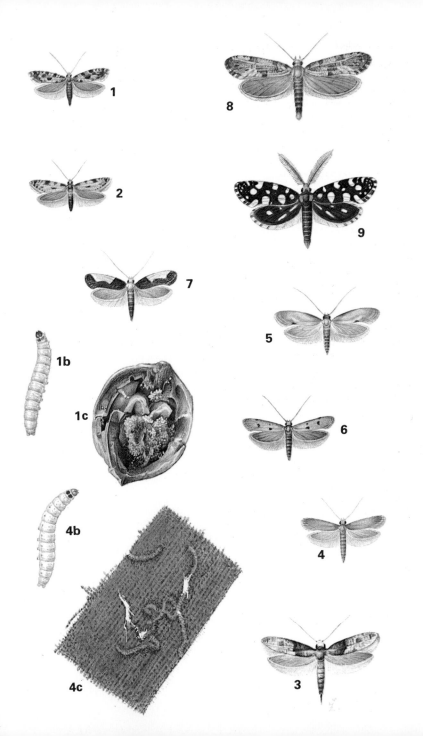

Family: **Psychidae — bagworms**

1 *Taleporia tubulosa* (Retz.). 16—18mm. Distributed over warmer parts of Europe and Asia Minor, this species is confined to deciduous and mixed forests. Males fly in May and June; the females are apterous. The caterpillar lives in a tubular case with three terminal valves (1c) and feeds on lichen attached to tree trunks.

2 *Solenobia triquetrella* (Hb.). 14—15mm. Distributed all over temperate Europe, the male of this species flies in April and May. The apterous female often reproduces parthenogenetically (without fertilization). Caterpillars can be found from summer until spring in a short triangular bag (2c), feeding on moss and plant remains.

3 *Psyche casta* (Pall.). 12—15mm. Distributed throughout Europe, eastwards as far as the Caucasus, the males of the single generation fly in May and June; the females are wingless. The polyphagous caterpillar lives in a case made of pieces of fine grass (3c).

4 *Epichnopterix plumella* (D. & S.) (= *pulla* Esp.). 10—12mm. Widespread throughout Europe, in Asia it ranges east to the Amur. A single-brooded species on the wing from April to July, depending on elevation above sea level. These small, black, diurnal moths can be found in grassy biotopes in lowlands and mountains. The caterpillar lives, in a case made of bits of fine grasses (4c), from summer till spring, in harsher climates taking as long as two years to develop. Polyphagous, it is mostly a grass feeder.

5 *Rebelia plumella* (O.). 12—16mm. A species confined to restricted, warmer localities of central Europe. The adult moths occur in May, the males flying in the evenings; the females are wingless. Caterpillars can be found from summer until spring in a simple bag (5c), feeding on grass or moss.

6 *Apterona helix* (Sieb.) (= *crenulella* Br.). 12—14mm. With a range extending over central and southern Europe eastwards to Turkestan, this species prefers warm localities. Males occur in more southern regions only; elsewhere only wingless females can be found — these never leave their bags, reproducing parthenogenetically. The adult moths live in June and July, at other times only the polyphagous caterpillars can be found, in their coiled cases resembling snailshells (6c).

7 *Megalophanes viciella* (D. & S.). 20—23mm. Ranges over much of Europe, eastwards to the Urals. A species of damp meadows and woodland clearings, the adults occur in lowlands from June to August. Females are apterous and often multiply parthenogenetically. The caterpillar, which has a barrel-shaped bag constructed of fine, transverse pieces of stalk (7c), occurs from summer until spring and is polyphagous.

8 *Leptopterix hirsutella* (D. & S.). 18—20mm. Widely distributed in Europe and Asia, this moth is confined to the zone of deciduous forests. Adults occur in June and July; the females are apterous. The caterpillar lives for two years inside its cylindrical case covered with particles of leaves and bark (8c), feeding on various deciduous trees and shrubs.

9 *Pachythelia villosella* (O.). 22—25mm. Found on heather moors of central and southern Europe, the males of this species are on the wing in early evenings during June and July; the females are wingless. The polyphagous caterpillar lives for one or two years, in a case made of quite large leaf particles (9c).

10 *Canephora unicolor* (Hfn.). 25—30mm. The largest European bagmoth, distributed in temperate Europe, the adults live from June to August; females are apterous. The polyphagous caterpillars inhabit large cases which differ in the male (10c) and the female (10d) in the material used; the cases terminate in a simple tube.

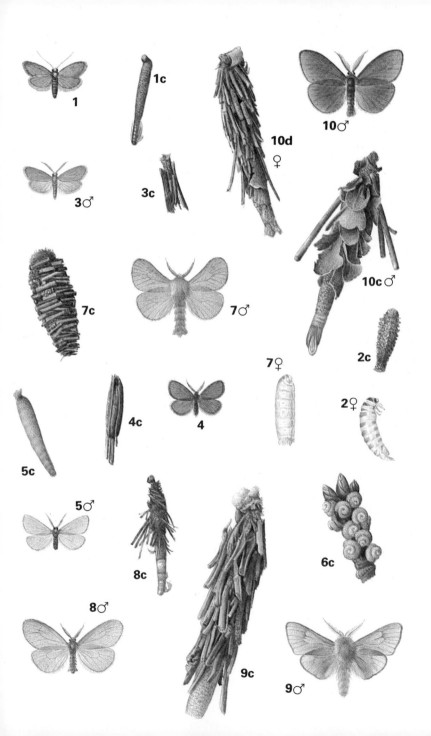

Family: **Cochylidae**

1 *Aethes hartmanniana* (Cl.). 14—25mm. Widespread in Europe and Asia Minor, there are two annual generations of this night-flying moth on the wing from May to August. The caterpillar, which lives from June and again from autumn until spring on scabious *(Scabiosa ochroleuca)*, occurs abundantly in woodland meadows and wooded hillsides rich in grassy clearings.

2 *Aethes tesserana* (D. & S.). 12—16mm. With a range similar to that of the preceding species, this moth is found locally in forest-steppes, meadows and slopes. It flies in two generations, from May to August; the caterpillars live in June and July, those of the second generation overwintering in rhizomes of hawkweed, hawk's beard and *Inula*.

3 *Eupoecilia angustana* (Hb.). 12—15mm. Occurring in central Europe and Asia Minor, the moths are on the wing from June to August; the caterpillars live in autumn, eating flowers and seed-pods of yarrow, thyme, plantain, goldenrod, and other plants.

4 *Eupoecilia ambiguella* (Hb.) — Vine Moth. 14—16mm. A thermophilic species distributed throughout the Palaearctic, most common in vineyards. Two generations of this moth fly annually: first in May and again in July and August. The caterpillars of the first generation develop on unfolding buds and flowers of grapevine (4b). The second brood live in August and September in webs spun among unripe grapes and leaves (4c) — but they will also feed on many other shrubs and plants.

5 *Cochylis posterana* Z. 12—15mm. An inhabitant of central and southern Europe, the moth occurs in two generations from May to August, haunting dry, grassy biotopes, hillsides and wasteground. The caterpillar can be found in midsummer, or from autumn to March in flowers and pericarps of cornflower, burdock and thistles.

6 *Agapeta zoegana* (L.). 14—22mm. Distributed over Europe and Asia Minor in warm, grassy biotopes, such as steppes, stony slopes, and wastelands, this moth is on the wing from June to August. The caterpillar passes the winter in the roots of scabiouses and cornflowers.

7 *Agapeta hamana* (L.). 16—22mm. Resembles the foregoing species in basic colouring but the pattern is less conspicuous. Occurs in Europe and Asia Minor, in damp meadow habitats and mountains. This single-brooded moth flies from June to August; the caterpillar develops in spring in rolled-up leaves of ice plant, thistle or clover.

8 *Stenodes straminea* (Hw.). 14—18mm. Lives mainly in central and southern Europe, inhabiting dry, even parched biotopes. Annually there are two generations, flying from May to August. One generation of caterpillars develops in summer, the other hibernates. The larvae feed either on motherwort leaves or in the inflorescences and ripening seeds of scabious and cornflower.

9 *Aethes margaritana* (Hw.). 10—16mm. A relatively abundant species, common in central and southern Europe in meadows and other grassy biotopes situated in lowlands and foothills. Moths are on the wing from June to August. The caterpillars hibernate and probably also occur in summer, but the number of generations is unknown; they have a liking for the leaves and flowers of oxeye daisy and yarrow.

1

2

3

5

4

6

7

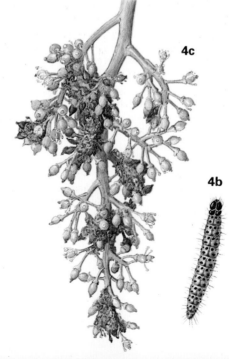

4c

8

4b

9

Family: **Tortricidae — leaf rollers (tortrix moths)**

1 *Pandemis corylana* (F.) — Chequered Fruit-tree Tortrix. 16—25mm. Distributed over Europe and eastwards to central Asia, the moth is on the wing from July to September. It overwinters in the egg stage; the caterpillars develop in spring among spun-up young leaves of various trees.

2 *Pandemis cerasana* (Hb.) — Barred Fruit-tree Tortrix. 16—25mm. This moths ranges across the zone of deciduous forests and forest-steppes of the whole Palaearctic (except northernmost regions) and extends to the Far East. The adults fly from June to September; the caterpillars develop in spring on webbed leaves of various trees, where they also pupate.

3 *Pandemis heparana* (D. & S.) — Dark Fruit-tree Tortrix. 16—25mm. Distributed throughout warmer parts of Europe and Asia as far as China and Japan, this very variable species occurs chiefly in lowlands but can also be found high up in mountains. Moths are on the wing from June to August, probably in two overlapping generations. The caterpillars develop in spring in a similar fashion to the previous species.

4 *Choristoneura sorbiana* (Hb.). 22—35mm. One of the larger species of the family, it is abundant in deciduous forests of Europe, and although not reported from regions east of the Urals, it is also widespread in Asia Minor, and perhaps Japan. The single annual generation of moths flies from June to August; the caterpillars (4b) develop in webs on oak and on fruit trees.

5 *Archips crataegana* (Hb.) — Brown Oak Tortrix. 20—26mm. Ranges all over Europe; locally distributed in Asia as far as Japan. This common inhabitant of forest-steppes, shrubby hillsides and orchards flies from June to August. The caterpillar develops in spring on a variety of shrubs.

6 *Archips oporana* (L.) (= *piceana* L.). 18—25mm. Common in warm coniferous forests all over Europe and Asia, as far as Japan, this moth flies in June and July; it shows marked sexual dimorphism, the male being smaller, and differently coloured to the female. The caterpillar lives from autumn to spring on various coniferous trees.

7 *Archips podana* (Sc.) — Large Fruit-tree Tortrix. 18—26mm. Distributed in Europe and Asia Minor, this moth is found in deciduous forests and orchards. On the wing from June to August, its sexual dimorphism is still more conspicuous than in the preceding species. The caterpillars develop in spring, on deciduous trees.

8 *Parasyndemis histrionana* (Frol.). 16—20mm. Reported only from Europe, living in areas of spruce and fir forests situated at higher elevations, this moth is on the wing from June to August. The caterpillar, which overwinters, feeds on the needles of spruces and firs.

9 *Ptycholomoides aeriferanus* (H.S.). 16—20mm. Distributed in scattered localities throughout temperate Europe and Asia, with records from the Urals, Baikal region, and Japan. Moths are on the wing in July and August; the caterpillars develop in spring on larch, probably also on maple and alder.

10 *Aphelia paleana* (Hb.) — Timothy Tortrix. 18—22mm. Distributed all over Europe, this species flies in June and July in damp meadows situated in lowlands, and also at high altitudes in mountains. The caterpillar develops in spring among spun-up leaves and young shoots of various moisture-loving plants.

Family: **Tortricidae — leaf rollers (tortrix moths)**

1 *Clepsis spectrana* (Tr.) — Cyclamen Tortrix. 16—22mm. Ranges over central and eastern Europe and Asia Minor as far as Transcaucasia, this moisture-loving species flies from June to August. The caterpillar develops in spring on a variety of juicy plants, including *Euphorbia palustris, Epilobium, Rorippa,* and *Rumex.*

2 *Adoxophyes orana* (F. v. R.) — Summer Fruit Tortrix. 14—22mm. Widespread throughout warmer Europe and Asia, extending to the Far East, this moth flies from June to September, the number of generations involved being uncertain. The caterpillar is also found throughout the summer: it spins together leaves of various trees and shrubs, or eats the young fruit of apricot, peach and other commercial trees. An extremely abundant species, it is of economic significance in fruit growing.

3 *Ptycholoma lecheana* (L.). 16—20mm. Its range extends throughout the deciduous-forest belt of all Europe and Asia Minor, extending to central Asia as far as Lake Baikal and southern Siberia. The moth is on the wing in May and June, frequenting damp deciduous forests, parks and orchards. Caterpillars develop in spring among leaves of trees and shrubs, which they join together with silken webbing.

4 *Paramesia gnomana* (Cl.). 12—18mm. Ranges over Europe and Asia Minor eastwards to southern Urals. The single generation produced per year is on the wing from June to August; the caterpillar lives in spring, eating leaves of bilberry, woundwort, plantain, etc.

5 *Periclepsis cinctana* (D. & S.). 12—16mm. Reported from drier and warmer localities of Europe, this moth flies in June and July. The caterpillar is believed to develop from summer until spring, feeding on greenweed *(Genista)*, broom, *Anthyllis,* etc.

6 *Isotrias hybridana* (Hb.). 12—16mm. Occurs in the warmer parts of central Europe, southern Europe and Asia Minor. This species produces two generations a year, flying in May to June and August to September. Warm deciduous forests, shrubby slopes and forest-steppes are among its favourite haunts. The caterpillars develop in summer and again from autumn till spring, feeding on hawthorn, maple or oak.

7 *Eulia ministrana* (L.). 18—25mm. Distributed in the more northern latitudes of Europe, the forest zone of Asia extending to the Far East, and in North America. Moths of this single-brooded species fly in June and July, mostly in mountain forests. The caterpillar lives from autumn until spring on oak, birch, alder, hazel, mountain ash, etc.

8 *Cnephasia interjectana* (Hw.) (= *virgaureana* Tr.) — Flax Tortrix. 10—15mm. Distributed throughout Europe and Asia as far as Japan (perhaps also in North America). A species native to forest-steppes, feeding on low-growing herbs when in woods, it has adapted well to agricultural areas. Moths are on the wing in June and July. In spring the caterpillars (8b) spin together (8c) and eat away the leaves and shoots of various plants.

9 *Exapate congelatella* (Cl.). 18—22mm. Locally distributed in central and northern Europe, it is found eastwards as far as the Caucasus. An abundant moth in restricted localities, particularly in mountains, the single annual generation emerges in October and November — however, only the males fly, the females having degenerate wings. The caterpillars (9b) live in spring on the shoots of various shrubs, including common privet, elm, hawthorn, currant and willow, spinning the leaves together (9c). The pupa is formed in the ground.

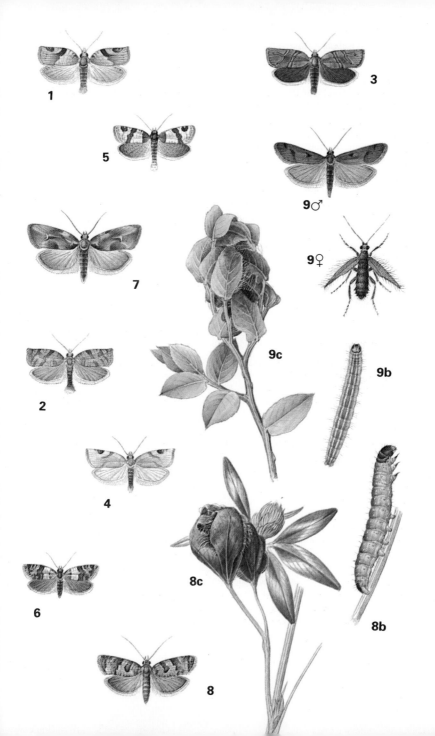

Family: **Tortricidae — leaf rollers (tortrix moths)**

1 *Tortrix viridana* (L.) — Green Oak Tortrix. 18—23mm. Distributed in oak forests in northern Africa, all over Europe and in Asia Minor, extending eastwards to the Caucasus. The moths fly in June and July, while the caterpillars (1b) develop in spring on young oak leaves (1c), frequently causing complete defoliation. They form black pupae, which can be found in rolled-up leaves.

2 *Croesia bergmanniana* (L.). 10—14mm. This species has a Holarctic distribution. The moths are on the wing in June and July; the caterpillars can be found in May among spun-up leaves and young shoots of roses.

3 *Croesia forskaleana* (L.). 12—18mm. Widespread in more temperate latitudes of Europe as far as the Caucasus, the single generation produced by this moth flies from June to August. The caterpillars grow during spring, feeding in rolled-up maple leaves.

4 *Acleris variegana* (D. & S.) — Garden Rose Tortrix. 14—18mm. Ranges from northern Africa across Europe and Asia Minor to central Asia. On the wing in autumn, from August to November, the caterpillars of this species live in spring and at the beginning of summer, feeding on bilberry, hazel, and various trees and shrubs of the family Rosaceae. This moth exhibits an extraordinarily wide range of colour variation.

5 *Acleris emargana* (F.). 18—22mm. Many individuals of this species have wings with a concave costal margin, but this feature is variable and may even be absent. A moth distributed in the deciduous and mixed forests of Europe and Asia, it also inhabits North America. First taking wing in July, it flies until hibernation, and then again in spring. The caterpillar lives in spring on willow, poplar or birch.

6 *Dichrorampha petiverella* (L.). 10—14mm. An abundant species distributed over Europe (except the north) and ranging east to the Amur basin. On the wing from June to August. The caterpillar develops from autumn until spring in roots of yarrow and oxeye daisy.

7 *Cydia splendana* (Hb.). 12—16mm. The occurrence of this species, inhabiting Europe and extending eastwards to the southern Urals and Volga basin, is associated with the distribution of oak forests. Moths occur in a single generation flying from June to August; the caterpillars, which hibernate, develop inside acorns, walnuts and sweet chestnuts.

8 *Cydia nigricana* (F.) — Pea Moth. 10—15mm. Distributed throughout the Palaearctic subregion and also in North America, everywhere except the cold north. The single generation flies from June to August. The caterpillars (8b) develop towards the end of summer on pea, vetch and vetchling pods (8c).

9 *Cydia pomonella* (L.) — Codling Moth. 14—18mm. A native of the western Palaearctic, from where it has been introduced to all apple-growing areas of the world. The moths fly in one or two broods, from May to August; caterpillars (9b) develop within ripening apples (9c), eventually forming their cocoons on tree trunks below the bark or in crevices, and pupate in spring. The prolonged flight period is caused by apples being taken into stores and households where they pass the winter under differing temperature conditions, the larvae inside developing at an unequal rate.

10 *Lathronympha strigana* (F.). 14—18mm. Widespread in Europe, Asia Minor and Siberia, this basically single-brooded moth flies from May to August. A partial second generation is assumed to occur. Caterpillars live from May to July, feeding on *Hypericum*.

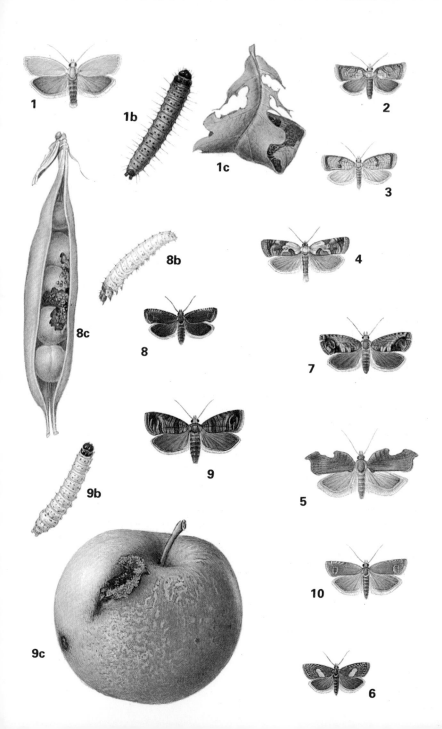

Family: **Tortricidae — leaf rollers (tortrix moths)**

1 *Enarmonia formosana* (Sc.) — Cherry-bark Moth. 14—16mm. Distributed over northern Africa, warmer parts of Europe, Asia Minor, and in Asia as far as Siberia. This moth is on the wing from May to August. The caterpillars, which are orchard pests, live from summer until next spring, boring into the bark of fruit trees — usually cherry, apricot or plum.

2 *Rhyacionia buoliana* (D. & S.) — Pine-shoot Moth. 16—20mm. Widespread throughout Europe and Asia in areas where pine grows, it also occurs in North America and has been recently introduced into South America. The moth is on the wing from June to August; the caterpillar (2b) lives in buds and shoots of pine trees, especially young ones (2d).

3 *Petrova resinella* (L.) — Pine Resin-gall Moth. 16—21mm. Distributed over the whole of Europe and in Siberia, this moth flies in May and June. The caterpillars develop, overwintering twice, in resinous galls on pine branches. The species is abundant in peat-bog areas.

4 *Spilonota ocellana* (D. & S.) — Bud Moth. 16—18mm. Abundantly distributed over the entire Palaearctic, and introduced to North America. Moths are on the wing from May to July; the caterpillars hibernate and develop during the spring inside the sprouting buds and young shoots of deciduous trees, often causing serious damage in orchards.

5 *Epiblema foenella* (L.). 18—23mm. Distributed in the temperate zone of Europe, and eastwards to Armenia. The moth flies in June and July in steppes and fields; the caterpillar lives from autumn till spring, feeding on wormwood. These moths are very variable in pattern.

6 *Epiblema uddmanniana* (L.) — Bramble Shoot Moth. 13—20mm. Ranges over temperate and southern Europe to Asia Minor. An inhabitant of forest-steppes, woodland margins and wastelands, this moth is on the wing from June to August, producing one or two generations per year. The caterpillars live in spring and in summer on the apical leaves of various species of blackberry, spinning the leaves together to make a tent.

7 *Epinotia stroemiana* (F.) (= *similana* Hb.). 16—20mm. Distributed over northern and central Europe, western Siberia and North America, this moth is on the wing from July to September. The caterpillar lives towards the end of spring among spun-up leaves of birch, alder and hazel.

8 *Epinotia solandriana* (L.). 18—20mm. Ranges over Europe and eastwards across the Urals and Caucasus to the Baikal. The moths fly from June to September, while the caterpillars live at the end of spring and beginning of summer, feeding on birch, hazel and sallow.

9 *Epinotia tedella* (Cl.). 10—12mm. Distributed in Europe and Asia in the spruce-forest zone, this moth flies from May to July both in plantations and natural spruce forests, up to high mountain altitudes. The caterpillars live on spruce, occasionally becoming pests.

10 *Ancylis mitterbacheriana* (D. & S.). 12—14mm. Abundantly distributed in Europe and Asia, this species is associated with oak forests. Moths fly in two generations, from May to August; the caterpillars develop in July and again from September to April, on oak or beech.

11 *Ancylis badiana* (D. & S.). 12—16mm. Widespread throughout Europe and Asia Minor as far as the Caucasus, this moth occurs in two generations, flying from April to July. The caterpillars develop in June and again in August, feeding on vetchling, vetch or clover, spinning the leaves together. Found abundantly in grassy biotopes situated either in lowlands or mountains.

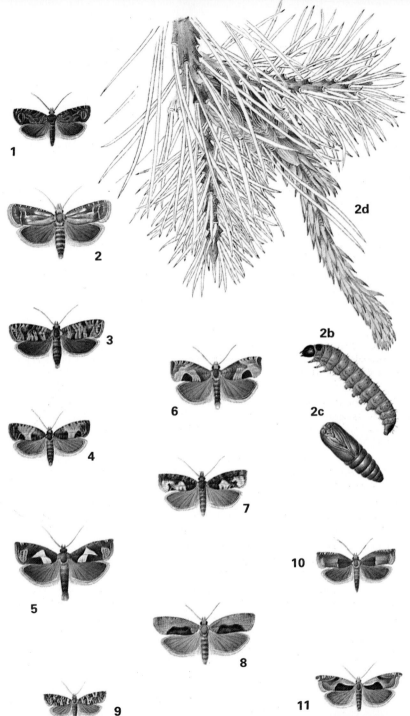

Family: **Tortricidae — leaf rollers (tortrix moths)**

1 *Hedya salicella* (L.). 18—22mm. Ranges over Europe (except the cold north) extending through Asia as far as Siberia. Moths fly in two generations, from May to August in lowlands and mountains, favouring damp localities and shrubby biotopes along rivers and streams. The caterpillar lives in spun-up leaves of willows and poplars.

2 *Hedya nubiferana* (Hw.) — Marbled Orchard Tortrix. 18—20mm. Ranging over Europe and Asia Minor to Armenia, this is a common insect of forest-steppes and shrubby slopes, and also occurs in orchards, where it causes considerable damage. The moth is on the wing from June to August, and when sitting on a leaf, looks remarkably like a bird's dropping. The caterpillar develops in spring, damaging buds and young shoots of deciduous trees.

3 *Apotomis betuletana* (Hw.). 16—20mm. Occurs abundantly in northern and central Europe, and Siberia. The moth flies in deciduous forests from June to August; the caterpillar lives in spring among spun-up birch leaves.

4 *Apotomis inundana* (D. & S.). 18—22mm. A relatively scarce species, inhabiting wooded and forest-steppe areas throughout most of Europe. Moths are on the wing in June and July in both lowlands and mountains; the caterpillars develop in spring in rolled-up alder leaves.

5 *Olethreutes arcuella* (Cl.). 16—18mm. Distributed throughout the Palaearctic in warm deciduous forests, this moth is abundant chiefly in oak woods. Annually a single generation is produced, which occurs from May to July, flying in the afternoon and evening. The caterpillars live from summer until spring, feeding on fallen leaves.

6 *Olethreutes siderana* (Tr.). 16—18mm. Distributed in temperate and more northern latitudes of Europe, and in southeastern Siberia, this moth shows a preference for peat-bogs and damp habitats by rivers, both in lowlands and in submontane regions. Moths fly in June and July; the caterpillar lives in spring in folded leaves of *Spiraea salicifolia*, *Aruncus* or *Filipendula ulmaria*.

7 *Olethreutes mygindiana* (D. & S.). 15—20mm. Widespread all over northern Europe, elsewhere in Europe confined to mountains and peat-bogs. The moths fly in June and July; the caterpillars live in spring, developing in spun-up leaves of various *Vaccinium* species.

8 *Olethreutes lacunana* (D. & S.). 16—18mm. Ranging throughout Europe and Asia Minor, and flying in two generations from May to September, this moth is abundant in damp, shrubby and grassy biotopes. The caterpillars live from April to July among spun-up leaves of birch, willow, raspberry, thistles, marsh-marigolds, and other plants.

9 *Olethreutes bipunctana* (F.). 16—20mm. Distributed over central and northern Europe and extends eastwards as far as Siberia. Found in great numbers in woods with an undergrowth of bilberry, mostly in mountains. Moth on the wing from May to July, caterpillar lives in spring on bilberry, *Pirola*, and perhaps even on *Rhododendron*.

10 *Olethreutes rivulana* (Sc.). 16—18mm. Extremely abundant in Europe and the whole of Asia, this moth flies from May to September in meadows, producing two or three generations. The caterpillars live throughout summer, feeding on a variety of herbs and sometimes on shrubs.

11 *Celypha striana* (D. & S.). 16—20mm. Abundant in central and southern Europe, this species has two generations, flying from May to September in grassy biotopes. The caterpillars develop in July and again in spring, feeding on dandelion roots; pupation takes place in the ground.

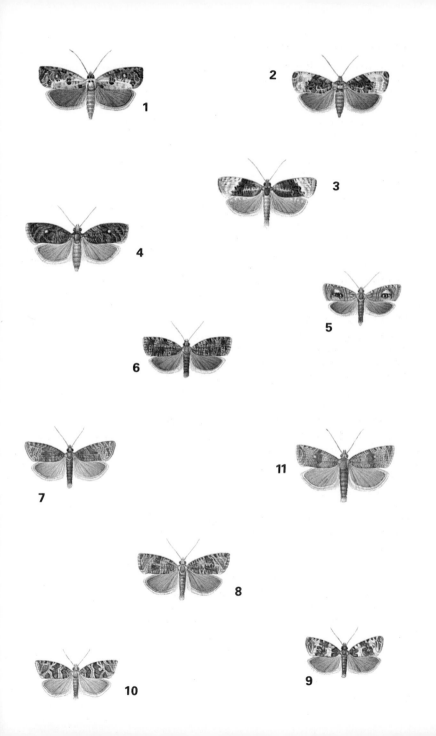

Family: **Cossidae** — **goat moths (wood borers, carpenters)**

1 *Cossus cossus* (L.) — Goat. 65—80mm. An inhabitant of all Europe except the northern regions, also temperate Asia and northern Africa, this large moth is found in deciduous forests ranging to high altitudes in mountains and in waterside habitats overgrown with trees. The adults fly at night in June and July. The caterpillars (1b) live for two years (hibernating twice), boring the trunks of various deciduous trees. Damage is caused mostly to willows and poplars but also to mountain ash, fruit and other trees. An infestation is recognizable at a distance by the smell of wood-vinegar; sawdust is also visible, ejected from the gnawed-out galleries. Before pupation, a caterpillar will burrow a large chamber in the wood, where it spins a soft cocoon of fibres and sawdust, in which it pupates (1c). Caterpillars can often be seen in spring, on their way to new trees or preparing to pupate.

2 *Parahypopta caestrum* (Hb.). 30—35mm. Distributed over warmer regions of Europe and in the Near East, central Europe is the northern limit of this moth's range. One generation is produced annually, the adults flying in June and July. The caterpillars eat the roots of *Asparagus* until autumn, and again after hibernation, until they pupate in May. This species occasionally becomes a serious pest to asparagus cultivators in France, Italy and the Balkans.

3 *Dyspessa ulula* (Bkh.). 18—25mm. Ranges from northern Africa across warm parts of central and southern Europe to Asia Minor, Armenia and Turkestan. One generation is produced per year, the moths flying in the evening hours of May and June. The caterpillars live in the soil, eating the bulbs of certain garlics from summer until the following spring. Most abundant in steppe localities, the moths vary greatly not only in pattern but also in size, depending on the size of the bulb in which they developed.

4 *Phragmataecia castaneae* (Hb.) — Reed Leopard. 27—50mm. Occurs locally in warmer parts of Europe and Asia, extending east as far as China and Japan. The life cycle of this species requires its association with stagnant or slow-flowing waters. There is only one generation per year, but it has a very long flight period, from May to September. The female differs from the male by being much larger and possessing a remarkably long abdomen, and in the shape of the antennae, but the wing colouration is the same in both sexes. These night-flying moths are often attracted to light, even far away from their habitat. The caterpillars live on reed *(Phragmites communis)* and hibernate twice. They pupate within reed stalks, after having prepared an opening for their eventual escape; this exit place is covered by a thin membrane.

5 *Zeuzera pyrina* (L.) — Leopard. 35—60mm. Distributed throughout Europe and Asia, it also occurs in North America where it was introduced during the last century. Most abundant in warm regions, the moths are nocturnal in habit, and on the wing from July to September. In daytime they lie at rest, often quite conspicuously, yet they do not take flight even when disturbed. The caterpillars (5b), which take two years to develop, have been discovered in about 150 kinds of wood. They are most often found on apple and other fruit trees, since here they attract attention as pests of orchards and gardens. This species is very variable in size, depending on the quality of food available to the larvae.

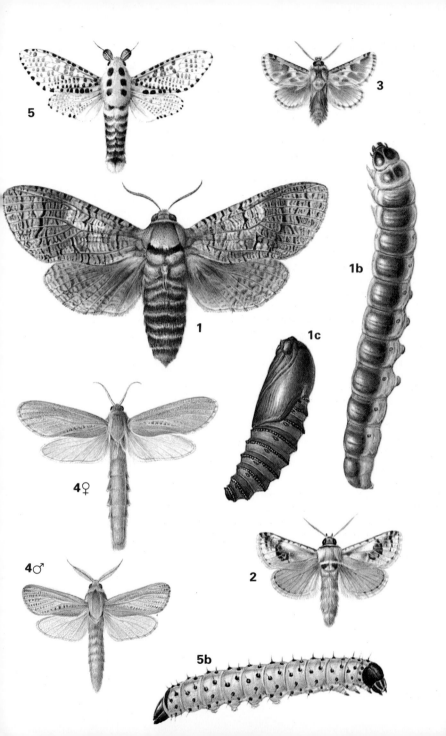

Family: **Adelidae — longhorns (fairy moths)**

1 *Nemophora degeerella* (L.). 16—21mm. Distributed over the whole of temperate Europe as far as the Caucasus, in areas of deciduous and mixed forests, it is found in damp localities, mostly at lower elevations and by water currents. The moths fly on sunny days in May and June, whirling in forest clearings and among trees in a similar fashion to some mayflies. Notable for its exceedingly long antennae (as is the case in many species of this family), their length exceeding that of the forewings about five times in males, about twice in females. The caterpillar lives from autumn till spring, on pasque flower *(Anemone nemorosa)*, mining the leaves at first — later it lives in a case.

2 *Adela reaumurella* (L.). 14—17mm. Inhabits all Europe and Asia Minor within the zone of deciduous, primarily oak, forests. There is one generation a year, the moths being on the wing early in spring — on bright days in April and May, whirling in swarms about sprouting twigs of oaks, maples, etc. The caterpillar lives from summer until early spring in a small case, feeding on the ground on dry, fallen leaves of oak, beech, hazel, etc.

3 *Adela fibulella* (D. & S.). 7—8mm. The smallest species of this family, it is widespread in temperate Europe, in parts of southern Europe, and in the north of Asia Minor. To be found in flowery and grassy biotopes, meadows, outskirts of woods and clearings within them, this moth is inconspicuous in nature. It flies by day among grasses and herbs, from May to July. The caterpillar develops from summer until spring, living in a small case, feeding on speedwell *(Veronica chamaedrys)*; later it remains on the ground consuming the remnants of its foodplant.

4 *Nemophora ochsenheimerella* (Hb.). 14—17mm. Found in fir forests at submontane elevations in Europe, this moth is on the wing in May and June. The caterpillars live from summer until spring, on fir trees.

5 *Adela croesella* (Sc.). 11—13mm. A fairly rare species, distributed over Europe, Asia Minor and Siberia. The moths fly in May and July, favouring deciduous forests with a lush, shrubby undergrowth. The caterpillar, found in summer until the following spring, at first mines privet leaves; later it lives in a small case, and feeds on the ground.

6 *Nemophora metallica* (Poda). 17—20mm. An inhabitant of damp, grassy biotopes throughout the temperate zone of Europe, this abundant day-flying moth often occurs in meadows, where it likes to settle on the flowers of scabious; it can be found from June to August. The caterpillar lives from summer until spring on devil's-bit scabious, field scabious or cornflower; later it moves to the ground.

7 *Nematopogon robertella* (Cl.) (= *pilulella* Hb.). 12—15mm. Distributed throughout Europe, it occurs wherever its foodplant grows — predominantly in mountains, up to the timberline. Moths of the single generation, both diurnal and crepuscular in habit, fly in June and July. The caterpillars develop on bilberry *(Vaccinium myrtillus)*, later living in a small case.

8 *Nematopogon swammerdamella* (L.). 19—21mm. The largest of several very similar species, it is found in deciduous forests over all Europe, east as far as the Caucasus. Moths are on the wing in spring, during April and May, and show a preference for open woodland. The caterpillar lives from summer through to spring, feeding on oak or beech. At first they mine the leaves, then each constructs a small, flat case from leaf particles, wherein to live on the ground.

Family: **Incurvariidae**

1 *Lampronia praelatella* (D. & S.). 11—13mm. Widespread in northern and central Europe, there is one generation of this moth annually, flying during June and July. The caterpillar develops from summer until spring, feeding on various species of the family Rosaceae.

2 *Lampronia rubiella* (Bjerk.) — Raspberry Moth. 11—14mm. Distributed throughout Europe, the moths are on the wing in June and July. Nocturnal in habit, it lays its eggs in raspberry flowers. The caterpillars (2b) live from summer until the following spring. At first they damage the receptacles of the ripening fruits; after hibernation they work their way into buds and young shoots (2c). An abundant species, it is capable of causing damage to raspberry plantations.

3 *Incurvaria masculella* (D. & S.) (= *muscalella* F.). 14—16mm. Distributed over Europe, east to the Caucasus, this moth is on the wing as early as April and May in deciduous woodland; it is common, especially in oak forests. The caterpillars are found from summer until spring on oak, beech, hornbeam, etc. At first they mine the leaves; later each uses bits of leaves to make a small case in which to live on the ground, feeding on fallen leaves.

4 *Incurvaria pectinea* Hw. 14—16mm. Ranging over temperate Europe and Asia across the Caucasus to the Altai, this inhabitant of mountain forests is on the wing in April and May. The life cycle is similar to that of the other species of this family; the larva eats birch, hazel, oak, etc.

5 *Lampronia capitella* (Cl.) — Currant Shoot Borer. 14—17mm. Ranges from central and especially northern Europe across the whole of Asia to the Far East; in central Europe this species is found in greatest abundance at submontane elevations. Moths are on the wing in May and June when green currant berries are formed, and oviposit in the middle of these berries. The young caterpillars live inside the berries, feeding on the seeds; then, after moving to the base of the shrub, they make ready for hibernation by forming a cocoon. In spring they re-emerge to eat the new flower buds of the currants. In northern Europe they are a serious pest, whole crops often being destroyed by them.

6 *Lampronia oehlmanniella* (Hb.). 13—16mm. Recorded from central and northern Europe, this moth extends eastwards to the Caucasus. A single generation flies in coniferous forests from May to July. The caterpillar lives from June to October, feeding on bilberry.

Family: **Tischeriidae**

7 *Tischeria ekebladella* (Bjerk.). 8—10mm. Lives within areas of deciduous forest all over Europe, eastwards to the Caucasus and Urals. Moths fly in May and June. The caterpillars make flat mines on the upperside of leaves of young oak and sweet chestnut *(Castanea sativa)* (7c); during September and October they may be found in great numbers, especially on 2—3 year-old seedlings.

8 *Tischeria gaunacella* (Dup.). 7—8mm. Ranges over central and southern Europe and Asia Minor to the Caucasus. The moths are on the wing in May and June, flying in woods, forest-steppes, shrubby slopes and in orchards. The caterpillars mine the leaves of various plants, favouring those of the genus *Prunus*.

Family: **Hepialidae — ghost and swift moths (hepialids)**

1 *Hepialus humuli* (L.) — Ghost. 40—70mm. Distributed all over temperate Europe, Asia Minor and eastwards to Siberia, this species is found in lowlands and at high altitudes in mountains, but occurs most abundantly in submontane regions, where it haunts meadows and grassy localities, flying close to the ground just before dusk; activity ceases after nightfall. The moths fly in June or July, according to elevation; in high mountains they may appear at an even later time. Development of the caterpillars (1b) takes two years. Until autumn they develop very slowly indeed; before the second winter they have almost attained full size, and pupate after hibernation (1c). They live in the ground, feeding on roots of various herbs, grasses and shrubs. Sexual dimorphism is very marked in this moth: the male is silvery-white, the female ochre coloured and marked with a brick red, very variable pattern. The size of these moths is also very variable, depending on the food quality available to the larvae.

2 *Hepialus fusconebulosa* (De Geer) — Map-winged Swift. 30—35mm. Distributed in more northern parts of Europe, this moth is confined in central Europe primarily to mountains and hills. Eastwards it ranges across the Urals to Siberia and the Far East. One generation is produced annually, flying from May to June. The female is somewhat paler and larger than the male. The caterpillar lives from autumn until spring, feeding on the roots of bracken *(Pteridium aquilinum)*.

3 *Hepialus carna* (Esp.). 30—45mm. Locally distributed in the mountains of central Europe, chiefly the Alps and Carpathians, this swift inhabits places near the timberline, in the dwarf-pine zone, and alpine meadows above 2,000m elevation. Considerable differences exist in the colouration of the males and females. There is a single generation per year, flying in July and August. The moths are active in early morning, and in dull weather they will continue their flight during the daytime. Nothing is known about the bionomics of the early stages.

4 *Hepialus sylvina* (L.) — Orange Swift. 25—45mm. Distributed throughout the milder parts of Europe, in the east the Orange Swift extends to Transcaucasia. There is one generation on the wing in August and September. The male differs considerably from the female, both in size and colouration. The caterpillars live in the soil, from autumn until the following summer, eating soft roots of a variety of plants. Adults fly in late evening, just as it is getting dark.

5 *Hepialus hecta* (L.) — Gold Swift. 22—33mm. Ranges over central and northern Europe and the whole of Asia to the Far East, to Sakhalin. One generation of this moth occurs per year, flying from June to August. The moths, active before dusk, when males are busy looking for females (sometimes they swarm) are very abundant in forests with a rich undergrowth of bilberry and oxeye daisies, be it in lowlands or in mountains. The polyphagous caterpillar lives from summer until spring, feeding on roots of bracken, bilberry, sorrel, and other plants.

6 *Hepialus lupulinus* (L.) — Common Swift. 22—35mm. Ranges throughout the temperate regions of Europe and Asia to the Altai. The moths of the single generation occur in May and June, flying before dusk over fields and meadows. The polyphagous caterpillars develop from summer to early spring, living underground and eating the roots of various plants. Lucerne, and some garden vegetables and flowers (e. g., lily-of-the-valley) are often infested.

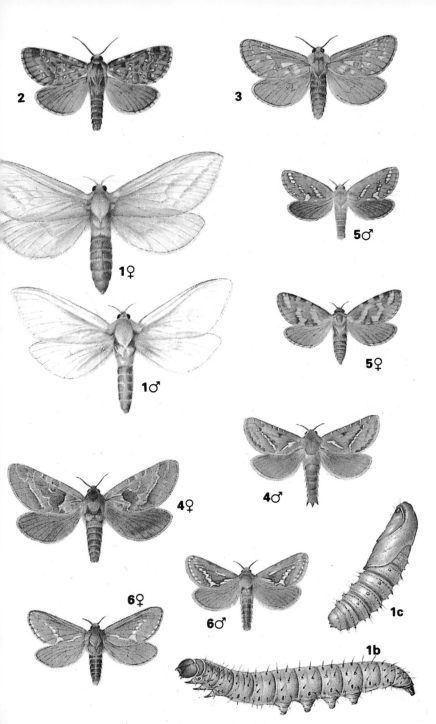

2

3

1♀

5♂

1♂

5♀

4♀

4♂

6♀

6♂

1c

1b

Family: **Micropterigidae** — **archaic moths**

1 *Micropterix tunbergella* (F). 8—9.5mm. An inhabitant of central and northern Europe, this moth produces one generation a year, flying in damp localities during May and June, where it likes to settle on marsh marigold. Hornbeam is assumed to be the foodplant of the caterpillar, but the life cycle is not well-known.

2 *Micropterix aureatella* (Sc.). 9—11mm. Little is known about the distribution of this moth; it has been recorded from western, central and northern Europe. Not rare in open woods, it flies in June and July. The caterpillar lives on bilberry, and the species accompanies this plant from lowlands to mountains.

3 *Micropterix calthella* (L.). 7—8.5mm. Known from all over Europe, it occurs in damp biotopes in lowlands and mountains. Most common member of this family, the moths fly in spring, during May and June. Caterpillars develop from June to October, on marsh marigold; various mosses are also considered to be foodplants.

Family: **Eriocraniidae** — **primitive moths**

4 *Eriocrania sparrmannella* (Bosc). 8—12mm. Distributed all over central and northern Europe, and also in Siberia, the moths of this single-brooded species fly in April and May. The caterpillars develop during May and June on birch, forming blister-mines on the leaves. An abundant species, both diurnal and nocturnal in habit.

5 *Eriocrania semipurpurella* (Stt.). 11—14mm. Windespread in the deciduous-forest belt of northern and central Europe, this moth flies early in spring, during March and April. The caterpillar develops in May, in blister-mines on birch leaves (5c). When full-grown, it falls from the mine to the ground, to pass the summer and winter in a flimsy cocoon. Only then does it pupate and soon the adult moth emerges. An extremely abundant species, active both by day and night.

6 *Eriocrania haworthi* Bradl. (= *rubroaurella* auctt.). 9—11mm. Reported from northern and central Europe only, it resembles the preceding species in its life cycle. The flight period is in early spring, during April. The caterpillar develops in May, mining birch leaves.

Family: **Nepticulidae** — **nepticulid moths (serpentine miners)**

7 *Stigmella malella* (Stt.) — Apple Pygmy. 4—5mm. A representative of an extremely extensive and hitherto insufficiently investigated family, containing many of the smallest Lepidoptera. These moths are all very similar to each other; they differ in bionomics, foodplants and type of mine rather than wing pattern. The Apple Pygmy is a very abundant species, occurring all over temperate Europe. There are two generations, on the wing in June and August. Caterpillars develop in July and again in autumn, within serpentine mines formed on the upperside of apple leaves (7c).

8 *Stigmella oxyacanthella* (Stt.). 5—6mm. A thermophilic species, occurring in the Middle East as well as in temperate Europe. There are two generations, flying in May and August. The caterpillars live in July and in autumn (until October), feeding in mines formed on the leaves of hawthorn, pear trees, and various species of the genus *Prunus*.

9 *Stigmella prunetorum* (Stt.). 4.5—5mm. A common species ranging throughout temperate and warmer parts of Europe to Asia Minor, and in eastern Europe as far as the Caucasus. Two generations emerge, their flight periods being in May and August. The caterpillars develop in July and again in autumn, within leaf-mines on various species of the genus *Prunus* or on hawthorn.

FURTHER READING

The literature on the Lepidoptera is vast, scattered, mostly published in very obscure books or journals, and to the non-specialist these are often unobtainable except from major science libraries. The works listed below can help serious students to further their knowledge of the biology, collection and identification of Palaearctic butterflies and moths — they include books with extensive bibliographies.

GENERAL

Common, I. F. B. 1970. Lepidoptera (moths and butterflies), in,
The insects of Australia — a textbook for students and research workers. Carlton, Victoria (Melbourne University Press). [An outstanding outline of the general biology and classification of Lepidoptera.]

Ford, E. B. 1945 (& editions). *Butterflies.* London (Collins).

Ford, E. B. 1955 (& editions). *Moths.* London (Collins).

Hering, M. 1926. *Biologie der Schmetterlinge.* Berlin. [In German, but no modern or English-language equivalent.]

Staněk, V. J. 1977. *The illustrated encyclopedia of butterflies and moths* (ed. B. Turner). London (Octopus).

STUDY AND COLLECTION

Bradley, J. D. & Fletcher, D. S. 1979. *A recorder's log book or label list of British butterflies and moths.* London (Curwen).

Cogan, B. H. & Smith, K. G. V. 1974. *Instructions for collectors, no. 4a, insects (5th edition).* London (British Museum [Natural History]).

Dickson, R. 1976. *A lepidopterist's handbook.* Hanworth (Amateur Entomologists' Society).

Oldroyd, H. 1970. *Collecting, preserving and studying insects (2nd edition).* London.

EARLY STAGES

Carter, D. J. 1979. *The observer's book of caterpillars.* London (Warne).

Fracker, S. B. 1967. *The classification of lepidopterous larvae* (reprint). New York (Johnson Reprint Corporation).

Moucha, J. 1974. *A colour guide to familiar butterflies, caterpillars and chrysalids.* London (Octopus).

Stokoe, W. J. 1948. *The caterpillars of British moths, including the eggs, chrysalids and food-plants* (2 volumes). London (Warne).

BUTTERFLIES

Higgins, L. G. 1975. *The classification of European butterflies.* London (Collins).

Higgins, L. G. & Riley, N. D. 1970. *A field guide to the butterflies of Europe.* London (Collins). [Translated in several European-language editions.]

Howarth, T. G. 1973. *South's British butterflies.* London (Warne).

Howe, W. H. 1975. *The butterflies of North America.* Garden City, New York (Doubleday).

Larsen, T. B. 1974. *Butterflies of Lebanon.* Beirut (CNRS).

MOTHS

Amsel, H. G., Gregor, F. & Reisser, H. (eds). 1965 — on. *Microlepidoptera Palaearctica.* Vienna (Fromme). [Multi-part, multi-author work, still being published.]

Bergmann, A. 1951—1955. *Die Grosschmetterlinge Mitteldeutschlands* (5 volumes). Jena (Urania).

Bradley, J. D., Tremewan, W. G. & Smith, A. 1973 & 1979 *British tortricoid moths: in two volumes*, London (Ray Society).

Forster, W. & Wohlfahrt, T. A. 1954 – on. *Die Schmetterlinge Mitteleuropas.* Stuttgart (Franckh). [5 volumes have appeared; others in preparation.]

Holland, W. J. 1968 (reprint edition). *The moth book: a guide to the moths of North America.* New York (Dover).

Newman, L. H. 1965. *Hawk-moths of Great Britain and Europe.* London (Cassell).

South, R. 1961. *The moths of the British Isles* (2 volumes; edited and revised by H. M. Edelsten, D. S. Fletcher & R. J. Collins). London (Warne).

Traugott-Olsen, E. & Schmidt Nielsen, E. 1977. *The Elachistidae (Lepidoptera) of Fennoscandia and Denmark.* Klampenborg, Denmark (Scandinavian Science Press).

INDEX OF COMMON NAMES

INDEX OF LATIN NAMES